WAR PLAN UK

Duncan Campbell

WAR PLAN UK
The Truth about Civil Defence in Britain

Burnett Books

First published 1982 by Burnett Books Limited
in association with
The Hutchinson Publishing Group
17 – 21 Conway Street
London W1P 6JD

Printed in Great Britain by The Anchor Press Ltd
and bound by Wm Brendon & Son Ltd
both of Tiptree, Essex

ISBN (hardback) 0 09 150670 0
ISBN (paperback) 0 09 150671 9

'If war should ever come, especially nuclear war . . . there would be scope for the application of management science in such fields as decision making or resource allocation, where the unit of cost may be expressed in terms of human life . . .

Management would have to accept and adapt to such new concepts.

The country would suffer widespread damage and disruption. But the nation would suvive any conceivable attack and would recover. . .'

From an advice note to Home Defence Scientific Advisers by the Chief Regional Scientific Adviser for London (1980).

Contents

List of Plates

Photographs by the author and others. Plates 4, 42, 43 and
44 © The Japanese Consumers Cooperative Union, from
their international travelling exhibition 'Nuclear Aftermath'.

List of Figures

List of Tables

Acknowledgements

Much of this book is a jigsaw puzzle for which many different people have supplied the pieces. Some, who can only be thanked anonymously, have taken risks with their employment in passing out information, and I thank them and respect them. A great deal has also been learned from the efforts of many researchers and campaigners across the country whose advice and information I am very grateful for. An exhaustive list of all those who have helped is probably not feasible, and I apologise in advance to any of those whom I have forgotten. I thank:

Jinty Knowling, Martin Spence, Jon Side, Steve Walker, Nick Anning, Professor Robert Moore, Albert Beale, Steve Peak, Malcolm Dando, Keith Lomax, David Ireland, Peter Marks, John Edwards, Ken Veitch, Peter Lipton, Frank Doherty, Guy Smith, Alan Hall, Evan Wylie, Wally Lloyd, Bill Arkin, Tony Bunyan, Duncan Campbell (of *City Limits* magazine, no relation), Ricky Hills, Paul Rogers, Peter Sommer, Mike Harris, Phil Jeffries, James Hinton and LEND, Professor John Erickson, Dr Desmond Ball, Owen Wilkes, Chris Rainger, Martin Kettle, Steve Wright, Phil Kelly, Keith Bryers, Ruth Davies, Neil Turok, Owen Greene, Nick Walter, Harry Dean, Aled Eurig, Stella Crewe, Jane Thomas, Jenny Edwards, Mary Kaldor, Alison Whyte, Kathy Fuller, Stuart Anderson, Chris Pounder and TAGS, Andy Haines, Chris Smith, Mike Gapes, Peter Pringle, Godfrey Boyle, Richard Kerley, Chris Horrie, Philip Weber, Michael Tracey, Professor Peter Nailor, Geoff Cotterell, John Hodgson, Gary Murray, Ursula Murray, and Sanne van der Toorn.

Some of the above attended the first *Researching State Structures* conference which I and others set up to promote more detailed research. Celina Bledowska made that happen, and I am grateful to Edward Thompson and END, Bruce Kent and CND, Patricia Hewitt and NCCL and Professors John Humphrey and Tom Kibble for their sponsorship of the conference, and for their encouragement. I am particularly grateful for, and inspired by, the developing scientific opposition to the government policies criticised here, in particular from Sir Martin Ryle and Mike Pentz and SANA (scientists against nuclear arms) and for the detailed work being done on the effects of war by Phil Steadman, Stan Openshaw, and other SANA groups.

I am indebted to Robin Cook, Chris Price, Frank Allaun, Jo Richardson, Bob Cryer and Michael Meacher for their continual support and assistance from the House of Commons, and to Lord Gifford and Lord Jenkins in another place.

Bruce Page, the former editor of the *New Statesman*, has lent his own determined support to these investigations. Hugh Stephenson, the present editor, and my *NS* colleagues have been kind in releasing me to proceed apace with this work. Piers Burnett and Hutchinson Publishing Group have made an urgent and valuable effort to lay the government plans for *Hard Rock* and civil defence efforts before the public as quickly as possible. Much of this report might not have been possible were it not for the efforts, four years ago, of Lord Hutchinson, Geoffrey Robertson, Andy Nicholl and Bernard Simons to keep the Official Secrets Act at a safe distance from the freedom of the press in the ABC trial.

A great many vital pieces for this jigsaw puzzle have been produced by Andy Thomas, whose investigations have been as painstaking as they are diligent. My own enquiries began eight years ago with Peter Laurie's report, *Beneath the City Streets*. Peter has now moved on to pastures new, but his early and imaginative investigation opened up not just these important avenues of enquiry, but also key methods of research.

I thank them all, most of all the 'moles'.

DC

Introduction

Civil Defence, as most people know it – or Home Defence, as it is officially styled, although there is an important distinction – should be about the means and methods of protecting the civil population. In some modern states, such protection is carefully planned. In Britain, the idea of 'civil' defence has been turned on its head. Home Defence is about the protection of *government* – if need be, *against* the civil population.

During and after a major thermonuclear exchange, there will be no time or place for the *camaraderie* of the Londoners and other city dwellers who endured the blitz. There will be no-one around to dig survivors out of the rubble, no medical care for most of the wounded and all of the dying, little energy for industry and none for heating, and a dwindling supply of food. In the year that follows an attack, many survivors will die. There will be little protection or succour that people have not provided for themselves.

This book documents the development and contemporary position of civil defence in Britain. I have tried to examine the subject, as far as possible, through the eyes of central government and its planners. Not, perhaps with their perspectives and motives, but certainly with the aid of much that they have written and circulated.

Much of this material has not willingly been put into the public domain. The more important details of the government's plans and expectations for nuclear war, described and revealed here, come from internal documents which are, at best, withheld and, at worst, formally classified to keep their contents from public view. Ironically, the emphasis placed on civil defence by the 1979 Conservative Government resulted in a considerable opening-up by the Home Office, and material such as guidance circulars to local authorities have in general been readily supplied to enquirers.

But the new openness masks what remains hidden, and what are being hidden are the most critical features. Guidance material for the public may advise that 'no place in the United Kingdom is safer than anywhere else'; in private, the same officials who write these words have planned and enacted dozens of exercises in which particularly likely nuclear targets are singled out, and exercises like *Hard Rock* are conducted on the basis of such assumptions. In private too, the bunkers for central government and the provincial dispersal centres for other officials have been selected with safety in mind. At no time has the government willingly offered the public its detailed view of the likely form of a Soviet nuclear attack on Britain. The implications – the need to create and service evacuation plans, or change defence policy – would be too demanding.

Such contrasts – between what is public and misleading and what is secret and more exact – illuminate what secrecy is actually for. It provides officials and their political chiefs with the facility to cheat, deceive, and sometimes downright lie. Although this use of secrecy is prevalent in all British institutions, it is illegitimate. It is the reason why many of those in possession of privy information have leaked it – to this author and others – in order to inform and educate public debate.

It is possible to view some of the contradictions and absurdities of government civil defence plans as merely part of normal bureaucratic ineptitude. But there are a set of fundamental aims. The primary purpose of Home Defence, laid out in Home Office circulars, is to 'maintain the internal security of the United Kingdom'. The details of how this is to be done, or why it is the *first* objective, do not often percolate out in material used by local authorities in planning for civil defence, for 'law and order' is not part of their responsibility.

This primary task of internal security has two important aspects. In the first place, the government has always maintained plans and disposed military forces in order to meet any internal threat of disorder or disruption. In the early 1970s, planning for internal security and for civil defence, already strongly overlapping, was made more homogeneous.

Secondly, it is not unreasonable to suppose that the greatest threat of mass disorder faced by the British government in the late twentieth century will not result from the organisation of a Bolshevik party, or even from the unprecedented level of unemployment and economic decay now prevalent. The one event which would undoubtedly turn the mass of the people against the government would be the imminence, or perceived imminence, of nuclear conflict. Resistance to the government, to NATO and the United States, is then anticipated on a wide scale.

In this context, a policy of nuclear deterrence places an impossible strain on democracy. If you believe in deterrence, there is no drawing back from the final brink. If you wish nuclear weapons to deter, then you must be ready, willing and able to use them, whatever the strength of public opinion against a posture of nuclear deterrence in a late stage of political crisis or conventional military conflict.

Planning for Home Defence thus places a primary emphasis on the control of the civil population. NATO, and Britain's, policy is one of no evacuation – 'stay put'. This policy, which will be enforced by police and military, keeps roads and transport facilities free for military logistic movements, which is a convenience. It *maximises* civilian casualties in the early stages of nuclear conflict, by maintaining population concentration in urban target areas where chances of survival during an attack and in the immediate post-attack period are lowest. On the other hand, it may perhaps be cynically justified by leaving, ultimately, a lesser number of mouths to feed and a consequently greater chance of stable 'survival' for the remainder.

At the same time, military plans to cope with and if need be, suppress, dissent are well advanced. A Cabinet Key Points Committee has identified each critical facility which needs to be guarded. Lists of 'subversive or potentially subversive' people are maintained, along with plans for internment areas. Troops allocated to Home Defence duties will counter pacifist demonstrations, and meet civilian obstruction, with weapons from CS gas to live ammunition. Most of the time during Home Defence exercises prior to *Hard Rock* – such as *Scrum Half*, *Square Leg*, or *Inside Right* – was spent not taking care of survivors *after* a nuclear attack, but with the transition-to-war (pre-strike) phase which comes first. In the pre-strike phase, it is resistance among the civil population which has to be fought and overcome. The preparations which have been made by both central and local government for dealing with the effects of attack have also been largely confined to the theme of control. A five-tiered government wartime command structure has been implemented with bunkers (of varying effectiveness) provided for central government, regional headquarters, sub-regional headquarters, and county and district headquarters (and, in London, Greater London Council 'group' and London Borough HQS). Communications systems have been installed. A great deal of planning has been done by compliant local councils, but is all on paper. No attempt has been made by the councils, for no money is available, to stockpile food or medical supplies or other neccessities for survival. The effect of such planning is thus a superficial palliative; it is designed to convince the planners and practitioners and their public that help is available, and would be effective.

In some areas, remote shire counties for instance, the chances for survival are a little better than elsewhere, and the planning process perhaps more useful to inhabitants. It is noteworthy that in these districts, the planners' thoughts have frequently – and publicly – turned to the problem of keeping out hungry town dwellers and other refugees by force.

There are many within the local authority and voluntary organisations for civil defence who are, nonetheless, sincere in a humanitarian purpose, and unselfish in the effort they may be making. They form the most useful part of Whitehall's sales force for civil defence as they are themselves convinced. It is often forgotten, with the emphasis Mrs Thatcher's Government places on boosting war preparations, that the emergency planning offices of local authorities do also have the quite proper task of preparing for peacetime disasters. These arrangements are not criticised here, save for one point; it is noteworthy that such contingency planning is at its most open when the disaster at hand is one about which we may do nothing. A good example of this is the London flood preparations, which are well-advertised. Contingency plans for nuclear reactor accidents are, in contrast, secret. For to admit to the possibility and circumstances of potential accident or disaster would be to arm the public with information which they might use to press for changes in policy. Above all, this is true of nuclear war planning and civil defence.

The government has sought to counteract criticism of its policy (in 1981) with a leaflet from the Home and Scottish Secretaries on *Civil Defence: Why We Need It*. This observed that:

Even the strongest supporter of unilateral disarmament can consistently give equal support to civil defence . . .

One does not have to adopt the more extreme type of dis-armament argument – which suggests that all defence prep-arations indicate an *intention* to have a nuclear war – to see the deep deception in this claim. Civil defence in its poten-tially palliative aspects is a means of persuading the public in favour of nuclear weapons and a policy of deterrence; and it is a means, if need be, of putting that deterrence policy, for those who believe in it, into practical effect.

Independent (but pro–NATO policy) defence strategists can be a good deal more honest about these objectives than the government or NATO. The International Institute of Strategic Studies' magazine *Survival* noted, in a discussion of the new theatre nuclear force (Cruise and Pershing missile) decision that:

The issue of defences is important for two reasons; because of their intrinsic potential for limiting damage and because of their potential for creating a greater degree of public support for a given strategy. . . . Both the potential values of civil defence are important to the creation of a more comprehensive and broadly supported theatre nuclear posture in the Alliance.*

Other equally pro-NATO commentators have disputed the value of civil defence to a population under attack, except from the point of view of government public relations. Law-rence Freedman, formerly of the Royal Institute of Interna-tional Affairs (Chatham House) and now Professor of War Studies at King's College, London, wrote in *The Times*:

It would be unwise to foster illusions that even a massive investment could significantly alleviate the consequences of war, especially if the enemy decided to compensate for this in his plans. . . . Passive measures to protect life and property are virtually useless to those caught in a target area. With vast expenditure, we might smother our environment with reinforced concrete, burrow underground, disperse to the remotest parts of the kingdom, and store huge quantities of foodstuffs and equipment. But for far less expenditure the enemy could make a mockery of all this by increasing the number of attacking weapons, especially against a country so small, centralised and densely populated as Britain. (*Times*, 26 March 1980)

In this book, then, the case is that civil defence as practised and preached by central government (although not necces-

* 'TNF Modernisation and Countervailing Strategy' by Christopher J. Makins, *Survival* July/August 1981, p 162.

sarily from other quarters) is essentially a public relations exercise for a pre-determined nuclear strategy. It also conveniently incorporates plans for coping with widespread disorder or dissent, in a war crisis or at any other time. I have set out to examine how we came here, and how, for example, the tables have turned since the 1930s, when scientific critics argued for Air Raid Precautions against an uninterested and unyielding Home Office, to the 70s and 80s when the same community of scientists and doctors are bitterly critical of 'civil defence'. The constant in the situation is the attitude of government officials; in particular, a willingness to place the maintenance of authority above all other goals.

This book contains what I hope is the most detailed and accurate acount of the British government's civil defence plans ever published. It is necessarily incomplete, as most of the contemporary information presented here has had to be retrieved from behind the walls of official secrecy. Much information has come by way of leaks, slowly building up the picture of the world behind those walls. I hope the leaks will continue to come, and thank those whose assistance, anonymous or not, has helped in this account. My experience on the *New Statesman* in reporting these affairs from within the Whitehall citadels suggests that secrecy, when it is illegitimate and against the public interest, is quite un-enforceable. There could be few more illegitimate aspects of official secrecy than covert plans for bottling up people in target cities, setting up internment camps for opponents of government, or death camps for diseased survivors, as described here. I will be grateful for any and all future guidance and correction, from quarters official or non-official, and will incorporate as much as possible in any subsequent editions.

London, June 1982

1
Hard Rock '82

Hard Rock is the largest Home Defence exercise exercise
planned for fifteen years – the latest in a series of rehearsals
for the nuclear devastation of Britain. According to the plans
of *Hard Rock*, war between the Soviet Union and NATO began
on 27 September 1982. Within a week, large tracts of the
United Kingdom would be a smoking, radio-active wasteland.
During the exercise, government and military planners would
operate their protected command bunkers and communications links, command their troops and subordinates in Home
Defence operations, and test their plans to keep government
going through a nuclear attack.

Hard Rock never happened. The bombs didn't drop. The
exercise did not happen according to plan, either. Two
months before it was to begin, this 1982 exercise was postponed. Too many local authorities refused to play – the bluff
of civil defence planning had been called. The Home Secretary, Willie Whitelaw, promised thereupon that the law
would be changed, in the course of time, so that uncompliant
councils could be *ordered* to play in *Hard Rock* and its successor exercises.

What follows are the complete scenarios of this official
rehearsal for World War 3. *Hard Rock* is the fourth such
excercise, and the most extensive since the Civil Defence
Corps was disbanded in 1968.

The official scenarios for *Hard Rock* have been drawn up
by the Home Office in conjunction with Britain's wartime
military commanders, the UK Commanders-in-Chief Committee (UKCICC). These scenarios draw out, for the benefit of the
'players' in the exercise, the circumstances in Britain as war
looms, and then commences. This is the timetable for the war
they have anticipated:

1 Sept:	Start of the crisis.
19 Sept:	NATO orders mobilisation and reinforcement of Europe; start of detailed plans of *Hard Rock 82*.
27 Sept:	War starts; Warsaw pact troops invade Europe, and conventional bombing starts on targets in Britain.
29 Sept:	Civil phase of *Hard Rock 82* starts; local authority war HQs and government bunkers are manned. Conventional bombing of British targets by Soviet bombers continues.
2–3 October:	Nuclear strike during the night – six hours of nuclear bombardment anticipated.
6 October:	*Hard Rock 82* ends, after officials have 'played' the scenario for conditions seven days and a month after nuclear attack.

Hard Rock 82 was preceded by a series of primarily military Home Defence exercises all with sporting titles: *Inside Right* in 1975; *Scrum Half* in 1978; and *Square Leg* in 1980. Before 1975, military Home Defence exercises were held in the autumn, but did not involve the civil authorities or their bunker HQs. *Inside Right* marked the 1970s revival of active Home Defence planning.

The title of the latest exercise is odd; most people would associate 'hard rock' with modern rock bands and their music. If the planners were strictly following their sporting nomenclature, then 'hard rock' means an area of particularly arduous and severe climbing. There is a more cynical interpretation, however. The term appears fairly frequently in analyses of nuclear weapons effects. Hard rock is simply the densest, most robust rock, in which underground bunkers for officials may most safely be built.

The official scenarios for these exercises are, as the government is now at pains to stress, fictional. They set the background scene for the planners in their war HQs. Everything happens on paper; the H bombs are not for real, and no police, fire or military columns are to be seen in the city streets during the exercises putting out fires or shooting looters. It is what the military call a 'command post exercise'. In this book, these scenarios form a useful introduction to what the planners expect nuclear war would be like.

At the time of writing, the government intended that *Hard Rock* would go ahead once local authorities could be legally compelled to play. That would take some time to arrange. The government cannot be certain of being successful. The Home Secretary has, nevertheless, stated that excercise *Hard Rock* will be 'held at a later date'. Readers can thus examine, at leisure, the nature and credibility of these intended plans.

One major boost to the nuclear disarmament movement during 1980 was the *Square Leg* exercise that September. It served to alert many to the mendacious, even sinister government plans which underlay so-called civil defence. A critical document, which was published in the *New Statesman** was the 'bomb plot' or target list for *Square Leg*. For the first time in many years, one could look at the government's expectation of the likely pattern of nuclear attack – how many targets, where, how severe the consequences. On the basis of the bomb plot, a great deal could be worked out by everyone from scientists to local CND and other campaigning groups on the real consequences of nuclear war.

In Chapter 12, 'Targets and forces', there are many examples of the kind of targets that would be struck in nuclear war. Chapter 2 gives details of previous civil defence or nuclear war exercises and their targets. The plans of exercises like *Hard Rock*, and the assumptions made in them, are critically important. There is no more vital aspect of planning any kind of civil defence than knowing where the bombs will fall.

Of course, no-one but the target planning staff of the Soviet Strategic Rocket Forces, and their naval and air force counterparts, know that for sure. And in practice no war will run according to anyone's plans.

One of the most absurd deficiencies in government planning since the H bomb has been a steadfast refusal to issue any kind of official guidance as to the likely form of a nuclear attack. Yet without such guidance, it is in fact impossible for local authorities and others, charged by regulation with making civil defence plans, to do their job. Do London's emergency planners, for instance, assume that the city is a prime target, or not? The Home Office line is that plans should be made in a general way, without official advice as to the likely form of attack. In a situation where resources are extremely limited this is absurd – what is available has to be stretched, by implication, to cover every contingency, however unlikely, whilst civil defence planners are poorly placed to deal with the most likely attacks.

It is this absurdity of government planning – amongst other things – which has driven many local authorities to abandon civil defence planning altogether and become 'nuclear free

---

* *New Statesman*, 3 October 1980.

zones'. It is those authorities who forced *Hard Rock* to be postponed. The cosmetic nature of the civil defence planning process is well illuminated by the fact that those responsible have to plan against an attack about whose weight and distribution the government will provide no clue. Such official estimates as exist are classified Secret or higher; they may only be seen, according to the Home Office, by those with a 'need to know'—a category which, in their view, does not include the British people.

That is why opening up the Pandora's box of real official expectations, as they are rehearsed in exercises, is so valuable. The war plans show us what contingencies our taxes spent on defence and home defence are allegedly designed to meet. As the exercise develops, the different parts of the official war machinery will be tested.

These scenarios provide details up to the start of the exercise. The 'players' are not allowed to see the next stages, for that is what they have to deal with from their bunkers. The *Hard Rock* scenario for the start of the war with the Soviet Union is flimsy and simple; a much more elaborate scenario was drawn up by NATO for the more extensive series of exercises (*Crusader 80*) – involving actual mobilisation – which accompanied *Square Leg*. The *Hard Rock* scenario includes daily summaries of the political situation for the week before war starts, together with daily radio and TV news broadcasts leading up to three days before nuclear attack.

The map of conventional bombing targets (pp. 34–5) has been prepared from target lists in the scenario.

When postponing *Hard Rock* until an indefinite later date, the Home Secretary told the Association of Civil Defence and Emergency Planning Officers, whose conference he addressed during July 1982, that:

It is of no advantage to anyone for an exercise on this scale to be held unless it has been consistently well prepared for, and this is unhappily not yet the case with *Hard Rock*. To hold this exercise this autumn (ie, September 1982) would do more harm than good, and I have authorised its postponement. . . . The key factor has been the failure of many local authorities – especially county councils – to pay more than lip service to civil defence, without being in breach of their present statutory duty. But that is simply the duty to make plans.

Whitelaw pointed out that the then current regulations on civil defence did not require anyone to 'play' in the *Hard Rock* exercise:

There is nothing in the regulations about keeping the plans up-to-date; nothing about taking part in exercises; nothing about the recruitment and training of volunteers; nothing about designating war headquarters so that we can equip them with proper communications. While we had hoped that encouragement, persuasion and advice would lead to councils attending to these things . . . many councils are still neglecting basic responsibilities. That is why I am informing Parliament . . . that we are urgently considering the need to amend the Planning Regulations made under the Civil Defence Act.

Battle lines are thus drawn, with *Hard Rock* at the centre. Parliament has to approve any change in civil defence laws. The *Hard Rock* plans which follow are the documents at the centre of this civil defence debate. They are followed by details of the aftermath, as rehearsed in previous exercises.

The first scene is an international disarmament conference in September 1982. The nuclear strike comes later.

Hard Rock 82

World background scenario
UK lead-in scenario
Start-of-exercise scenario*

1–18 September 1982

1. Throughout 1981 and 1982, encouraged by the growing capacity of its military power, the Soviet Bloc systematically strove to advance its objectives to the detriment of NATO influence. On 1 September, the Soviet Union introduced a draft resolution at an international conference, urging delegates to take

* 1. The scenarios are preceded by a note that 'Exercise scenarios are fictional and are designed solely for the purpose of creating a setting in which selected plans and procedures can be tested thoroughly. The scenario for *Hard Rock* 82 is not intended and should not be taken to be a realistic description of possible causes of war, nor the government's response to such a crisis or of the weight or distribution of an enemy's attack.'

2. These three scenarios were provided separately, but have been combined here as a single documentary. The exercise terminology, whereby NATO is referred to as BLUE, and the Warsaw Pact as ORANGE, has been dropped for the sake of clarity, and the proper names are used instead.

3. Comments made by the author are based on *Square Leg* and earlier scenarios, and are intended to restore some of the cosmetic erasures which have been made from these plans. All passages not marked 'Comment' are the full, unabridged Home Office exercise scenarios.

immediate action to dissolve military alliances. NATO nations dismissed this initiative as being aimed at misleading world public opinion and opposed the resolution. The Soviet Bloc immediately launched a major diplomatic offensive urging NATO to adopt the resolution and thereby remove a major source of international tension.

2. By 16 September, nations on the flank of the NATO alliance detected signs of Soviet mobilisation in the areas facing them which coincided with intensified Soviet pressure on them to adopt the resolution. Concerned with these moves, they requested the deployment of NATO forces to their respective countries, and this was approved on 17 September, when NATO issued a statement emphasising the defensive and non-provocative nature of these measures, appealing to the Soviet Bloc to refrain from any further steps that could increase tension and ending with an assurance that the NATO alliance would recall its reinforcements as soon as the Soviet Union ceased its course of action.

3. On 18 September the Soviet Bloc Political Consultative Committee issued a communique condemning the NATO alliance in strong terms for increasing international tension by reverting to the discredited display of military force, demanding an immediate unconditional reversal of the NATO decision concerning the deployment of troops to those nations on the flanks of the alliance, and warning NATO nations of the possible grave complications of non-compliance.

The same day, the NATO alliance met to further discuss the situation. Soviet actions, including the forward deployment of some ground forces and the extension of conscript periods of service, posed a growing military threat to the flanks, whilst Soviet activities were increasingly threatening vital sea-lines of communications. In the view of the alliance, these actions, if not countered, would inevitably lead to Soviet military domination of NATO members. The armed forces, the emergency services, the local authorities, public utilities and central government departments were instructed by HMG to review their emergency plans.

19 September 1982

NATO concluded that, whilst intensifying its efforts to defuse the crisis by negotiation with Soviet Bloc leaders, it had no alternative but to undertake the general reinforcement of Europe.

General Situation: During September 1982, public awareness of the growing seriousness of the world situation resulted in (massive) support for Her Majesty's Government in its role as a voice calling for commonsense to prevail. The period was characterised by:

a. Sabotage – a number of isolated and uncoordinated acts causing local disruption;
b. Peaceful rallies, urging the government/NATO alliance to reach a negotiated solution, cause problems with traffic disruption. Some isolated demonstrations cause some law and order problems;
c. Localised fuel and food shortages – some areas suffered from a series of runs of certain food items. Disputes between shoppers and stores, while not uncommon, were not of a serious nature. There were some fires through the hoarding of petrol in private garages despite clear warning to the public of the danger involved;
d. Population movement – a tendency of some urban families with connections in the west country, Wales and Scotland to move to those areas manifests itself.

Late night news broadcast, 19 September

In a statement to Parliament today, the Prime Minister announced that it had been decided, as a result of a NATO decision, that the UK would help reinforce Europe and the first contingent of British troops are now leaving the UK. The Prime Minister added that efforts to seek a peaceful solution were being intensified but as the Soviet Union was increasing its military preparedness there was no alternative. The government has arranged to provide facilities for the reinforcement of Europe and has introduced emergency legislation to enable reinforcement to proceed smoothly.

In an evening broadcast to the nation, the Prime Minister urged the country to remain calm and support the government in its efforts to persuade the Soviet Union to draw back from the point of no return. Public opinion polls continued to show a substantial majority of the population agreed with the firm line being taken by the government.

On the industrial front there is concern over industry's ability to face a prolonged crisis. In the aftermath of last month's heavy destocking and the loss of production caused by the holiday period, the country is not well placed to face the loss of essential imports.

There is also concern over the increased number of terrorist incidents. A number of incidents occurred in which explosives and detonators had been stolen from quarries. Postal bombs addressed to high ranking service officers have also been discovered.

Many service HQs and stations were the target for subversive leaflets last night.

Comment: The *Hard Rock* scenario has been re-written a number of times since defence planners originally drafted it. This version was prepared by the Home Office, and has been repeatedly 'sanitised' of unwelcome and embarassing references; further 'sanitisation' was to take place before final versions were made available to local authorities. In the draft obtained by the author and published here, some sanitisation had begun. References to emergency powers had been toned down, and qualified support for the British government became 'massive' and confirmed by opinion polls. Such soothing insertions were made because the Home Office had assumed that the *Hard Rock* documents would 'leak', and therefore removed rougher parts of the Home Defence plans first. Another deletion dealt with the beginning of the flight of refugees from the cities.

The references to terrorism and subversion emphasise that during the pre–nuclear attack ('pre-strike') phase, Home Defence is primarily concerned with an *internal* enemy.

20 September 1982

NATO nations requested direct negotiations between NATO and the Warsaw Pact in order to lower tension. However, a seemingly conciliatory attitude and positive response by the Soviet Bloc was not borne out by any evidence that the Soviet Union was preparing to reduce its military posture. On the contrary, there were reports that Soviet reservists were being mobilised in areas bordering the NATO alliance.

The Soviet Union intensified its campaign by calling for a debate in the UN Security Council on NATO's reinforcement action. The Soviet Union claimed that the buildup of NATO troops in Europe indicated NATO's warlike intention to which the Warsaw Pact was forced to respond in kind. Meanwhile North Sea oil and gas installations came under close Soviet surveillance and reports were received of increased numbers of Soviet naval vessels in the area. NATO shipowners' organisations requested guidance and protection for their shipping which was reporting harassment from Soviet vessels.

Late night news broadcast, 20 September

The day has been marked by a number of rallies throughout the country, reflecting support for and against the government's decision to reinforce Europe. In some cases, demonstrations were held; these passed off without incident. Some groups have called for NATO to agree to the UN Security Council debate suggested by the Soviet Union and to cease its reinforcement activity prior to that debate.

British holidaymakers abroad are facing severe delays in returning to the United Kingdom in response to the government's advice. Relatives at home are seeking information on when the holidaymakers will return.

There has been a run on tinned food, sugar and other storeable items causing shortages in some areas. A spokesman representing the largest chain food stores said that this sort of panic buying was quite unnecessary. He admitted that fuel shortages were hindering resupply in some areas but that overall there was no shortage of stocks and the public should calm down and buy sensibly.

As a result of yesterday's announcement in Parliament that military mobilisation was to take place, orders calling out the Reserves were signed in the afternoon. Country-wide reports indicate that reporting-in by reservists is going well.

21 September 1982

There was widespread public concern throughout NATO concerning the military buildup by the Soviet Union and her satellites. Opinion polls conducted throughout the NATO alliance nevertheless reported substantial public support for NATO actions. It was reported that large scale Soviet exercises and troop movements were taking place; mobilisation of reservists was reported to be occurring in the whole of the Soviet Union and observers spoke of large numbers of men moving towards the NATO/Warsaw Pact borders. Aircraft normally stationed well inside the Soviet Union were also said to have been seen flying near the border areas. Soviet radio broadcasts claimed that these exercises were routine and that the NATO alliance was deliberately misinterpreting them. The Soviet Union declared maritime danger areas in the Atlantic and the North Sea and informed NATO that her shipping entered these areas at their peril.

Late night news broadcast, 21 September

Further rallies have been held throughout the country.

The emergency services, the local authorities, public utilities and central government departments (have been) instructed by Her Majesty's Government to start implementing their emergency plans. Local authorities have been given the power to suspend certain peacetime functions and close educational establishments and to requisition premises and materials for civil defence purposes. Radiac instruments are available for collection from Home Office stores. Chief Constables have been asked to ensure that the (Attack) Warning System is at full operational readiness and to recruit additional Special Constables.

22 September 1982

In the North Sea gas fields, Soviet warships circled gas platforms operating powerful sonars which caused scheduled diving operations to be abandoned. NATO merchant ships reported an increase in incidents involving Soviet naval shipping manoeuvring closely and dangerously to them.

Late night news broadcast, 22 September

In response to parliamentary pressure, the Home Office 'Protect and Survive' guidance is to appear as four page inserts in tomorrow's newspapers. Guidance is expected to be broadcast on radio and TV throughout the coming week. The Home Offices emphasises that these steps in no way imply that a nuclear attack on the United Kingdom is regarded as likely, let alone imminent.

The plans for the return of servicemen's dependents to various ports and airfields are working well. However some individuals are having difficulties with accommodation and local authorities have been asked to provide assistance should this become necessary.

There have been meetings in major cities at which public anxiety over the international situation has been expressed. There have been some isolated acts of sabotage at military installations.

There are unconfirmed reports of mine-laying in home waters by the Soviets.

The Prime Minister praised the way in which the country was going about the task of conducting the reinforcement arrangements.

Comment The new powers given to local authorities imply (although the scenario doesn't state) that the enabling Defence Regulations under the Emergency Powers Act (which was passed by Parliament on 19 September) have come into effect. Internment and other war measures now begin. The reports of demonstrations indicate that the police and army are engaged on 'public order' problems, but this is not spelled out. The *Square Leg* scenario of two years earlier was more specific:

There has been continuous left and right wing political activity since the beginning of September. . . .Pacifism as a front for subversion has been the main theme. Some demonstrations called for the use of troops in support of the police (Military Aid to the Civil Power). . .

In *Hard Rock*, the emphasis is on terrorism and sabotage – either by Soviet frogmen or otherwise orchestrated by the Soviet Union – to draw the *Hard Rock* local authority players' attention away from the real tasks of law and order being undertaken; simply, the suppression of dissent, and 'persuasion' of the public to stay put.

23 September 1982

The Soviet Union further intensified her propaganda campaign reiterating her claim that NATO's aggressive intentions were evident by her actions in reinforcing Europe. The Soviet Union stated that unless these actions were stopped, she and her allies would have to deploy troops in defensive positions in their own interests.

Late night news broadcast, 23 September

The situation at home is much as yesterday with public meetings continuing to make most of the news. There is growing evidence of anxiety among the civil population as they realise that hostilities between NATO and the Warsaw Pact may be inevitable. There is increased evidence of movement to holiday accommodation in the west.

Some government personnel and local authority staff are reported to have moved to secret wartime locations to get them ready for use should the international situation deteriorate further.

24 September 1982

Soviet forces were reported to be massing on NATO borders. North Sea oil installations were subjected to increasing harassment by Soviet naval forces.

Late night news broadcast, 24 September

The UK Offshore Operators Association has announced that all exploration rigs, crane barges and other mobile offshore installations are to be withdrawn from the North Sea. This is a direct result of the harassment experienced in the past week and marks the virtual end to further oil exploration in the area.

There have been a number of reports of frogmen coming ashore who, it is suspected, may be Soviet saboteurs.

Use of some ports on the east coast has been affected by the stranding of Soviet vessels. This is apparently a deliberate attempt to block reinforcement ports.

25 September 1982

There were increasing signs of general mobilisation in Soviet Bloc countries whose governments were now known to be activating civil defence procedures and other measures involving warning to their population.

Late night news broadcast, 25 September

Throughout the day various reports of sabotage have been received. They appear to be well planned and professional suggesting that Soviet-trained saboteurs are responsible.

The motoring organisations report that there is increased traffic out of London towards the west. Ministerial television and radio broadcasts last night emphasised the disadvantages of leaving home.

Early this morning a major oil refinery in Wales was attacked. A number of simultaneous explosions resulted in the destruction of the majority of the fuel tanks in the refinery.

Comment: According to projections of refugee movements attached to the *Hard Rock* 82 scenario, 200,000 people have now fled from the cities, and London in particular. This flight continues to grow. Ten per cent of the population cannot get the food they want, and a run on building materials for 'Protect and Survive' precautions has started. Although public order aspects are suppressed from these scenarios, earlier exercises had troops confronting pacifist demonstrations by this stage, and every military unit was given extensive stocks of cs gas, as well as conventional ammunition.

26 September 1982

Soviet military preparations opposite the NATO flank nations had reached such a point of readiness that it was clear that an invasion of those NATO nations was capable of being launched within hours.

Late night news broadcast, 26 September

Further reports are being received of mines being observed near to UK coast. These reports indicate that the mines are not of a type kept by the NATO nations.

Petrol is in short supply in some parts of the country and today there are reports of shortage of food in some cities. In rural areas, the petrol shortage is causing difficulty over restocking stores.

Earlier this morning a senior Army officer was about to step into his car when there was an explosion seriously injuring the driver. The General escaped with only minor cuts and bruises.

Most newspapers carry (officially sponsored) features on elementary air raid precautions.

27 September 1982

The war starts.

At 0600 hours the Soviet Union launched air attacks against the United Kingdom. Targets were airfields and air defence radars; nuclear weapons were not used. In Europe, Soviet forces attacked NATO throughout the length of its borders. The attack, which was preceded by a twenty minute artillery bombardment, started at 0450 when main battle elements crossed the border on a broad front. At sea, the Soviet Navy conducted a coordinated air and submarine pre-emptive attack on NATO fleets. High level talks commenced in the UN Security Council in an effort to end the fighting but it quickly became clear that Soviet representatives were taking up an intransigent attitude and were demanding the recognition of permanent Soviet control over certain territories which were to be 'liberated'.

Late night news broadcast, 27 September

At 6 o'clock this morning the Soviet Union launched air attacks against the United Kingdom. Details of damage have not been disclosed yet, but the government has issued a statement to the effect that only military installations have been hit. Although civilian casualties have been reported the civilian population as such is not being subjected to deliberate attacks.

Every effort is being made to locate saboteurs. Many service installations have come under attack and the situation is made more difficult owing to the conventional bombing attack by Soviet aircraft. There are reports of (large numbers of) people moving away from urban areas.

The Prime Minister has formally announced in Parliament and on radio and TV that a state of war exists between the United Kingdom and its allies and the Soviet Union.

Air Raids on civil targets, 27 September*

Time	Target	Number of bombers	
		Attacking	*Shot down*
7.22 am	St Fergus	6	—
7.24 am	Peterhead	3	—

Comment: Ironically, the *Hard Rock* scenario makes it clear that the government statement about attacks on military targets only would have been untrue. St. Fergus (North Sea gas terminal) and Petermead (a port) are, of course, civil targets.

28 September 1982

The exact depth of Soviet penetration (in Europe) remains hazy. It was known however that heavy fighting was continuing on all fronts with significant losses to both sides. Late that night the Soviet Union rejected NATO's response to her demands. It was strongly believed that the Soviet Union was deliberately dragging out the talks to enable her forces to advance as far as possible before the war was brought to an end on her terms, namely recognised control of all territory taken in the war.

Late night news broadcast, 28 September

The bombing raids on the United Kingdom have continued during the past twenty–four hours. Yesterday, Soviet forces attacked RAF stations. The raids lasted for half an hour. This morning Soviet aircraft struck again. In a short space of time Soviet raiders

*Times of raids on military targets are not given (see map for targets).

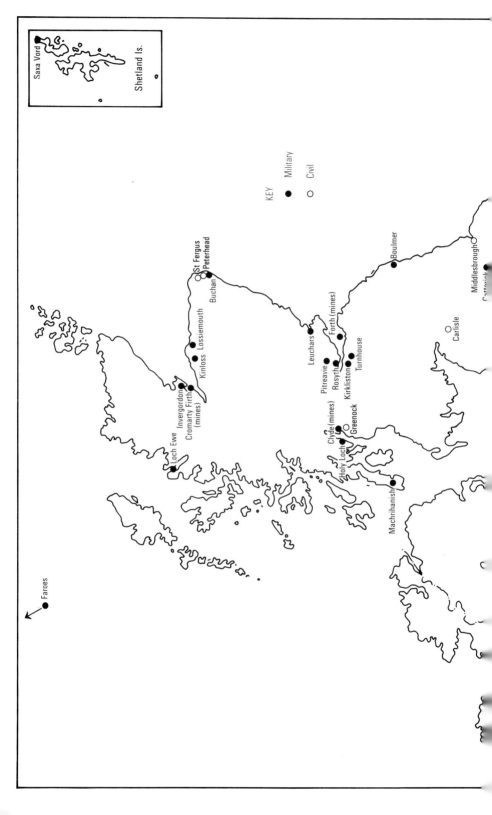

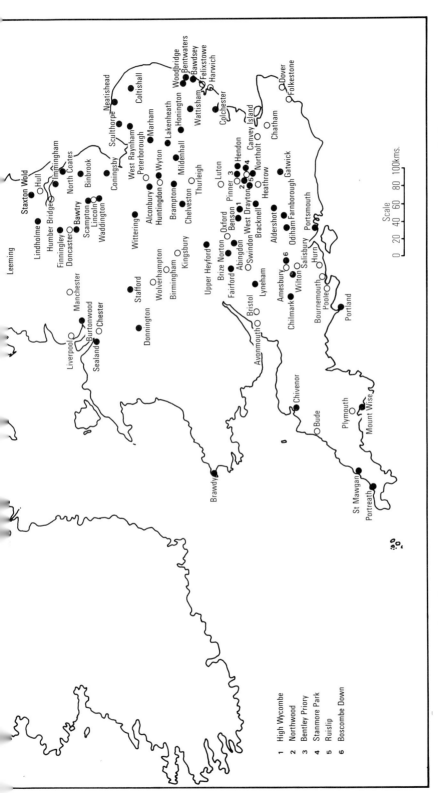

Figure 1 *Hard Rock* 82 conventional bombing targets were to have included civil and military installations. In a realistic exercise most would subsequently have been attacked with nuclear weapons.

attacked nearly fifty targets including RAF stations and naval ports. Details of damage are not yet known but it is understood that Rosyth Naval Base was attacked and the Forth Main Channel and the Cromarty Firth were mined from the air during the raids.

A number of incidents throughout the country demonstrated that sabotage attacks continue. In the early hours of the morning a major port on the south coast was attacked. A series of small but very discriminate explosions seriously disrupted port activity.

At a rally in support of HMG peace moves this morning, there was strong opposition to Soviet objectives, but a call was made to NATO to redouble its efforts to seek peace for fear of an escalation to nuclear war.

Traffic leaving the cities is still causing difficulties. In addition to the sheer volume of traffic on the roads, the situation is being exacerbated by vehicles running out of fuel.

Air Raids on civil targets, 28 September

Time	Target	Number of bombers Attacking	Shot down
6.30 am	Felixstowe	8	1
	Greenock	4	
	Huntingdon	1	
6.34 am	Manchester	1	
	Liverpool	4	1
6.35 am	Chester	1	
6.40 am	Oxford	1	
6.45 am	Swindon	2	
6.30 pm	Ruislip	2	
	Luton	2	
	Thurleigh	2	1
	Salisbury	1	
11.30 pm	Felixstowe	10	2
	Harwich	10	3
	Canvey Island	10	1

29 September 1982

In response to the failure of the talks, the Warsaw Pact stepped up the severity of its attacks against NATO naval units and against land forces in Europe. Heavy fighting continued on all fronts.

Late night news broadcast, 29 September

The United Kingdom continues to be a target for Soviet bombing. Yesterday afternoon, several RAF stations and the Army headquarters at Wilton were bombed. Again, shortly before midnight heavy conventional air attacks were directed against Portsmouth naval dockyard and naval installations in the area suffered some damage. At the same time, Canvey Island came under heavy air attack, as did the ports of Avonmouth, Felixstowe and Harwich. The third raid in twenty-four hours came at first light this morning. RAF stations and naval ports were bombed and the London airport area has also come under attack.

Some twenty-five sabotage attacks have been reported during the past twenty-four hours, not all of them successful. Some sections of the population continue to move to the countryside. (There is) late news of further conventional air attacks.

Air raids on civil targets, 29 September

		Numbers of bombers	
Time	Target	Attacking	Shot down
6.30 am	Avonmouth	3	1
	Bristol	1	
6.45 am	Amesbury	1	(Bombers could not reach
7.00 am	Bude	1	assigned target of Bristol.)
6.30 pm	Hull	2	
	Humber Bridge	1	
	Doncaster	3	
	Middlesborough	4	
	Lincoln	2	
6.34 pm	Doncaster	4	
	Swindon	2	

Comment: The exercise starts with the opening up of war HQs and briefings of 'players'.

30 September 1982

The exercise 'play' starts at 9 am with a review of the overall home defence situation

General Situation Report

Morale: There is deep concern amongst the population that the war may escalate from conventional to nuclear.

Voluntary services: The number of people volunteering their services grows. There are some areas with many volunteers and few tasks and vice versa. In addition to numerous offers of help from individual citizens, established welfare and civil defence organisations are eager to become fully involved.

Armed forces: Reinforcement of Europe is almost complete. Delays to completing some movement is being caused by aerial mining of ports. Troops at home are fully committed to guarding tasks. Reserves have (not) been deployed. Some personnel have moved to wartime locations (but command and control continues to be exercised through peacetime locations).

Emergency powers: Parliament has given the government sufficient powers to conduct the defence of the country. The

Plates 1 & 2 *Hard Rock* 82 conventional bombing targets: the northern Shetland radar station at Saxa Vord (above) and a missile control centre at Bawdsey, Suffolk (below).

emergency services, local authorities, public utilities and central government departments are in the process of completing their plans to go on a war footing and (are) urgently engaged on completing their mobilisation tasks. Country Controllers have been given requisitioning powers for premises and goods.

Wartime locations: All designated staff have gone to their Sub–Regional Headquarters. They have no operational role for the time being. Local government headquarters are similarly manned.

Self evacuation: This is still limited in the main to those with somewhere specific to go, eg relatives or holiday homes in the west.

Absenteeism: Absenteeism is almost entirely due to difficulties in getting to work through shortage of fuel or disruption of public transport, although some people are remaining at home to prepare fallout rooms and shelters. Those working for large organisations are reporting to branches in their home areas.

Food: Foodstuffs continue to be moved from ports. Some fat refineries and compounding facilities have been destroyed. Deliveries of animal feedingstuffs have been disrupted following damage to mills at ports. An overall assessment of foodstocks indicates that there are (eight to ten) weeks supply in the pipeline including intervention stocks. Buffer depots have been doubled and there are now some 250 spread throughout the UK. Manufacturers have increased production of basic items, eg flour, sugar, powdered and canned milk for babies. The most serious problem centres on panic buying and hoarding which is on the increase.* Government announcements through the media have not yet had any marked effect. Most shopkeepers have initiated a form of rationing. There is some profiteering.

'Protect and Survive' materials: Advice is being given on the provision of suitable materials. In some areas there are shortages of suitable materials. In some areas there are shortages which have led to self provision (eg removing fences) and the emergence of a few black marketeers.

Petrol, oil and lubricants: The main problem has been a rush on petrol. Garages have imposed various forms of rationing such as limiting sales, supplying regular customers only or cash limits. However the trend is for re-supply not to keep up with demand and motoring to the station or to work is impossible in many places. Priority users are required to determine minimum requirements for essential operational use.

* This is an absurd comment, *Protect and Survive* tells householders to 'stock enough food for fourteen days'. Then, it appears, the government complains of food 'hoarding'.

Plate 3 Scottish Eastern Zone HQ at Kirknewton, a massive surface concrete bunker developed on a 1950s War Room site.

Communications: Prior to the first Soviet attacks on the United Kingdom, there were no difficulties in telecommunications (telephones, teleprinters and telex lines). However, after the air attacks on 27 September, loss of communications of the order of five per cent were experienced in attacked areas because of damage to the system. Further degradation was experienced on 28 and 29 September. There is little difficulty for local authorities, the police and fire services or government departments who are receiving priority attention for the repair of their lines but private telephone subscribers are experiencing difficulties. Arrangements are being made by official sources to assist relatives who are unable to contact families in bombed areas.

Broadcasting: Television and radio entertainment is continuing – interspersed with public guidance delivered at frequent intervals.

Policing: Throughout the country the police are responding to a wide range of activities and incidents and individual calls for assistance as well as pursuing such specific war functions as the protection of important installations, UKWMO (UK Warning and Monitoring Organisation) liason, and completing force mobilisation. In effect, most police forces are engaged at the 'major incident' level with major calls being made on their resources for traffic arrangements and the investigation of reports of saboteurs.

Fire services: The absence of some armed forces fire brigades who have gone to Europe has placed considerable extra demands on the local fire brigades in coping with fires arising on military establishments subjected to direct attack. RAF airfields still have fire brigades stationed there. The brigades are also prominently engaged in measures to rescue trapped civilians and to restore disrupted water supplies in civilian areas. There are difficulties in obtaining fresh stocks of foam, etc. In addition, brigades continue their war mobilisation measures.

Health: In the areas attacked, NHS staff are fully stretched. Difficulties are encountered discharging long-stay patients for care in the community, and (in) restricting admissions. There is an incipient outbreak of flu.

Social Security: Many local DHSS offices are being inundated with requests for 'special needs' allowances to enable householders to obtain their 'Protect and Survive' materials.

Cash and credit: are in demand generally and banks, Post Offices and building societies report widespread withdrawals from accounts.

Transport: The rail and road network have not been severely affected by bombing raids although some local damage has been sustained. There is severe congestion on some roads to the west; a problem made worse by vehicles running out of fuel and being left abandoned. Despite some bombing damage, trains are running virtually at normal capacity although normal schedules have been disrupted.

Prisons: Most inmates have been released on parole. The exceptions are those with a substantial term of imprisonment still to serve whose immediate parole would be likely to put the public at serious risk. They number (one thousand) and are to be held in not more than five high security establishments.

Saboteurs: There now exists a very low level of unattributable sabotage.

Air raids on civil targets, 30 September

		Number of bombers	
Time	*Target*	*Attacking*	*Shot down*
7.00 am	Oxford	4	
7.30 am	Carlisle	5	
	Birmingham	5	
	Wolverhampton	5	
	Kingsbury	1	
7.33 am	Manchester	5	
	Peterborough	5	
7.36 am	Liverpool	5	1
8.00 am	Dover	5	2
	Chatham	3	
	Plymouth	4	1
	Folkestone	2	

Comment: This briefing concludes the run up to the 'play' of *Hard Rock*. Even in this very optimistic view, the scenario outlines a grim picture of fleeing refugees, food and other supplies becoming exhausted, and public disorder. These versions of the *Hard Rock* scenarios were produced in December 1981 by the Home Office, and they omit many features of Home Defence planning, including the control of roads, and the early 'control' of food and petrol. As we see later, plans for these moves are quite explicit. The *Hard Rock* exercise is different from its predecessors in that it is intended (from the Home Office point of view) to be a public relations campaign almost as much as a serious exercise. Thus, many features of earlier exercises have been dropped or distorted, and the scenario itself altered to present the best achievable image of civil defence. Thus, *Hard Rock* features a public granting NATO and the government full support, largely obedient to instructions to 'stay put' even in target areas, and a minimum level of disorder and chaos and rioting. The alterations to the scenarios made on the draft obtained by the author show some of the public relations work going on – references to *Protect and Survive* (the discredited Home Office pamphlet on household precautions against the bomb) have been deleted; the new official term is 'DIY public civil defence'. The 'inundation' of '*Many* local DHSS offices' with supplementary benefit claimants asking for money so they could built shelters was altered to just '*Local* DHSS offices'. The general point is worth noting too – it would be those who didn't have money or employment or food stocks or 'vital' skills, or indeed cars for 'motoring to the station' from the home counties (as the *Hard Rock* planners appear to do) who would stay in the cities and die in the nuclear strike. As in the Second World War, it would be the urban working class who would have to bear the brunt of the aerial bombardment.

Other cosmetic changes to the scenario concern policing, public order, and morale, but it has not been possible to determine what the original and, presumably, more pessimistic assumptions may have been. Some 'facts' such as the level of the wartime prison population (one thousand), or the over-optimistic suggestion of eight to ten weeks supply of food in the pipeline are placed, tentatively, in brackets for argument and later revision.

The target map for *Hard Rock* conventional bombing includes both military targets and civil targets for which full details of air raids are given above. When the nuclear attack comes on October 3, many of the nuclear targets will have been conventionally bombed first.

The long phase of conventional bombing before nuclear attack (six days) and the comparatively short warning period for reinforcement before war (eight days) reflects changes in NATO policy made during the early 80s. The Home Office *Civil Defence Review* circular (ES1/81) had stated:

Changes in strategic thinking mean that we must be prepared for conventional as well as nuclear attack on this country and for the possibility of hostilities occurring at short notice. Emergency plans will have to be maintained at a higher state of readiness and be capable of dealing with a variety of forms of attack, ranging from the effects of conventional aerial attack with high accuracy weapons against a limited number of targets to the devastating consequences of strategic nuclear attack.

The government suggested that Britain now faced:

. . . as little as seven days warning of attack . . . . The basic essentials of plans should be capable of implementation within forty-eight hours.

Hard Rock takes on board some of these assumptions, with more than a good measure of optimism about the ability of emergency services to come into effective operation.

In appendices to the scenario, the 'players' in the war game were given estimates of various critical developments. These included, by 30 September:

- A thirty per cent shortage of foodstuffs;
- A thirty-two per cent shortage of *Protect and Survive* materials;
- A twenty-five per cent shortage of petrol and oil;
- Five per cent of communications out;
- About 1.4 millions refugees fleeing from likely targets, mainly London and the South East, the West Midlands, East Anglia and Lincolnshire. (Home Defence Regions 3–6 and 9). By the time of the 2 October nuclear attack, these figures would probably have doubled.

2 October 1982, 2 pm: Before the nuclear attack

In Europe heavy fighting continues on all fronts and there has been a sharp increase in the number of casualties on both sides. The extent of present Soviet penetration is not clear but second echelon forces have been committed and NATO forces are under extreme pressure. (All the NATO front forces have also suffered heavy attack.) Intense diplomatic pressure to end the fighting continues but efforts are persistently thwarted by Soviet prevarication and the refusal to retreat from territory she has 'liberated'.

In the United Kingdom conventional air attacks on military airfields, communications centres and headquarters have continued. Large numbers of casualties have been suffered in these areas and widespread damage caused in areas adjacent to these targets. Localised disruption of transport and fuel supplies has brought about some shortages of food. Public reaction to the continued failure of peace initiatives is muted, but fear of an escalation to the possible use of nuclear weapons is now uppermost in everyone's minds. As a result the population fears that nuclear attacks are imminent. All remaining home defence measures have been implemented and, where applicable, remaining staff of government departments and military headquarters have been deployed to their post strike positions.

Comment: In this standard and much-rehearsed NATO scenario, the next moves are clear. NATO forces are giving way across the central front in Germany and falling back on the Rhine. Reserves will not survive long. NATO has no policy of 'no first use' of nuclear weapons; on the contrary, NATO policy is to use tactical nuclear weapons in precisely such a situation, to destroy and repel attacking conventional forces. Even though the Red Army has, in this scenario, now overrun large parts of West Germany, SACEUR (Supreme Allied Commander Europe) will now have sought and obtained reluctant permission from the NATO Council and the United States President for 'release' of nuclear weapons. H–hour, from which time NATO military commanders are empowered to begin nuclear fire, is late this afternoon. If they do not get release, soon the nuclear missile and artillery units will themselves be overrun.

Strike aircraft, howitzers and Pershing missiles fire concentrated 'packages' of tactical nuclear weapons – from thirty to one hundred weapons at one time – to destroy the Soviet advance. Soviet scenarios are clear on the response at this point; a retaliatory salvo will *not* be limited. Successive Chiefs of the British Defence Staff have explained that no 'limited' NATO nuclear war exercise has ever stopped short of an all out exchange – Armageddon in Europe and the northern hemisphere.

In the rear, and in Britain in particular, longer range, more devastating nuclear weapons are readied. Ten flights, each of sixteen Cruise Missiles, are dispersed throughout Britain, and dozens of airfields are choc-a-bloc with US bombers and fighters which have arrived as part of NATO's reinforcement measures. Soviet Bloc rocket and air forces in Poland, Czechoslovakia and the western republics of the USSR, in the Baltic and the Atlantic are at a high state of readiness.

There are only a few hours left.

The Attack

The Home Office plans for *Hard Rock* are polite, aseptic and remote from reality. As the pamphlet, *Civil defence – Why We Need It** proclaims:

War would be horrific. Everyone knows the kind of devastation and suffering it could cause . . .

Everyone knows, indeed, but it is both easy and convenient for officials to forget the appalling horror of war – any war – from remote offices and windowless, isolated bunkers. The reason why we all want to avoid war, whether we favour nuclear deterrence or nuclear disarmament, is because it is so awful, so bloody and so futile. Yet the military planners, and the glib theorists of *Hard Rock* and other rehearsals for war, seem only too ready to forget their – and our – humanity in the mechanics of paper shuffling. A 'standard' 200 megaton attack on the United Kingdom alone would be the greatest and most fearful catastrophe that the human race has ever experienced – irrespective of the effect of nuclear war on any other nation, and there would be many involved at that level of war. For the 20,000 official 'players' who may eventually play the Home Defence game from their bunkers and Regional HQs, there are fifty-five million outside who have no choice but to take all the risks and all the consequences.

The tortuous, mechanistic language of official Home Defence planning robs us all of humanity just as much as the jargon of megadeaths and Mutually Assured Destruction. Before examining how Britain will ultimately fare in the aftermath of an attack, and the real details of Home Defence plans, it is worth remembering the quantity of suffering that is involved. J. B. S. Haldane described one of the first modern air raids in 1938:

Air raids are not only wrong. They are loathsome and disgusting. If you had ever seen a child smashed by a bomb into something like a mixture of dirty rags and cat's meat you would realise this

* Distributed free by the Home Office and Scottish Office in 1981.

Plate 4 Nagasaki after the bomb.

fact intensely . . . I find it unpleasant even to write about what babies look like when you dig their bodies out of the ruins of a house, or pick them up so terribly mutilated that you wonder whether it would not be an act of mercy to complete the fascists' work by dashing out their brains on the wall, as you would do if they were animals.*

The quantum of suffering has since increased:

(Mr Tanimoto) was the only person making his way into the city; he met hundreds and hundreds who were fleeing, and every one of them seemed to be hurt in some way. The eyebrows of some were burnt off and skin hung from their hands and faces and hands. Others, because of pain, held their arms up as if carrying something in both hands. Some were vomiting as they walked. Many were naked or in shreds of clothing. On some undressed bodies, the burns had made patterns – of undershirt straps and suspenders and on the skin of some women, the shapes of flowers they had on their kimonos. Many although uninjured, supported relatives who were worse off. Almost all had their heads bowed,

* J. B. S. Haldane, ARP (Left Book Club, 1938.) Haldane was writing about his experiences of the first aerial bombing of civilians, in Madrid Durango and Guernica, during the Spanish civil war.

looked straight ahead, were silent, and showed no expression
whatsoever. . . . All the way he overtook dreadfully burned and
lacerated people.*

Historians have yet to chronicle a major nuclear exchange.
There are only the Prophets:

I beheld the earth and it was without form and void, and the
heavens and they had no light. I beheld the mountains, and they
trembled, and all the hills moved lightly. I beheld and there was
no man, and all the birds of the heavens were fled. I beheld, and
the fruitful place was a wilderness and all the cities thereof were
broken down. . . . A noise shall come even to the ends of the
earth. . . . Evil shall go forth from nation to nation, and a great
whirlwind shall be raised up from the coasts of the earth. And the
slain of the Lord shall be at that day from one end of the earth
even unto the other end of the earth; they shall not be lamented,
neither gathered, nor buried; they shall be dung upon the
ground.**

2 October 1982, 7.55 pm (comment)

Across the darkening face of Britain, seven thousand power
sirens come to life, emitting the powerful banshee wails last
heard more than a generation before. But no vivid white
pencils of searchlights cross the sky now; they have been
replaced by the silent watch of the ballastic missile early
warning radar station at Fylingdales, Yorkshire. Three missile
trajectories have appeared on the Fylingdales tracking con-
soles; trajectories heading towards London, the south coast,
and Yorkshire. There are six minutes left.

* John Hersey, *Hiroshima* (Penguin, 1946).
** *Jeremiah 5*, 23–26 and *25*, 31–33).

2
Attack and aftermath

In the *Hard Rock* scenario, the first sign of the arrival of the long-expected Soviet attack on Britain would be the false dawn of new suns across the streets and houses of West Drayton, Middlesex; Newhaven, Sussex; and Catterick, Yorkshire. Only minutes would have passed since the sirens first howled their warnings. The *Hard Rock* bombardment continues for a further six and a half hours, as incoming nuclear warheads strike targets from Sussex to the Shetlands. At the end of the bombardment 54 nuclear weapons have devasted the United Kingdom, releasing some 48½ megatons of nuclear explosive power – 3000 times the power of the prototype bombs which destroyed Hiroshima and Nagasaki.

The spread of the warheads across Britain is remarkable. (The nuclear bomb plot is on pp. 50–1.) *Hard Rock's* plans are the preparations for the largest and most important civil defence exercise since the Civil Defence Corps was abandoned in 1968. Included in the plans, for the first time, are many of the civil departments' officials who would run the SRHQ bunkers and later the Regional Government HQs planned after a nuclear attack. Also included is the first exercise period which deals in detail with the so-called 'recovery' phase of a nuclear war – a month and more after the bombs. It has been planned as the first test of the new and supposedly more effective civil defence arrangements of the 1979 Conservative government. It is the first exercise which has not been purely military in its origin and planning. It is therefore all the more remarkable that the *Hard Rock* plans postulate the most absurd nuclear strike ever seen in a serious civil defence exercise.

The bomb plot has apparently been constructed with public relations in mind. Since it bears little resemblance to a realistic pattern of attack, it is of no value for testing civil defence plans. Its principal purpose appears to be the production of statistics for public consumption on the 'value' of government

Figure 2 (overleaf) *Hard Rock* 82: the nuclear strike
Compared with 130–140 bombs in previous exercises, and 180 in
a 'typical' Home Office scenario. *Hard Rock* was to be miniscule
in scale and – especially – effects. There are fifty four bombs on
the plot; total yield 48.45 megatons. Many bombs missed their
apparent targets, especially cities.

Major strategic targets: none

Major military targets: Catterick, Wyton, Wittering, Honington
(miss), Scampton (miss), Prestwick (miss), Lossiemouth (miss),
Portsmouth (Spithead, in sea)

Minor military targets: Waterbeach, Netheravon, Defford (miss)

Cities hit: Plymouth, Hastings, Leicester, Glasgow

Cities missed: Liverpool, Carlisle, Perth, Nottingham, Leeds,
Bradford, Birmingham, Stoke on Trent, Swansea, Colchester,
Brentford, Aylesbury, Bedford

Industrial: Shotton (steel), Sullom Voe, St Fergus, Fawley,
Fishguard, Falmouth, Milford Haven (oil), Runcorn
(chemicals), Forth Bridge (transport), Newhaven (port),
Eglinton, Sydenham, Staverton (minor airfields), Heathrow
(miss), Gatwick (miss)

Non–targets: Mallaig, Builth Wells, Downham Market, Bideford,
Skipwith, Sandbach, Weston, Stowmarket, Mersea

The map shows a city or other target seperately when a bomb
aimed at it 'misses'. Many bombs, particularly on cities, have their
ground zeroes (centre of the explosion) from six to ten miles from
the city centre, which results in a considerable reduction in
casualties. Sometimes, these shifts have been extremely artful.
The bomb on Walsall has its ground zero on the M5/M6
motorway intersection, perhaps the least populated area it is
possible to find within the West Midlands conurbation. The same
effect can be seen, when the bomb plot is examined in detail, at
Swansea, Carlisle, and Nottingham.

The 'non targets' are places without any population
concentration or military or industrial significance. Even these
bombs have sometimes been oddly moved; the bomb on Builth
Wells, for example, explodes three miles away on a mountaintop
called Carneddau. This is a 500 kiloton hydrogen bomb, but it
causes only trivial casualties. In this, and a multitude of other
ways, the *Hard Rock* exercise became a public relations effort on
behalf of the Home Office, and not, in any way, a test of the
effectiveness of its civil defence plans.

---

policy. Certainly, the Home Office scenarios do warn players
that the exercise plans 'should not be taken as a realistic
description . . . of the weight or distribution of an enemy's
attack'. That is not a mistake that anyone who examines the
Hard Rock bomb plot in detail would make.

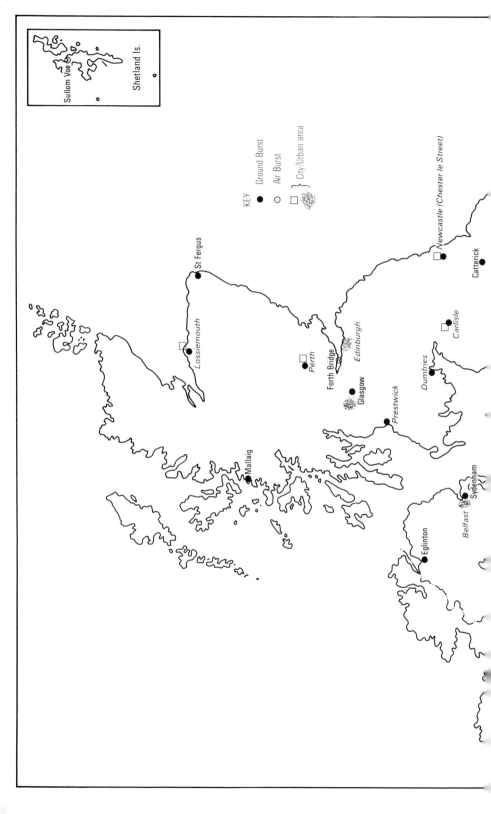

KEY

● Ground Burst
○ Air Burst
□ City/Urban area

Sullom Voe

Shetland Is.

St Fergus

Lossiemouth

Perth

Forth Bridge

Edinburgh

Glasgow

Prestwick

Dumfries

Carlisle

Newcastle (Chester le Street)

Catterick

Mallaig

Sydenham

Belfast

Eglinton

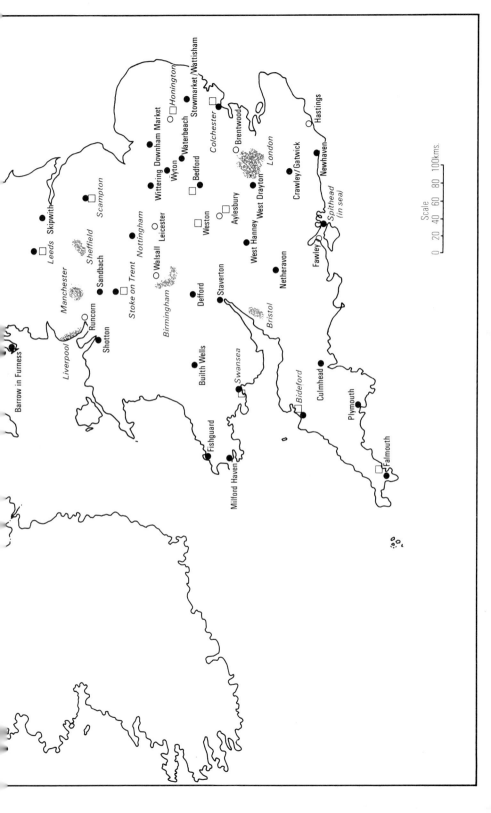

The major features of the attack pattern are:

- No bombs on vital strategic military targets – US or NATO bases, command centres, cruise missile or submarine bases;
- There are seven bombs on lesser military targets, plus three which 'miss'. In previous comparable exercises there were at least fifty attacks on major military targets;
- Twenty cities *are* attacked. But only four bombs strike near city centres (Hastings, Glasgow, Leicester and Plymouth). In every other case, the bombs are placed on a sparsely populated area of land near the city concerned, minimising the casualty figures.
- The only bomb aimed near London explodes on part of the M4 motorway, far west of London, near Heathrow airport (also missed). The bomb intended for Nottingham lands on the M1 motorway eight miles west of the city.
- Many bombs land on tiny towns of no significance – whether military, urban or industrial. Examples are Mersea in Essex, Builth Wells in Wales, and Mallaig in Scotland.
- The major 'realistic' targets are oil refineries and industrial installations. Except for Fawley on the Solent and Shotton, these targets are all far from significant population concentrations.

It is hard not to conclude that this bomb plot was prepared with two considerations in mind. Firstly, because of the close public attention these exercises draw, the Home Office did not wish to appear to confirm that any particular site – for example a United States Air Force nuclear bomber base – might be a potential nuclear target, however blindingly obvious such an observation might be.

Secondly, the premeditated 'adjustments' to the bomb plot which were made during 1981 and 1982 result in convenient and comparatively small casualty figures. Even on more pessimistic (and unofficial) models of the effects of such an attack, the dead would amount to 3–6 million. This sort of result could be given useful play by the Home Office in its publicity campaigns, were its detailed assumptions not to be closely scrutinised. In fact the casualty toll previously suggested publicly by Home Office ministers generally has been put at between 26 million and 41 million, depending (they claim) on whether 'Protect and Survive' precautions and other official plans are implemented.

The Home Office exercise specification for *Hard Rock* says that it is 'intended to practise and test selected civil and armed forces procedures post-strike'. The nuclear attack is to be followed by 'various stages within the survival and recovery periods'. The objectives include:

- To exercise designated wartime staffs and other personnel in relevant roles at all levels of headquarters in the system of wartime regional government.
- To test the Emergency Communications Network, the UKWMO, and military home defence communications systems.
- To practise preparations for survival of selected headquarters.
- To practise and test the armed forces chain of command and procedures for home defence. To exercise the employment of armed forces in support of the civil authority, especially when residual fallout is still critical.
- To exercise logistic and resource allocation problems when movement is partly inhibited by residual fallout.

Very few of these tasks have any real impact on the 'ordinary' survivor; no life saving, emergency or medical services will be supplied in any attacked area for many days, because there are no resources available to deal with operations in heavy fallout areas.

The bomb plot illustrated here was, according to exercise specifications, 'devised by UKWMO (the UK Warning and Monitoring Organisation) to meet Home Office requirements' and 'political clearance' was given by the Ministry of Defence. It was drawn up in outline in June 1981, and was supposed originally to have had about one hundred and five bombs: eighty groundbursts, twenty airbursts, five underwater bursts. Gradually the numbers of bombs were whittled away as the Joint Emergency Planning Staff at Army headquarters at Salisbury circulated the plot to different ministries and regions for 'adjustment'. What finally emerged as the bomb plot for final issue in June 1982 was a wholly bowdlerised attack scenario. The final bomb list is marked 'Distaff (Directing Staff) eyes only' and was not intended to be seen by exercise players in advance, or by the public at all.

As the map on pp. 50–1 shows, the 130-plus bombs of *Scrum Half* or *Square Leg* have been reduced, not to a hundred, but to a mere fifty-four as a result of the process of 'political clearance'. I am obliged to Philip Steadman, Director of the

Centre for Configurational Studies at the Open University and Dr Stan Openshaw of Newcastle University, for having carried out an analysis of the effects of the *Hard Rock* strike using the computer programmes they have developed to assess casualties after a nuclear attack. (These assessments, and the deficiencies of similar Home Office analyses, are described in more detail in Chapter 11.) This enables us to assess the political effectiveness of having made the bomb plot subject to 'political clearance'. A Soviet attack on the lines of *Hard Rock* would kill 7.9 million and leave 5 million injured. *Square Leg*, in contrast, caused 29 million deaths and left 6.4 million injured.*

As government protagonists are pleased to assert, this casualty toll demonstrates that even a major nuclear attack, at the two hundred megaton level, does not immediately end all life in the British Isles, or even the vast majority of all lives. This is evident, of course, to those on both sides of the debate about nuclear deterrence and civil defence. As an argument about 'survivability' in nuclear warfare, however, any presentation of a claim that fifty per cent would survive the first days of the strike is criminally deficient in understanding.

In the first place, most of the data on nuclear weapons effects which have been used to assess the death and casualty tolls are frail indeed, because there is little rigorous scientific data on the effects of nuclear weapons on cities. This is as it should be; it is hard not to feel considerable repugnance at the eagerness with which Hiroshima and Nagasaki survivors were studied by doctors and scientists to discover the bomb's effects. But it means that data on biological effects of nuclear weapons are largely confined to this sole source; and that concerning the effects of blast on buildings confined to a few US and British tests made before the Partial Test Ban treaty was signed. No-one can really say for certain whether or not

---

* These calculations assumed a 15 mph (24 Kph) southerly wind, a standard nighttime population, and an average protective factor of 5. The Home Office usually uses an implausible PF figure of about 20, which would, for example, reduce the *Hard Rock* casualties further – to 3 million dead and 3.8 million injured, almost half the realistic figure.

Figure 3   *Square Leg* nuclear targets. The exercise used a relatively realistic target list, probably based on one of the 'standard' Home Office lists. Shaded areas indicate the extent of fallout after three hours.

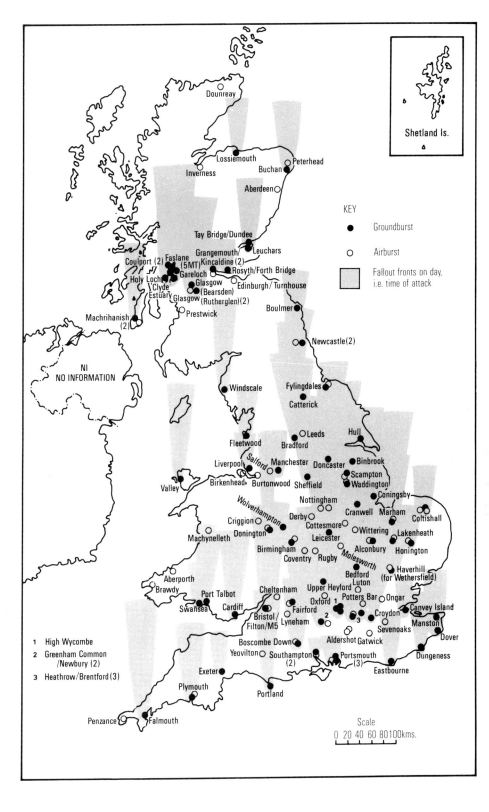

KEY

● Groundburst

○ Airburst

▨ Fallout fronts on day, i.e. time of attack

Shetland Is.

Dounreay

Lossiemouth
Inverness
Buchan
Peterhead
Aberdeen

Tay Bridge/Dundee
Leuchars
Grangemouth/
Kincaldine (2)
Coulport (2)
Faslane
(5MT)
Gareloch
Holy Loch
Clyde
Estuary
Glasgow
(Bearsden)
Glasgow
(Rutherglen)(2)
Rosyth/Forth Bridge
Edinburgh/Turnhouse
Machrihanish
(2)
Prestwick
Boulmer

NI
NO INFORMATION

Newcastle(2)

Windscale
Fylingdales
Catterick

Leeds
Hull
Fleetwood
Bradford
Liverpool
Salford
Manchester
Doncaster
Binbrook
Scampton
Birkenhead
Burtonwood
Sheffield
Waddington
Valley
Coningsby
Nottingham
Wolverhampton
Derby
Cranwell
Marham
Coltishall
Criggion
Donington
Cottesmore
Wittering
Lakenheath
Machynlleth
Birmingham
Leicester
Alconbury
Honington
Coventry
Rugby
Molesworth
Aberporth
Brawdy
Bedford
Haverhill
(for Wethersfield)
Luton
Port Talbot
Cheltenham
Upper Heyford
Potters Bar
Ongar
Canvey Island
Swansea
Cardiff
Oxford
1
Croydon
Manston
Bristol/
Filton/M5
Fairford
2
Lyneham
3
Sevenoaks
Dover
Boscombe Down
Aldershot
Gatwick
Dungeness
Yeovilton
Southampton
(2)
Portsmouth
(3)
Eastbourne
Exeter
Plymouth
Portland
Penzance
Falmouth

1 High Wycombe
2 Greenham Common
   /Newbury (2)
3 Heathrow/Brentford (3)

Scale
0 20 40 60 80 100 kms.

Plates 5 & 6 *Square Leg* nuclear targets were far more realistic than those selected for *Hard Rock*. They included Windscale with its plutonium reprocessing facilities (top) and RAF Scampton, Lincolnshire, with its nuclear weapons store (above).

megaton weapons detonated over many west European cities will, or will not, raise a firestorm, for example.

The more important issues concern ultimate survival, after the first few days, weeks, and even months, in the face of the destruction of all social infrastructure and a minimum of eighty per cent of industrial facilities. What will be the consequences and death toll, not one week or one month after attack, but after a year or eighteen months?

Public statements on civil defence do not even begin to contemplate anything beyond the immediate aftermath. Privately, official studies, such as the diaries of exercises like *Hard Rock* or *Square Leg*, begin to. Through such sources, we can appreciate what, albeit on an unreasonably optimistic view, the aftermath of nuclear attack may be like in Britain. First, however, it is important to note a number of very serious problems:

- There is no good reason to believe that a two hundred megaton attack is anything other than a 'moderate' assessment of Soviet intentions if nuclear war begins. Since the 1960s, a total yield of some 200 megatons has been anticipated – but as discussed in Chapter 12, this could easily be much higher.
- There is a tendency, understandable psychologically, to consider an attack pattern involving only one brief strike. Then the war stops. But this does not accord with either Soviet or NATO doctrine. Unless all central command and control facilities had been completely destroyed on both sides, and field commanders forbore from further nuclear fire, there is every reason to believe that hostilities would continue, both conventionally and with nuclear weapons. Just as even a major nuclear strike will not wholly end the world or the western and eastern hemispheres, it need not end the war and its warriors.

  The US Office of Technology Assessment report on *The Effects of Nuclear War* asks, rhetorically, 'How much worse would the situation of the survivors be if, just as they were attempting to restore some kind of economy following a massive attack, a few additional weapons destroyed the new centers of population and of government?' This is a most probable late course for an all out nuclear exchange, as some embittered, detached and as yet undestroyed nuclear units and their commanders (perhaps a few missile-carrying submarines) carry out final acts of epic revenge. Could the ragged, starving and dying bands of survivors on each side assert themselves sufficiently to enforce a peace on what remained of the warring governments? One suspects not.

• British military planners have not taken an interest in the long term consequences of a major exchange, beyond assessing whether NATO has the weapons with which to deter or, ultimately, 'win'. There is therefore no assessment in British official plans of the regional or global atmospheric and ecological consequences of a major nuclear exchange. The US National Academy of Sciences, in a 1977 assessment, reported on the damage the weapons would inflict on the ecosystem – which would be the only lifeline for the reconstruction of any kind of society – or even for the maintenance of life, at all. The most serious effect would be the destruction of the ozone layer (or about seventy per cent of it) and the massive ultra violet bombardment which would ensue – burning skin, blinding, destroying crops, and causing major damage to agricultural production due to a change in global weather conditions.

The Royal Swedish Academy of Sciences published a new report in June 1982, confirming many of these effects. The global destruction of the food supply could kill three billion people in the southern hemisphere, while those in the north would face slow decimation through starvation, medium and long term radiological effects, disease and adverse changes in climatic conditions.

This account does not set out to repeat these long term assessments, which have not been challenged – just ignored. They do however compound the absurdity of the British government's civil defence policy, which consigns the whole issue of what happens during 'reconstruction' after the war – if ever it ends – to a near void in official thinking. In early 1982, there were some signs that officials had begun to realise that life after nuclear attack did not stop after one month, although to read the sixty accumulated Home Office circulars issued to local authorities since 1972, one would be excused for thinking that it did. There has been no discussion of the 'long term recovery' phase; it was merely presumed that it existed, and would somehow be better than the phase that survivors had just endured.

Phase 1 of *Hard Rock* was to begin with briefings in more than a hundred bunkers all over Britain on the morning of 29 September, two days into the 'war'. During this phase the main jobs of the local authority controllers would be to tackle the problems of damage by conventional bombing – which on the scale described, with no more than a handful of bombers attacking each target, may well be handled remedially and casualties evacuated and cared for. They would also have to supervise operations such as road clearance, and controlling refugee movement – or, as the briefing puts it, 'consider the implications of self–evacuation by the general public'. Food and fuel rationing under emergency powers would also be administered, but with difficulty since there would not have been time to set up a formal rationing scheme. But with the nuclear attack, Phase 1 ends, and Phase 2, post-strike, begins.

The *Hard Rock* bombs stopped falling at 2.46 am on Sunday, 3 October. At 3 am, from the sector controls of the UK Warning and Monitoring Organisation, facsimile charts detailing the bombs and the fallout they are causing come to the twenty-seven Sub-Regional Headquarters (SRHQS) and Armed Forces Headquarters (AFHQS) in England and Wales, and six equivalent centres in Scotland and Northern Ireland. The first post-nuclear attack play in *Hard Rock*, as with its predecessors, concerns 'survival' – the first twenty-four hours after an attack, while fires and fallout bar most surface movement and the population's suffering begins. Then a few hours break is taken, and play jumps to a much later period when 'recovery' supposedly starts. In *Hard Rock* this period was to be played on October 4 and 5, but represented the time four weeks after the attack, when fallout is reducing, millions of dead have been buried, many of the injured have died, and long term problems are emerging. Each embunkered team plays through lists of events and problems that portray a grim, devastated and suffering society.

The immediate aftermath of the attack is lucidly described by a military circular about the situation at D+7 days (a week after attack) in an earlier exercise which used a 'moderate' 130 nuclear weapons (*Scrum Half*, 1978).

Plates 7 & 8 Sub-Regional Headquarters for the administration of England after a nuclear attack: SRHQ 102, Southport, Lancashire (top) and SRHQ 72, Bold Head, Devon (above).

The overall situation within UK is one of vast destruction
enormous casualties and widespread chaos as must be expected
after the arrival of some 130 nuclear weapons.
Conditions vary, however, from complete obliteration and no
signs of life in the main target areas to almost normal conditions
in those areas not affected by weapons bursts or fallout. Over
most of the country normal services and public utilities are non-
existent. There is no central government control of any national
facilities.

2. Military operations have ceased both on the continent and in
the UK though there is no guarantee that further small scale air
attacks and naval skirmishes could not occur. The armed services'
post-strike arrangements are in being and emergency
communications systems where applicable are in operation. AFHQS
are in contact with . . . the surviving units of all services. . . .

3. There has been a great exodus of refugees outwards (and
particularly upwind) from all centres of population and this shows
no signs of abating. Most main roads are blocked by fleeing
pedestrians and traffic. Considerable numbers of refugees are
beginning to arrive on the south and east coasts of England from
the continent.

This breathless, official romance of the holocaust is continued
in vast, detailed briefings which are prepared by military
commanders for each Home Defence Region and county
council area. Many of the briefings would make books on
their own, such are the elaborate histories that they chart.

The world they describe is one of huge, wild mobs, roving
the country in search of food stores and government targets.
Medical centres are overwhelmed within a few hours of the
start of the attack, and begin the process of *triage* – or
sorting. Those who can survive without medical aid are sent
away for 'care in the community'; those who would need
major treatment – for third degree burns, serious blast injuries, severe radiation sickness and the like – are put to one
side to die. Many huge refugee camps have been established
by fleeing city dwellers, who are short of food and shelter and
arouse the anger and aggression of local residents.

In the attacked cities and target areas, nothing at all is done
to stop fires, to rescue the injured or trapped, or help those
stuck in the so-called 'Z Zones' – where fallout will quickly
give them a lethal dose of radiation – even inside government
recommended 'Protect and Survive' style shelters. Most

police and military units are taking shelter, and the streets are left to those who chance their lives by moving in the open. Inside the Sub-Regional HQs, and military and local authority bunkers, officials slowly assemble reports about the wild world outside. Some areas, of course are hardly suffering at all, perhaps only with the milder levels of fallout being deposited from bombs striking elsewhere.

Emergency food supplies will not be released by Sub-Regional Commissioners to Food Depots and Feeding Centres until two weeks after the attack. Until then, the people would have to survive with what they had stored or carried with them as they fled. Many people had not been able to obtain enough food in the days of panic and shortages before the attack, of course, and the situation for them and their families rapidly becomes critical. As for refugees, some Commissioners may choose to feed them. Some may not. But if they are positioned in an area where, without significant fallout shelter, they are likely to receive lethal or near-lethal radiation doses, it is very unlikely that they will be fed. They will rampage and loot for food, and, their activities may threaten sheltering survivors, or government depots, bunkers, communications facilities or other key points.

In areas of light fallout, a few days after attack, Emergency Works Organisation teams will try and repair damaged bridges, clear some major roads, and restore communications cables. Compulsory billeting might alleviate some of the refugee problems if the police enforce the arrangements. Meanwhile, a huge drift of walking, even cycling refugees from the urban target areas would be building up – the 'survival trek'. Many would be seriously injured with blast or burn wounds, others, even all, might be walking dead, having already absorbed near-lethal radiation doses.

For many refugees from the urban periphery there will be no survival in the long term. Radiation doses of 300-600 rads (see Chapter 11) will result in death in a month or more, as the blood forming system of the bone marrow gives out. Faced with such survivors, casualty centres will – at the first signs of radiation sickness – refuse treatment for other injuries (other than palliative treatment, if available). They would be advised to refuse such casualties food also.

As is the case with almost all of this book, these vignettes of post-nuclear British society are not the author's guesses, expectations or analysis. They are drawn from government

scenarios and the diaries of *Hard Rock, Square Leg, Scrum Half,* and a multitude of other official sources. In the case of walking dead, for example, there are telexes sent shortly after the strike in *Scrum Half* by the Essex county control, which stressed the problem of:
'. . . attempting to keep zombies separate from clear local residents.' The 'zombies' in question were largely the half million refugees from bombs on London and south east Essex who were tramping north east, away from the havoc. Other requests in the same set of telex messages from the control advised that a particular route was 'passable but difficulties with refugees (so) inadvisable to send unprotected food convoy by this route'. Soon after the attack, the Essex Controller had reported that:

Stay put policy near bomb bursts being ignored. . . . Pre-attack advice concerning food acted upon by public and food suppliers quickly overrun and emptied. MAFF food plan (i.e. the emergency feeding arrangements) *not* implemented. Assume some public have large food stocks and many very little.

Later, the same Controller described plummetting police morale as the problems of controlling the public slipped beyond reach. Forty fire stations were beseiged by mobs trying to get at their food supplies. Hundreds of prisoners were being held, with difficulty, by police, for crimes of murder and organised looting. The 'zombies' were put away out of sight to await their deaths – the County Controller minuted that he had 'requested military to hold irradiated cases at refugee camps'.

Later, in other notes, the problems of the spread of infectious disease are tackled by similar means. Given the critical shortage of antibiotics and the primitive conditions in which the populations would be subsisting, major diseases, once started, would spread like wildfire amongst refugee populations. As local survivors ran out of the food and joined the queues for water and at the Emergency Feeding Station Centres, the conditions for the spread of epidemics could scarcely be better.

Suspected disease carriers, like the 'irradiated cases' above, would be taken aside to 'Special Rest Centres' and prevented from leaving by military guards. Since the suspicion of disease carrying would no doubt be correct in at least some cases, the 'Special Rest Centres' would become, fairly rapidly, death

MESSAGE FORM

FOR COMM CEN SIGNALS USE

PRECEDENCE—ACTION	PRECEDENCE — INFO	DATE — TIME GROUP	MESSAGE INSTRUCTIONS
Routine	DEFERRED	192200	
FROM	ROCHFORD		PREFIX GR
TO	County Control		SECURITY CLASSIFICATION
			Restr.
INFO			ORIGINATOR'S NUMBER
			?

SITREP 2120 19 Oct

Survivors 70000 pop. 5000 dead 15000 die in 2 months 1000 houses damaged

in GT. WAKERING area(.) Refugees estimated 15000 accommodated at

airport hanger(.) Many severely affected by radiation and blast(.) 3000-

4000 at RAYLEIGH Industrial Estate housed in factories fed in canteen(.)

Rest centres those previously reported are still open in addition rest

centres 36 & 37 have been opened(.) Rest centre 68 still occupied by

armed youths(.) Many able bodied volunteers from Safe area have been

obtained(.) Food sufficient for few weeks to feed whole pop. local

residents have been asked to stay at home and eke out food stocks(.) No

food facilities for 15000 moving into airport(.) Grain and Fleur stocks

could serve other areas(.) Transport: Fuel stocks requistioned Petrol(.)

Vehicles: 100 vehicles 30 bicycles 20 meter cycles(.) Transport Officer

collecting apples and potatoes at night(.) Water: O.K. Sewage: O.K.

Health: bury dead main problem(.) Worried mental attitude of zombies(.)

Page 1 of 2 pages	REFERS TO MESSAGE CLASSIFIED ☐YES ☐NO	DRAFTER'S NAME	OFFICE	TEL No.

FOR OPR'S USE	R	DATE 19	TIME 2220	SYSTEM P	OPERATOR PT	D	DATE	TIME	SYSTEM	OPERATOR	RELEASING OFFICER'S SIGNATURE
											RANK

M.F.P. (1643)

Plate 9 Civil defence planners refer to London refugees as 'zombies' in these telegraph message forms sent during the 1978 exercise, *Scrum Half*. All home defence exercises since 1970 have been entirely conducted on paper.

MESSAGE FORM

FOR COMM CEN SIGNALS USE

PRECEDENCE—ACTION	PRECEDENCE — INFO DATE — TIME GROUP DEFERRED	MESSAGE INSTRUCTIONS
FROM		PREFIX GR
TO		SECURITY CLASSIFICATION
INFO		ORIGINATOR'S NUMBER

Attempting to keep zombies seperate from clear local residents(.) Many
local communities are being asked to take refugees from other parishes
Reads: (1) route A130 BATTLESBRIDGE TOA127 cleared (2) route BATTLESBRIDGE
to ROCHFORD via Watery Lane HULLBRIDGE ASHINGDON passable (3) route
BATTLESBRIDGE Rawreth Lane HAMBRO HILL HAWKWELL ROCHFORD GREAT WAKERING
passable but difficulties with refugees inadvisable to send unprotected
food convoy by this route(.) What has happened to other districts
MALDON, CHELMSFORD, CASTLE POINT

		REFERS TO MESSAGE	DRAFTER'S NAME	OFFICE	TEL No.
Page 2 of 2 pages	CLASSIFIED ☐YES ☐NO				

FOR OPR'S USE	R	DATE	TIME	SYSTEM	OPERATOR	D	DATE	TIME	SYSTEM	OPERATOR	RELEASING OFFICER'S SIGNATURE
											RANK

camps. The Home Office circular on the *Machinery of Government in War* (ES7/73) makes this point:

Post-attack decisions should not be compared with the more deliberate and often prolonged peacetime decision-taking processes of government. Inevitably post-attack plans would be crude and simple. The urgent decisions of County Controllers would be arbitrary, and, to some people, would appear harsh and inequitable.

Critical areas of decision for Controllers would concern the shelter, feeding and support of refugees from outside; the voluntary civil defence organisation of the 1980s has been directed to repelling refugees from devastated urban areas as much as to supporting them. Indeed circular ES7/73 comments that, 'Initially at least, County Controllers should concern themselves with the position in their own county . . . it is unlikely there would be any significant scope for mutual aid.'

   This sort of view is implicit in the assumptions made, for instance, in the *Hard Rock* scenarios, that it was legitimate for those with 'holiday homes in the west' to evacuate themselves to relative safety; but the rest of the urban population should return to their homes, 'stay put', and face the consequences. No doubt the *Hard Rock* planners in the Home Office were not intending to suggest that those who could afford second homes should thereby have a better chance of survival in war, but it is difficult not to rank such an observation alongside their comfortable home counties concern with fuel shortages causing problems for those 'motoring to the station' when much of the population go to work by public transport.

This vision of the post-holocaust society accords very well with Peter Watkins' celebrated film, the *War Game*. Different scenes in the film showed rioters attacking police lorries, a mob assailing a food depot and killing its guards, police firing squads shooting looters and a kindly policeman providing euthanasia for moribund casualties by means of a revolver bullet through the head. Various official or 'expert' critics have dismissed the film as inaccurate or exaggerated; and a disgraceful lobby has kept it off public television for over sixteen years. It is difficult not to get angry at such hypocrisy, for a few Controller's logs, military incident lists or exercise scenarios from the dozen or so major Home Defence exercises held since the *War Game* was made, could provide enough material for a hundred such films.

Table 1 (p. 68) illustrates this point with a selection from the daily War Diary of exercise *Square Leg*; 11–25 September, 1980. Each section of the history comes from a different source: the pre-strike details from a national Main Event List; the post-strike 'survival' phase is from regional military records for Warwickshire; during a longer term 'recovery' phase two weeks later, the record of activities carried out by troops in support of the civil authority in Gloucestershire over two days shows the level of disturbance prevalent.

A few pages of the War Diary, extracted from a much larger mass of material, contain almost all the facets of the *War Game*. Watkins' message was not that no-one would survive; merely that survival itself would be a grim struggle, in a food-starved radioactive hell.

The civil and military Controllers of Gloucester County foresee that kind of hell too. In two days, they anticipated thirty-five possible or actual onslaughts by mobs, looters and refugees against food depots, a government bunker and government offices. Asked to provide medical aid, the military refused. But two mechanised platoons set off to defend the Government Communications Headquarters intelligence centre in Cheltenham, whilst a helicopter and twelve men flew to defend some MAFF (Ministry of Agriculture, Fisheries and Food) Food Officers who were supervising supplies from a market garden.

I have spoken to former members of the Royal Military Police who have been briefed on a 'Home Defence' role involving one of the *War Game* scenes almost precisely as shown. The RMP, obviously one of the army's more disciplined units, would carry out brief patrols through the urban and damaged area peripheries to reconnoitre and deal with any isolated 'law and order' problems. Looters would be shot, they were instructed, and so would any injured survivors they encountered. This, the RMP soldiers were told, was a policy both of expediency and humanity. The immobile and or partially mobile injured would inevitably be accumulating a sufficiently large radiation dose to ensure their deaths, from compound injury if not radiation alone. A bullet was kinder, and quicker than a lingering radiation death. More mobile casualties would not be evacuated by these patrols. Bodies would not be collected; they would for some days or weeks remain as 'dung on ground.'

Table 1   Exercise Square Leg: main events and civil and armed forces actions

---

Britain: before the war

---

15 August	Cabinet instructs all departments and specified authorities to review their plans for Transition to War (. . .)
16 August	Fuel rationing imposed.
27 August	HMG requests preparations to be made to remove art treasures.
31 August	Industrial unrest and large scale activity by extreme left and right wing parties.
1 September	Considerable cross channel movement into UK by expatriate families on a self-evacuation basis (. . .)
7 September	Prime Minister speaks to nation on TV/radio.
9 September	Secretary of State authorises power of direction over British Airways.
11 September	Prime Minister again speaks to nation.
12 September	'Protect and Survive' instructions issue through the media.
	Cabinet approves Queen's Order 2.
	Directed food buying (by government departments, police and military services, etc).
	Noticeable run down of industry.
	Local authorities, MPS, police and the services swamped with offers of help in forming some sort of civil defence/Home Guard organisation.
13 September	Prime Minister again speaks to nation.
	Panic food buying breaks out in some areas.
15 September	General Alert and war declared. Fighting breaks out on continent. Conventional bombing on defence related targets in UK. Public reaction to bombing is mixed . . . those living in high rise flats and in areas generally thought to be obvious targets leave home quickly.
	Industry seriously affected. Schools close in afternoon.
17 September	Government authorises local authorities to man their Wartime HQS.
	Public passenger transport operating at fifty per cent of capacity.
	Government orders manning of HQS in the Regions.
19 September	Attack Warning Red 11.55 am. Nuclear strike starts at 12.01 pm.

'Survival': extracts from the War Diary of Warwickshire County

D+ 1 (20 September)	Daily food requirements – 680,700 rations. Eighteen thousand people (in refugee camps) suffering third degree burns; Isolated reports of refugees leaving West Midlands area.
D+ 3	Casualty aid points swamped. Hospitals and improvised hospitals full. Decision taken to conserve police strength with a view to deployment of Police Support Units later.
D+ 4	Commence mass advice to achieve public order. Reappraise triage. Request medical aid from military.
D+ 5	Establish additional casualty aid points close to existing where possible. Commit to home nursing casualties who will probably die. Commence grave digging operations. (Transport) Remove dead from casualty aid points; remove dead from damaged areas as radiation levels permit. Fire situation in county under control.
D+ 6	Identify rationing levels of food and water. *Identify additional rationing requirements of workers.* Flow of refugees from the West Midlands is indicated; 31,000 to North Warwickshire, 12,000 to South Warwickshire.
D+ 8 (27 September)	Casualty figures Rugby area is indicated 30,000 plus estimate, Nuneaton area 17,000 plus. Large numbers of persons suffering first stages of radiation sickness. Arrange for establishment of decontamination units. Consider variations to law – liase with police.
D+ 9	Estimate 100,000 plus refugees coming from West Midlands – most injured/shocked/irradiated. Consider disinfection in Rugby/Coventry area to avert disease. Liase with military for aircraft for spraying. Control of refugees in the west of the county impossible at this state. (Via Wartime Broadcasting System) advise public on measures being taken to alleviate rioting and looting. *Produce advice to encourage 'Good Neighbourly' behaviour towards refugees.* Advise public with regard to disposal of dead bodies. Advise populace not to leave their areas.
D+10	*Numbers increasing at casualty aid points, priority being given to savable under thirties.* Anticipate refugee figures to be 200,000 plus. Further request to Sub-Regional HQ for additional food; SRHQ directive received – conserve fuel.

'Survival': extracts from the War Diary of Warwickshire County

D+11	Arrange collection of food from Buffer Depots. Liase with police and military for convoy guards. Food to be held and guarded in district stores. *Deaths becoming a serious problem, liase with transport and works for speedier removal of bodies from casualty aid points.* Advise public on action to be taken re looting – particularly theft of food. Call for volunteers to assist with transport and works tasks.
D+12	Notification from SRHQ; twenty five per cent of food requirements for refugees to come from local Buffer Depots. Police Support Units established and deployed to areas where refugees are known to be located. Consider establishment of interim police controls in known trouble areas.
D+13	Feeding to commence at 1800 hrs. *Calorific content of meals will be six hundred* + *one pint of water (non-workers), 800* + *two pints of water (workers).* Meals provided for infant feeding totally inadequate, request additional supplies. Known casualty figures 37,000; seriously injured 67,000. Radiation sickness entering third stage. *Disease control absolute priority.* All Essential Service Routes cleared. Identify and prepare additional burial resources. Advise public on location and times Feeding Centres will be open, safe routes to them, (and) emphasise subsistence level of feeding in operation.

'Recovery': extracts from the War Diary of Gloucestershire County (Military Liaison)

	Request to military staff	*Response*
D+14 (3 October)	Request for air reconnaissance at Little Rissington food depot.	No response
	Provide armed troops to assist police at ten locations on M5 Motorway.	Thirty men deployed.
	Provide coils of barbed wire.	Barbed wire requested.
	Provide armed troops to assist troops at Gloucester to:-	
	(a) quell disturbance involving eight thousand persons	Twenty-five troops sent.
	(b) guard a food warehouse at Hare Lane.	Twenty-five troops despatched.

Request to military staff	*Response*
Provide ambulances, trained first aid personnel and medical supplies.	No ambulances, trained first aid personnel or medical supplies available. Some vehicles and drivers only.
Provide armed troops to assist police with law and order problems at Cirencester, Cinderford, Lydney and Newham.	Thirty armed men made available for Cirencester. Due to radiation hazard, (it is) not considered effective to send armed parties into other areas at this time.
Provide armed guards to secure MAFF warehouse.	County Militiary HQ requested AFHQ 7 to provide assistance from east of county due to radiation levels.

	Request to military staff	*Response*
D+15 (4 October)	Provide assistance to police at Gloucester to deal with law and order problem.	Fifteen men from Hare Lane detailed for this task.
	Secure and guard a food warehouse at Cirencester.	Twenty armed men despatched from Innsworth at 0930 hrs.
	Provide guards at twelve food supply and cooking centres throughout the country. Provide escorts on ten food supply vehicles.	Five armed guards provided at each location. Two armed guards provided for each vehicle.
	Assist police to prevent hostile crowd gaining access to Gloucester District Wartime HQ.	Twenty armed men made available.
	Assist police at GCHQ (Government Communications Headquarters in Cheltenham) which is under attack by looters and refugees.	Two mechanised platoons despatched at 1400 hrs.
	Accomodate five thousand homeless at RAF Innsworth.	Cannot accomodate at RAF Innsworth but could take four thousand two hundred at RAF Quedgely. Vehicles available at Aschurch, but no drivers or fuel.

Request to military staff	Response
Provide hygiene and sanitation teams and equipment at Cheltenham. Provide rodenticides and disinfectants.	Unable to assist.
Provide security patrols and barbed wire at *Special Rest Centre* at Stroud for *suspected disease carrying refugees.*	Two platoons despatched to Stroud. No stocks of barbed wire available.
Provide assistance to Ministry of Agriculture officers who have been prevented by hostile crowd from arranging the despatch of food from a market garden.	1630 hrs. Wessex helicoper and twelve soldiers sent to scene.

Sources: The pre-strike event list is drawn from the national Main Event List for *Square Leg*. The post-strike 'survival' phase reports are a very small selection of the daily summaries used during *Square Leg* by Warwickshire's emergency planners. The 'recovery' phase reports are drawn from the Gloucestershire log of requests for military support; both exemplify the detailed planning done in most HQs during the exercise. Emphases are made by the author.

The identification of the moribund by these patrols would be left to the commander – an NCO, perhaps a sergeant. He would not have had any special medical training.

The Warwickshire diary provides an equally grim pictures. Casualties at collecting centres rapidly built up, most of them moribund. 'Deaths becoming a serious problem,' the medical staff reported in their log at D + 11. When emergency feeding was introduced, it was at sub-subsistence level: one pint of water and six hundred calories worth of food for non-workers, and only a pint and two hundred calories more for workers. (A normal requirement for an adult is at least two thousand calories; more if heavy work is undertaken) In such circumstances, none of the workers could expect to continue working for very long; for many it would be death by slow malnutrition. Hunger would exacerbate radiation sickness, injuries, and psychological problems faced by survivors.

The *triage* of casualties had become equally fraught – by

this stage merely singling out those who could benefit from highly limited hospital care, or at most twenty minutes surgical attention, would be insufficient. Age became a new criterion, and only those in their twenties or younger got treatment. Similar features appear in the rules for doing essential work in highly radioactive zones; the higher doses should be taken by those over thirty-five, suggests *Protect and Survive*; the increased longer term hazards, of cancer and leukaemia, which such exposure brings, will cost them less life-expectancy than the more youthful.

The same sets of notes (not reproduced in the table) also point up the other cynicism in *Protect and Survive's* glib advice to stay put. In many areas, scientific advisers reported that the 'general public remaining in their own homes will be absorbing lethal doses (of radiation) but this cannot be avoided.'

Those condemned to die this fashion would be families and others who would sicken again in the late stages of *Protect and Survive's* fourteen day sheltering period. Shortly after hearing, over the regional Wartime Broadcasting System run from the srhqs, that it was now safe to make their way quickly to a refugee Rest Centre, they might have to leave their homes as their food supplies ran out. Perhaps they might not be identified as moribund radiation casualties until a few days later, when scientific advisers at the local county wartime hqs would point out to their Controllers that food, medical and welfare resources were certain to be wasted on evacuees from heavy radiation zones. Generally speaking, anyone who had remained in an area where the initial fallout radiation exceeded a thousand Roentgens an hour* would have little chance of survival.

Any attempt at self-evacuation (none would be provided officially) would merely mean that the lethal dose would be absorbed more quickly than otherwise once people left the relative shelter of houses. The Home Office circular on *Health Services in War* (esi/77) is clear about the non-provision of medical aid in such circumstances:

. . . General life-saving operations in areas of fallout might not be possible, therefore, until *days or even weeks* after a nuclear strike (Author's emphasis).

---

* The medical aspects of radiation are discussed in Chapter 11.

At Casualty Collecting Centres (such as the aid points described in the Diary, Table 1):

Casualties retained at a CCC would have to provide as much basic nursing care *for each other* as their injuries allowed.

Before the final 1968 abandoment of British civil defence, medical planning for war was significantly more advanced. Although the same principles of casualty sorting and *triage* would apply, emergency civil defence recovery and medical teams hoped to rescue many injured and trapped survivors in the aftermath of attack. Although plans might have been unduly optimistic, it was hoped that Forward Medical Aid Units, working continuously, could deal with as many as one thousand casualties per shift, sending three-quarters of them on to hospital. Each such unit would have been equipped with seventy or more ambulances. They would aim to move inwards into zones of increasingly high initial radioactivity, as the actual radiation levels declined over time. Eventually, there would only be areas of such complete devastation and high mortality that rescue and medical operations would no longer be worthwhile, and casualty collecting parties would be withdrawn.

These plans have now been utterly set aside in Britain. The emphasis is solely on conserving a few doctors and other medical staff, and a residue of surviving medical equipment and stocks. Patricia Lindop has observed in her study (see page 388) that:

In effect medical care will not be available in fallout areas to people who (have) suffered injuries in the cramped conditions of life in shelters, so that for days or weeks broken limbs will bleed and become infected, a trapped uninjured person will die slowly from acute radiation sickness – vomiting, diarrhoea and haemorrhage, knowing that no-one can come to them.

This, then is the nature of the world outside the bunkers that *Hard Rock*'s planners envisage, – the officially-expected aftermath of a major nuclear attack on Britain.

Inside the control centres will be not just the local authority and central government, police and military staff but coordinators from all manner of other public enterprise – fire and ambulance services, British Rail, Gas and Electricity Boards, Water and Health Authorities, the NCB and British Telecom, transport and construction enterprises, public and private – each acting out scenarios for their part in the 'survival' and 'recovery' phases. Outside the bunkers, nothing, generally, happens – these are 'command post exercises'. A particular role in *Hard Rock* is given to the RAF and the Royal Navy, to act out this war plan in the field. Under Home Defence plans, the RAF provides each AFHQ bunker with the services of a Regional Air Squadron for reconnaissance work (they can also transport VIPs or undertake such jobs as airborne spraying of disinfectant onto areas where large numbers of decaying dead, and dying, pose a hazard.) After attack, the RAF is also responsible for mustering all available transport aircraft into an Air Despatch Wing, providing a few squadrons of helicopers and aircraft to move troops and valuable supplies around.

Royal Navy ships which have survived the naval battles of the Atlantic will attempt to clear mines from ports which could be of use, escort merchant ships, and requisition empty vessels to assist in the redistribution of the surviving population to less damaged parts of the country. During exercise *Scrum Half*, for example, many hundreds of thousands of refugees from London and the south east, and those living in East Anglia where heavy fallout from dozens of nuclear strikes against US and British air bases threatened ultimate survival through high radiation levels, are gradually embarked for Scotland. At ports which survived – Harwich, Felixstowe or Ipswich, or even resorts like Southend and Clacton – refugees might be ferried off to Scotland in requisitioned container ships. The move relies, of course, on the Scottish Regional Commissioner and his military commanders and food advisers being willing to accept them.

Other countries and areas could expect similar problems – many refugees from Belgium, the Netherlands and France might opt to flee west to Britain, upwind (generally) of the monstrous zones of fallout towards central Europe. In the same fashion, many Britons with any chance of getting on a boat would doubtless endeavour to set sail for the Irish Republic which they would presume, as a non-belligerent, to have survived undamaged. It does not appear that the Irish government have ever considered the possibility of millions of British refugees fleeing their devastated homeland.

The central government (if it survived) at Hawthorn (see Chapter 8) might hope for supplies of oil and goods by ship. A central bunker HQ for Ports and Shipping, coordinated by NATO, might still be in operation but no food and little oil could be expected a few weeks after the war had begun. NATO policy, 'if Saudi Arabia (and OPEC) turned down the wick' after a war, according to a former head of the Home Office's Home Defence Division, Duncan Buttery, would be the 'equalisation of misery'. Britain's own North Sea oil resources would, as the *Hard Rock* target lists suggest, be a major early target of Soviet strikes. It would take ten years at least to manufacture and install new production platforms in the North Sea.

Food is the ultimate problem, and likely to be the major factor affecting the post-attack population at its nadir. Government plans for food supply centre on the minimum held in Buffer Depots, and beyond that on the themes of 'control' – that is, government and military control. Although unspoken and unwritten, the long term implications of government food 'control' are writ large across the plans; Controllers and Commissioners will have to move from the relatively easy decisions – to supply only subsistence rations of less than a thousand calories and the *triage* of casualties at an early stage – to inescapable life-and-death decisions. Policies, mentioned in the War Diary, for example, of withholding medical care from those aged over thirty might have to become more general and extend to food supplies – only those with special occupational skills would be exempt, or perhaps those who had viable families to raise. Human beings would be judged on their worth to the government in the most rigorous and ruthless way – there would be no other course.

The long term 'survival' problems facing Controllers a few weeks after attack could include the establishment of opposing centres of power to the government, sustained perhaps by the government's failure to avert war, and the self-centred policies for the maintenance of authority which Controllers would administer – however expedient these might be in the long term. A recent assessment of essential objectives in Regional and Sub-Regional Commissioners' home defence plans* listed, firstly:

The need to establish themselves as the recognised, legitimate and effective government.

Although no exercise has yet explicitly embraced this possibility (largely because none of them continue long enough),

* 'Scientific Advice in Home Defence', by Sid Butler, Deputy Director of the Home Office Scientific Advisory Branch. British Association, September 1981.

Scrum Half did include scenarios of tracking down and assailing 'illegal' (ie non-government) broadcasting stations.

The same official paper listed other problems facing postwar administrators besides challenges to their authority:

The assessment of the *viability* of the different areas of areas of their Region

The conflicting priorities of using scarce resources for short term problems, and conserving them for the future

The contrast between the complexity and fragility of pre-attack society and the post-attack impoverished community struggling for survival.

In the course of time (how long it might take is not specified):

Commissioners would also need to look forward to the problems of national regeneration, aiming at creating a stable democratic society, inevitably substantially reduced in economic and social terms.

Aspects of this phase of government would include the 'choice of long term objectives which are realistic,' the 'establishment of sustainable living standards,' with or without international aid (a fairly unlikely idea), and the 'selection and development of appropriate technologies' for a post–nuclear society. The ultimate aim is piously identified as:

The formation of a national government and the restoration of democratic procedures and freedoms. . .

Whether such hopes are remotely realisable has never been properly analysed, and what analyses have been done are maintained as highly secret by the Home Office. But some analyses have been suggested.

In 1974, the head of the Home Defence Divison (F6) at the Home Office gave a 'background' (ie, unattributable) briefing to a *Times* reporter in which he suggested, mischieviously, that the Home Office were building up stocks of 'millions of contraceptives' on 'the advice of psychologists, who suggest that people are brought closer together in emergencies. . . . It would be unwise for any births to be allowed for at least a year'. 'The young are also very susceptible to radioactivity', the *Times* report concluded.

This was black humour, in the nature of a joke at the expense of the reporter and his paper. No such contraceptive stockpile has been planned, or implemented.

Eventually, exercises like *Hard Rock* peter out with a few comments on the long term prospects. A final summary of the situation in Essex after *Scrum Half*, for example, noted that despite shipping off refugees *en masse* to Scotland, there was a 'likelihood that in excess of a quarter of a million will remain and this will tax existing food stocks to the extreme.' There are many comments like this, but no further 'play'.

The long term future is thus absent from official war plans. The future may be no future for some races and many nations, and the unknowns in the equations of survival are perhaps too large and often too awesome to contemplate. We might jump, as Nevil Shute did in *On the Beach* to the final stages of planetary life as a consequence of the transport of massive fallout around the globe. That is not now seen as a likely outcome, even if all the arsenals are used. If death came to mankind as a whole, it would be through more subtle, less direct modifications of the ecosystem.

There are just a few writers on this subject, of whom the first was Herman Kahn. *Thinking about the Unthinkable* (1962), was at the time a controversial assessment of a post thermonuclear war world. Another American, Fred Iklé, had four years earlier reviewed the *Social Impact of Bomb Destruction*. Emmanuel deKadt followed Kahn with an account of *British Defence Policy and Nuclear War* (1964), and a Rand theoretician, Norman Hanunian studied the prospects of survival in detail (*Dimensions of Survival: post-attack survival disparities and national viability*). Of these, only deKadt offered a view of the British situation: and immense extensions in the size and scale of the arsenals, as well as in the philosophy of nuclear war have long surpassed his estimates. Two more recent writers, Peter Goodwin, a scientist working for the government Central Office of Information (*Nuclear War: the Facts*, 1981), and Magnus Clarke, an Australian lecturer (*The Nuclear Destruction of Britain*, 1982) offer views of high plausibility but with no better basis than guesstimation.

Goodwin suggests that, 'Britain is likely to fare badly under a large nuclear attack, with perhaps no more than a few million people surviving the first month.' This is a pessimistic, but far from hysterical, view. Clarke examines the presentation of a Home Office analysis to NATO planners, and modifies them by assuming that the claimed effects of 'Protect and Survive' civil defence measures are null and void; thus reaching a post-attack population, a year later, of 15–17 millions.

This is in fact the same figure, for the same reasons, that Home Office ministers such as Lord Belstead have offered as the ultimate 'survivors' figure if the wholly questionable virtues of *Protect and Survive* were not realised.

Somewhat late in the day, in 1981, the Home Office ordered a wide range of special reports from the United States concerning the effects of nuclear attack. The reports had been prepared by the US National Technical Information Service in the late 1960s and early 1970s, and ranged from studies of 'organising after nuclear attack', 'models of economic capability after nuclear attack', and 'recovery from nuclear attack' to the 'effects of nuclear attack on local transportation'. All the reports had been openly available since their first publication. No equivalent studies have ever been carried out in Britain. One American games company has even turned out a board game – *Holocaust* – in which players can compete for economic and military domination in the (dis-) United States ten years after nuclear war.

Shoulder-shrugging guesstimation may be an unreliable means of assessing the impact of thermonuclear war, but it seems about as worthwhile as the politically motivated assessments of home defence 'science', as conducted by the Home Office. Some of the methods used, described in Chapter 11, bear as much relationship to nuclear and biological reality as medieval alchemy does to the modern electronics industry.

Official students of nuclear weapons effects in Britain are concentrated in two centres, the Ministry of Defence scientific staff, and in particular the Atomic Weapons Research Establishment (Aldermaston), and the Home Office Scientific Advisory Branch (SAB)*. The former take the lead in designing bombs and advising on their military and physical effects for the offensive; SAB on the other hand have prepared a long list, with up to three hundred British targets, from which various attack patterns can be profiled and their effects studied by computer. The computer programmes used suffer from massive deficiencies, both in assumptions and method, but they do represent an assessment of sorts – a highly optimistic one.

There are two standard Home Office attack patterns, as follows:

---

* Renamed, in 1982, the Scientific Research and Development Branch (SRDB).

1. Sᴀʙ 'standard unclassified attack': a mixed military and urban industrial selection of targets. The total yield is 193 megatons, from 179 weapons (50 airburst, 129 groundburst). The list excludes military targets of a classified nature – primarily the less obvious nuclear weapons–associated sites, such as command and control centres in London and elsewhere. But well-known nuclear weapons centres such as the Holy Loch or Faslane, or the ꜰ-ɪɪɪ bomber bases at Upper Heyford and Lakenheath appear to be included.

   This is sometimes identified as a 'standard two hundred megaton' scenario.

2. More highly classified attack models, using 80–84 more powerful weapons, all groundburst, with a total yield of 180 megatons.

The casualty totals derived from the Home Office's standard current casualty computer standard model are shown in Table 2. Given their origin, these figures are highly speculative, to say the least. The estimate of long term survivors after Attack 2 (military) is given in the ɴᴀᴛᴏ briefing prepared by the Home Office merely on the basis of a guess that 'perhaps two thirds of the population will have survived' a year after attack. The same paper comments that if 'sound' civil defence plans were not put into effect before the attack, then 'the number of survivors *might be cut in half*' (author's emphasis). Applying this assertion and estimate to the last column in the casualty table, one reaches a long term post-attack ᴜᴋ population of twelve to fifteen million.

This sort of figure accords with more reasonable calculations of the death toll from attacks like those in the sᴀʙ estimates. The exact targets used in the sᴀʙ estimates have not been published or otherwise made available. Nevertheless, we have available from previous exercises some of the attack patterns which have been used. A particular example is the 1980 *Square Leg* exercise, which Steadman and Openshaw have analysed on a preliminary basis,* and their results are shown in Table 2.

These analyses all point to a rapid death toll of well over fifty per cent, taking due account of methodological difficul-

---

* Their analysis is based on the reports by the author in the *New Statesman*, and which are reproduced Figure 3. This is not quite the complete *Square Leg* bomb plot, and the Home Office and Ministry of Defence have refused on numerous occasions to supply an accurate version. Apart from minor inaccuracies in the positions of ground zeroes resulting from replotting from photographs of ᴍᴏᴅ charts, the plot is also incomplete; specifically it does not include any airburst weapons which

Table 2 Survivors after nuclear strike

Attack pattern	Immediate Dead	Seriously injured	Short term survivors	Long term survivors
SAB: *Standard Unclassified Attack* (Mixed targets)				
193 MT	–		–	
129 GB				
50 AB	16		38	26
SAB: *classified attacks* (i) (Mainly military)				
180MT	–		–	
80GB	3–4		5–9	
	8–13		41–46	28–29
SAB *Classified Attacks* (ii) (Counter city)				
181MT	–		–	
84AB				
	20		34	23
Square Leg (1980) Steadman and Openshaw casualty model				
200 MT	29	7		
68 GB				
59 AB	36		19	not assessed

GB: Groundburst AB: Airburst MT: Megaton

Sources: Butler, *op cit*; NATO briefing papers quoted by Magnus Clarke, *The Nuclear Destruction of Britain* (1982); S, Openshaw and P. Steadman 'Models for predicting the effects of nuclear attack on Brtiain' (reseach memorandum, 1982).

ties. An ultimate constraint on population in the first few years post-attack will be the sustainable population level for subsistence agriculture – which does not seem likely to be able to exceed, at most, twenty million. During this period survivors will face high mortality through radiation sickness and epidemic disease, starvation and exposure, and probably through armed struggle for available resources and social control. The old and the very young will have been virtually eliminated from the post-attack population, and few infants conceived in the months before or after attack will have any

---

arrived more than an hour after the attack started, except in Scotland and Home Defence Regions 5 and 6. Thus the total number of weapons actually used in *Square Leg* could have been as many as the in the 'standard unclassified attack'. On this occasion, however, the yield would have been much higher – between 260 and 350 megatons. This yield may usefully be contrasted with the 48 megatons which was postulated for *Hard Rock*.

chance of survival. Part of a generation might be lost. The lowest level of population might be reached three to eight years after attack, after a slow decline below ten millions – provided, that is, that accumulated fallout and atmospheric dust had not so altered the ecosystem as to decimate potential agricultural production, even at subsistence level.

It is worth reviewing, briefly, the development of the attack scenarios. Only once has the government ever issued a suggested attack pattern, although some, like *Hard Rock*, have of course leaked. In recent years, extensive bomb plots have been prepared for the renewed series of autumn home defence exercises, in particular *Inside Right* (1975), *Scrum Half* (October 1978), and *Square Leg* (September 1980). The only comparable exercises, in the era of major civil defence preparations, were the *Fallex* series, which were broadly similar in scope and purpose. Three or four times a year, the UK Warning and Monitoring Organisation holds bomb plotting and fallout monitoring exercises. A series held with NATO liaison is called *Intex*; more recent national exercises have been held in the *Warmon* series. But *Intex* and *Warmon* exercises do not aim at the production of 'realistic' bomb plots, but merely test the mechanics of the UKWMO's plotting work.

Assessments of Soviet atomic capabilities in the early 1950s predicted (probably correctly) a relatively slow growth of the atomic arsenal which the Soviets could successfully deliver to British targets. Planning papers in 1950 and 1951 regarded the threat as manageable. In discussions soon after with the House of Commons Select Committee on Estimates (First Report on Civil Defence, Session 1953–54) the suggested attack took the form of a bomber raid with forty low-yield (twenty kiloton) Hiroshima type bombs. Of these the RAF pronounced that it would shoot down three-quarters, leaving ten cities attacked – a disaster, but nothing compared with what was to come.

The United States' view of the likely fate of the UK in atomic warfare was less sanguine. By the early to mid-fifties, there was a considerable array of US bomber bases scattered throughout Lincolnshire and the south east. Britain's own nuclear capacity, in the form of V bombers and crude, early atom bombs was beginning to become operational, although in a highly limited way. (The bombs were produced very slowly.) For the first time, the Soviets had what would now be called 'counterforce' targets in the UK – opposing nuclear forces which had to be the first priority for nuclear destruction in any future war.

In 1949, us planners had produced a blueprint for a potential global war with the Soviet Union, to take place during or before 1957 – Operation *Dropshot.** This plan credited British fighters with the ability to down only ten per cent of the attacking Soviet bomber force. A related assessment suggested that forty atomic bombs would destroy Britain militarily – one hundred and twenty, completely. Strategic Air Command, whose presence in Britain was largely responsible for its new significance as a strategic target, estimated that Britain and its bases could not be relied on at all after the first sixty days of atomic war.

As hydrogen bombs became available for Soviet bombers and the pace of ballistic missile development became clear, civil defence and other projections of possible attacks on Britain rapidly moved towards total destruction. Exercise *Four Horsemen*, whose title clearly reflected the Apocalyptic gloom then starting to take root, was held in May 1958. Six months before, the bomb plot for one of the first projected H bomb attacks on the British Isles, *Dutch Treat*, had listed (megaton) bombs on Glasgow, Liverpool, Sheffield, London, Belfast, Dublin, East Kilbride, Aldermaston, Aberporth, Brawdy and Shannon (the last three being airfields). The inclusion of targets in the Irish Republic was an unusual feature of the exercise.

Shortly after this the Royal Observer Corps began a major series of exercises to rehearse plotting the heavy fallout of the new H bombs. One series was given titles such as *Dust Devil* (1959), *Dust Storm* (1963), and *Dust Bath* (1964) – an early exercise in 1959 was called *Cloud Dragon*.

In 1960, for the first and only time, a British government department issued to local authorities a projected attack scenario for planning purposes. The scenario was contained in a Ministry of Health circular (No 9/60) and suggested a minimum retaliatory counter – city strike. Some four icbms (each carrying a ten megaton warhead) and eleven medium range missiles (one megaton) were used. The high yield warheads were distributed onto Britain's major conurbations; the total yield was larger than in *Hard Rock*. The targets were:

---

* See *Operation: World War III*, by Anthony Cave Brown (1979). The book consists almost entirely of reproductions of the us plans.

Ten megaton warheads: London, Manchester, Birmingham and
  West Midlands, Leeds and West Yorkshire
One megaton warheads: Portsmouth, Southampton, Bristol,
  Cardiff, Swansea, Coventry, Nottingham, Liverpool and
Merseyside, Sheffield, Middlesbrough, Tyneside
Total yield: fifty-six and a half megatons

Scotland and Northern Ireland were not included in this circular, but on the same basis there would have been a ten
megaton warhead on Glasgow, and one megaton missiles
aimed at Belfast and Edinburgh, and probably Dundee and
Aberdeen.

When the *Spies for Peace* raided the Warren Row Regional
Seat of Government in 1963 (see Chapter 8), they discovered
many details of 1962 civil defence exercises. In one, coden-
amed *Parapluie*, planners had anticipated the bombing of
London with ten megaton weapons – a pattern of three across
the capital. Birmingham received a single five megaton
groundburst, and sub-megaton weapons fell on Aldershot,
Oxford and Chetwode. *Fallex 62*, however, was the first major
British government exercise utilising the then newly operating
Regional Seats of Government during a major thermonuclear
attack. The exercise mirrored plans such as *Square Leg* and
Hard Rock. Mobilisation in the face of a deepening crisis
began on 15 September 1962; six days later, after Regional
Commissioners had theoretically taken up their emergency
powers, the bombs rained in. Within a few days, the casualty
toll was over fifteen million across Britain. Ultimately, reported the *Spies for Peace*, the *Fallex* players estimated that
three-quarters of the population of their region had died.
'Large heavily populated areas like London were called Z-
zones and then abandoned to their fate.' The 1957 Defence
White Paper had, after all, stated that there was 'no defence
against nuclear war.'

Similar exercises were held regularly until 1968 when the
Civil Defence Corps was scrapped. Between then and 1975,
so far as is known, most exercises consisted of the somewhat
idiosyncratic and less realistic UKWMO plots. Large scale
Home Defence/civil defence exercises began again in earnest
with the secret and wholly military *Inside Right*. Gradually,

---

Figure 4 *Fallx* 63 was a CND exercise to identify likely nuclear
targets. The title was adopted from that of a series of NATO
exercises. No detailed official assessments of likely military targets
were released by the government after 1960.

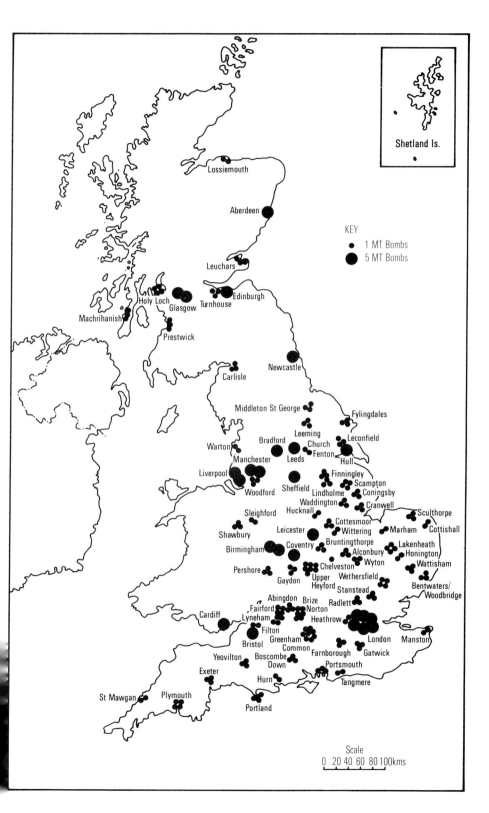

KEY
● 1 MT Bombs
● 5 MT Bombs

Shetland Is.

Lossiemouth
Aberdeen
Leuchars
Edinburgh
Holy Loch
Glasgow Turnhouse
Machrihanish
Prestwick
Carlisle
Newcastle
Middleton St George
Fylingdales
Leeming
Leconfield
Warton Bradford Church Fenton
Manchester Leeds Hull
Liverpool Finningley
Woodford Sheffield Scampton
Lindholme Coningsby
Waddington Cranwell
Sleighford Hucknall Sculthorpe
Cottesmoor Cottishall
Shawbury Leicester Wittering Marham
Birmingham Coventry Bruntingthorpe Lakenheath
Alconbury Honington
Pershore Wyton Wattisham
Chelveston Wethersfield
Gaydon Upper Heyford Bentwaters/
Stanstead Woodbridge
Abingdon Brize Radlett
Fairford Norton
Cardiff Lyneham Heathrow
Filton London Manston
Bristol Greenham Common Gatwick
Yeovilton Boscombe Farnborough
Down Portsmouth
Exeter Hurn Tangmere
St Mawgan Plymouth
Portland

Scale
0 20 40 60 80 100kms

these have become more public, and more 'civilian' in orientation.

The 1978 *Scrum Half* strike, involving 130 weapons, was very similar to the *Square Leg* plot. The plans for *Hard Rock* took the implied level of Soviet attack back to pre-1960 days, and inserted a great deal of nonsense for public consumption. The size of the Soviet arsenal is now many hundreds of times larger and more effective; as Chapter 12 suggests, an attack on the *Square Leg* or *Scrum Half* level would probably still leave the Soviet Union with a considerable oversupply of weapons to use against other British and western European targets.

When the figures are not fiddled with, the societal impact of the attack and its aftermath is not in much doubt. An Assistant Chief Constable attending a Home Defence College course explained:

Given the nuclear holocaust that is in the scenario, we may be back in the Dark Ages, a new society with new rules. . .

Home Office planners don't care for talk of 'holocausts', but the College's former principal, Sir Leslie Mavor, has been more forthcoming:

One thing that is as near as dammit certain, is that after a nuclear war we will never pass this way again.*

* *Observer*, 12 July 1981.

3
War on civilians 1914–1949

The problem of forecasting the scale of destruction in future war is not new. The same roads which civil defence planners – and their critics – now follow have been well charted by earlier writers and officials, particularly in the 1930s as the effects of the coming air war were assessed. Many official planners of the 1930s anticipated damage and death on a scale comparable with what was, subsequently, feared from the use of atomic weapons. The casualties would have been spread out over a period, there would not have been radiation, but the toll predicted was as heavy.

Other factors in official perceptions have been signally constant through many decades. For many centuries Britain had faced no serious threat of invasion, and the civil population, whilst accustomed to the raising of armies for remote European or imperial expeditions, had not experienced direct attack. The First World War changed that. Civilians in the homeland came under aerial attack; and unlike disciplined fighting armies, civilians were expected by political and military leaders to become enveloped in widespread neurosis and panic. Industrial production, it was feared, would be disrupted, the military effort diminished and diverted, and administrative effort consumed in dealing with plummetting public morale.

Such fears developed and sustained an aloof and cynical attitude on the part of government, well expressed in the history of civil defence, from the First World War to the present. Evacuating populations at risk was a task always far lower in priority than its antithesis: preventing wholesale flight.

The central theme of civil defence – control – concerned preventing civilians from behaving in ways the government considered to be against their interests, or against the national (ie government's) interest. It would be necessary in future war to coerce and contain civilian misbehaviour. This could be done overtly by a campaign of cajoling propaganda, and covertly, by preparations for control by police and military force. Later chapters in this book examine these methods as presently applied. They may be best understood, however, not as a cynical and brutal *de novo* design of some particular cell of Home Office and Ministry of Defence planners with Dr Strangelove-like perceptions, but as the continuation of policies and attitudes of the British administrative system, with a long historical tradition and many precedents.

The theme of control has brought together the two major strands which now make up Home Defence. The first is the control of public morale and behaviour under aerial attack; the second consists of preparations for dealing with a general strike, revolution, or insurrection. To deal with the latter, organisations to maintain supplies were set up, whilst police and military forces were adapted, in preparation for armed conflict with part of the population, to a system of regional administration. This planning began in earnest in 1919, after the Russian revolution, as the growing strength of the labour movement in Britain alarmed the country's traditional rulers.

These two historical roots have now fused into a single system of Home Defence measures. Home Defence is a wider term than 'civil defence', although the two are often used (including here) without very much distinction. However Home Defence is the broader term because it explicitly embraces circumstances where the use of coercive measures or military force are *not* related to external hostile attack – for example internal security operations of the sort presently conducted in Northern Ireland. Civil defence should mean only measures for the passive defence of the civil population, by way of providing protective systems, succour and relief. As we have seen, the British government takes a great deal of liberty with such a definition. Most of what is stated publicly to be concerned with 'civil defence' really belongs in the wider ambit of Home Defence, where the chief objective is the maintenance of internal security.

Another constant of civil defence policy is the freedom officials and politicians have allowed themselves to broadcast and distribute innumerable appeals to the public to 'remain calm' and, generally, to 'stay put' with minimal protection at a time when they themselves have constructed or occupied shelter accommodation on a substantial scale. Such attitudes are not in any sense the exclusive province of Britain's rulers – indeed the arrangements made for the protection of key cadres of the Communist Party of the Soviet Union in contemporary war would seem to go rather beyond what any western power has officially planned for its ruling classes. These attitudes are generally justified by reference to the national importance of the officials concerned, the economic impracticability of a large scale shelter construction programme, and the fact that the officials will not, as a class, be wholly excluded from risk. These claims are specious. They place the maintenance of administration as the highest goal any country in war can have.

The hard core of civil defence plans reflect constitutional arrangements of earlier, less democratic times. At an early stage in war preparations, all democracy vanishes. Regional Commissioners are enabled to act, ultimately, under the Royal Prerogative – it is merely preferable, if there is time, that Parliament passes an Emergency Powers Act first. Throughout the country, the system of Commissioners and subordinate Controllers, which began in its present form in 1920, would be one of authoritarian rule, using coercive force when required.

The first aerial bomb fell on Britain on Christmas Eve, 1914. One German aeroplane dropped one bomb, near Dover Castle, and broken glass was the only damage. London's first experience of aerial bombardment was in May 1915, when a German airship dropped a ton of bombs on the East End; seven were killed and thirty-five injured. From that summer onwards, Zeppelin raids became frequent and reached their zenith early in 1916. Much greater casualties, in London, in particular, were caused by bomber aircraft raids in 1917: one raid in June killing 162 and injuring over 420. The public began to take shelter in underground stations, and also 'trekked' nightly into safer, west London. Public demands for a warning system and shelter arrangements grew. According to the official history of civil defence* 'the government only gave in gradually and reluctantly to demands for public warnings in London.' An *ad hoc* system was eventually devised using (as usual) minimal resources:

* T H O'Brien, *Civil Defence* (1955) HMSO (Official history of the Second World War series).

Warning were distributed by maroon . . . and by policemen on foot, on bicycles, or in cars carrying *Take Cover* placards, and blowing whistles or sounding horns.

Towards the end of the war, there were considerable fears of further havoc to come. Gas had been widely used in the trenches; it seemed only a matter of time before it was dropped on cities. Incendiary attacks by hundreds of aircraft, some in the War Cabinet feared, might even have turned the tide of war in 1917–18. But the air war ended after the spring of 1918. Three hundred tons of bombs had been dropped, killing 1400 and injuring 3400 others.

The effect of the bombardment was noted by the British Committee of Imperial Defence. These were techniques which British forces should use (and did use many times in imperial 'police bombing' in India long before 1939); and they were techniques which, in any future European war, would be used against Britain. Selecting the French Air Force as the protagonist-to-be, the Committee's planners set about working out the impact of one thousand five hundred tons of French bombs on London every month. Casualties, scaled up from wartime figures, looked alarming, and secret planning for Air Raid Precautions began in 1923. Nothing, however, was made public until twelve years later, lest the population be unduly alarmed.

The same years saw the formation of plans and organisations to deal with a General Strike or insurrection. Political and industrial struggle had begun on a large scale in 1917, and continued after the war. Action was not limited to industrial workers. In 1919 there were military riots in Folkestone and Calais, while soldiers in London once attempted to blockade the War Office. On another occasion, a party of three thousand troops *en route* through the capital marched on Whitehall, and were disarmed by the Guards.

During the war, an emergency committee for supplies and transport had been set up, in case of invasion. It was reconstituted in 1919, and charged with planning to break strikes affecting any area. A circular to Military District commanders throughout Britain warned them that troops might soon be called on for this work. The new committee, under Sir Eric Geddes, proposed the establishment in emergency of sixteen Districts, under District Commissioners, who would have full devolved powers of civil government. The plan went into action during September 1919, in anticipation of a nationwide rail strike against wage cuts. The army and police were on alert, and a 'Citizen Guard' of seventy thousand enrolled to assist. Powers of requisitioning and other authority were derived from the Defence of the Realm Act ('DORA') passed at the beginning of the war. Full use of the scheme was not, in the event, required, as the strike only lasted a fortnight.

Early in 1920, a British revolution seemed a not inconsiderable risk to the Tory government. A ministers' meeting in February 1920 assessed the risks and the role of the army and the Geddes system in defending the government. The Geddes committee was strengthened as the Supply and Transport Committee; it later became the Emergencies Committee, and has continued in existence ever since. In circumstances faintly reminiscent of 1920, it evolved into the Civil Contingencies Unit after the successful miners' strike of 1972, and the police withdrawal from confrontation at Saltley Gate.

Military preparations to counter insurrection remained in the hands of the Committee of Imperial Defence and the government as a whole. A new act, the 1920 Emergency Powers Act, made permanent some of the provisions of DORA. Still in force today, and often used by the Heath Government, it enables the proclamation of a 'State of Emergency', consequent creation by decree of new regulations (to be approved by Parliament within a week), and the appointment of officials such as District (later Regional) Commissioners. The first state of emergency proclamed was a year later, in response to the miners' strike of 1921.

The schemes for emergency powers and the maintenance of supplies and transport came into frequent use and were finally fully deployed for the General Strike in 1926. From these beginnings came the regional government system in more or less its present form. Regional government was established during the General Strike; it was used again during the Munich crisis in 1938; and went into operation throughout the war. But none of these occasions tested the system to the limit; the TUC leaders of the General Strike did not press on to a general revolutionary confrontation, and there was no German invasion. Lines of communication to London were never cut and Regional Commissioners did not have to assume full powers to run their parts of the kingdom.

The Emergency Committee, chaired by the Home Office Permanent Under-Secretary Sir John Anderson, set up the system in 1925, and details were communicated to local authorities in a government circular (from the Ministry of Health, whose curious responsibility such communications then were). The territory of each regional 'Division' and its headquarters were much the same as in the nuclear age. The HQS were at Newcastle, Leeds, Nottingham, Cambridge, London, Reading, Bristol, Cardiff, Birmingham and Liverpool (Scotland had five 'Districts', based on Edinburgh, Glasgow, Dundee, Aberdeen and Inverness). When atomic bomb proofed 'War Rooms' were set up in 1953, they were, with two exceptions, in those same towns.

The new headquarters were to be staffed by the 'Civil Emergency Organisation', which would organise the work of the civil ministries in each region. The Major-Generals commanding each Military District would provide troops if the Commissioners needed them. The Commissioners – all junior ministers – were designated by the end of 1925. By Royal Proclamation, they were in their jobs, with powers, on the 30 April 1926.

The Commissioners ruled only for days, whilst strike-breaking transport and supplies were organised by volunteers who swelled the ranks of both the Voluntary Service Committees which had been set up (taking in the privately-organised Organisation for the Maintenance of Supplies) and the Special Constabulary. Many volunteers joined, including some two hundred thousand enrolled as special constables. It is this voluntary strand that the government expects to reappear as nuclear war looms – scenarios for *Square Leg* and *Hard Rock* anticipated the police and other organisations being 'swamped' with offers of help.

The theory of a 'civil general staff' which Sir John Anderson's Emergency Committee had created for the General Strike through the Civil Emergency Organisation was studied by the Air Raid Precautions Committee, which the Committee of Imperial Defence had set up in 1924 (also under Anderson). The provisions for regional government were maintained 'on a skeletal basis' from then until the 1938 crisis, and the outbreak of war.

Advice on the likely scale of bombardment came from the Air Ministry. As the only source of expertise on the subject its estimates were unchallengeable and they portrayed – even in 1924 – a gloomy picture. Total casualties would start at five thousand in the first day, and subsequently run at half this number. One third would die, two thirds would be wounded.

In a spirit of despondency perhaps not seen again until the Defence White Paper of 1957 (which said that no defence save the 'tripwire' of a massive nuclear deterrent could be offered in missile war) the Air Staff said that air defences could not significantly diminish such an assault. 'To plan adequate precautions', the official history records, 'seemed almost impossible.' The ARP Committee's report stressed the problem of a collapse in public morale in words which echo the more robust and absurd pronouncements by US and (and also Soviet) strategists on the matter of 'victory' in thermonuclear warfare:

It has been borne in upon us that in the next war it may well be that nation whose people can endure aerial bombardment the longer and with the greater stoicism which will ultimately prove victorious.

Various themes concerning ARP were agreed by the Committee. On 'the education of the public opinion to realisation of the menace', it was thought undesirable to broadcast widely the fearsome prospects of aerial bombardment. On the outbreak of war, however, a Royal Proclamation would

call on the people loyally to obey any orders and instructions the authorities might make (and) exhibit their well-tried qualities of courage and endurance in danger.

But the education of the public in this matter, the Committee thought, should be slow, gradual and deliberate. They examined how local services could be extended to meet wartime tasks, how the public would be 'controlled' to curb flight and the evacuation that might be needed for government departments in Whitehall.

Within this ambit, plans were drawn up for the medical treatment of casualties, and tests were carried out on gas warfare techniques and defences. The first step towards an Air Raid Department was taken in 1933, when an Air Raids Commandant (designate) was appointed for London and a report prepared. The scheme – including new fire fighting organisations and exercises early the next year – was turned down. Civil servants thought it would cost too much money.

It was not that the perception of the effects of war had in any way diminished They were shortly to increase. H. G. Wells had already written widely of one vision, more appropriate to our own era, of 'great cities wiped out in a single air raid, and areas poisoned for years on end'.* Winston Churchill had also become concerned about mass neurosis among civilians, and in 1934 publicly warned:

> We must expect that under the pressure of continuous air attack upon London, at least three million or four million people would be driven into the open country around the metropolis. This vast army . . . would confront the government with an administrative problem of the first magnitude, and would certainly absorb the energies of our small army. . .

Expert opinion warned the government of the psychological debilitation of the population, with people 'behaving like frightened and unsatisfied children', who would 'regress to an earlier level of needs and desires.' This contempt for, and misjudgment of, 'undisciplined' civilians persists – for example in the minds of exercise planners (p. 64) who write off the refugees of nuclear-bombed London as 'zombies' to be kept away from a 'clear' local population.

Money for ARP was first provided in 1935, and spent mostly on research into precautions against gas rather than high explosive attack – the latter posing some more intractable problems of shelter provision. A first circular on ARP went to local authorities in July 1935, and could also be bought for 2d. Handbooks were to be issued, it promised, to advise the public on precautions. An ARP Department was set up inside the Home Office and Regional Inspectors of Civil Defence took up their posts in the government's regional offices, following the example of the London Air Raids Commandant (who had by then resigned).

The first training school for anti-gas precautions opened at Falfield in Gloucestershire in 1936, and a second school followed at Easingwold, near York the next year (Easingwold is now the Home Defence College, and centre for all courses and training on the subject). While continuing to argue with local authorities about the costs of most of the ARP provisions, the cabinet nevertheless agreed to pay for a scheme to issue most of the population with gasmasks; a production target was set of some thirty million masks by March 1939.

There remained, however, a preoccupation with public morale as the dominating factor. The expected panic, of which Churchill had spoken, had to be dealt with. For over a year prior to the Munich crisis in October 1938, the Com-

---

* Quoted in J. B. S. Haldane, ARP (p. 38).

missioner of the Metropolitan Police was pursuing a request for seventeen thousand troops to deal with the London population. An additional twenty thousand special constables would help prevent panic at rail and underground stations and restrain public movement. Official consideration of evacuation policies had always concentrated on restricting, rather than assisting, evacuation; in 1931, the Evacuation Sub-Committee had proposed a massive enlargement of the police force (to one hundred and twenty thousand) to provide a complete cordon around London.

Much the same spirit was conveyed to Military District Commanders by the Army Council in 1938 and 1939. The 'initial preoccupation' of home defence troops would be to 'sustain public morale'; moreover:

The public should be aware that there are available formed and disciplined bodies of troops ready to assist in minimising the effects of air raids.

The minimisation would be achieved with bayonets, not shovels. At the same time the Ministry of Health anticipated a 'probable menace' in the form of civilians with air-raid-induced neurosis which would necessitate restricting hospital admission 'to prevent the organisation from being swamped'. The Ministry of Food was alarmed at the problems of emergency feeding which a large scale exodus would create and proposed the creation of 'concentration camps' into which refugees would be herded, and then redirected back to the cities to continue industrial work and vital tasks.*

These attitudes persist: the police and military retain a strong preoccupation with controlling refugee movements, as the plans for *Hard Rock* and *Square Leg* show clearly, in particular through the Essential Service Route system (see pages 188–195). The present day food ministry, MAFF, has explicitly prohibited the use of any emergency food stocks before nuclear attack for refugees who have left cities or other target areas, thus choosing to 'ignore government advice'.

Another modern artifact which echoes earlier times is the derided official advice pamphlet, *Protect and Survive*. Its progenitor, with which it shares many family traits, is the gov-

---

* The quotations in this and later sections come from three Official Histories of the Second World War: T. H. O'Brien on *Civil Defence* (1955), R. M. Titmuss on *Social Policy* (1950) and R. J. Hammond on *Food* (Vol. 2) (1956).

ernment handbook of 1938, *The Protection of Your Home Against Air Raids*. Although in some ways useful in promoting the ARP debate and wider precautions, it was the subject of widespread and well-deserved ridicule.

This episode of national history has now been repeated three times. *The Protection of Your Home* drew a lengthy and well-reasoned riposte from Professor J. B. S. Haldane, FRS in the form of his book, ARP (Left Book Club, 1938). In 1963, the pattern was repeated with the issue of *Advising the Householder on Protection Against Nuclear Attack* which won the well-publicised contempt of the House of Commons Select Committee on Estimates. And, in 1980, the rebirth of the nuclear disarmament movement received one of its greatest boosts when the government printed *Protect and Survive* for public sale. Edward (E. P.) Thompson riposted with *Protest and Survive*, and the original pamphlet has rapidly become the butt of such ridicule that (as the *Hard Rock* scenarios show), the Home Office planners now wish to disown their progeny. Publication of each of these epic works of public information and propaganda was preceded by a more limited, officials–only circulation.

The Protection of Your Home like its successors, did not even mention total evacuation as a possibility, despite the scale of devastation expected in urban areas, and in London in particular. It did suggest that

If you live in a large town, think whether you can make arrangements for children, invalids and elderly persons *and pets* to be sent away the moment danger threatens so that they may be in a place of greater safety (Author's emphasis).

The booklet offered a great deal of advice on the creation of gas-proof refuge rooms, and had a few words to say on incendiaries. It had no precautions to offer against blast (ordinary high explosive) bombs, which were going to be the principal weapons used, with or without the addition of gas and incendiaries. No shelters were proposed for the civil population, and the booklet did not include more than minimal instructions on blast strengthening homes. The single most useful tool to have with you in your refuge room – a pick to dig yourself out of the rubble – was not on the list of 'Things to have in your refuge room'. It still does not appear in the 'survival kit' of useful items and necessities in *Protect and Survive*, fifty years later, even though the abandonment

Plate 10   Advice to the public changed little between 1938 and 1980, the years in which these two pamphlets were issued by the Home Office. Many of the instructions remain the same – because the underlying policies are the same. In the Second World War, however, there was time to persuade the government to change its policy.

of those 'trapped' by nuclear war is a (novel) feature of the civil defence of the seventies and eighties. It seems the government can be slow to learn, even when no costs or changes in general policy are required. *Protect and Survive* does suggest the inclusion of toys and magazines. *The Protection of Your Home* included these, plus books, cards and a radio set or gramophone (with records). Haldane was appropriately scathing:

The official handbook does not distinguish sharply between an air raid and a picnic. In Spain the distinction is quite obvious

The experience of air raids in Spain lent considerable weight to Haldane's comments, whereas, as the official history by Titmuss records (dealing with the government's expectations regarding public morale):

It is difficult to find even a hint (in sifting many thousands of government papers) . . . that this fear of a collapse in morale was based on much else than instinctive opinion.

There were occasional references to the First World War and Spanish civil war experiences, all passed through a 'dense and reduplicated veil of human interpretation'.

So it was with the effects of bombs. Haldane proposed a system of trench shelters, billeting arrangements, and ARP precautions to be undertaken by a Labour government. (As a socialist, he had no faith in any other administration seriously contemplating the task on behalf of the vast majority of the civil population.) Although Haldane formed part of the spearhead of a left wing and communist campaign for deep shelters, the campaign was by no means the exclusive province of the Left. Duncan Sandys, a prominent Conservative MP, told the House of Commons on 1 June 1938:

It is very reassuring to everybody to be told that they have only to put some transparent paper on their windows and take a few other elementary precautions in their upper floor refuge rooms in order to make themselves – as they imagine – relatively immune from the dangers of air attack. . . . When the first bomb falls, it is going to explode the whole of this policy.

Sandys was later threatened with a court-martial for attempting to disclose a shortage of anti-aircraft guns to protect the cities.

An unofficial ARP Coordinating Committee, including architects and engineers, began to develop ideas for public shelters. Meanwhile, an ARP officer for Chatham in Kent was sacked for his advocacy of digging shelters in the chalk hills nearby. The deep shelter campaign became a serious embarrassment for the government, especially as such policies had been wholly endorsed by both Labour and Liberal parties by the end of 1938. The London Borough of Finsbury unveiled, to wide publicity, schemes for sheltering its population; the Coordinating Committee worked out a proposal for tunnel shelters, as suggested by Haldane, in the Paddington district.

The government manifestly deplored the widespread public agitation for shelters and a credible ARP policy. The tone had been set well before the late 1930s; for example, Earl Baldwin told the House of Commons in 1932, in words that might apply today to the nuclear strategy of Mutually Assured Destruction:

There is no power on earth that can protect (the man in the street) from being bombed. Whatever people may tell him, the bomber will always get through. . . . The only defence is offence, which means you have to kill more women and children quickly if you want to save yourselves.

The development of ARP from late 1938 was directed by Sir John Anderson, who had departed from the Home Office to become Governor of Bengal, returned, been elected to Parliament and become Lord Privy Seal.* Anderson chaired the ministerial Committee on ARP, now called Civil Defence (Policy). That Committee is still in being today (as Home Defence (Policy)); it is chaired by David Heaton, the Home Office Deputy Secretary in charge of the Police Department.

In the summer of 1938, after Hitler had invaded Austria, a 'Civil Defence Emergency Scheme' of Regional Commissioners, based on the old Civil Emergency Organisation, was set up; plans were complete by August. In September Hitler

* The personality of Anderson is stamped indelibly on the entire development of British civil defence and nuclear policy. His role in civil defence is chronicled here and during the war, initially as Lord President of the Council, he chaired the committee responsible for the British contribution to the atomic bomb programme. He continued this job after the war in the Labour Government. Although an 'independent' MP, he sat on the Opposition front bench and was, according to Margaret Gowing's official history of the British atomic energy programme 'in most affairs an implacable enemy of the Labour Government'. On the suggestion of the Cabinet Secretary, Anderson was reappointed to this job *under Labour*, three days before Hiroshima. He was the British signatory of the Anderson-Groves agreement of November 1945 which gave Britain the

threatened the invasion of the Sudetenland, and the plans were put into action – secretly, in advance of any other civil defence measures. The scheme, 'Scheme "Y"' was, according to the official history, 'an unpopular form of central control (and) made no concessions over secrecy.' Towards the end of September, ARP work began in earnest with the digging of trench shelters, the fitting of gas masks, and the setting up of warning organisations. Although official preparations were distinguished first by secrecy and then by muddle, much – including the issue of thirty–eight million gasmasks – was seen through to the end, despite the resurgence of optimism after Chamberlain's retreat from Munich.

The sudden crisis of 1938 had brought to most of the adult population an acute perception of imminent personal danger, and the issue of deep shelters was soon to resurge. *The Protection of Your Home* was distributed to fourteen million householders the day after the Prime Minister's return from Munich. A 'pickaxe and shovel' were now shyly included in the revised list of 'things to have' together with other amendments to take account of criticism of the first edition.

The scheme for Regional Commissioners was made public in February 1939, to some considerable criticism of its unusual and undemocratic nature; there were unwelcome comparisons made with Napoleon's *Prefets*, Hitlers *Gauleiters*, and Oliver Cromwell's Major-Generals. Indeed the entire scheme bore close resemblance to the seventeenth century plans; eleven districts were created by Cromwell, with boundaries close to those adopted in the 1939 scheme. Even Anderson conceded, after the names of Commissioners had been announced without any Parliamentary discussion, that 'no attention was paid

---

vital right, later carelessly and quickly discarded, to 'prior consultation' before atomic weapons were used against 'other parties'. Anderson reported directly to the Prime Minister, and provided the continuing momentum that kept the British project going until a decision had been taken that a bomb should, in fact be produced. The decision was taken by a committee, GEN163,* (See Margaret Gowing *Independence and Deterrence*, Vol. 1: *Policy Making* (1974), p. 182) which met only once, agreed to a secret programme of A bomb work, and disbanded. Meanwhile the gross absurdity of the situation of British atomic energy policy being chiefly in the hands of an elected opponent of the Labour Government had become manifest, and Anderson faded out completely by the end of 1947. He became a director of ICI, which carried out much of the subsequent work of producing the enriched uranium required for the atomic bomb.

to the elective principle'. The regional scheme had more or less reached its present day form; the headquarters of the north west region moved from Liverpool to Manchester and the vulnerable contemporary Region 6 (South East) divided into two – a new Region 12 was created comprising Kent and Sussex (it disappeared again after 1963).

On August 25 1939, nine days before war was declared, the Regional Commissioners took up their posts. The Emergency Powers Bill had been passed the day before; Defence Regulations were shortly framed. The Commissioners remained in place until 1945. Communications were never disrupted on the scale anticipated, Britain was not invaded, and the Commissioners' main job became the coordination of ARP and other civil departments. At first, each Commissioner answered directly to Anderson, now Minister of Home Security. The Commissioners could, at their own discretion take over the full powers of civil government if the need arose; 'they would be indemnified for everthing done in good faith.' Meanwhile, the criticism of the government's shelter policy had to some extent bitten. In addition to the free distribution of gasmasks and stirrup pumps (for small fires), the government announced plans to provide poorer families in vulnerable areas with a household shelter formed out of corrugated steel plates, bent to form an arch. The shelter was quickly dubbed the 'Anderson'. Two and a half million were ordered in the first phase of the programme.

The Andersons were useful blast shelters. They would not protect against a direct hit, but properly assembled they provided far better blast protection than most surface accommodation. Although originally conceived for indoor use, they had almost universally been dug into the ground out-of-doors, and were not always used. A new design, the 'Morrison' (Herbert Morrison had become the new Minister of Home Security), was introduced in late 1940, for use indoors. It consisted of a strong steel table with a plate providing protection from falling debris; a steel mattress formed its base, and it was surrounded in strong wire mesh. The shelter, measuring about six and a half feet by four feet by three feet, would accommodate two adults and one child (or two young ones), lying down, without great comfort. Nearly a million Morrisons were initially produced.

With a degree of consummate cynicism and bureaucratic inertia that is hard to credit, the Andersons and Morrisons were offered again to the British public in 1981 as suitable designs for mass produced nuclear shelters for the population, as specified in *Protect and Survive*. They were in fact the only two near-viable designs contained in a 1981 publication on nuclear shelter design issued by the Home Office. The major new feature of the Morrison, 1981 nuclear model, was the use of metric dimensions.

Before the start of the Second World War, Sir John Anderson soon perceived a 'grave danger that the policy of deep underground shelters may be prejudged in the public mind.' He therefore arranged an 'independent' conference as a public relations measure for his policy. This conference, the Hailey Conference, which reported in April 1939, examined the issue of deep shelters in detail, and generally recommended against them. The Conference is reported, particularly in the official history, as an evaluation of government policy by impartial outsiders. It was nothing of the sort, as the formerly 'secret' papers of Anderson's committee, now in the Public Records Office, make clear.* Anderson proposed and convened the Hailey Conference as an explicit means of winning public acceptance of his extreme hard-line policy against deep shelters. At the same time, of course, the government was urgently constructing and completing a series of citadels for key officials, in total secrecy (Chapter 7 describes the wartime citadels).

Anderson stressed that a 'balanced view must take into account many considerations' other than engineering. He had in mind 'mass psychology', of which much has already been said, and 'the strategy of enemy air bombardment' designed to cause civilian panic. Haldane, he told the Civil Defence Committee, 'had no real knowledge of the problem' and had 'misled' people. The government should merely announce that 'for certain types of work (that is, key officials) deep bomb proof shelters should be provided' while for the rest a 'representative body' would consult and report. Anderson's policy appears to have been based on the belief that people under bombardment would be unable to achieve a higher level of social organisation than a flock of sheep. Deep shelters would create 'stampedes leading to very heavy and demoralising casualties' and the population were better off without them, he explained. Not even the underground stations should be available: 'it would be a mistake to suppose that the tubes generally could be used'. Only three of the

* PRO File CAB16/197.

Committee's nine members supported Anderson, but he nonetheless prevailed:

If (deep shelter) accomodation was provided, it would be impracticable to carry on effectively and work in the area concerned and we might as well give up the war.

Although:

He realised the political necessity of giving some evidence of (official activity on shelters).

The Hailey Conference recommended against deep shelters on broadly the same grounds as Anderson had urged on his Committee. Anderson reported back:

The Report was highly satisfactory. It provided the strongest justification for the present Government policy. . . . The Conference ruled out the widespread provision of deep shelters.

He was obliged, in consequence, to follow a minor, less welcome recommendation:

He had hoped that so far as refuges for persons working above ground were concerned, the recommendations of the Conference would stop at the provision of splinter and blast-proof shelters, but actually the conference had gone further and recommended heavier protection for vital industrial establishments and in addition special protection for skilled workmen.

Hoist to some extent with their own petard, the Committee agreed this recommendation. Anderson hoped that political pressure for deep shelters would now subside, the Hailey Report having 'proved' them 'not a practicable possibility'. For the Treasury, a Captain Walter said that:

The Treasury was naturally gratified that the policy of deep shelters for all had been effectively killed.

Six months later, the government started work on the first phase of the Whitehall tunnels. Within eighteen months, the policy on deep shelters was reversed, and construction of some twenty-five tunnel shelters was commenced by the Ministry of Home Security. Government resistance had remained entrenched, but the formation of the new National Government and the need to maintain public support for all aspects of the war effort had displaced the patrician indifference to public feeling of the immediate prewar period. A broadcast by Morrison, the new Home Security Minister, early in November 1940 announced the change:

Anything like a universal policy of deep shelter . . . is beyond the bounds of practical possibility . . . (But) in some places and in some circumstances the construction of deep shelter is practicable, and will be undertaken. The deep shelter provided in London by the tubes will be extended by tunneling. . .

Eight deep tube shelters, each to accomodate eight thousand people, were dug below existing tube stations. Several, however, were never opened to the public.

The background to wartime planning was the estimates made by the Air Staff of the weight of a German bombardment. The German air force had been built up at an enormous rate,

---

Figure 5   The Chamberlain government began the Second World War determined not to provide deep shelters for the public. Eventually the policy was reversed and eight identical shelters (right) were completed below London Underground stations in 1943. But many of the shelter places never went to the public, as the table below shows.

Table 3   *Deep level tube shelters*
Each shelter was built below the underground station of the same name
Each accomodated (for sleeping and welfare only) 8000 people.

Belsize Park	Public shelter	Leased in 1976 by Security Archives Ltd, who operate a commercial security records store.
Camden Town	Public shelter	Ditto (since 1980).
Goodge Street	Converted for war headquarters by General Eisenhower; known as COSSAC	Leased by British Museum as book store.
Chancery Lane	Invasion citadel; headquarters for resistance if London was overrun	Renamed, deceptively, 'Kingsway' in 1951 conversion to atom bomb protected underground trunk exchange.
Stockwell	US troops' hostel (1000 places)	Unused.
Clapham North	Public shelter	Unused
Clapham Common	Invasion citadel	Unused.
Clapham South	Public shelter	Unused; was children's hostel for 1951 Festival of Britain.

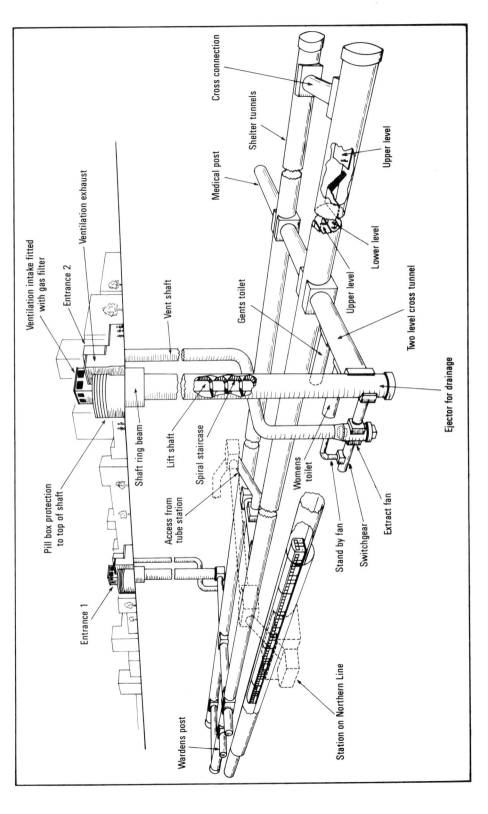

Pill box protection to top of shaft

Ventilation intake fitted with gas filter

Entrance 2

Ventilation exhaust

Cross connection

Shelter tunnels

Medical post

Upper level

Lower level

Upper level

Vent shaft

Shaft ring beam

Lift shaft

Gents toilet

Spiral staircase

Two level cross tunnel

Access from tube station

Entrance 1

Womens toilet

Stand by fan

Switchgear

Extract fan

Ejector for drainage

Wardens post

Station on Northern Line

and the bombing of Barcelona and other Spanish cities had occasioned considerable alarm. The Air Staff assessed casualties on the basis of fifty per ton of bombs dropped, a figure based on tenuous data and sheer error in both statistical assumptions and arithmetic. Nevertheless, in 1938 they revised it – upwards. On this basis, the effects of two months' air attack were calculated by the Committee of Imperial Defence in that year at 600,000 dead and 1.2 million wounded. The total is in fact slightly more than the Greater London Council's chief Emergency Planning Officer, claims would have resulted from the hydrogen bomb attack postulated in the 1980 exercise, *Square Leg*. (Just as the assessments for the casualties expected in the Second World War went wildly high because of scanty, ill-used data from the First, so the casualty assessments for a future war are now based, at considerable risk of error, on the experiences of the blitz and Hiroshima (see Chapter 11)).

Once the 1939 aerial bombardment had begun, health planners expected to have to provide more than a million hospital beds. Mass burials and cremations were planned as insufficient wood would be available to make coffins. A million burial forms were distributed by the Ministry of Health in April 1939. These estimates were based on a delivered total of some 36,000 tons of high explosive bombs, about half of the eventual total delivered to British targets. Instead of killing a million people, however, they killed 60,595 and seriously injured 86,182.

Evacuation policies had been contemplated in an early stage of planning. One and a half million schoolchildren, mothers and infants, invalids and the blind, teachers and helpers were initially evacuated – it was later estimated that self-evacuation had accounted for the same again, with private arrangements having been widely made in Wales and 'safe' parts of Scotland and England. During and after the blitz, more were evacuated until, eventually, four million people in the selected classes had been dispersed under government schemes.

The scenes of schoolchildren with labels attached crowding railway stations is as much a part of the common (and valid) image of the Second World War as the efforts of ARP wardens and rescue teams during the blitz. Evacuation schemes for the 'priority classes' survived until 1965, well into the nuclear age. A major cause of their abandonment was the closure of significant sections of the railway network, which disturbed long-established plans and timetables for evacuation.

Volunteers, and later those compulsorily recruited to ARP or the National Fire Service, swelled to 1.7 million. The ARP forces were divided into Rescue, First Aid and Stretcher, and Welfare parties. Mobile reserve units, trained in these skills and in gas decontamination, could be brought in to assist heavily bombarded areas. Backing up the almost one million ARP personnel (nearly ninety per cent of them part-time) were the fire services and expanded casualty help, chiefly the Emergency Ambulance Service. The effect of incendiary bombs, used on a wide scale, was countered by fire watching regulations and a Fire Guard.

ARP precautions were not cheap. The total cost of civil defence between 1939 and 1945 was a billion pounds, the vast majority of it being grants to local authorities to pay for new services. Some £125 million was spent on evacuation schemes, and slightly more on casualty and disease prevention services.

As the Allies invaded and reconquered Europe in 1944, the threat of air attack progressively diminished. Early in September 1944, Fire Guards in all except the southern and eastern regions were stood down, and civil defence was progressively reduced in strength. The V1 cruise bomb attacks had abated since their July peak, as the landing sites were overrun. However, a worried War Cabinet reacted to the imminence of the V2 with the same degree of official panic and overestimation that had charatised the early, pre-war days and the height of the blitz on London. The Home Secretary, explained that V2 rockets, which were presumed to have a seven ton high explosive warhead, would kill eighteen thousand for each one thousand missiles arriving, and

civil defence resources would be quickly exhausted, hospital services might be swamped, and police, transport and emergency services for accomodating and feeding evacuees might be overwhelmed by an exodus of people from the capital. Rockets might well . . . affect the conduct of military operations.

The old plans for the evacuation of government departments were again dusted off. The plans had been in two stages; a 'yellow move' of 44,000 less essential Whitehall staff to the provinces which had begun quickly in September 1939, but had never been fully implemented; and the final, 'Black Move' of the remaining 16,000 key staff to dispersal sites which had been selected around Stratford-upon-Avon,

Worcester, and the West Midlands. (see p. 234). Like many
of the initial evacuees, many government staff soon came
back to London – although new exoduses started with each
new threat.

Although the new evacuation plans went ahead in 1944,
and the deep tube shelters were finally opened to the public,
the experience of the blitz and the V1 flying bombs tempered
the worst-case views of the Home Secretary. From September
1944, until the Allies crossed the Rhine six months later, 1150
V2 rockets fell on Britain. Their warheads, and destructive
power, however were no worse than the V1s had been: the
death toll from the rockets was 2754 – rather less, once again,
than had been anticipated. Civil defence was finally stood
down and disbanded in May 1945, with only a few reserve
units continuing to operate. There were then two months
before Hiroshima. The machinery which had been created in
wartime was soon again to be recreated, at first slowly and
reluctantly, and then in great haste and with public support,
during the Cold War revival of civil defence.

The issue of public shelters remained contentious throughout the war – the tube stations were only opened to the public
after determined struggles had taken place with the authorities. But by the start of the blitz, 177,000 were sheltering
there nightly. The fact that the destruction wrought by German bombers was on several counts less than had been expected meant that many of the ARP services were not as
overstretched as had been anticipated. The feeling was created in the blitz that 'London can cope'; and if the authorities
again expected that that new onslaughts would end this ability
to cope, they did not intend to let on.

Regional Commissioners had twice been called in: once to
deal with 'trekking' out of Southampton in 1941; and to cope
with the aftermath of heavy raids on Plymouth. They too left
their posts in June 1945, and soon only a skeleton organisation
of civil defence remained.

The Emergency Powers Act was exercised twice by Clem-
ent Attlee, to counter the docks strikes of 1948 and 1949.
Troops were called out both times; on the latter occasion an
Emergency Committee was once again in operation, run by

Plates 11 & 12 The Second World War saw much construction
above and below London's streets. A view (top) of the
underground cable tunnels and (below) the 'stronghold' bunker
being built behind the BBC headquarters.

a former Home Office Permanent Under Secretary. Regional Commissioners were not again to be appointed, although they may well have been (secretly) designated. The system which Attlee used, however, has since spawned a chain of Regional Emergency Committees (RECS; see p. 00) which now form the civil arm of the emergency planning system, and whose members form a major part of the contemporary wartime regional government system described in Chapter 5.

As the optimism of 1945 passed and the schism deepened in east-west relations, a new Civil Defence Act was passed in 1948. The 1948 Act remains the principal statute concerning civil defence measures. A first set of regulations, in July 1949, empowered local authorities to appoint Civil Defence Committees and recruit members for the new Civil Defence Corps. The scale of spending and precautionary measures gradually increased. They were given a sharp boost on 23 of September 1949, when it was discovered that the first Soviet atomic weapon had just been tested.

4
Home defence in the nuclear age 1949–1972

In the aftermath of the Second World War, the British Chiefs of Staff judged – and the government agreed – that no general war in Europe was likely for ten years. By the end of the decade, however, this assumption looked less cosy. The US Strategic Air Command bombers based in Britain, for 'temporary' duty, in July 1948, had begun to have an air of permanancy. Radar stations, and the network of Royal Observer Corps posts (then observing only with eyes and ears) had begun to be revived in 1947. The autumn of 1948 saw the first large scale exercise in which Britain was again under simulated air attack.

The British atomic weapons programme had begun immediately after the war, and continued in April 1950 when the first land was cleared at Aldermaston near Reading. After a lengthy debate over the moral questions posed by the bomb, and discussion about handing all atomic energy over to the United Nations, the subject went quiet. The determination of the military establishment, whose investment in strategic bombing in the war had been considerable, to have a British bomb was quite apparent. Within official circles, there was only one voice of dissent, that of Professor P.M.S. Blackett, a physicist of distinction who sat on the atomic advisory and technical committees. As early as 1945 he had warned:

Much further consideration will need to be given to the military situation of the United Kingdom, considered as a forward base and as an advanced airfield in a war between the USSR and the United States, in which atomic bombs were used by either or both sides. . . . Simple arguments would seem to show that the United Kingdom would suffer far more than either of the two main contestants.

The object of having bombs, he warned 'could only be interpreted as defence against the USSR'. Given that 'the special
property of the bombs is that they are very efficient for the
destruction of cities and civilian lives,' the likely consequence
of British possession of atomic bombs 'may well be to leave
the United Kingdom more vulnerable than before.' He called
for the open declaration of a British policy not to produce
atomic weapons.

Blackett was overruled. The decision to press ahead was as
much a product of the postwar American mood, which saw
nuclear weapons as the coercive means of imposing a US
organised world order, as it was of British fear of the Soviet
Union. The Americans were not expected to supply Britain
with atomic bombs, and they were not going to be asked.

In consequence, British defence planners soon came to
accept that future war would be prolonged and involve extensive use of nuclear weapons. It is often forgotten in the
present age that the idea of a 'spasm' nuclear war, involving
only a few hours of exchanging nuclear salvoes, is a wholly
modern concept. The planners of 1950 and 1960 had a perception of war which was partly based on the long campaigns
of previous wars. The Second World War had lasted six years;
World War Three was not going to be over in a day.

When civil defence re-entered the British order of battle in
1948, it was, therefore, to operate in a way which might now
be seen as repugnant. The recreation of civil defence and
later many other precautions and systems described here, was
intended to provide Britain with a capacity to fight an atomic
war lasting months. In the course of this war, major cities like
London and Birmingham, Manchester, Leeds and Newcastle
would suffer the fate of Hiroshima and Nagasaki on a much
larger scale. Ports and airbases, particularly those leased to
the US Strategic Air Command, would be attacked early in
the war. There would soon be casualities far in excess of
Second World War levels, with hundreds of thousands of
wounded to be treated. The overall war aim, which is reflected both in declassified British plans, such as those for
setting up the UK Commanders-in-Chief Committee (pp. 205–
8), and in US plans such as *Dropshot* (for a general nuclear
war with the Soviet Union, circa 1957), would be to maintain
the UK as a forward air base, and a main offensive base *as
long as possible.*

The UK base would not tenable in a war of several months'
duration unless the British government itself was able to op-

erate securely from citadels proof against atom bombs; these were constructed (Chapter 8). They would need secure communications systems, which were provided by tunnels under London, and by new communications links throughout the country (Chapter 9); these were constructed. Above all, a system of civil defence would be needed to help the survivors of major atomic attacks on the great cities and other target areas. Recruiting advertisements for civil defence were later to be quite specific about what might now be called the 'war-fighting' role of CD:

To talk of all the *three* services is out of date. In the H bomb age, we have a fourth arm too – Civil Defence. Like the peacetime Navy, Army and RAF, peacetime Civil Defence is part of our essential national preparedness.

(National newspapers, 10 October 1957)

Stressing the now revived slogan that 'Civil Defence is common sense,' prospective recruits were advised that training would be useful because:

You learn some of the basic, fundamental *facts* of this nuclear age, and you learn to face these facts as a responsible citizen should. You learn to live with your eyes open in the same world as the H bomb.

To single out the war-fighting aspect of civil defence planning is not to deny its humanitarian intention, or indeed, in the early days of the atomic age, humanitarian effect. It will be remembered that official resistance to effective shelters for the civil population was founded primarily on distrust of the endurance and spirit of the civil population. During the war, that strand of official opinion was tempered by national coalition, and the discovery of an unexpectedly low toll of death and injury and a high popular spirit. But distrust of the endurance of the population remained the dominant official perception, as it is today.

Although, too, it is generally specious to equate preparations for war with an intention to wage war, that was not the case in the late 1940s. There was widespread talk of 'preventive war' on the Soviet Union, talk briefly and irrationally supported by even Bertrand Russell, later to lead in CND. It then mattered very much whether Britain could sustain and survive an atomic attack.

The first Soviet bomb in 1949 was the sixth and final A bomb test of the decade. Early in 1951, the United States began testing again – this time, with an increasing array of equipment and structures around the ground zero of the bomb. At first such tests were intended to discover the destructive effects of the bomb, as they might be used against Soviet targets. Later, there was an increasing emphasis on discovering the effects of bombs on the sort of buildings and structures found in American and European cities. Most books on the effects of nuclear weapons contain illustrations of houses being blown apart in the shock wave from such test explosions.

For a short while, in 1950, the British Chiefs of Staff thought of increasing military (air) defences to resist atomic air attack, in preference to constructing Britain's own nuclear deterrent. At a critical conference on 'Global Strategy' at Greenwich in 1952, however, this thinking was reversed. The document resulting from the conference said that:

it was now clear that there was in the foreseeable future no effective defence against atomic air attack. . . . The primary deterrent must be Russian knowledge that any aggression would involve immediate and crushing atomic retaliation.*

The words were almost the same as those Stanley Baldwin had spoken twenty years before; a successful defence must be measured in terms of rival abilities to slaughter women, babies and non-combatants.

Meanwhile, the target list in Britain had begun to notch upwards. The presence of SAC aircraft was now permanent, at least for the duration of the Cold War; late in 1949 older bombers in Britain had been swapped for atomic bomb carrying types, and in the summer of 1950 nuclear weapons were stockpiled in Britain for the first time. For many years, this was categorically denied.** But all over Oxfordshire and East Anglia, at the air bases of Brize Norton, Fairford, Upper Heyford, Greenham Common, and later at Wethersfield, Woodbridge, and Bruntingthorpe, there were now erected the watchtowers, double fences, searchlights and underground storage 'igloos' which protected the bombs. On 1 October, 1952 SAC consolidated its presence in Britain with the opening of an underground command post in the western part of High Wycombe – now in operation as the computer

---

*Margaret Gowing, *Independence and Deterrence* (1974), *Vol. 1*, p. 441.
**One semantic device which facilitated lying about the presence of atomic weapons was the construction of the bombs in two parts – with the nuclear core stored separately (and at first kept in the US). Officially, these weapons were not 'atomic bombs'.

programming centre for cruise missiles and F111 bombers. Two days laters, the first British atomic *device* was detonated at Monte Bello in the Pacific. The first A *bombs* – 'Blue Danubes' – were delivered to the RAF within two years. Commitment to atomic weaponry and nuclear deterrence became complete.

The critical decisions about Britain's defences and civil defences under atomic attack had been taken in 1950. Enormous sums of money had been poured into reviving the Civil Defence Corps, to little visible effect. All over Britain (as Chapter 8 describes) critical parts of the war machinery – including dozens of radar stations and anti-aircraft gun controls, army, RAF and navy HQS, and new War Rooms for the (unappointed) Regional Commissioners – were being fortified to withstand atomic blast, fire, and radiation. These War Rooms were two storey concrete bunkers, generally located beside the hutted government offices remaining from the war. War Rooms were built near Edinburgh, and in Newcastle, Leeds, Nottingham, Cambridge, Reading, Bristol, Cardiff, Birmingham, Manchester, Belfast and Tunbridge Wells. The neighbouring huts contained the regional administrators for the new civil defence organisation, and representatives of many other government departments besides; in war, they would become complete centres of administration – Regional Seats of Government. The overall direction of civil defence operations was all that would be done from the War Rooms themselves, and space was provided for police, military, fire and ambulance officers.

Between £50 and £100 million was spent during the early 1950s on building bunkers, so far as it is now possible to estimate. The cost was shared by the Home Office, the three services and the Defence Ministry, and the General Post Office. During 1953, considerable publicity was given to a scathing 340-page report on the state of civil defence by the House of Commons Select Committee on Estimates. The report condemned the organisation of civil defence thus far as 'extravagant and inefficient', with uncertain training standards, poor leadership, a proliferating and top heavy Home Office bureaucracy directing CD, and little control over spending levels in the hundreds of authorities which organised local sections of the CD Corps. The government resisted most of the criticism, and said it intended to press on as before.

The shape of civil defence in 1953 was much very according to the wartime specification, and comprised:

- Plans for *evacuation and dispersal*, involving moving millions of people in 'priority classes' to 'neutral' or safe zones.
- The Civil Defence Corps (over 300,000), divided into five sections for:
  - Rescue and First Aid teams: trained to evacuate, as quickly as possible, as many people as possible from the wreckage of houses and shelters, and provide the first, simple medical aid.
  - Ambulance and Casualty Collecting: to provide further medical care and ferry the injured to hospitals or emergency centres.
  - Welfare: to house and feed evacuees or refugees, and look after the homeless.
  - Warden: directing emergency services in damaged areas
  - Headquarters: coordination of emergency services
- Emergency billeting arrangements: Ministry of Health asked for widespread arrangements for emergency accommodation, but 'because of economic considerations', no new building.
- Food stockpiles kept in buffer depots, and protection for electricity HQs, ports and other civil installations.
- An Auxiliary Fire Service.
- New respirators for civilians in case of gas attack.
- Forward Medical Aid Units for the NHS.

The wartime effectiveness and value of this organisation (and the extensions it would gather during a war) may well be questionable. But it is certainly worth comparing the scale of effort which had been mounted in 1953, to meet a threat assessed at perhaps a dozen Hiroshima-sized bombs, at a time of considerable economic restraint in Britain, with the non-existent civil defence measures of the 1970s and 1980s. All that is listed above – save diminishing food depots and ageing supplies of 'Green Goddess' fire engines and other Home Office stores, such as Radiac intruments – has gone.

The Select Committee report of 1953 concentrated its fire on the preponderance of administrative and planning activities in civil defence, compared with the training and equipment of field staffs. Their comments in 1982 or 1983 might have been rather more succinct and abrasive.

A month after Britain tested its atomic bomb, a megaton range hydrogen bomb was exploded by the United States at Eniwetok Atoll in the Pacific. When the Soviet Union followed suit a matter of nine months later, the western planners were horrified. For the second time running, their lead in nuclear technology had turned out to be far less than was anticipated. The gap between American and Russian technology had apparently closed from four years to less than one. In the next major development, inter-continental ballistic missiles (ICBMs), the Soviet Union would soon appear to be in the lead. Moreover, the Soviet bomb of August 1953 had been airdropped, implying an ability to deliver such a weapon. The Americans did not test the prototypes of their first air-dropped H bomb until May 1956.

American test results from Eniwetok, and then from the 'Castle' series of H bomb tests at Bikini Atoll in the early spring of 1954, produced details of the huge quantities of fallout created by H bombs. A fallout reporting study was convened at the then Civil Defence Staff College at Sunningdale, to study the effects of a ten megaton bomb groundbursting on Birmingham. The prospects were grim, and civil defence policy was re-evaluated. The Home Secretary, Gwilym Lloyd-George, warned CD officers that he would not 'venture to predict the difficulties for civil defence that lie ahead. The development of the hydrogen bomb has posed, for those concerned with planning and organising the defence of the United Kingdom, problems quite unprecedented in scale and complexity.' A colleague added that it 'would undoubtedly be a struggle for survival without precedent in the history of mankind.'

The H Bomb involved, firstly, enlarging considerably the scale of civil defence resources, in order to cope with destruction across areas one hundred times larger than an A bomb would produce, and posed new problems of fallout and preventing firestorms. For some years, the government tried to increase resources in civil defence to keep up with the scale of the threat. Then they gave up.

The second need was to create a stronger system of bunkers and communications to protect the government. There were already extensive government shelters and cable tunnels under London, linked to the underground telephone exchange, *Kingsway*. Two more underground exchanges, Birmingham *Anchor* and Manchester *Guardian* were also under construction. Nevertheless, these would not be enough. The Defence White Paper of 1954 anticipated that a future war 'would begin with a period of intense atomic attacks lasting a relatively short time but inflicting great destruction and damage;'

subsequently, the war could continue at reduced intensity between the mortally injured protagonists with

a period of 'broken-backed' warfare . . . during which the opposing sides would seek to recover their strength.

To cope with the need to keep military defence and CD operations going after attack, Britain was to get – literally – some *Backbone*. This was the codename given by the Post Office to a chain of new microwave radio stations, which now form an extensive communications network throughout Britain. The development of *Backbone* system during this period is referred to indirectly in *Attack Warning Red*, the history of the Royal Observer Corps (Derek Wood, 1976):

The Home Office (was) engaged in setting up eleven Civil Defence Regions with regional and sub-regional headquarters capable of taking over in the event of breakdown of central government control following a nuclear attack. Essential food and fuel were stockpiled, while Civil Defence rescue and salvage columns were set up. The Post Office worked out plans for a complete emergency network, based on microwave techniques and repeater stations.

The *Backbone* network was first planned in late 1954, and appears, from its subsequent development, to have had a dual purpose. For wartime use – as is evident from the layout of the emergency network (p. 308) – it is arranged to provide bypasses around key target areas – London, Manchester, Birmingham, Leeds and, later Bristol, Newcastle and Tyneside. But it appears also to have been arranged to provide extensive facilities for feeding international communications to the United States National Security Agency monitoring base at Menwith Hill, near Harrogate.* The two uses are not incompatible, and indeed provide an economy of effort by making use of the emergency communications system during peacetime. The network was referred to in the 1955 Defence White Paper:

The Post Office are planning . . . a special network both by cable and by radio, designed to maintain long distance communications in the event of attack.

The same White Paper offered further gloomy assessments of the consequences of nuclear war:

* See Duncan Campbell, 'America's Big Ear in Europe', *New Statesman* 18 July 1980; reprinted in *Big Brother is Listening, NS Report 2*, 1981.

Central and local government would be put out of action partially
or wholly. . . . . There would be grave problems of control (ie, of
the public), feeding and shelter. Public morale would be most
severely tested. It would be a struggle for survival of the grimmest
kind.

Nowadays, bland references to remote if awful catastrophes,
and the invaluable role of official advice as contained in *Protect and Survive*, are much preferred to this kind of plain
speaking in official circles. Indeed for the following quarter
of a century, Defence White Papers have avoided dwelling
on the nature of thermonuclear war.

Britain's new *Backbone*, which did not in fact substantially
come into service until the early 1960s (owing in part to
problems with the intelligence aspects, it appears), comprised
twenty-two stations, including the Post Office Tower in central London. Later an eight station *Northern Backbone* extension linked Harrogate to Dundee, bypassing Edinburgh,
and a western extension ran southwest, bypassing Bristol.
The key point of the new system was the Central Government
War HQ at Hawthorn, near Bath (see Chapters 7 and 8).

Although British Telecom now denies that the system was
built exclusively for military purposes, the opposite view was
repeatedly stated by Post Office witnesses at planning enquiries. In 1956 a Post Office* letter explained that:

the reason for providing (the towers) in these particular places
and at this time is in order to safeguard vital national
communications in the interests of defence. Having provided
them, we propose to make the best use we can of them for
general telecommunications traffic.

Backbone provided, it was hoped, the means by which the
separate military and civil defence HQs in an H bomb blitzed
Britain might stay in contact after attack – to conduct a
continuing war, or to plan for 'survival' and 'recovery'.

In order to deal with the new problems of fallout, the Royal
Observer Corps, whose previous task of logging aircraft
movements by visual observation had been become redundant
in an age of high speed jets, were given the job of observing
nuclear explosions and fallout. Eventually, the ROC were incorporated into the Home Office–run UK Warning and Monitoring Organisation (UKWMO), which distributes details of
bomb bursts and fallout to military and civil war
headquarters.

* To the Council for the Preservation of Rural England.

The military provided the major new facet of civil defence to cope with H bomb. Everyone in the armed forces was to be trained in civil defence work; part of the RAF reserve was to operate a new emergency fire service; and there were to be, to start with, forty-eight new military battalions of a Mobile Defence Corps (about 30,000 men) who would provide military aid to civil defence work – not in controlling the population, but in 'fire fighting, rescue and ambulance work'. A new Director General of Civil Defence (a former General) was appointed to coordinate the new forces. In the autumn of 1954, the Home Office launched a new recruiting campaign for the Civil Defence Corps.

For four short years, the government continued to believe its own propaganda about civil defence providing succour to the population. By the end of 1959, they harboured no such illusions. The advent of the H bomb was closely followed by the first operational developments in long range missiles; soon, despair was complete. The Home Office estimates of the magnitude of nuclear attack on Britain had changed, over the course of five or six years, from perhaps a dozen Hiroshima-type weapons (240 kilotons) to a vision of Hell illuminated by the fire of anything from a hundred to three hundred megatons or more of H bombs. By 1960, in the official view, civil defence was a means of providing marginal relief to the population, whilst ensuring that the policy of nuclear deterrence remained effective and convincing; the preservation of administration wholly supplanted the provision of relief to survivors as the paramount objective.

The first official published details on the H bomb went out to the public in 1956 when HMSO issued a descriptive manual on *Nuclear Weapons* (revised and still in print), and an illustrated 9d booklet on *The Hydrogen Bomb* was published a year later. Scarcely optimistic, the latter did, however, suggest that the thermal radiation danger of H bombs was 'not as much as might be expected'. In the spirit of cheerful lunacy which has often characterised such Home Office advice to the public, *The Hydrogen Bomb* pointed out that clothes contaminated by fallout after thermonuclear attack were better washed in 'a bucket or tub' rather than by an (electric) washing machine, and that:

If a vacuum cleaner were used, radioactive material would collect in the bag and the whole machine would have to be put where the radiation could do no harm. . . . Many of the fires caused by a hydrogen bomb could be put out by the methods familiar in the last war, by beating or with a stirrup pump, or with a bucket of sand or water

In 1958, the government published details of the 'provisional scheme for the control of the public under fallout conditions'; belts of radioactivity were successively divided up into W, X, Y and Z zones. At each, higher, level, the possibility of rescue or survival in shelter become more remote.

In January 1956, a new full time post of Commander-in-Chief, UK Land Forces was created specifically to provide for the supervision of the new military units. In 1957, new 'Sub-Regional Controls' were introduced into the regional civil defence organisation, normally located on the outskirts of industrial areas which would be likely H bomb targets. These would administer civil defence operations in and around areas like London: they were necessary because the extent of damage and casualties, and the difficulties of moving under heavy fallout, required speedy and well coordinated action. New vehicles were purchased to assist civil defence sectors in these operations.

Every autumn, throughout the 50s and 60s, the Home Office staged a week of recruitment propaganda for Civil Defence, under such slogans as 'Our survival might depend on Civil Defence' or 'The H bomb: What about the Millions of Survivors?' (a talk by Mr R. A. Butler). On occasions, local authorities organised recruitment canvassing door-to-door.

But inside the bowels of government, a very different view of civil defence had emerged. The Defence White Paper of 1957 was the last to be blunt about the future in the nuclear missile age:

There is at present no means of providing adequate protection for the people of this country against the consequences of attack with nuclear weapons.

The 1957 White Paper set up the 'tripwire' policy of nuclear retaliation, and, as deliberate policy, ran down the fighter and air defences of Britain in order to pay for the V bombers and their weapons.

The build-up of military support for civil defence, and the Mobile Defence Corps, came to an abrupt end in January 1959 – the first step in dismantling civil defence (although the immediate impetus then had been the cessation of conscription). However, in secret, the government had begun the construction of new, underground Regional Seats of Government from which much larger staffs of central government would administer what remained of Britain after H bomb attack. The military involvement remained strong, and was no longer oriented towards the rescue or succour of survivors. A CD briefing on the 'Chain of Control' issued in 1958 gave a few hints of the construction of the twelve new RSGS and the controlling Central Government War HQ:

Central Government Headquarters: (Hawthorn, see page 270*ff*)
A Central Government War Room, representative of all Government Departments, will be established and will have a dual responsibility: Control of Civil Defence operations, and Civil Administration.

Regional Headquarters: (RSGS, see p. 266)
In each civil defence region, there will be, in war, a Regional Commissioner appointed by central government. . . . To enable a Regional Commissioner to discharge his responsibilities he will have a staff appointed by the central government and a specially equipped regional headquarters which wherever possible will be a joint headquarters with the corresponding Army District. An arrangement of this kind will be particularly desirable because of the increased importance of the part which the armed forces are to play in civil defence operations.

The briefing also described how some headquarters were also being provided for Sub-Regional Controllers 'with operations room, signal office, liason, and other facilities'.

Five of the RSGS were indeed built on army sites, and although all have now been given back by the Home Office, the military role in protecting government authority and suppressing dissent or lawlessness has become the paramount feature of contemporary Home Defence.

During the early 1960s, the Civil Defence Corps continued to maintain its strength, peaking in 1961 when it had 375,000 members. At the same time, the other civil defence organisations mustered 145,000 members – 19,000 in the Auxiliary Fire Service, 55,000 in the Special Constablulary and 70,000 in the NHS reserve (including the St John Ambulance Society and the British Red Cross). There were also some 4000 units in the Industrial Civil Service. None of this organisation – except, of course for police special constables and the independent medical aid societies – now exists. The turning point for the Civil Defence Corps was reached in 1963, after which membership plummetted at increasing speed, until its disbandment in 1968.

Shortly after the Mobile Defence Corps and other supporting units had been disbanded in 1959, the government withdrew regulations allowing local authorities to requisition shelters, and proposed new schemes for youth training – starting with a Duke of Edinburgh's Award. The role of civil defence at the end of the 50s was summarised in a report in the *Municipal Yearbook* (1961).

The defence policy of Her Majesty's Government, based as it is on the nuclear deterrent must, in this era of the ballistic missile, rely more than ever upon our home defence. . . . No effort should be spared in building up in every locality a strong and efficient Civil Defence organisation. *Without it the deterrent is seriously weakened* (Author's emphasis).

In fact, Civil Defence had reached the watershed of its existence.

As proper civil defence began to decline, considerable amounts were spent on other areas during 1960–63. The RSGS and the Central Government HQ were nearing completion, and the *Backbone* Post Office network, (although not directly connecting to the RSGS) was well under way. The Home Office was paying for a network of 1500 three-person underground posts for the Royal Observer Corps, equipped with nuclear burst detectors, plotters and measurement equipment, as well as radioactive fallout meters. There were new protected headquarters for ports and shipping, for British Rail and the energy industries – gas, electricity, coal and oil. The new network of Home Office 'hilltop' radio stations to link civil defence controls together began in earnest in 1962. There were also various stockpiles – ambulance equipment, radiac instruments, food and so on. The 1963/64 Home Defence budget came to £23 million. Linked to the development of the Royal Observer Corps posts was the Warning Broadcast system, ultimately to be linked to the joint US/UK Ballistic Missile Early Warning Station then under construction at Flyingdales Moor, near Scarborough. The Warning Broadcast system (see p. 289*ff*) distributes attack warnings nationally to 250 police stations from where the automatic sirens and other warning devices are controlled.

During 1961, a number of exercises in 'Military Aid to the Civil Power' rehearsed the control of civilians in war. In 1962 NATO organised a major international exercise, *Fallex 62*, which anticipated a major nuclear war. It was reported to have been disastrous: every hospital in the southern region was quickly out of action through destruction or fallout, and civil defence support had to withdrawn from a wide area around London. Most Z zones proved unclearable, even after the level of radiation reduced to ten Roentgens per hour two days later (by this time, only those in substantial shelter could hope to have avoided a lethal dose of radioactivity).

These points (which were revealed by the *Spies for Peace*) did not however reach the 1963 Defence White Paper, which reported that:

(Civil Defence) plans, which provide for the close cooperation of the civil and military authorities, are an integral part of our defence plans, and are kept under constant review. They were fully tested, both at the central and regional level, during the major NATO exercise *Fallex 62.*

The paper also reported that accelerated progress was being made with the provision of 'buildings and communications for emergency controls' (ie the RSGs and other bunkers). Home defence expenditure was to be increased, but most of it went to the building of emergency bunkers and other controls for separate departments. Instructions to civil defence officials emphasised that mere rescue was now the minor part of their work:

Modern Civil Defence goes far beyond the popular conception of the rescue, treatment and removal of casualties and the care and feeding of the homeless. At a time when normal channels of communications would be non-existent or seriously disrupted, the Civil Defence organisation would be needed not only to provide essential supplies and services, but for the restoration of good order and local government. (*Municipal Yearbook*, 1963)

At this point in 1963, the government decided to release the householders' handbook on protection against the H bomb which had been in preparation for six years. Called *Advising the Householder on Protection against Nuclear Attack*, it rapidly attracted the same notoriety and criticism as *Protect and Survive* and the 1938 leaflet *The Protection of Your Home*. Like its predecessor and successor, *Advising the Householder* had no advice whatsoever to offer on protection against the blast effects of bombs – conventional or nuclear. Like *Protect and Survive*, *Advising the Householder* only offered instructions on how to equip a 'fallout room' inside suitable houses. Householders in bungalows, or the top or bottom storeys of flats were recommended to find shelter elsewhere, preferably in a cellar, or in a room with as few exterior walls as possible.

Although the booklet did not discuss details, the intention was to maximise the protective factor (PF) by cutting down radiation penetrating into the 'fallout room'. It was an extremely rough and ready approach, and extended the principle of writing-off blast casualties to potentially writing off many whose homes would provide insufficient radiation protection. Unlike *Protect and Survive*, however, *Advising the Householder* still held out some hope. It reminded those who might be caught in (perhaps undamaged) heavy Y and Z fallout zones to be ready for speedy evacuation:

After an attack you and your family might have to be moved away from where you had taken shelter. Pack necessities and any small valuables. . . . Remember that you may be out in any weather and that your belongings may need protection from the rain. . . . Keep your luggage down to a weight you and your family can carry. If you have a car, make sure that the petrol tank is kept full and that the car is ready for a journey at any time.

There was, in 1963, at least a hope that CD rescue teams might move into a damaged or fallout stricken area, organise the evacuation of the uninjured, and the rescue and provision of first aid to as many as possible, even under conditions of relatively heavy fallout. The Medical Research Council suggested in 1956 that CD workers and other could in 'relative' safety be exposed to a 'War Emergency Dose' (WED) of seventy-five Roentgen – roughly 150 times the peacetime maximum permissible under international standards for any member of the public. The advice also suggested that, after an eight hour shift and a rest, CD workers or other staff could, if need be, receive a further seventy-five Roentgen. At this level, in fact, some six to ten per cent of the workers so exposed would die within weeks or months (and perhaps rather more in the conditions of deprivation and inadequate medical care after nuclear attack). But it provided a basis for deploying CD rescue teams into serious fallout areas; even in Z zones, for example, each rescue team could work one or two 4–6 hour shifts in order to remove survivors. Such an operation depended, of course, on the existence of a massive infrastructure of transport, communications and coordination, which no longer exists.

Amongst various inanities and inadequacies in *Advising the Householder* was the profuse use of sandbags suggested for barricading windows in a 'fall-out' room. It was soon calculated that the supply of sandbags for even a medium sized town (Hull was the example taken) would entirely exhaust the national supply. An illustration of an attacked population taking shelter featured terraced north of England urban housing – wholly undamaged, and the people silent behind sandbagged walls.

The House of Commons Select Committee on Estimates, in its 1962–63 11th Report, singled out a particularly absurd passage giving advice about parking cars while under nuclear attack:

Driving a vehicle: Park off the road if possible; otherwise alongside the kerb, but not near crossroads or in narrow streets.

The Committee commented:

The average householder who reads what to do in the event of an imminent nuclear attack . . . will not form the impression that the civil defence measures taken by the government are of any value whatsoever.

The Committee did not think many householders would want the handbook or be convinced of the effectiveness of the measures proposed.

In the event, considerable changes in civil defence organisation were already under way. At the local level, membership of the cd Corps had begun to fall by about ten per cent a year; by the time it was disbanded it was at half its 1962 strength. Events, in particular the Cuban missile crisis and the installation (and in 1963, the removal) of *Thor* medium range missiles in Britain, had not, it seemed, inspired more to join cd's ranks.

Inside government, a similar view had been taken. Exercises like *Fallex* 62 suggested very clearly that there was no match between possible civil defence resources and the scale of devastation anticipated. At the central government level of regional and sub-regional organisation, the administration of civil defence now lost all of its residual humanitarian nature. Medical and rescue services would have to be withdrawn from sections of the community in order to make them effective elsewhere. Essential supplies and services would have to be withheld from some groups of survivors, so that others could live instead. The dying and those condemned to die would, so far as they were able, fight for a share of existing resources – they would have to be met by military force. The government's power and authority to govern would be widely challenged 'in conditions of anarchy' and, in the government's view at least, the 'maintenance of administration' would be the paramount objective. Post-attack, the Regional Seat of Government staffs would assess surviving resources – food, medical, transport, fuel, industrial and so on, – and design a society for 'recovery' around that basis.

In April 1963, the *Spies for Peace* disclosed the existence of the Regional Seats of Government (see p. 264); coincidentally, the RSGs were quickly reorganised on a different basis.

A new plan in July 1963 (Home Office circular CDC17/63) outlined three phases of home defence plans:

- *Operational* or life-saving phase, when civil defence units, largely under local authority control, would rescue as many as possible, and evacuate them away from fallout zones.
- *Survival* phase: administered from new 'Sub-Regional Controls' (SRCs), remaining resources of the sub-region would be marshalled and assessed, and plans laid for the organisation of remaining population and industry into a 'survivable' social system.
- *Recovery* phase: directed from Regional Government HQs to be set up weeks after attack, the recovery phase would last years and aim at the gradual restoration of some society and industry.

Circular 17/63 was fairly blunt about these circumstances, in contrast to the cosy domesticity of *Advising the Householder*:

The survival period might be long and would certainly be grim. . . . The organs of government would continue to do everything possible to save lives immediately after attack but would also preserve a framework of administration to use remaining resources in the best way to keep the rest of the people alive, to maintain law and order, and to prepare for the restoration of a more normal life.

In September 1963, in the annual advertising campaign for civil defence, the Home Office gave away more information than ever before about its secret emergency plans. The advertisement listed 'ten vital points' including 'wartime regional headquarters . . . provided and equipped in England and Wales, and similar headquarters in Scotland', and an 'emergency chain of control' extending from them.

The 'ten points' also included references to the *Backbone* system:

Important telephone cables are being re-routed away from the big population centres and special radio links installed to bridge gaps that might be caused by bombs.

Also mentioned were:

- A chain of self supporting (BBC) broadcast transmitters
- A national warning system
- Alternative supplies from deep wells (with) standby water pumping and piping equipment
- Stockpiles of essential food
- Emergency moorings, strategically sited around the coast, away from likely target areas, with cargo equipment stockpiled
- Reserve supplies of fuel oil and medical equipment

The Home Office had also provided transport and communications equipment to move huge 600-strong civil defence and police Mobile Columns to bomb–struck areas. The Home Office also published details, separately, of quite extensive schemes of evacuation which were then in force. Overall, they said, some 10.5 million people would be 'voluntarily' dispersed before attack to reception areas. Those covered by the scheme were primarily children and adolescents under eighteen, mothers of school children and expectant mothers. Besides the evacuation scheme, new regulations in 1964 asked local authorities to draw up lists of rest centres for other refugees, and for those evacuated from fallout zones. An official film, *Operation Exodus*, showed this process in operation.

The replacement of succour with survival also affected local authorities in 1964; they were told that a wartime Emergency Powers Act would require them to become, in effect, part of central government. Their Town or County Clerk (now Chief Executive) should be appointed as wartime Controller, and would form part of a 'chain of command' from central government HQS. The democratic role of local authorities was more or less dispensed with; they were to select an Emergency Committee of not more than three members to whom all the power of the Council would be deputed in war. In fact this was really a sop, as the Controller would only have to 'account for his activities in relation (only) to local government functions *as soon as it was feasible for him to do so*' (author's emphasis).

A new, hardened and authoritarian form of government con-

Plates 13 & 14
Regional Seat of Government 6 at Warren Row, site of many CND demonstrations in the 1960s. Right, the first visit to RSG 6 during the 1963 Aldermaston march. Below, Julie Felix sings at RSG 6, Easter 1968.

trol was thus erected within the previous framework of home defence plans. District Controllers would answer to county and county boroughs Controllers; they in turn would answer to Sub-Regional Commissioners; and after an attack abated and fallout radiation levels were reduced, the SRCS would answer to the new, devolved Regional Governments. Until these governments were set up, however, the only regional administration would be from Military District commanders.

The names of Regional Commissioners were never published, and there was never any official statement during the 1960s that these would even be elected politicians, such as junior ministers. The Sub-Regional Commissioners were to be senior civil servants. By 1965, in less than ten years, the wartime model of coordinated civil defence for rescue and succour had been totally transformed; the Civil Defence Corps itself had little time left, and a reappraisal of defences was also taking place under the new Labour government.

This was also the year in which the discussion of the effects of nuclear attack reached some prominence after the banning by the BBC of their documentary, *The War Game*. The film had been made during 1965 by Peter Watkins, whose prodigious ability to put the dirt and devastation of battle or disaster onto film had first been demonstrated with *Culloden*. In late 1963, he had proposed a film about the aftermath of nuclear attack, in Kent, and it was accepted – not without awareness of the controversial nature of the proposal: a note in the BBC archives by Watkins' superiors argues:

So long as there is no security risk, and the facts are authentic, the people should be trusted with the truth. There are views at experienced levels that since nothing can be done to save Britain from annihilation, it is better not to portray such probable occurrences or to give frightening facts . . . the film is bound to be horrifying and unpopular – . . . but surely necessary.

It was made, banned, and has never subsequently been shown on television. The BBC still refused to show it in 1980. They contemplated a new version, given the renewed interest, and a special showing was held for News and Current Affairs executives. But nothing was done and the ban – also applying to other TV channels – remained in force.

When the ban was announced by the BBC Director General, Hugh Greene, in November 1965, he claimed that:

This is the BBC's own decision. It has been taken after a good deal of thought and discussion but not as a result of outside pressure of any kind. . . . The film (was) too horrifying for the medium of broadcasting . . . one cannot guarantee that there would not be children, the very old, or the unbalanced in the audience who might be seriously disturbed. . . .

It was the BBC's own decison, but it had been made after a great deal of outside pressure had been brought to bear on the 'independent' Corporation. The pressure was directed, chiefly through the Chairman of the BBC Governors, Lord Normanbrook, who as Cabinet Secretary had been responsible for overseeing the development of Home Defence and nuclear weapons policy over much of the previous decade. Normanbrook secretly called in a panel of top government officials to see the *War Game*; after they had reviewed it and reported back to their ministries, Normanbrook wrote to Greene that 'Whitehall will be relieved if we do not show it.' Normanbrook then resolutely ensured that it was not shown.

The mechanics of the ban, and the true reasons for it, were only disclosed after BBC archives were examined in 1980. Far from it being an independent decision in the interests of public health, it was an explicit move to withold such a powerful account of the consequences of nuclear warfare from the public – chiefly on account of risks to government policy. This was made clear in a letter Lord Normanbrook wrote to his Cabinet Office successor, Sir Burke Trend, in September 1965. Normanbrook observed that 'the film is not intended as propaganda; it is intended as a purely factual statement, and is based on careful research into official material.' He might have added that the Home Office had determinedly resisted the making of the film, refusing to answer questions Watkins had put to them about their expectations, and banning the official cooperation of local Civil Defence groups – even though many of them later used the film for training purposes (!).

Normanbrook warned, however:

The showing of the film on television might well have a significant effect on public attitudes towards the policy of the nuclear deterrent. . . .

Late in September a party of Whitehall's highest visited the Television Centre, unannounced. The party included Cabinet Secretary Sir Burke Trend, Home Office Permanent Under Secretary Sir Charles Cunningham, and three other officials from the Ministry of Defence, the Defence Chiefs of Staff, and the Post Office. The officials felt that the film 'whatever its intention' would lend support to CND. Although the officials pointed out a few inaccuracies, these could be corrected; they agreed that 'the major question of policy was whether it would be expedient, in the public interest, that any film of this kind should be shown on television.' Although Labour government ministers declined to see the film or express a view on banning it, the consensus of Whitehall opinion was quite clear to its former chief, and the film was banned.

The Defence Ministry said in its 1963 White Paper:

> The government have always recognised the importance of informing the public about the effects of nuclear weapons and the steps that could be taken to mitigate these effects. . . .

Sir Charles Cunningham, who had personally superintended the conduct of *Fallex* 62 and other exercises, was also well aware of the grim accuracy of the *War Game*. But taken to the brink of openly disclosing their visions to the public, Whitehall reverted to its traditional policy of 'not in front of the children' when government policy might be disagreeable. Home Office spokesmen, according to some accounts, went so far as to reassure press correspondents, off the record, that psychologists had anticipated a 'wave of 20,000 suicides' if the film were shown.

The rest of the media tended to side with the BBC; the *Daily Sketch* suggested that the film was 'irresponsible' as 'it excluded hope. . . . It excluded any reasoned argument on why we must have the Bomb.' The case for letting the public, as a whole, see the power of the *War Game* for themselves, and judge, was best put by Kenneth Tynan in the *Observer*:

> The War Game stirred me at a deeper level than panic or grief. So long as adequate warning is given to depressives . . . it should not only be televised but screened in cinemas, not just here but everywhere on earth, especially in countries that possess (or would like to possess) the bomb. The BBC is like a doctor witholding the truth from a patient who is suffering from a portentially fatal disease; silence may preclude panic, but it also precludes cure.

In the event, *The War Game* reached its audience (and continues to reach it), if not its full impact, through thousands of showings in Britain and abroad.

*

The rundown in 'steps to mitigate the effects' of nuclear attack continued through the rest of the 60s. Development of the SRC bunkers and their communications did continue apace, and the UKWMO warning chain continued to be developed. But stockpiles were being run down, work on new self-supporting BBC transmitters was abandoned. The evacuation and dispersal scheme would be 'reviewed', it was said in 1967, but since it would take a week to complete, the new policy was to have a scheme which did not require moving children to the 'neutral' or 'reception' areas of the country; instead they should be found 'suitable existing accommodation near at hand'. There was also a new statement about shelter policy:

The Government had reviewed their shelter policy and concluded that to provide shelter against blast was impracticable and for most people the best protection against radioactive fallout would be achieved by staying in their own homes and acting on the advice that would be given them.

Communal fallout shelters for those in bungalows or other lightly constructed dwellings might be contemplated, but it was made quite clear to local authorities that they should go no further than thinking about possible places to use.

The government planned in its 1967 review to scale down the CD Corps to 75,000 and cut out entirely the rescue and aid teams. The community would have to provide these for themselves, based on a 'nucleus' of CD control staff. In effect, the policy decision which had been taken was that henceforth all those trapped or injured by the blast or fire effects of an explosion should either be left to die, or rescue themselves by their own or neighbours' efforts. This remains the policy today.

A year later, in January 1968, Harold Wilson announced that 'Home Defence – Civil Defence' would be reduced to a care and maintenance basis. Despite protests by some local authorities and members of the Civil Defence Corps and the Auxiliary Fire Service, disbandment was completed by the end of March. Ex-members were given their uniforms free to keep; it would have cost more to collect them back and clean them for a stockpile.

The closure also applied to the Home Guard, which had only been recently reorganised from being the 'Territorial Army', to become the Home Defence Force, or Territorial and Army Volunteer Reserve 3. The TAVR3 Home Defence Force, 28,000 strong, was to have 'assisted the police in the

Plate 15 A modern bunker; srhq 42 is under Sovereign House, Hertford.

maintenance of law and order' and act generally in support of the civil authorities. It would have been comprised of 'lightly armed infantry type units' from which its primary role – to provide government with defences against sabotage or insurgent or rioting civilians – was obvious. Tavr 3 would have been wholly unable to combat a landing of frontline Soviet forces, whether on a sabotage raid or invading.

In the event, tavr 3 was closed along with the cd Corps – or it appeared to close. In the event, a number of ta units continued to be assigned to Home Defence including at least two volunteer Signals Regiments.

Three Civil Defence schools and colleges closed, leaving only Easingwold, and all the government and local authority bunkers were put onto care and maintenance. One or two new srcs which had started construction in the mid 60s underneath new provincial office blocks were completed and put into service. The whole of local authority civil defence activity was reduced to a rump of paper plans for the redeployment of local authority staff in time of war. They were authorised to demolish old wartime shelters. Stockpiles of emergency equipment or supplies were maintained at a minimum level. The Home Office closed all its regional civil defence offices, and kept only a Whitehall 'central planning staff'; no capital spending of any kind was permitted, and if communications systems fell apart and stocks rotted, so be it. Civil defence was, thus, 'dismantled'.

The extensive networks of warning sirens and receivers, and the UK Warning and Monitoring Organisation, was kept going, although the number of Royal Observer Corps bunkers was halved, and a few higher group controls closed. But reporting the arrival and weight of nuclear attack remained of key importance to military headquarters, even if there was no substantive civil defence organisation to do more than pass out warnings. (The UKWMO network is described in Chapter 9). Police training in war duties continued, and there was no reduction in the police reserve of Special Constables.

Between 1968 and 1972, and in many ways until much later, civil defence completely disappeared from the public eye. The view, presented by James Callaghan in defending the closures, was that 'the danger of nuclear war had lessened significantly enough' to permit the reduction. (This statement was not however held to justify any reduction in spending on British nuclear weapons or strike forces.) The prevalent public attitude appeared to be a desire to forget that nuclear weapons and the possibility of nuclear war still existed. The conclusion of the SALT 1 talks in May 1972, and the creation of limitations in at least one minor department of the arms race (the number of strategic weapons carriers), appeared to support this view into the 70s.

Yet the dangers had not abated, they had merely consolidated. Where once, in the early 1950s, there were only half a dozen 'temporary' US air bases, there was now a ramified network all over Britain, supporting US nuclear submarines, main and reserve air bases, army stockpiles, headquarters, marine and anti-submarine bases, communications and intelligence facilities. Britain now deployed nuclear forces from dozens of bases. The withdrawal of France from NATO's military structure in 1967 meant that Britain had become the United States' primary support or 'rear' area in Europe, and yet more bases were to be built. Living in Britain did not put the citizen in the nuclear firing line as much as in Braunschweig or Nordrhein-Westphalia, but there could be no denying that the risks for the citizens of London, Lincoln, or Lancashire had been multiplying exponentially for twenty years.

The huge arrays of Soviet missiles, which had not existed

when us politicians proclaimed the 'missile gap' in 1960, were in being by 1970, along with their us counterparts. Some 750 medium range missiles, 180 long range missiles and hundreds of medium and long range Soviet aircraft were in positions from which they could mount nuclear attacks across Western Europe. Soviet pronouncements left no doubt that once someone started the nuclear shooting, their response would be 'massive', annihilatory.

When Civil Defence had been revived in 1948, it had retained its wartime character – a thick layer of welfare and rescue services surrounding its heart -- the primacy of administration. To the extent that the government maintained its legitimacy by providing and organising necessary welfare services, it was entitled to remain the centre of the organised community. But gradually all but the hard core had been stripped away, partly through public disinterest and partly through government economy – serious sums of money in defence went, as always, to the nuclear deterrent and to grandiose 'conventional' projects of the three services. When 'Emergency Planning' was resurrected in the 1972, it was as the bastard child of the old civil defence organisation – producing plans about plans, without, of course, spending any money and yet endeavouring to convince the public.

5
Machinery of government 1972–1983

Home Defence retired into the carapace of central government after the 1968 dismantlement, and emerged again four years later in its present form – without Civil Defence Corps, without shelters or emergency fire or medical services. In 1971, the Home Office reorganised its former Civil Defence Department as the Emergency Services Division (F6) in the Police Department. Including the Supply and Transport Branch, part of the Scientific Research and Development Branch, and the UK Warning and Monitoring Organisation, some 160 people now work for the central organisation of Home Defence – still a statutory duty of government under the 1948 Civil Defence Act.

In 1972, the Home Office set out anew the objectives of Home Defence. The first listed was the *internal* threat to government. The four objectives (contained in circular ES3/73, *Home Defence Planning Assumptions*) are:

(to take) those defensive measures necessary in the United Kingdom:

a. to secure the United Kingdom against any internal threat;
b. to mitigate as far as practicable the effects of any direct attack on the United Kingdom involving the use of conventional nuclear, biological or chemical weapons;
c. to provide alternative machinery of government at all levels to increase the prospects of, and to direct, national survival; and
d. to enhance the basis for national recovery in the post-attack period.

These tasks are seen to occur successively. First, there is the threat from sabotage, subversion and public opposition to the government. In this phase, government plans (see below) explicitly define lawful opposition to their war plans as the 'enemy', including 'dissident groups', 'anti-war demonstrations', and even 'adverse public reaction to government policies'. As exercises like *Hard Rock* and *Square Leg* demonstrate, Home Defence planners show deep concern about the mobilisation of anti-war opposition in the United Kingdom. This concern also appears in NATO's general civil defence plans, with which those of the United Kingdom are integrated.

The second task is to provide relief for the citizenry during attack – 'as far as practicable'. This is the task primarily allocated to local government, and for which no resources are provided, save to build bunkers and make plans.

The third task concerns the maintenance of the machinery of government, by means of the network of protected controls, supported by military aid. This has as its objective the survival of the *nation*, which in context is wholly distinct from the survival of the *people*. 'National survival' does not mean endeavouring to keep each member of the nation alive. Then follows the fourth, 'recovery' phase. There are few plans for this phase, and little idea of its likely dimensions or difficulties.

Most of the visible, local face of home defence in the 80s is concerned only with planning for the second and third phases. In circulars, the government has explained to local authorities that 'the main responsibility for the internal security of the United Kingdom rests with central government supported by the police and, where necessary, the armed forces'. Little more is said about the problems of law and order, which do not normally concern local authority Controllers or their staff – only the Commissioners at SRHQS and RGHQS (see Chapter 6).

In a few cases, such as the pre-strike phases of *Square Leg*, the nature of these problems is glimpsed. But the most exact gloss on these government objectives is provided in a *Training Manual for Scientific Advisers* issued in 1977. A section of this manual, on 'Policy and Planning', identifies the public as the enemy of government with unusual precision. The *Training Manual*, strangely, isn't even classified which is the customary protection for indiscreet official thought. The overall threat is defined as:

(a) internal threat (sabotage, subversion, and possibly *adverse public reaction to government policies*)
(b) conventional attack
(c) nuclear attack:
(d) chemical attack
(e) biological attack

On sabotage, the *Training Manual* suggests, there is:

a potential threat to the security of the United Kingdom arising from acts of sabotage by enemy agents, possibly assisted by *dissident groups*. The acts could be aimed . . . directly at the population. *Their aim would be to weaken the national will and ability to fight.* One result of sabotage would be to tie down large numbers of men on static guard duties. . . .

On subversion, it explains:

There exist in the United Kingdom *certain dissident extremist groups* which are *known to be in sympathy with our potential enemies* and which can be expected to react against the good of the national in times of tension. The groups are small and for the most part exercise little influence. . . . Their significance should not be underestimated.

The threat posed by subversive groups includes formenting strikes in key industries, *promoting anti-war demonstrations* to turn the populace against the government and disruptive activities connected with war preparations (Author's emphases).

In conclusion:

So long as the threat of attack on the United Kingdom exists there will be a need for flexible, realistic and practical home defence arrangements to secure the country against the internal threat. . . . Credible home defence plans prepared in peacetime by both national and local government are an essential part of the total defence posture.

These comments make it difficult to see how current British Home Defence plans can do other than regard any popular opposition to imminent war as wholesale treason – and react accordingly. The internal security task of dealing with 'adverse public reaction' would end as war began; once an all out nuclear attack had begun there would be little point in popular protest against the government of the day's suicidal lack of foresight or judgment. In the subsequent, operational (1–7 days), survival (1–8 weeks) and recovery (after 1 or 2 months) phases, the prime objective would still remain the maintenance of administration and the 'elimination of hostile elements'.

Local authorities' part in this design consists in providing the civil defence measures which they are directed to plan for. These include:

• Operating the specified Controls, and gathering information
• Advice to the public (ie 'Protect and Survive' measures)

- Providing Rest Centres and billeting arrangements for (post-strike) refugees and the homeless
- Burial of the dead, and controlling the spread of disease
- Providing a food distribution and emergency feeding service
- Clearing highways, maintaining essential services where possible and general works services
- Training

Chapter 2 gave a picture of these services in operation after an attack. Local authorities get no resources, other than wages for planning staff, and (recently) grants to build and equip their bunkers, with which to provide these services. Local authority Controllers will, in fact, have no control over resources such as food, fuel, or water which remain entirely in the hands of central government HQs.

Over a decade, the Home Office's new Emergency Planning Division have issued over sixty circulars to local authorities, suggesting the manner in which they should carry out civil defence plans. Until the recent movement for 'Nuclear Free Zones' in the cause of nuclear disarmament, there was generally little opposition to these plans (and little enthusiasm either). Home Office grants in any case, covered half or three-quarters of the cost.

The first phase of detailed planning lasted from 1972 to 1974. The 1974 reorganisation of local government reconstituted England and Wales into a handful of giant county authorities, and Scotland into similar regions (the term is used in a different sense from that of home defence planning; the whole of Scotland forms one Home Defence Region). During 1972 and 1973, the new authorities-to-be were advised of the future structure of civil defence. England and Wales continued to be divided into ten Regions, each comprising one or two Sub-Regions. Scotland was divided as before into three Zones, equivalent to English Sub-Regions. Northern Ireland was one Region, making twelve in all. Each English or Welsh Sub-Region was to have a protected SRHQ, some seventeen in all. Each Scottish Zone has a protected Zone HQ (ZHQ); in addition there is a Scottish Central Control; Northern Ireland is administered from a single Northern Ireland Central HQ.

Figure 6 (p. 142) shows British Home Defence Regions, Sub-Regions and Zones. Figure 7 shows the contemporary machinery of wartime government – a five tier integrated structure of civil and military controls, from central government to district council and below. The locations and nature of the bunkers concerned are described in Chapter 8.

The 1973 restructuring of Home Defence Regions to take account of local government reorganisation reduced the number of Sub-Regions in England and Wales from twenty-six to seventeen. This was just as well, as in 1971 a majority of Sub-Regions did not have an SRHQ. This is perhaps a measure of how seriously the government took its own plans. Shortly before the change occurred, London (or what was likely to remain of it) which had previously been parcelled out to the five adjacent sub-regions, was reconstituted as a Home Defence Region again, at the request of officials of the Greater London Council (whose function, understandably, was somewhat negated by the implicit and evidently realistic assumption that London could not survive as a single entity).

The apex of the machinery of government tree is the central government war HQ, at Hawthorn near Bath. This has been the nerve centre of the British government's war plans for over twenty years. It is difficult to believe that no higher or reserve centre of government exists, although all the evidence one can muster suggests that this is not so; virtually all the wartime central government of the UK is concentrated into a bare hundred underground acres. This contains the central defence and government staff who will supervise the war, and conduct foreign relations and control trade, ports and shipping in war. The concentration of command and control into this centre and a few major military HQs, equally well known to a potential enemy, does in fact raise severe and serious questions about the British nuclear deterrent. If it is truly intended to be used to avenge a first strike on Britain, then it is clearly of importance that command, control and communications centres survive even a massive first attack, in order to be able to order the launch of an avenging salvo of Polaris. But even official military home defence manuals warn that central command and control agencies may not survive a nuclear strike. If that is so (and I suspect it is), then British nuclear weapons are highly destabilising in crisis; a moment wasted in ordering the use of the nuclear armoury may be a moment in which the opportunity to order such a strike is lost (or would be). Although further discussion is beyond the scope of this book, it is apparent that, because of this factor, British military commanders would wish either to launch a pre-emptive strike, or order an all-out response on receipt of early warning of the first stages of an attack.

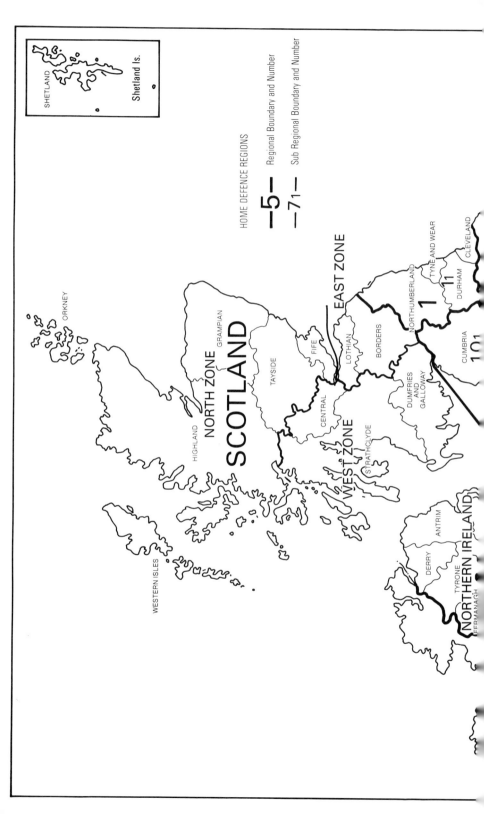

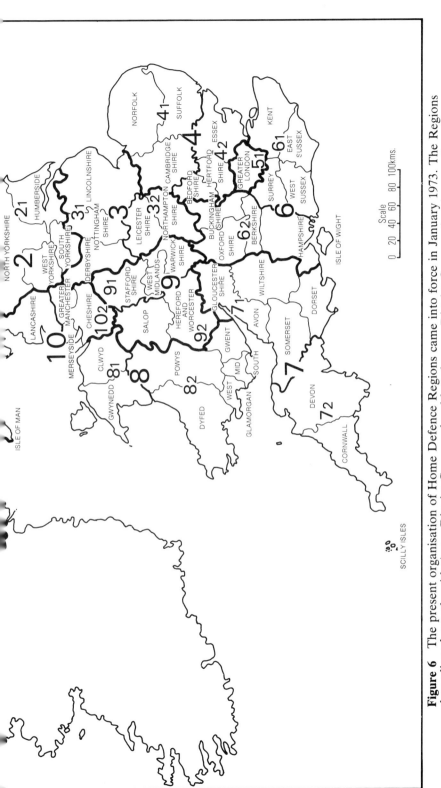

Figure 6 The present organisation of Home Defence Regions came into force in January 1973. The Regions then aligned exactly with Army District Commands, although some District Commanders in peacetime are responsible for two Regions (North East District covers Regions 1 & 2, Eastern District, Regions 3 & 4).

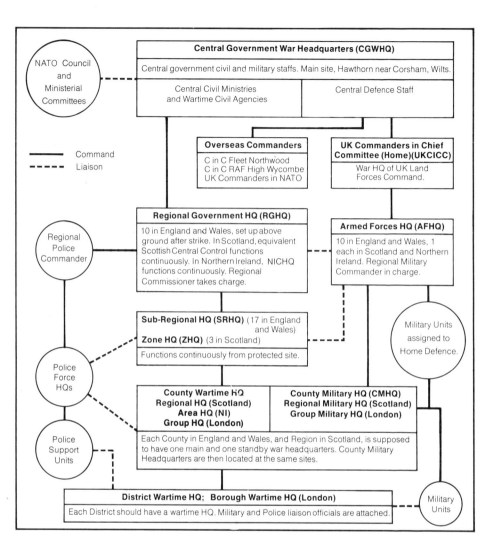

Figure 7 The diagrams in military manuals of Home Defence, on which this Figure is largely based, warn that 'central command and control agencies may not survive a nuclear strike'; in other words, regional government may be all that is left after an all-out attack. Each of the five layers of government answers to the layer above. In war, District and County Controllers are officials of central, not local, government.

Regional Government HQs are *not* bunkers. Staff designated to serve in Regional Government are dispersed to 'Group Locations' in the Region, thought to be relatively safe. Between D+2 weeks and D+3 months they then gather at a suitable surviving location to establish the RGHQ.

The central government HQ coordinates military action with the NATO Council dispersed across Europe and the North Atlantic, in whose hands the final decision to go nuclear rests. It also coordinates civil defence measures through a series of NATO Wartime Civil Agencies (NWCAS) that would function internationally when war seemed imminent. There are six NWCAS – for ocean shipping, transport, refugee handling, energy (mainly oil), aviation, food and agriculture. Two NWCAS – for oil, and ocean shipping (eastern hemisphere) – apparently have their wartime European headquarters in Britain, and a D Notice asks for no mention of their whereabouts (which are presently unknown, although the Ocean Shipping NWCA is probably either at Northwood or Hawthorn). The other NWCAS have, clearly, more relevance to the continental NATO allies, whose national boundaries would have little meaning after the flight of tens of millions of refugees in a major land war and a thermonuclear exchange.

At central government level, only the military commanders-in-chief would initially exercise any direct control over the UK's Regions. The Sub-Regional HQs would take over after 'an attack which destroyed the effectiveness of central government in its normal peacetime location'. The *Machinery of Government in War* circular (ES7/73) explains the function of SRHQS:

Sub-Regional Commissioners would be concerned with the administration of justice, with the maintenance by the police of law and order, and with the general behaviour and morale of survivors . . . the function of Sub-Region would be to process and disseminate information on the extent and effect of attack; to determine priorities and arrange for the re-allocation, where appropriate, of resources to meet immediate needs . . . and to prepare the administrative groundwork for the establishment of regional government. . . . Local priorities would be left to the County and District Controllers

The chief function of the SRHQ would, in fact, be to withhold resources from the worst hit areas, and conserve them for elsewhere, later, whatever the human cost. As the GLC scientific advisers' advice note (quoted at the beginning of this book) observed, in the wartime bunkers:

there would be scope for . . . decision making and resource allocation where the unit of cost may be expressed in terms of human life. . . .

The SRHQS would withold the government food stockpile until as late as possible, and avoid feeding those refugees who were injured or dying; it would fall to the local authorities to explain to some groups why no food was forthcoming and to the army to suppress their reaction. Efficacious lying, early on, might save on the number of bullets required. In the same way, available fuel supplies would be conserved and not used for rescue, and police and other units 'saved' from undue early radiation exposure by mounting no welfare or 'control' operations in areas of fallout.

Circular 7/73 explains:

Although Sub-Region would rule on conflicting priorities, its intervention would aim at the *conservation of resources*, both manpower and materials, for longer-term survival – rather than immediate short-term aid to the hardest hit areas.

Each County Controller (peacetime Chief Executive) would have complete dominion over the county territory, except for police and military forces. By 1973, the wartime role of any elected councillors had vanished altogether; if an emergency committee was constituted (and found suitable accomodation, about which there was no stipulation), then the Controller might report to them 'from time to time'. But he would be a *regional*, not local government official, the third level in the hierarchical chain of control.

Each county was asked in 1973 to provide both a main and a standby wartime HQ; but plans for these are highly varied. When this advice was first issued, for instance, only about 150 out of 300 local authorities had provided themselves with protected controls (in fact a better average than central government). Although every council has nominated premises since 1972, not all have actually provided them, and the majority of council war HQS do not meet the Home Office's standards for ventilation, standby power or other facilities. When the Nuclear Free Zone movement started with the rekindling of the Campaign for Nuclear Disarmament, many councils opted to end capital spending on building or refurbishing their bunkers. County Council War HQS (as far as they are known), are listed in Appendix 3.

In *Home Defence Planning Assumptions* (ES 3/73) local authorities were asked to make plans which could be implemented in a three to four week warning period, based on 'current NATO assessment' of 'weeks rather than days' before an attack came. In a statement by Home Secretary William

Plates 16 & 17 London has its own control network, including Group Controls, such as that at Wanstead Flats for north east London (above), and its own SRHQ 51 at Kelvedon Hatch in Essex (below).

Whitelaw in July 1980, this warning period was abruptly short-ened to 'days rather than weeks', and forty-eight hours was the stipulated period in which local authority plans could be put into preliminary operation. No strategic explanation was given for this drastic – and, on the face of it, extremely alarming – cut in the warning period. It might have been in large measure a fiction designed to spur others into greater preparation for war; but if so, it was probably a NATO-wide ploy, and it had been some years in coming.

Circular ES7/73 stressed that if purpose-built or cellar accommodation could not be found for local authorities' bunkers, improvised plans (along the lines of *Protect and Survive*, only better organised and with priority access to supplies) should be made to build in radiation protection. A county council might, typically, seek to accommodate up to ninety people, with up to sixty more in the standby HQ. For large metropolitan district councils, eighty might be the maximum, while a small rural district might need only twenty.

Below district council level there were no explicit plans to be formulated. However a circular on *Community Organisation in War* (ES2/76, and later ES2/81) suggested that local authorities might prepare plans for 'community leaders' and committees to organise small communities (such as parishes and town or city neighbourhoods) for civil defence. These leaders or committees could then liase by telephone or, event-ually, by bicycle or improvised semaphore with district council HQs. Councils were asked to decide what type of organisation might be the most useful for adaptation to war planning 'having regard to the social and economic nature of the area'. As might be expected, this has produced plans of widely divergent character from 'a chain of District Soviets' (as Ro-bin Cook MP styled the Lothian Regional plan in Scotland) to Church guilds, and vigilante groups, such as the West Sussex 'Peacekeeping Forces'. The Conservative government elected in 1979 placed a growing emphasis on voluntary effort in civil defence, and the role of community organisation was stressed in the second circular on the subject issued in 1981. The encouragement of volunteers and the 'Voluntary Aid Socie-ties', led by the newly appointed Coordinator of Voluntary Effort, Sir Leslie Mavor, was an attempt by the government to magnify the public profile of civil defence at (virtually) no cost.

The essence of home defence plans in the 70s and 80s remains as it was when civil defence of the old sort died in 1968. The key planks of this policy are (from ES3/73).

- A 'stay put' policy, strongly advocated by the government. (in private meetings, however, Noel Law, the mid 70s head of F6, qualified this as a 'stay put policy for all but a few' – meaning officials).
- No evacuation, of any kind. 'Formal planning for the possible dispersal and reception of people in certain priority classes of the population from one area to another is no longer consistent with the (new) policy.'
- No public shelters (and until 1981, no encouragement of private shelters). 'Families could expect better protection by staying in their own homes. . . . The requirement for communal shelters would be limited to those who, for one reason or another, could not in the time available find adequate protection at home.'
- Nuclear war was 'the overriding consideration. . . . Few, if any parts of the country could expect to be completely unaffected.'

The Home Office also moved to a position of refusing even to discuss what the likely pattern of attack might be, and left all such hypotheses to be made at a local level. This policy is an essential corollary of the 'stay put' advice and, naturally, maximises casualties in a likely target area (the population of which would otherwise be evacuated and dispersed). This strategy is justified to the public by a mixture of carrots, sticks and keeping-in-ignorance. The carrot is stressing the psychological advantage of familiar surroundings; the stick is the threat of what happens if you go: 'the local authority may need to take your empty home for others to use'.

This threat is on page 7 of *Protect and Survive*; in fact there are *no* local authority plans to identify and use for billetting homes left empty *before* an attack, and the government has *not* suggested that local authorities make any such plans. Indeed, in *Homelessness in War* (ES7/76), the government specifically prohibited local authorities from doing the kind of pre-attack billeting hinted at in the dishonest passage from *Protect and Survive*.

It would be imperative for the police and local government officials and members to discourage those, whose personal arrangements for their own accommodation were inadequate, from any belief that, before an attack occurred, they would become a charge on the local authority in whose area they happened to appear. . . .*

Such persons should whenever possible be persuaded to return to their homes before any hostilities began. The public mass information campaign would reinforce local persuasive efforts.

The stay put campaign materials were designed by the Central Office of Information in 1974 and 1975 as, perhaps, the ultimate exercise of twentieth century marketing skills. The marketing concept for *Protect and Survive* was a non-specific, 'nuclear family' (sic). The *Protect and Survive* 'logo' of the words encircling father, mother, daughter and son was adopted for the official pamphlet, the prepared newspaper layouts of advice, and more than twenty video films and similar sound recordings, all of which have now been stock-piled. The video films cover all the topics in the *Protect and Survive* pamphlet and include such themes as: 1: Nuclear Explosions explained . . . 4: Stay-at-home . . . 8: Make your fallout room and refuge now . . . 20: Casualties.

Each video would be broadcast repeatedly in the 'low level phase' a few weeks before attack; in the last few days of deepening crisis, they would reach 'saturation coverage'. The 'mass information campaign' would include already prepared layouts of *Protect and Survive*, which would be published as a two page insert in broadsheet newspapers, or a four page insert in each of the tabloids. The layouts 'have a high pic-torial content', another aspect of the coi's marketing strategy for the stay-put campaign. Using newspapers to distribute the information would also be rather more rapid than printing and distributing ten to twenty million copies of *Protect and Survive* itself.

The pamphlet which finally emerged to something less than acclaim in 1981 was a reprint, slightly edited, of the original version which had accompanied a circular on *Advice to the Public on Protection Against Nuclear Attack* (ES9/76) ('for research purposes only and . . . not for publication').

---

* An incidental dishonesty is that the 'Digest of Home Defence', which is issued by the Easingwold Home Defence College to council members (not officials) who attend seminars there, says that the policy is that 'the homeless must be looked after. . .whatever their composition and wherever they come from.' Later, it points out that this is a reference to 'survivors', not refugees.

Not much was changed, although the 1976 version contained some even more extraordinary idiocies than its successor. The familiar illustrations of stairs or shelter tables for the 'inner refuge' were protected, in 1976, in part not by bags or boxes of earth but by *pillows, cushions and mattresses*. These would have prevented neither blast nor fire and provided no radiation fallout protection either, however comforting hiding under a mattress might be psychologically. One suggestion was technically utterly incompetent; shelterers were asked to take a portable radio with them, and to switch off 'until after attack (to avoid damage)'. The writer apparently thought that this might protect a radio against damage from the electromagnetic pulse (EMP) effects of explosion; it couldn't and wouldn't (it would have no effect at all); the next edition pointed out, more sensibly, that the aerial should be pushed in or disconnected.

Protect and Survive was created as a modern counterpart of the 1963 booklet, *Advising the Householder*, but was intended more to reinforce obedience to government policy than to give advice. Gone, now, are exhortations to help neighbours or others caught in the open (or to receive such help); gone is any plan for evacuation, either in advance, or from zones of lethally heavy fallout. It should be said that some of the minor underlying assumptions of *Protect and Survive* are sound. It devotes most of its thirty-two pages to advice on the construction of fallout shelters within houses, and what to take into them. In certain cases, this is indeed the proper point to emphasise, as increasing the average protective factor (PF) of the population makes an enormous difference to the level of radiation casualties. Its suggestions for filling drawers and suitcases with earth are slightly more useful advice than was given in 1963 concerning sandbags. Some advice on avoiding contamination is generally sound. For people living in rural areas, away from the direct effects of any bomb burst, who have ample food, means of heating and a suitable dwelling, *Protect and Survive* helps. If that group cuts down its radiation exposure, some of those who would have died will live in the short term.

The government's policy cannot, however, be justified on the basis of its utility to a tiny part of the population, since the policy multiplies the risks for all the rest. Implicitly the following categories of people are killed by *Protect and Survive* policies:

- Everyone staying put in target areas whose homes are within the main blast and fire damage zones. For a one megaton groundburst, those extend 5–6 miles (8–10 km) from the ground zero. In the outer areas, not everyone is killed, but. . . .
- All the trapped and injured are written off through non-provision of rescue services or Forward Medical Aid Units; and . . .
- More will die through fires and perhaps firestorms, starting in the peripheral, damaged areas, since there is no emergency fire service support for householders, who, if they are uninjured, have to do what they can with buckets of water or domestic fire extinguishers. Even if such fires are not widespread, and there are no firestorms, there will be more deaths since. . . .
- Those sheltering anywhere in the blast zone (which extends beyond 11 miles (17 km) from the ground zero of a one megaton airburst) will lose the protective factor of their housing through windows and roofs being damaged and blown out shortly before the heaviest fallout starts. Those who may escape from burnt out homes, with or without injury, will, unless they can evacuate themselves, die without radiation protection unless they are well upwind of Ground Zero.
- Others, not so near the centre of the explosion, will die from radiation because, even in their undamaged fallout shelters and refuge rooms, they do not have a high enough PF for the heaviest radiation zones. Others will have been unable (through shortages) to obtain the necessary materials to carry out the official advice, and suffer the same fate.

  This factor can be quite serious. The mushroom cloud of a one megaton bomb will extend across over 10 miles (16 km). The blast effects of the bomb in damaging and destroying houses will extend well beyond this area, and those downwind of Ground Zero would rapidly suffer from the heaviest fallout, against which they would have inadequate protection. They could attempt quickly to evacuate upwind, but *Protect and Survive* gives no guidance on patterns of fallout.
- Even those in secure refuge rooms in areas of minimal fallout may die, perhaps through hypothermia, if an attack occurs during winter. A major attack would cut off electricity and gas, nationwide. Oil and coal would be

impounded in guarded stockpiles, and only the most provident or fortunate householders would have calor gas heaters, or coal stocks, or be able to forage for wood when fallout permitted. Fuel could not be burnt inside the refuge room.

• Others might face extra injury or difficulty, since they had been unable to get enough food. *Protect and Survive's* advice on purchasing fourteen days' stocks of food would be unattainable for many householders. Supermarkets, on average, hold three days' stocks; they would not generally be able to resupply since their wholesale depots would have been requisitioned. The government might allow some releases to prevent pre-war food riots, but would not want large stocks of food from the distribution chain to be wasted by being stored by city centre households where provisions would be destroyed at the same time as their owners.

In consequence, yet more people might die of lack of food or through the interaction of semi-starvation and other individually non-lethal effects; minor injuries and burns; lack of heating; less than lethal radiation doses; and, ultimately, disease.

Although not directly part of the 'Protect and Survive' plans, the harsh measures implied in the general policy extends also to the expeditious abandonment of unproductive members of the civil population. For example, the Home Defence College's *Digest of Home Defence* (1976) stressed unpleasant if realistic aspects of conserving medical staff and supplies:

This conservation would rate a high priority – more so indeed than ensuring the safety of the chronically sick or mentally abnormal patients.

Similar priorities apply to environmental health measures:

(Environmental problems) should never take priority over arrangements for provision of emergency accomodation or food or medical treatment for the living . . . to be more precise, for those who showed signs of being likely to go on living for a reasonable time. Priority for the most useful members (of the surviving community) is a policy that goes against the grain somewhat when considering the problem today, but a serious long term view should soon dispel doubts about its necessity and lend support to this as an unavoidable theme in planning.

Should there be resistance to such 'themes', a subsequent passage explains:

Plans do exist to assist solution of (the main problems of law and order) but, as might be expected, these are classified.* . . . Some modification of the penal code might be called for.

Prior to the Second World War, civil servants writing about such delicate matters usually took refuge in French – the phrase *les bouches inutiles* described those earmarked for abandonment.

Current civil defence policies have value only in two respects; the provision of a warning system may save some of those who might be caught in the open, and consequently suffer fatal burns or blast injuries; secondly it has marginal value to those who are at risk only from medium levels of fallout. In fact, however, many of those 'saved' by the warning system will, in the event, be in areas where the ultimate prospects of survival are minimal; they merely enjoy a slower death. Sir Leslie Mavor, then the Easingwold Principal, explained in a NATO seminar in Mary 1977:

The main target areas would be so badly knocked about as to be beyond effective self-help. They would have to be more or less discounted. . . .

(*The Times*, 16 January 1980)

Some early idiocies of government advice have been given a cosmetic upgrade by the Central Office of Information. Instructions in the 1960s to cover windows in 'whitewash' now refer to 'diluted emulsion paint of a light colour'. This precaution was widely criticised because of the certainty that blast would shatter windows in areas where the heat rays of the explosion were a threat (by shining through windows and igniting items inside); the government, correctly, defended itself by pointing out that the heat flash would come *first*; then, some seconds later, the blast wave. However the precaution still remains useless in many cases since several target areas will be covered (as, for example, the *Square Leg* bomb plot suggests (p. 55)) by more than one burst; this is a standard measure against major military targets.

Suggestions made in 1963 that the family should take all its personal papers into the fallout room have also been dropped. But the COI have not been above visual, as well as textual dishonesty. *Protect and Survive's* most distinctive contribution to shelter design is the 'three doors' lean-to shelter. This is illustrated considerably larger than it would actually be (given

* The plans are described on pages 202–5.

that the normal British door is 6'6" (2m) high). The nuclear family of the *Protect and Survive* logo – two adults and two five to ten year olds – could only be accomodated in grave discomfort, yet may be expected to spend days inside.

A fundamental fallacy of Home Office policy is that it purports to take no account of the likely behaviour of the population. Those who live in urban areas, or near major targets, will not need to read Edward Thompson's *Protest and Survive*, or an analysis of the likely categories of imminent self-destruction in order to resist 'stay-put' policies. Up to a point (the point at which it does not interfere with military preparations) self-evacuation may be allowed when the refugee has a known destination. But there will certainly be no petrol supplies; there will be road blocks on major 'Essential Service Routes' (pp. 188–95). No amount of mass information campaigning by the coi is going to alter that. To judge from the way in which *Protect and Survive* has generally been received, the issue of such government advice might well induce at least as much flight as it prevents.

At the time of attack, therefore, hundreds of thousands, if not millions, of people may be on the road, stranded, walking or driving. Others will be established in local refugee camps, perhaps tolerated, perhaps in open conflict with local police and vigilante groups. Some will be besieging local authorities for emergency accomodation, or seeking to appropriate it. They will have no protection if a bomb or fallout affects their area.

The Home Office view is that those who 'choose to ignore' government policy deserve their fate, and such incipient deaths cannot be laid at the government's door. Not so. If government policy was manifestly honest, and consistent, that might be reasonable. As it is, it presupposes that the public will obligingly behave like a group of imbecilic, thoroughly disciplined sheep. That will obviously not happen. The Home Office has to plan (and does plan in secret) for the real world in which flight will be prevalent. Pre-war refugee movement is, indeed, a feature of both *Square Leg* and *Hard Rock*.

For a considerable period, perhaps wisely, *Protect and Survive* was withheld from public scrutiny, a step for which the government was widely criticised. Alan Clark, a Conservative MP, commented in 1977 that he found it 'difficult to penetrate the various layers of obstruction which both the Home Office and the Department of Defence set up on this subject.' Once it was out, however, the emperor's lack of clothing was apparent for all to see. If the booklet was short on advice in some areas, the inclusion of half a page of advice (at the end) on labelling the family dead disposal might have left some in no doubt as to where its advice might lead. From the political centre, David Owen of the SDP was as scathing as E. P. Thompson:

Having decided that home defence must be geared to what the country can afford, and yet having decided that it can afford £5,000 million for Trident, the Government should not be unduly surprised to find a considerable measure of scepticism about the genuineness of their intentions to protect against nuclear attack – or as a result of that scepticism – opposition to their defence policy. . . .

The Home Secretary reveals the paucity of his approach (and) goes on to advocate spending to ensure that the ruling establishment survive – the Royal Family, central government and local government politicians, the admirals, generals and air marshals and senior administrators all survive. But millions of others lose their lives. Money is to be spent on Sub-Regional Headquarters; the governors will go underground, the governed will stay on top. We should not attempt to hide the horror of nuclear war, nor should we pretend that with good civil defence the concept of limited nuclear war is acceptable.

(David Owen, *Negotiate and Survive*, 1980)

The whole row has deeply embarrassed Home Office planners, and their embarrassment was manifest when they removed references to the offending pamphlet in the final issues of the *Hard Rock* scenarios (Chapter 1). In consequence there has been some tinkering with policy. A Home Office Working Party on shelters was set up around 1977, under Home Office scientist James Cotterill. It did little public work until required to produce a report for the 1980/81 Home Defence Policy Review ordered by William Whitelaw. Its first function was to produce an elaborate justification of a public policy of no shelters, and this was done by finding suitable straw men amongst shelter policy options. The results (or some of the results) of the Cotterrill Working Party report were leaked to the press by Mr Whitelaw and his officials early in August 1980, five days before he announced in Parliament the results of the Review. A national shelter policy, journalists were told, had been found to cost between £60 and £80 billion. That figure was reached on the basis of providing every single household (ten million) in Britain with an individual, concrete

Plate 18 Huge underground spaces were constructed to store ammunition and other supplies in old stone quarries near Bath. Access was usually via steep slope shafts such as this one, running a hundred feet (30m) into the ground.

underground shelter costing £6000–£8000. Such a suggestion is absurd, and a programme of communal shelters could reduce the cost of each place to less than a tenth of the figure preferred – say £5 billion – at which level it would have equalled the cost of the Trident programme, and invited unwelcome public comments on defence policy priorities.

Part of the Cotterill Working Party report was published late in January 1981 as advice on the construction of 'Domestic Nuclear Shelters'. The report showed remarkable paucity of original thought. Of the five shelters examined, two were trench or field shelters of great discomfort and no blast protection, one was the expensive individual underground concrete type, costed at £6,000 – £10,000; and the remaining two were merely the Anderson and Morrison shelters of the

Second World War re-offered as suitable mass assembly 'kits'.

Late in 1980, another Working Party was set up, this time answering to the Cabinet's Home Defence Committee and led by Robert Wade-Gery of the Cabinet Office, to review mass evacuation from strategic areas. Various hints have been dropped in public about this study, but nothing is likely to come of it. The Cabinet Office planners are only too well aware of the slippery slope and the policy chasm that opens up once one group, geographical or otherwise, is admitted to need evacuation. Where would it stop? Which potential target area, or social group, could not claim equal need?

A further difficulty is that evacuation plans would require spending on reception, transport arrangements, accomodation facilities and special food stocks. Despite the 'priority' given by Mrs Thatcher's government to Home Defence, the spending increase announced in August 1980 amounted to only £4 million (it was also planned to increase overall expenditure from £27 million in 1980/81 to £45 million in 1983/84). Unless an ingenious suggestion is made for evacuation plans at no cost, then it is certain that no policy or new findings by the Cabinet Office Working Party will be forthcoming.

Not the least of the difficulties would be explaining a new, very high, level of expenditure on civil defence at the same time as justifying the government's attack on other public spending.

Means, other than official propaganda, of controlling what the public sees and hears during the late stages of a crisis are planned as part of the general government transition-to-war measures. Two committees are proposed; the first, the Information Policy Committee, would exercise formal powers of censorship when Emergency (Defence) Regulations came into force. It would be chaired by the Prime Minister's Press Secretary (in 1982, Mr Bernard Ingham) and would also advise on the issue of information (such as press releases) by other government departments, through the COI. The second committee, of officials, would supervise and plan government information releases and carry out the censorship policy. The two committees would also coordinate the release of 'Protect and Survive' information.

Later, these and other officials at sub-regional, regional and national levels would form information 'cells' – particularly inside SRHQS where they would issue broadcasts and information bulletins to the public. According to *Information Services in War* (ES2/75), in the pre-attack period:

> Very little material would be released to the public. . . . Government broadcasts might give the first indication of the possibility that war might not be averted, but the emphasis would on assurances that everything possible was being done to prevent war, and on references to the effectiveness of the nuclear deterrent.

Later, after the information campaigns, and the nuclear attack:

> If there were . . . a complete absence of news and advice . . . the reaction of survivors might range from an initial stunned apathy to more aggressive behaviour. . . . People would need to be told what was being done for them. . . . Information and guidance would also be directed towards maintaining law and order, improving morale, and countering defeatist and alarming rumours.

The transitional machinery for press and broadcasting are only part of more general arrangements for every aspect of both local and central government. Some of these would be deliberately concealed from the public. The 'restricted' circular on *Home Defence Planning Assumptions* (ES3/73) explained that some transition measures 'could be carried out without becoming public knowledge ('covert measures') while others ('overt measures') obviously could not.' In early stages of crisis, only covert measures might be enacted to 'avoid causing unnecessary public disquiet'; on the other hand the Cabinet might order overt measures since:

> An important element of deterrence might be a demonstration that we were not only redeploying military forces but also bringing our home defence organisation to the appropriate level of readiness.

In general, for 'convenience and speed of action in the event', there are long lists of civil and military steps to take in the War Books of all government departments. 'These lists are constantly revised and kept up to date.' One important 'covert' measure would be the need for each government department and local authority to ensure that they had obtained their stocks of food, water, fuel and protective materials before the public were fully aware of the crisis. Minutes of a Regional Home Defence Controllers meeting in Preston in 1978, attended by Noel Law, then head of F6, stressed this point:

(We) need a fairly active covert period of activity for effective dispersal. . . . If we wait for the overt period, (we) will clash with *Protect and Survive* re sandbagging, fourteen days supply of food, etc. . . .

Figures 8 and 9 (pp. 162 & 167) shows how peacetime functions of central and local government adapt to war roles. In many sectors, from oil and construction to supermarket chains and the banks, there are places in the bunkers and the regional governments for 'senior executives' of private industry and commerce. All officers of Regional Government (which includes Sub-Regions, Counties and Districts) including those of the Post Office and the BBC, would be answerable ultimately to the Regional Commissoner. The exact position of such staff, whether from private industry, public corporations or local councils, was clarified by the Home Office in a 1977 letter to local authority associations:

Full powers of constitutional government would be vested constitutionally in the Regional Commissioner on behalf of the Crown. . . . In addition to being able to exercise within his region all the powers vested in any Minister in peacetime, (he) would have the power to make emergency laws by ordinance. The powers exercisable by local authority Controllers will derive directly from the abnormal powers of the Regional Commissioner.

In the late stages of crisis, local authorities would check their controls and communications were operating, collect radiac (radiation monitoring) instruments from the Home Office, and emergency feeding equipment from 'buffer' and store depots run by MAFF. They would check prepared plans, turn council and public buildings into emergency feeding centres and rest centres, and requisition stores and other premises.

Controllers would have their authority, and democracy would be suspended for the duration, as soon as the government had used Emergency Powers. The *Machinery of Government in War* circular (ES7/73) warns that nothing in current proposals for Emergency Powers 'should be construed as pre-empting the discretion of Parliament at the time to decide the content of emergency legislation.' But it does, of course, as there will be little opportunity for fine points of debate during a deteriorating pre-nuclear war crisis.

Appointees to regional or sub-regional government posts are generally senior civil servants, at least of the rank of principal. The names of many of the office holders can be deduced or guessed from the annual *Civil Service List*. For example, the Regional Director of Works in war is the peacetime Regional Director of the Property Services Agency. The 'Regional Principal Officer' is probably the peacetime Regional Director of Environment and Transport. These officials, who also chair Regional Economic Planning Boards, are responsible for the Regional Emergency Committees which deal with anti-strike action on behalf of the Civil Contingencies Unit. Most subordinate officials of these regional DOE offices would also have wartime government posts; for example, the Chairman of Traffic Commissioners would become the wartime Regional Inland Transport Administrator ('RITA').

Wartime local authority appointments follow a similar pattern, although each chief executive can make his or her own plan. Some transitions are particularly common; library service directors, for example, are usually appointed to be Chief Information Officers, while Directors of Parks and Recreation, with a staff accustomed to the wielding of spades, are usually given the task of burial of the dead or disposal of human remains by other means. Local authorities are advised to divide their staff into three groups. There is, firstly, a group of controlling staff, responsible for welfare (rest centres), food distribution and emergency feeding (normally the responsibility of education directors), works, and other essential services; secondly a 'support services' group, running, *inter alia*, the communications and administering the HQ; thirdly, a 'liason group' of representatives from other organisations. At county level these would include representatives of British Telecom, MAFF, water authorities, health authorities, police and military liason staff (both with their own communications systems), regional transport and works, an oil industry Petroleum Officer and, in appropriate areas, a representative of the NCB. There might also be representatives of the voluntary aid societies, such as the St John Ambulance Brigade.

The *Machinery of Government in War* circular (ES7/73) explains that some local authority peacetime functions would, unsurprisingly, be redundant in war: 'For example, schools, libraries and parks would not be operating as in more normal times.' Schools would be closed for the duration; the still current policy is contained in *Education Service in War* (Min. Ed. circular 3/64), which sets out the circumstances and policy:

Each side would have the capacity to inflict upon the other a degree of devastation which has never before in human history

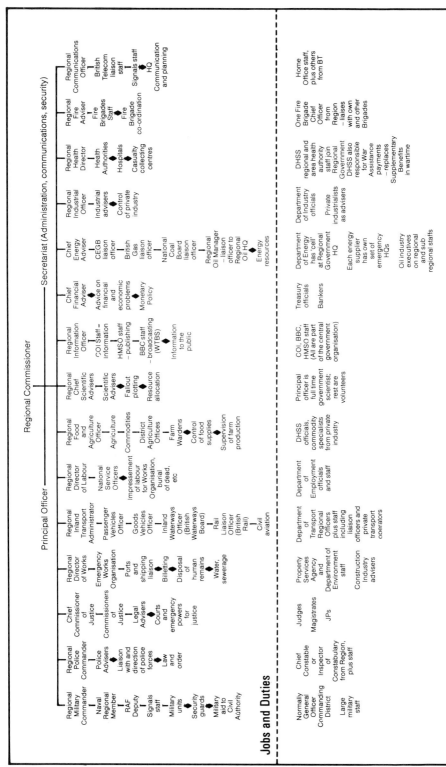

Regional Commissioner

Principal Officer ———— Secretariat (Administration, communications, security)

Officer	Jobs and Duties	Official/private sector appointees
Regional Military Commander	Naval Regional Member; RAF Deputy; Signals staff; Military units; Security guards; Military aid to Civil Authority	Normally General Officer Commanding District; Large military staff
Regional Police Commander	Police Advisers; Liaison with and direction of police forces; Law and order	Chief Constable or Inspector of Constabulary from Region, plus staff
Chief Commissioner of Justice	Commissioners of Justice; Legal Advisers; Courts and emergency powers for justice	Judges; Magistrates; JPs
Regional Director of Works	Emergency Works Organisation; Ports and shipping liaison; Billeting; Disposal of human remains; Water, sewerage	Property Services Agency and Department of Environment staff; Construction Industry advisers
Regional Inland Transport Administrator	Passenger Vehicles Officer; Goods Vehicles Officer; Inland Waterways Officer (British Waterways Board); Rail Liaison Officer (British Rail); Civil aviation	Department of Transport Regional Officers plus staff including liaison officers and private transport operators
Regional Director of Labour	National Service Officers; Impressement of labour for Works Organisation, burial of dead, etc	Department of Employment officials and staff
Regional Food and Agriculture Officer	Agriculture; Commodities; District Agriculture Offices; Farm Wardens; Control of food supplies; Supervision of farm production	DHSS officials, commodity specialists from private industry
Regional Chief Scientific Advisers	Scientific Advisers; Fallout plotting; Resource allocation	Principal officer is full time government scientist; rest are volunteers
Regional Information Officer	COI Staff – Information; HMSO staff – publishing; BBC staff – broadcasting (WTBS); Information to the public	COI, BBC, HMSO staff (All are part of the central government organisation)
Chief Financial Adviser	Advice on financial and economic problems; Monetary Policy	Treasury officials; Bankers
Chief Energy Adviser	CEGB liaison officer; British Gas liaison officer; National Coal Board liaison officer; Regional Oil Manager – liaison officer to Regional Oil HQ; Energy resources	Department of Energy has 'cell' at Regional Government HQ; Each energy supplier has own set of emergency HQs; Oil industry executives on regional and sub regional staffs
Regional Industrial Officer	Industrial advisers; Control of private industry	Department of Industry officials; Private industrialists as advisers
Regional Health Director	Health Authorities; Hospitals; Casualty collecting centres	DHSS regional and area health authority staff join Regional Government; DHSS also responsible for War Assistance payments – replaces Supplementary Benefits in wartime
Regional Fire Adviser	Fire Brigades Staff; Fire Brigade co-ordination	One Fire Brigade Chief Officer from Region – liaises with own and other Brigades
Regional Communications Officer	British Telecom liaison staff; Signals staff; HQ Communication and planning	Home Office staff, plus others from BT

Official/private sector appointees Principal officer and Secretariat includes Home Office, Treasury (Civil Service Department), and Department of Environment staff.

been either possible or imaginable. An armed clash involving the interests of either side is, therefore, likely to lead to the virtual destruction of both and not merely to conquest or defeat.

A few extra days of holiday for the children, would, clearly, be both justified and sensible in exceptional circumstances, as the Ministry of Education wisely foresaw:

> In the light of these considerations the Government have come to the conclusion that education could not be continued in the sort of conditions expected to follow a nuclear attack.

There is, obviously, some official doubt about how easily peacetime office-holders will adapt to the catastrophe of war. There is even some doubt as to whether many of them would, in the event, turn up. Nowhere in official plans is there provision made for families or dependents, and most council Emergency Planning Officers foresee considerable difficulties in assembling their staff on the day. Most EPOs have arranged for their bunker staffs' families to either move to special accomodation near to the site of the control; or for a service of special supervision of their needs and welfare to be carried out after attack. Both policies are fraught with danger if they are not kept secret from the general public; the first is in effect an official evacuation measure, and contrary to the 'stay-put' advice with which most of the public would be bombarded. Special attention paid to the welfare of council officers' dependents might, post-attack, come to the notice of neighbours, provoking a 'law and order' problem.

Nevertheless, one or other appears officially necessary. In 1980, the Home Office also decided to evacuate dependents of their SRHQ and Regional Government officials to accomodation with improvised protection in the vicinity of the controls concerned. Hotels near to the SRHQ site would perhaps be used for the officials' families. The fact that such a requirement did not, apparently, occur to the Home Office until 1980 is a further measure of the ill-preparedness of home

---

Figure 8   War roles, local government. Home Office circulars to local authorities suggest that most senior officers should be trained for a wartime role, preferably allocated according to a specific pattern. Library Directors specialise in public information; Parks and Recreation Directors in waste disposal and mass graves. This Figure shows a typical form of organisation. Each County Controller would normally have about 80–90 staff.

defence. Indeed, at that time, the majority of civil servants who were designated for bunker places (by office and not by name) were unaware of this, and had apparently undertaken no courses. Simple training for senior SRHQ officials was arranged during 1981.

The structure of wartime government in the London region is different from everywhere else, as it covers the territory of just one super-county, the GLC. It was agreed by the Home Office, GLC and borough officials in 1972 that London should continue to be divided into five groups – three in the north and two in the south – in the fashion of slices of apple pie. The GLC was to provide 'Group Wartime HQs', which would be interposed between the Borough HQS and SRHQ51, at Kelvedon Hatch, east of London. This plan really resulted from earlier schemes to divide up London into slices administered by adjacent Sub-Regional Controls, since the centre of London (and consequently communications across the region) would cease to exist in almost any attack. Premises (away from the city's centre) were found for four Group HQs, but plans for a fifth were scrapped by the 1980 Labour-led GLC, in the course of a wide-ranging review of civil defence policy. The reluctance of the GLC, or indeed any metropolitan authority, to accept the credibility of government civil defence plans is severely tested by such features which demonstrate that urban populations are 'written off'. Further problems would arise, particularly in London, when city dwellers observed the dispersal of police, fire and medical teams, the removal of food and other stockpiles, and the evacuation of officials and their families to SRHQS and places of relative safety in other regions. It might be particularly hard for local officials to explain such moves in the context of claims made in 'Protect and Survive' video film 5, *Stay-at-home*:

No place in the UK is safer than anywhere else. No one can tell you where the safest place will be. In fact, you will be far better off at home. . . .

Most council chief executives have now attended a Chief Officer's home defence course at Easingwold. A major feature of this course is a 'game', called *Hot Seat*, in which the participants spend two days playing the role of post-attack Controllers of 'Naptonshire', whose capital of Napton is struck by a two megaton bomb at the start of the exercise. (The scenario plans and detail are in fact based on Nottingham and Nottinghamshire.)

The game is supposed to teach prospective Controllers the difficulties of resource allocation – that is its fundamental purpose. However the parameters of the game (it was devised by the Royal Military College of Science Operations Research Group in 1977) are such that there is not an underlying shortage. There is only one bomb; it kills 340,000 but 640,000 survive, and the county has diversified industry and agriculture, as well as coal; it pulls through. The attack takes place in the spring, so that (if the players get it right) the harvest comes in at the time when food resources are becoming scanty. Malcolm Dando, an operations research specialist, prepared a report on *Hot Seat* whilst contemplating accepting a Home Office contract to help redesign its successor, a new game called '*Regenerate*'.* (He refused, although he had previously worked on the use of games and games theory in home defence.)

Dr Dando observed that the game was more oriented towards inducing acceptance of government deterrence and civil defence policies than training executives to take decisions that would be considerably more fraught in reality. The same view was reached by a journalist** watching the game:

The game is arranged, if played right, so that there is just enough to go round all the living – though the participants aren't told this. So they do not have to make some of the more unpleasant decisions that might be required of them – such as who gets the food. . . .

Occasionally the game players get it wrong, as they did during another journalist's visit; after a month had elapsed in the game play:

Rations sank to 1200 calories a day, subsistence level, then sank further, with the harvest still months away. At the final discussion session, an army officer said 'Did you realise that from then on, everyone was starving?'†

The results of the game, players are told, show the success of government policy, proving: (i) the need for planning now (ii) the need for exercises to test plans (iii) the need for the post of Emergency Planning Officer at county level to help

---

* M. R. Dando, *Hot Seat, a critique of the use of a training game*, Bradford University School of Peace Studies, 1981.
** Polly Toynbee, *Guardian*, 5 January 1981.
† Paul Ferris, *Observer*, 12 July 1981.

coordinate overall plans. The Vice-Principal of the College, a retired army major, told the players, finally, that:

Home Defence is part of a credible deterrence policy . . . and that the credibility of Home Defence was confirmed by their success in the game.

There is also a much more gentle game, *Emblem*, for elected councillors who go to Easingwold for shorter three-day courses on Home Defence policy. It is an ' "action game" designed to enable council members to identify and debate in a simulated setting some problems associated with war and peacetime emergencies'. Since elected councillors have no role in decision-taking in war these courses can only be described as, at best, 'educational'. More bluntly, they provide propaganda for government policy.

The 1972 re-organisation of civil defence included provision for more general emergency planning. Local authorities had been asked in 1969 (by the then Ministry of Housing and Local Government) to make plans for floods and other peacetime disasters, and such planning was included as part of the responsibility that council Emergency Planning Officers were asked to undertake in 1972. However, such planning has, in comparison to war planning, scarcely been a priority at the Home Office. Of more than sixty guidance and information circulars issued by F6 division since 1972, only six have not been connected with war. One of these concerned London flooding (ES6/72), two concerned arrangements for accidents involving radioactivity (ES7/72 and 3/77), one involves satellite accidents (ES5/79) and one concerned police use of the tele-

---

Figure 9   War roles, regional government. The staff are almost all from the upper ranks of the civil service, a few selected industrial managers and 'advisers' are included. The Figure shows the structure of the staff, perhaps 5–600, which would form the government of each of the twelve Home Defence Regions. The structure at Sub-Region level is similar, but the staff is lower ranking and smaller – standard size is 180.

Only the Regional Commissioner is an elected minister, the rest are civil servants.

The Figure draws on many government circulars and not every designation may be accurate; besides Regional and Sub-Regional HQs, there are many public (or even private) organisations with emergency HQs.

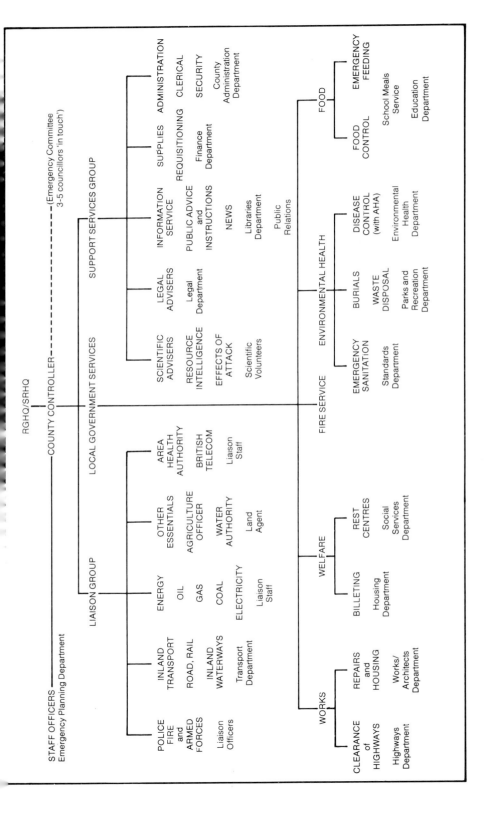

STAFF OFFICERS
Emergency Planning Department

RGHQ/SRHQ

COUNTY CONTROLLER - - - - - - (Emergency Committee 3-5 councillors 'in touch')

LIAISON GROUP

LOCAL GOVERNMENT SERVICES

SUPPORT SERVICES GROUP

POLICE FIRE and ARMED FORCES
Liaison Officers

INLAND TRANSPORT
ROAD, RAIL
INLAND WATERWAYS
Transport Department

ENERGY
OIL
GAS
COAL
ELECTRICITY
Liaison Staff

OTHER ESSENTIALS
AGRICULTURE OFFICER
WATER AUTHORITY
Land Agent

AREA HEALTH AUTHORITY
BRITISH TELECOM
Liaison Staff

SCIENTIFIC ADVISERS
RESOURCE INTELLIGENCE
EFFECTS OF ATTACK
Scientific Volunteers

LEGAL ADVISERS
Legal Department

INFORMATION SERVICE
PUBLIC ADVICE and INSTRUCTIONS
NEWS
Libraries Department
Public Relations

SUPPLIES
REQUISITIONING
Finance Department

ADMINISTRATION
CLERICAL
SECURITY
County Administration Department

FIRE SERVICE

ENVIRONMENTAL HEALTH

WORKS

CLEARANCE of HIGHWAYS
Highways Department

REPAIRS and HOUSING
Works/Architects Department

WELFARE

BILLETING
Housing Department

REST CENTRES
Social Services Department

EMERGENCY SANITATION
Standards Department

BURIALS
WASTE DISPOSAL
Parks and Recreation Department

DISEASE CONTROL (with AHA)
Environmental Health Department

FOOD

FOOD CONTROL

EMERGENCY FEEDING
School Meals Service
Education Department

phone preference scheme in peacetime (ES6/75). A full list of Home Office circulars since 1972 is contained in Appendix 1. The main circular on peacetime accidents was issued in 1975, three years after Home Defence planning had begun anew: *Major Accidents and Natural Disasters* (ES7/75). This circular reviewed a spectrum of possible disasters from floods, gales and hurricanes to air crashes and chemical industry accidents. It *excluded* plans for nuclear reactor accidents or other accidents involving nuclear sites: these are the responsibility of the CEGB (or the SSEB or NSHEB in Scotland), the UK Atomic Energy Authority, or the Ministry of Defence. But their exclusion removes the onus from authorities like the CEGB to supply local authorities with internal accident or safety studies.

The circular also excluded industrial disputes, because of their political character, although countering national strikes affecting services or supplies is a responsibility of the Home Office F6 Division; its head (in 1982, F. A. Howard) attends meetings of the Cabinet Civil Contingenices Unit. During major strikes, for example the 1977 firemen's strike, the Home Office arranged for cooperative Chief Executives and their Emergency Planning staffs to provide information about local activities and incidents. Some of the information the Chief Executives were asked to gather appeared intended for propaganda purposes; there was a particularly unhealthy interest expressed in early news of any fire casualties. Regional officers of the Central Office of Information, who are responsible for providing government information to the provincial press, would then rapidly disseminate any information disadvantageous to the striking firemen. There is little doubt that planning for peacetime disasters comes a poor third in Home Office priorities, after war planning and the maintainance of supplies and services during industrial action.

Throughout the 1970s, government spending on real civil defence measures was a tiny portion of public expenditure. Out of an average £15–20m budget during these years, only £2–3 million went to local authorities for their plans to provide welfare services – and all of that was spent on plans, bunkers and communications. Much of the Home Office money pays for the Royal Observer Corps and the UK Warning and Monitoring Organisation, and most of the rest pays for the central planning staff, the Home Defence College, the stockpile kept in Supply and Transport Stores, and the maintenance and development of the bunker network. A new provision of £14.5 million was made in 1979 to buy new, extra stocks for the MAFF food stockpile.

The Home Office has always faced as much criticism from the (pro) civil defence lobby about the insufficiency of its plans as it has from other quarters about their futility. Nationwide shelter building is frequently suggested as a useful occupation for the recipients of unemployment benefit, or those working in job creation schemes. (The proponents of such proposals appear to have a general aversion to productive industrial investment of such time or resources.) Early in 1980, the 'Civil Aid' organisation (which was formed by former CD Corps members who wanted to carry on in 1968) accused the Home Office of aiming at 'the complete abolition of the volunteer bodies as well as the destruction of practically all equipment held.' They pointed out that large quantities of surplus radiac instruments and dosimeters had been disposed of by the Home Office at auction rather than by allowing their use by volunteer emergency organisations. Civil Aid also claimed that the Home Office had intended to sell off the 'Green Goddess' fire engines shortly before they were found useful in the 1977 fire strike.

The same year saw several other *ad hoc* civil defence organisations assail the Home Office. The 'Campaign for Civil Defence', led by Mr J. A. Hibbert, an ex Parachute Regiment Major, EPO for Devon, and leader of the 'Devon Emergency Volunteers' suggested to Mr Whitelaw, shortly before the Home Defence Review was announced, that *Protect and Survive* was 'ineffective and misleading'. It sought, the 'Campaign' said:

to persuade people that safety lay in huddling under a ramshackle collection of table tops and sandbags.

A Conservative Political Centre pamphlet in 1978, *Britain's Home Defence Muddle* proposed a new national civil defence organisation; whilst the same party's Bow Group produced a 1980 paper asking, as many other organisations had, for compulsory construction of shelters in new buildings, and government grants for domestic 'Anderson-type' shelters. Greater London Young Conservatives recommended a new civil defence corps in a report, *A Place Called Armageddon*, in January 1980. They also called for extra stocks of freeze-dried food and communal sub-surface 'hardened' shelters. Even relatively conformist organisations like the County Emergency Planning Officers Society were moved to comment a little later (through their Chairman):

> One sometimes get the opinion that the government's home
> defence policy is to protect the government and not the
> people.   (*Times*, 2 April 1980)

Gradually, that part of the campaign for extended civil defence based on the political right has come to stress the need for the government to use greater coercion to get local authorities to obey their policies.

In what some saw as remarkably bad taste, a new national magazine, *Protect and Survive Monthly*, was launched in January 1981, intended to capitalise on advertisements for nuclear shelters and growing public concern. It was, eventually, increasingly taken over by a right wing lobby organisation, the 'National Council for Civil Defence' for its propaganda, much of it aimed at CND and the Labour councils. *Protect and Survive Monthly* eventually went bankrupt in June 1981 after the private nuclear shelter market turned out to be less profitable than had previously been supposed.

From the left, the Labour Party denounced the new emphasis on civil defence as, according to Robin Cook MP, 'an attempt to foment a war psychosis . . . making the population more willing to contemplate war.' A party policy statement and 'advice note' in June 1981* denounced the government proposals as a 'fraudulent waste of scarce resources', and gave the party's new policy:

> For a densely populated country like Britain, there can be no
> effective civil defence against nuclear attack. The only effective
> civil defence is to ensure that Britain is not involved in a nuclear
> war, and to oppose all nuclear weapons and nuclear war
> preparations by Britain or any other country.

The note also recommended the creation of further Nuclear Free Zones, and urged local authorities 'to reject attempts to use so called civil defence to condition people to accept that a nuclear war is somehow "survivable".' Much of the British left takes the view that civil defence would be appropriate and possibly worthwhile if Britain were not nuclear armed, did not provide bases for United States forces, and – prefer-

---

* The author is a member of the Defence Study Group of the National
Executive Committee of the Labour Party, which prepared the 1981
policy advice.

ably – disengaged from NATO, as part of a process of European disarmament.

The utter inadequacy of the government's paper plans to help the population to survive is recognised in every quarter except government itself. The 1980 review provided little of value for the critics who wanted more. All they got was a new Minister of State in the House of Commons (originally Leon Brittain; in 1982, Patrick Mayhew) instead of a peer. A Conservative backbench committee was to be allowed to investigate, but got nowhere. Local authorities got £3m more for their planning, but overall, the increase in expenditure (£4 million added on to a planned £22 million) was so derisory that Home Office announcements did not mention this – stressing instead that they hoped to climb to £45 million a year in three years' time. In fact, the 1980-81 expenditure level was, even after the review, still *less* in real terms than was spent during the Labour administration, from 1974 to 1977!*

Two new Coordinators of Voluntary Effort in Civil Defence appointed in 1980 (Sir Leslie Mavor in England and Wales and Mr R. G. Armstrong in Scotland) turned out to be occupied primarily as touring recruiters rather than as office-bound coordinators; they thus provided high visibility for civil defence without actually providing any. Where money could not be found to help such organisations as 'Civil Aid' the 'Devon Emergency Volunteers', or the 'Wiltshire Community Advisers', they were at least lavishly praised instead.

The first fruits from the Shelter Working Party appeared in public late in 1980. The Department of the Environment circulated proposals to drop Building Regulation restrictions which might prevent people building certain kinds of nuclear shelter. The regulations were dropped provided the shelter was constructed 'solely as a wartime emergency shelter', was not under publicly accessible land, and was detached from existing buildings.

Two months later, the DOE's Ancient Monuments Secretariat, which had been approached by authorities wanting to turn medieval castles into nuclear shelters, circulated a memorandum advising against this:

There appears to be a mistaken belief that all castles are of sound construction and with deep cellars or dungeons which make them

* At 1978 prices, civil defence expenditure in 1973/4 was £21m; 1974/75 – £25m; 1975/76 – £25m (Source: *The Government's Expenditure Plans 1979–80 to 1982–83*, Cmnd. 7439, January 1979).

ideally suited for such use. This is a fallacy, since such structures may not necessarily withstand blast conditions. . . . Moreover, modifications (such as) stockpiling food supplies . . . would almost invariably cause unacceptable damage to the monument.

The Department therefore advised shelterers to stay away:

In line with government policy not to provide public anti-nuclear shelters, such enquiries and applications should be diplomatically declined on grounds of general unsuitability. . . .

In January 1981 a pamphlet, *Advice on Domestic Shelters* was released. The accompanying *Technical Guidance* was certainly one of the more detailed assessments of nuclear weapons effects released by the British government. But it was not without mistakes and deliberate omissions. It did not say how much radiation would be lethal, which made assessing the efficacy of some shelters' protection in different fallout zones quite impossible. It also provided, on two separate pages, two different tables describing the blast effects of airburst H bombs. One table gave the data based on widely accepted US government 'standard' accounts; the other table, inadvertently, gives different – and inaccurate data – for the same situation based on Home Office advice to the public.

The US figures are one third greater than the Home Office's own figures, which is embarrasing for them. Further, the Home Office's 'scientific' assessments of the casualties and effects of a nuclear attack on the UK, widely circulated in ministerial and other announcements, and Home Office circulars, are based on their own erroneous figures. (This is discussed in more detail in Chapter 11).

The non-technical pamphlet – *Advice on Domestic Shelters: providing protection against nuclear explosions* – contains a number of errors. In summarising the detail in the *Technical Guidance* it includes a number of serious and misleading inaccuracies, as well as absurd mathematical mistakes not normally tolerated in those expecting to pass an O Level arithmetic examination. The writers (the Cotterill Working Party on nuclear shelters) fail, for example, to distinguish between *distance* and *area*.

Both publications explain the difference between the effects of a *groundburst* and an *airburst* nuclear weapon. The blast and thermal and other radiation from an airburst will, naturally, go further. *Technical Guidance* explains that:

Distances would be increased by about thirty per cent for airbursts (p. 9).

Advice on Domestic Shelters says, on the same point:

The *areas* affected will be about thirty per cent greater than a groundburst bomb of the same size (p. 5) (Author's emphasis).

Not so. The area is sixty-nine per cent greater. For the type of bomb illustrated, the difference in area covered is one hundred square miles. (256 km²) – which would make a significant difference.

Advice on Domestic Shelters also provides erroneous and dishonest information on the extent to which blast might affect the United Kingdom (not contained in *Technical Guidance*).

The pamphlet says:

Estimates suggest that around five per cent of the land area of the UK might suffer seriously from the effects of blast . . . about eighty per cent of the land area might suffer no blast effects at all. Any part of the country might suffer fallout therefore radiation protection would be needed everywhere.

This appraisal is directly contradicted by the Home Office's own *Training Manual for Scientific Advisers*, the Introduction to which is provided by the head of the Scientific Advisory Branch, Mr J. K. S. Clayton. This Introduction specifies the 'standard' two hundred megaton attack, and explains:

Heavy damage (areas) will amount to approximately five per cent of the land areas of the UK. Another fifteen per cent will suffer extensive but by no means total damage by blast and fire; another forty per cent will suffer superficial damage. In other words, four-fifths of the land area will suffer no more than minor physical damage. Of course many undamaged areas would be affected by fallout but this inconvenience would diminish with the passage of time.

The gradual process of constructively altering meaning in rewriting, as exemplified here, is known in the civil service as 'massage'; the less sophisticated call it lying. Both the statements above are based on the same analyses. 'No blast effects at all' is not the same thing as 'no more than minor physical damage'.

The comments made in the *Advice* pamphlet were criticised in an article in the *New Scientist* by Philip Steadman, which appears to have provoked the Home Office to new heights of fabrication and absurdity. Steadman pointed out that the figure of eighty per cent could only be derived by ignoring the outer areas of 'minor' damage; and that sixty per cent of the land area was in fact affected by blast, the same figure as given by Clayton, although reached independently.* The criticism was taken up and put to the Home Office by the EPO for Cambridgeshire County Council, amongst others. He received a reply from Mr K. A. Day, of the F6 Division and the Cotterill Working Party, saying that Steadman had visited the Home Office and had withdrawn his criticism. This was wholly untrue. The letter from Mr Day also commented:

Mr Steadman makes much of the possibility that a large number of people reside in the areas directly attacked. But that is not really relevant. The point being made is that in many parts of the country a shelter designed against radiation rather than blast effects may provide in the event all the protection needed.**

The general observer would be forgiven for supposing that since shelters are to be provided to shield *people* from weapons effects it is material as to whether the people who would use them live in the 'areas directly attacked'. Shelters will not be built in some abstract random smear across the countryside.

The terms of reference for the shelter Working Party excluded discussion of introducing a planning requirement for shelters to be provided in new buildings (as is, for example, required in Switzerland), or possible communal shelter designs. Since these are the most cost effective ways of providing shelters (and the most commonly advocated suggestions by protagonists of more civil defence) they would have been worth examining, if shelter policy was being seriously re-evaluated.

It is, consequently, difficult to take the published work of Cotterill's group at all seriously. They were tasked to ignore the most viable shelter options, constructed advice on the basis of quite contradictory data, massaged up a selection of statements to support the 'stay-put' policy, proved incapable of avoiding fundamental mathematical error, and ended up offering the public a selection of shelters half of which were invented in the blitz, and whose dimensions have been reproduced, unaltered, forty years later. (The only change to the 'Morrison' was to put its dimensions in metric units.) On the

* *New Scientist*, 18 June 1981.
** Letter to Mr Graeme Bushell, Cambridgeshire EPO, from K. A. Day, 30 July 1981.

other hand, this kind of home defence 'science' is a worthy continuation of traditional government shelter policy over the past fifty years.

The government's ultimate advice to the public was published in November 1981. Half a million copies of a four-page pamphlet, *Civil Defence – Why We Need It*, were distributed to libraries and local authorities to promote acceptance of civil defence. The pamphlet, in question and answer form, mixed silly homilies with minor deceptions, and emphasised a new theme: the protection that civil defence measures give against conventional attack – 'protection against *any* sort of attack'. This new tack in official propaganda is, once again, absurd. 'Protect and Survive' type or other improvised shelters are intended only to protect against fallout; they do not provide protection against blast (which is what comes from most 'conventional' bombs), incendiaries and fires, nerve gases or biological weapons, or even the gases feared in World War II.

Why We Need It soon attracted the customary and well-deserved criticism, which several groups, both for and against civil defence, produced in the form of mocking lookalike *pastiches*. In Parliament, lapdog Conservative MPs lauded the pamphlet with a motion commending the fact that it:

draws attention to the provisions of civil defence made by
Switzerland and Sweden, notwithstanding that these countries
follow a policy of neutrality.

The proposers of this motion failed to note that the Home Office had in fact completely *refused* to enact any civil defence provisions on the Swedish or Swiss pattern – or that neutrality significantly lessens the risk of direct nuclear attack.

At other times, Home Office officials have suggested new home defence measures more in keeping with the British administrative tradition. The head of F6, J. A. Howard, suggested to a conference of Emergency Planning Officers that the authorities might be 'armed with more flexible Emergency Powers,' so as to 'avoid the "trauma" of public debate'*. Sir Leslie Mavor told the same group in 1976 that 'the full possibility of the present internal threat is only just sinking in.'

In the 1980s, it would be entirely in keeping with the historical development of Home Defence policy for the government now to identify the chief planning 'threat' as too much

---

* *Guardian* 4 July 1980.

freedom of speech, thought, or action in a war crisis. Such a review might go further and identify the root cause of the problem as parliamentary democracy, and look to an early adoption of Emergency Powers and suspension of Parliament in any crisis.

At the same time, planners have not lost sight of their fundamental values. In the most remarkable circular of all to local authorities, *Briefing Material for Wartime Controllers* (ES3/76), the Home Office offered its views on a post nuclear economy:

Collapse of the monetary economy
14. A large scale nuclear attack on this country would completely disrupt the banking system on which the whole monetary economy is based. Even a small scale attack on London and the location of the major facilities of the big clearing banks would have a similar effect. . . . Money in its present form would cease to have any significance.

The circular proposes that barter and, for the government, release of food or clothing, would quite rapidly replace the use of money 'as a means of purchasing goods or rewarding services'. It then stress that:

15. It would be an essential part of the policy for national recovery to re-establish a new monetary system as soon as possible. This might take a year or more, depending on the scale of the attack, and it could not be assumed that the old currency would be redeemed, *except possibly at a considerable devaluation of its earlier purchasing power* (Author's emphasis).

The circular also explains that Regional Commissioners would have assistance from 'financial advisers drawn from the Treasury and the private sector'. This statement confirms evidence produced by the *Spies for Peace* that, in 1963, it had been intended to include representatives of the 'big five' banks amongst the staff of Regional Seats of Government.

The official plans for the determined relaunch of industrial capitalism into a brave, new, post-nuclear world contrasts strangely with the inadequacy of official thinking on shelters. Other aspects of civil defence policy are considered in the following chapters, starting first with the central and essential theme – law and order, maintained by the police, with martial aid.

6
Martial order

Few aspects of government plans for Home Defence have more chance of being effective than those concerned, broadly, with 'law and order'. The army and police are in general better prepared, trained and exercised to carry out their war duties, with far better and more flexible communications systems, than the civilian agencies of sub-regional government; and they hold a near monopoly of coercive power, and will continue to do so until or unless social disintegration in Britain is complete.

A feature of the regional government structure, described in Chapter 5, is that police and military units are commanded at the *regional* level whilst post-attack civil government (from the SRHQS) is organised at the lower, sub-regional level. The parallel regional power structures of police, military and civil agencies has been directly modelled on the British colonial experience; in general a 'triumvirate' is created to deal with the emergency situation. Official statements stress that the civil power should remain paramount above police and army. That may not necessarily happen.

In the early period after a nuclear attack, there is what even the Home Office concedes to be a 'problem'. Regional Commissioners, dispersed with their staff at their evacuation locations, are not in charge until the planned regional governments are formed. Sub-Regional Commissioners, embunkered in the SRHQS, cannot direct their military and police staff. At sub-regional level, they may only ask liason staff. The former principal of Easingwold, Air Marshall Sir Leslie Mavor, has acknowledged that this could be a 'nasty situation . . . there could be a long time while communications are assembled in which the Regional Military Commander might start disposing of his forces in the light of a purely military appreciation.' 'A local military takeover' was possible but 'surely no more than a passing local aberration.' On another occasion Mavor suggested that 'we just have to ask the Generals to be good boys.'

The Regional Police Commanders and Regional Military Commanders already hold their designate appointments, just as do their civilian counterparts, the local authority chief executives who will become Controllers. Tables 4 and 5 list the peacetime posts (they are normally appointed *ex officio*) of these Commanders, and the present incumbents. There are ten Regional Commanders for each service, plus one each for Scotland and Northern Ireland.

The organisation and role of police and military units in war are generally similar, with each service undertaking guard duties of various kinds, and primarily enforcing Commissioners' and Controllers' orders. A few tasks are not shared: providing firing squads to execute the sentences of wartime 'special courts' will be the job of the military alone, for example.

Most of the armed forces will, during a pre-war crisis, have gone abroad. One front-line army unit, the 8th Field Force (recently reorganised as the 5th Infantry Brigade), is however earmarked for service in Britain, together with a few units of the Territorial Army (signals regiments being a particular example). Until their disbandment in 1969, the 'Home Guard' section of the Territorial Army and Volunteer Reserve (TAVR 3) had home defence responsibilities, and were particularly allocated to the work of guarding 'key points'. In March 1982, Defence Secretary John Nott announced that such a force was to be reformed, known as the Home Service Force. Some 4,500 recruits were to be sought, and in addition the size of the existing Territorial Army was to be expanded by over twenty per cent, from 70,000 to 86,000.

Most military units which eventually come under Regional Military Command will be those, such as training or support units, which do not have a direct war role. They will include not just the army, but any naval or RAF training or admini-

---

Table 4 Regional Military Commanders would control all general military units in their Regions, whether army, navy or RAF. Special Composite General Reserve (CGR) companies would be formed out of pre-attack volunteers, reservists not required for NATO and other available units. Protected headquarters were built for most army commands during the 1950s, and these, or more recently adapted premises, serve as the Armed Forces HQs (AFHQS) Bold type denotes a confirmed AFHQ location.

Home Defence Region	Regional Military Commander (designate) Peacetime location	Wartime location (Armed Forces HQ)
1	Brigadier Spreckling OC Royal Signals Training HQ, Catterick	**Ouston, Northumberland**
2	Major General I. H. Baker Imphal Barracks, York	**Imphal Barracks, York**
3	Air Vice Marshall A.C.F. Peirse RAF College, Cranwell	May be (Chalfont Drive), Nottingham
4	Major General R. E. J. Gerrard-Wright Flagstaff House, Flagstaff Road, Colchester	May be (Brooklands Avenue), Cambridge
5	Major General H. D. A. Langley Horseguards, London SW1	**Wilton Park, Beaconsfield, Bucks**
6	Lieutenant General P. A. Travers HQ South East District Steels Road, Aldershot	No AFHQ; several sub-District HQS; may include: Warren Row; Guildford; Dover Castle; Wilton Park, Beaconsfield
7	Major General Sir John Acland Bulford Camp, Salisbury	Unknown
8 Wales	Major General L. A. H. Napier The Barracks, Brecon	**The Barracks, Brecon**
9	Major General J. A. Ward-Booth HQ West Midland District, Shrewsbury	Unknown
10	Major General W. M. E. Hicks Fulford Barracks, Preston	**Fulford Barracks, Preston**
Northern Ireland	Lieutenant General Sir Richard Lawson Magheralave Road, Lisburn, Co Antrim	Probably NI Central HQ, Armagh
Scotland	Lieutenant General Sir David T. Young Craigiehall, Edinburgh	Craigiehall, Barnton Quarry, Edinburgh

Scottish Zone Military Commanders:

Northern Zone OC Highlands, Perth

Western Zone OC Lowlands, Edinburgh

Eastern Zone IOC Highland Division, Edinburgh

Table 5   Regional Police Commanders would have overall command of a group of police forces after attack. Although the Home Office says a list of prospective appointees is 'not available' it is, in fact, published, in the *Police Alamanac.*

Home Defence Region	Regional Police Commander	Force and War Duties HQ
1	Chief Constable S. E. Bailey	Northumbria Police, Ponteland, Newcastle upon Tyne
2	Chief Constable R. Gregory	West Yorkshire Police, Wakefield
3	Chief Constable C. McLachlan	Nottinghamshire Constabulary, Sherwood Lodge, Arnold, Nottingham
4	Chief Constable S. L. Whiteley	Suffolk Constabulary, Martlesham, Ipswich
5	Commissioner Sir Kenneth Newman	New Scotland Yard, London; (War Duties (D11) Branch ‚– 337 Old Street, London EC1; War HQS: Lippettshill, Essex (North); Merstham, Surrey (South)
6	Chief Constable J. Duke	Hampshire Constabulary, West Hill, Winchester
7	Chief Constable B. Weigh	Avon and Somerset Constabulary, Bristol
8	Chief Constable J. Woodcock	South Wales Constabulary, Bridgend, Glamorgan
9	Chief Constable Sir Philip Knights	West Midlands Police, Lloyd House, Colmore Circus, Birmingham
10	Chief Constable A. Laugharne	Lancashire Constabulary, Hutton, near Preston
Scotland	HM Chief Inspector of Police for Scotland Edward Stizzell	Edinburgh (at Scottish Central Control)
Northern Ireland	Chief Constable Jack Hermon	Royal Ulster Constabulary, Knock, Belfast

strative units in the Region. Army reservists called up without a specific unit to go to will also into composite General Service Units (GSUs). As police and military planners are ready to admit (in private at least), the role of their forces within the United Kingdom will be vastly different from the experience of the Second World War. Mr F. Jobson, a war planner on the staff of No 1 Regional Police Commander Designate (then the Chief Constable of Durham) told a gathering of north of England Home Defence planners in 1972:

In the 1939–45 war . . . there was nothing (the police) did not do, from moving people out of threatened shelters, to mounting guard over unexploded bombs, first aid, rescue work, shepherding the homeless, incident control. . . . The police turned their hand to every task of civil defence.
A future war would present a vastly different problem from that of 1939–45 bombing attacks. Apart from the terrible threat of nuclear weapons, a failure in common communications may result in much uncertainty and fear in the public and introduce an apathetic attitude to Home Defence during the critical mobilisation period. This would have an untoward effect on the changeover from a peacetime to a wartime economy and organisation. Some peace organisations by demonstrations and public disorder may show dissent with this objective in mind.

The military role is oriented wholly towards the NATO alliance and the security of its military facilities. The *Armed Forces in War* circular (ES11/74) and related briefings make military Home Defence priorities clear:

1. At all times, the Armed Forces have an inherent duty to support the Civil Authority in the United Kingdom.
2. Plans for defence are geared to the fact that the United Kingdom is part of the NATO alliance and in any major war will fight as such.
3. During any Warning Period prior to nuclear attack on this country, the Armed Forces have to mobilise, deploy to war stations, ensure that our nuclear strike forces are operational, and maintain the security of the United Kingdom base.

(Home Defence College Notes, 1976)

As we will see from other official documents, the highest priority military task is to keep Britain going as an 'unsinkable aircraft carrier' for NATO and the US, and as a forward nuclear strike base.

To these ends, once the pre-war warning period begins, and mobilisation is ordered, the key objective for police and military units is efficiently to accomplish the 'transition to war'. As we see in the *Hard Rock* and *Square Leg* scenarios, the Defence and Home Office planners anticipate a period of days to weeks in which war measures take effect. During this period, the police, with military support, are primarily concerned with controlling a public which will panic as supplies

Plate 19 Armed Forces HQ 8, in Brecon. This building, part of the barracks at Army HQ, Wales, was originally fortified as RSG 8 in the early 1960s. It was refurbished again in the late 70s. The roof sports VHF and UHF transmitter aerials to link with mobile columns or aircraft of the post-strike Regional Air Squadron.

become increasingly short, try to flee obvious target areas, and organise in resistance to a coming nuclear holocaust. As supplies become critically short and the pre-war crisis deepens, government control and military mobilisation will inevitably be increasingly threatened by public disorder and dissent.

These concerns of the planners are scarcely disguised, The *Police Manual of Home Defence* is the basic police guidebook issued to PCs and other ranks during War Duties courses (which all police officers have attended at least once). Class-ified 'restricted', it gives rudimentary details of the effects of nuclear weapons and home defence arrangements. It also gives a list of the 'urgent additional tasks' the police would undertake 'in the enforcement of the many wartime regula-tions imposed by the government'. Prominent amongst these tasks are setting up internment areas and sealing off cities to prevent refugee movement. The tasks are:

a. Special measures to maintain internal security, with particular reference to the detention or restriction of movement of subversive or potentially subversive people
b. The guarding of key points and the maintenance of protected areas
c. Manning carrier control, and carrier receiver points
d. Supplementing public warnings
e. The control of Essential Service Routes
f. Assisting the Armed Forces in their mobilisation plans
g. Advice to the public
h. Collection and distribution of radiac instruments and maroons
i. Freezing of petrol filling stations

Task (a) is of course an unnecessarily wordy reference to the planned arrest and internment of dissidents and 'subversives'. The guarding of key points, and the control of petrol stations are part of the government's general plan to take control of large stocks of food and other supplies at the earliest possible stage. Although even 'restricted' and police only sources such as the *Manual of Home Defence* are unspecific about the use of the word 'internment', it crops up elsewhere – for example in the *Square Leg* list of police and military tasks.

The arresting of internees would be one of the govern-ment's earliest acts once Parliament had passed the Emer-gency Powers Bill – perhaps two weeks before war. The preparation and maintenance of lists of alleged subversives to be interned is one of the key wartime tasks of the Security Service (MI5). Its plans are supervised by the Official Com-mittee on Security, and the Transition to War Committee, both chaired by Cabinet Secretary Sir Robert Armstrong. Similar internment orders were made in the 1939–45 war under Defence Regulation 18B. Although Regulation 18B was used to intern fascist sympathisers, the dragnet which was spread for 'enemy aliens' enmeshed Jewish and left-wing refu-gees alongside Nazi sympathisers in a fashion that scarcely suggested discrimination or even forethought on the part of the authorities.

Some 20,000 names are thought to be on the arrest lists maintained by MI5. The 5,000 or so strong organisation, with headquarters at Curzon Street in Mayfair, London, compiles extensive political data and other information on millions of people on its central computer facilities. It also directs the activities of each police force's Special Branch in obtaining local information from agents and surveillance. In wartime, the Security Service would coordinate intelligence about anti-war movements and other political opposition. The paper by Jobson (p. 181) explains

Normally there is close co-operation between the police and the Security Service in matters affecting the security of the state. In a time of war this collaboration becomes increasingly more vital and Chief Constables must be prepared to comply immediately with any request made by the Security Service on matters of civil security. . . .

A threat of war may be treated by subversive organisations as an occasion for provoking civil disturbance and sabotage, perhaps under the guise of anti-war propaganda. This will call for action by the police. . . . The risk of sabotage should be largely met by measures taken to protect key points, and keeping close watch on persons of doubtful loyalty employed in or living near key points.

In times of war it would be necessary to take special steps to restrain the activities of persons or organisations likely to engage in subversion. . . . The main step would be the detention of named individuals.

Jobson also quotes from draft Emergency Powers regulations, which would provide for:

The restriction by order of the movement of named individuals or restriction of their possession of certain articles or animals and of their employment in places of importance to the war effort.

In the exercise plans of the *Inside Right* to *Hard Rock* series, military activitity against subversives and saboteurs is a prominent feature. Although there is a real possibility of some armed incursions by Soviet ('Orange') forces, the main threat is dissident Britons. Soviet Special Forces or 'Strategic Diversion Forces' (similar in principle to the SAS) are expected to make some secret raids, perhaps coming ashore from trawlers or submarines. But their impact is minor.

Coordinating the roundup of internees appears to be a special wartime task allocated to the Police National Com-

Plate 20 Rollestone Army Camp near Larkhill, on Salisbury Plain, turned into a prison camp. Plans for 'internment areas', which would probably use similar facilities, are well advanced.

puter, based at Hendon in North London. In normal times, this computer maintains some forty million records on individuals and vehicles which are almost instantly available from a nationwide network of more than 750 video terminals and printers, located in every force headquarters, and also many police Divisional HQs. In war it will provide a rapid means of checking up nationally on individuals who may have evaded callup or internment. It also provides a fast and effective communications system between police forces.

The speed with which internment plans could be brought into operation was vividly demonstrated during the 1980 prison officers' strike, when the army was rapidly able to provide suitably equipped camps and trained soldiers to handle the prison overflow. Two army camps were quickly turned into prisons, at Rollestone on Salisbury Plain and Beckingham in Nottinghamshire.* It is not known what internment

* Other sites, not used in the event, included camps at Bicester, and Bordon near Petersfield.

sites have been pre-selected (and it is tempting to suppose that they may have been located in likely major target areas). However Emergency Powers legislation is expected to provide for the release on parole of almost all of the normal peacetime prison population, leaving inside, according to some Home Office estimates, only one thousand or so dangerous prisoners at a few maximum security sites.

Emergency Powers and government decrees will also give the police new tasks from an early stage in the warning period. *Square Leg*, for example saw POL (Petrol Oil and Lubricant) rationing imposed as the very first of Britain's transition-to-war measures, on August 16, more than a month before nuclear strike (19 September). During the next month, requisitioning of ships, aircraft, vehicles, and premises was introduced. Food supplies at central factories and warehouses (such as the distribution centres of supermarket chains), and at MAFF Buffer Depots were placed under central government control, and guarded. So, too, were military bases, fuel depots, power stations, major industries, government buildings and other 'key points'. These and other facilities might become prohibited zones to the public under emergency defence regulations. Violators could lawfully be shot.

The police also have statutory responsibilities for enforcing billeting arrangements made for troops or refugees, and also (under the Army and Air Force Acts of 1954) for impressment, (ie enforced military service). It would be an offence to obstruct the police or military when requisitioning goods, or enforcing billetting or impressment.

A major police task, pre-strike, would be to keep clear the 'Essential Service Routes'. The full nationwide network of Essential Service Routes is shown in the maps on pages 188 to 195. The ESR system is a coordinated network of major roads, which would be kept clear for essential traffic. According to the *Police Manual of Home Defence*,

the police would give priority to keeping these roads open for the free flow of essential traffic. In addition to help given to essential movement, the police would be concerned with the planning and co-ordinating of large scale movements.

The ESR system was most recently described in Civil Defence Circular 4/71, originally classified 'restricted' but now declassified (although the ESR maps remain classified). ESRs would be:

controlled by the police, possibly assisted by the armed services, to facilitate the free movement of essential traffic of all kinds engaged in the implementation of transition-to-war measures . . . and subsequently to meet the likely post strike requirements should the need arise.

The ESRS were amended in 1973 and again in 1976 and 1979. Details of the most recent Scottish version of the ESR system was circulated to local authorities in 1979 (ES(SCOT) 1/79).

The government has on occasion denied that it plans to use the ESR system to enforce a 'stay put' policy. Home Office Assistant Secretary J. A. Howard, who headed the F6 (Home Defence) division in 1981 for example claimed in an open meeting in Oxford that 'roads would be left open to people to move wherever they choose'. This, to be plain, is not true. (And it should be noted that he added that in any case refugees should not expect to get any food or shelter provided at the far end of their journey.)

The *Police Manual of Home Defence*, for example, states:

Priority would be given to the Essential Service Routes which, so far as is possible, should be kept clear of refugees and non-essential traffic . . . (Para 9–30, p36)

The paper on police War Duties by Jobson also notes:

An instinctive survival trek of members of the public away from likely targets to (other) areas would create problems – ie, clearing of Essential Service Routes.

He also noted that the refugee movement problem will require police manpower to ensure that NATO military units have 'trouble free journeys to stations, airfields and ports'. One more example comes from exercise *Scrum Half*, where police officials and the County Controller in Essex grappled with the refugee and ESR problem:

Conference 20.30 Hours: *Police*: Main problem has been to keep Essential Service Routes clear; road blocks set up to keep back refugees from London area . . . *Army*: Main problem at the moment (is) protection of food stocks – discussions now with Police to decide who best able to cover this. . .

Controller's Conference, 19 September 1978, during *Scrum Half*

Such nitty-gritty details of Home Defence planning in operation strongly illuminate the life-and-death decisions that would be required from the very start. Refugees from London would not get out unless other counties were willing to accept

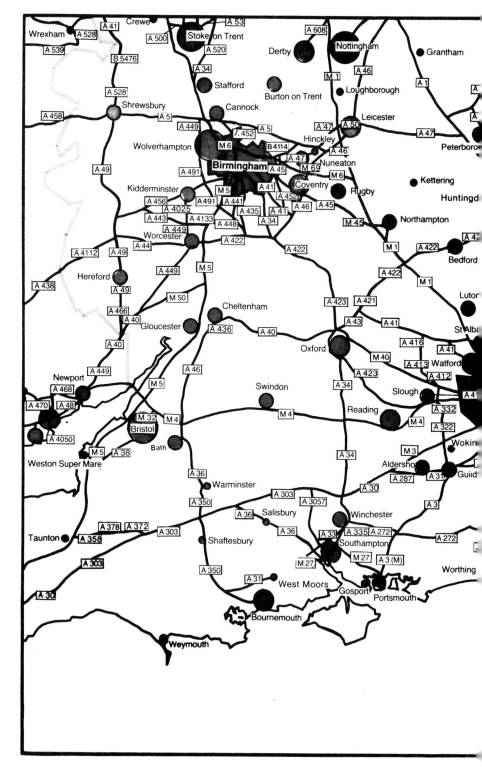

Figure 10 Essential Service Routes, South East

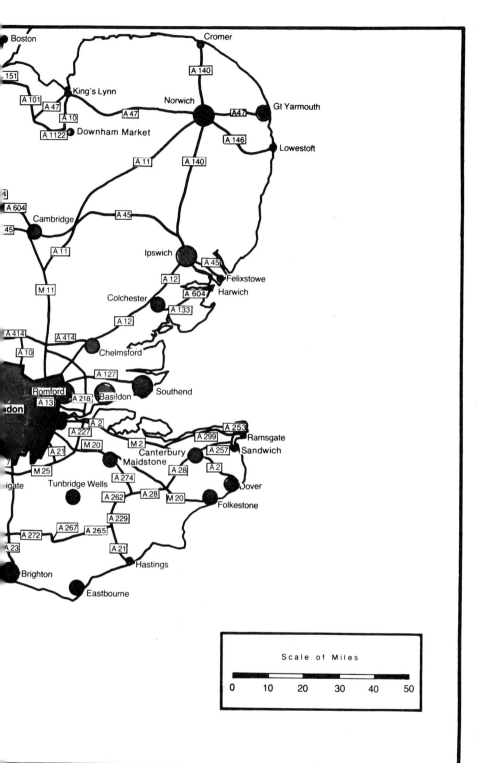

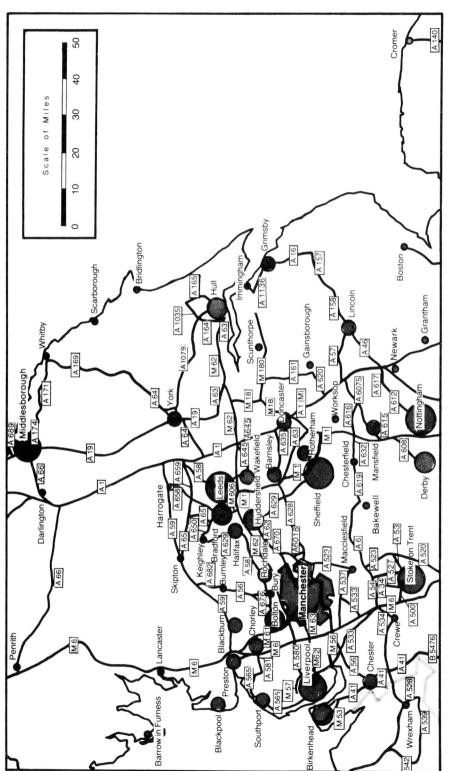

Figure 10 Essential Service Routes, Northern England

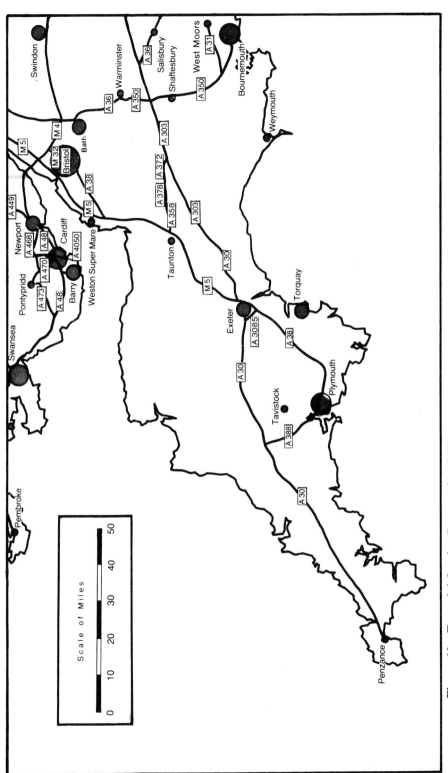

Figure 10 Essential Service Routes, South West

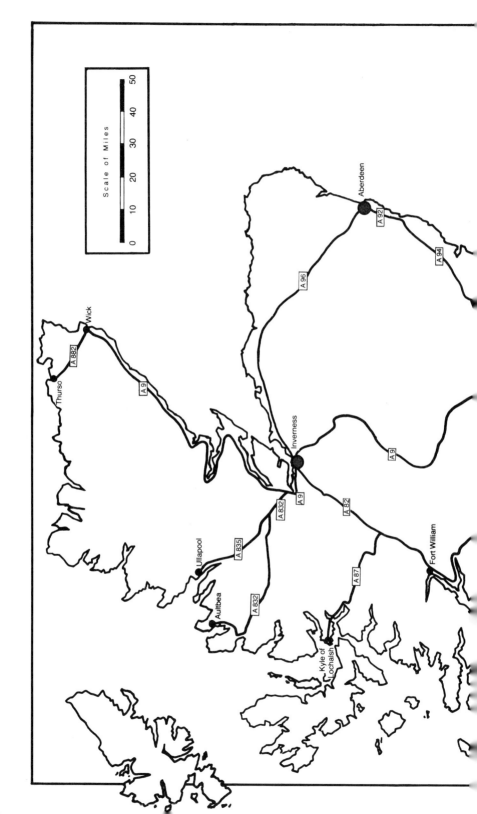

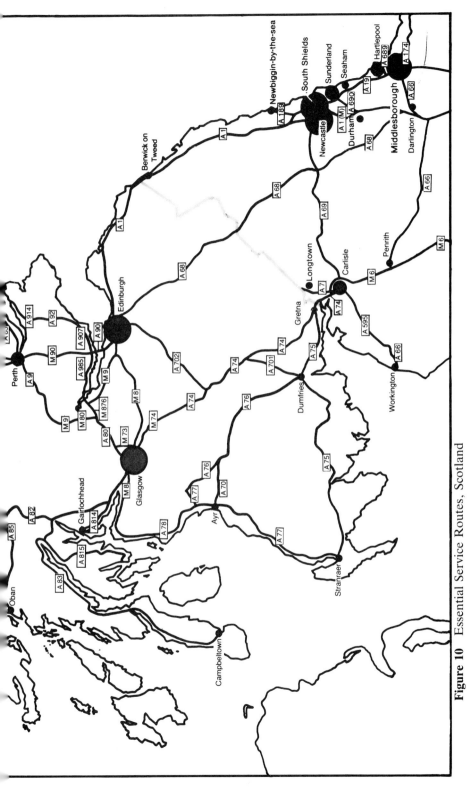

Figure 10 Essential Service Routes, Scotland

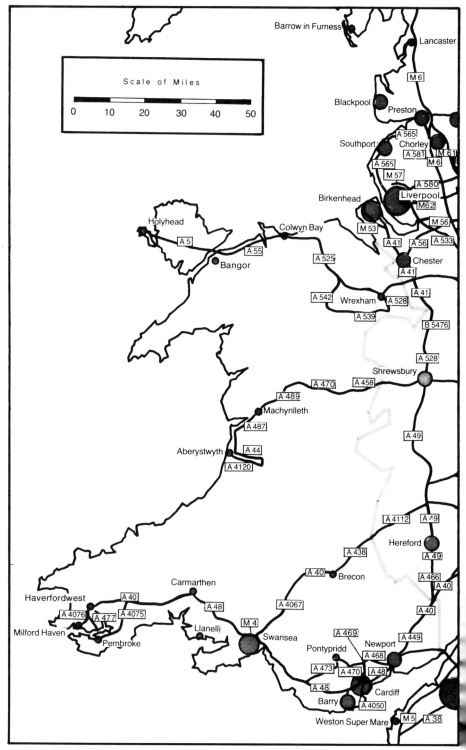

Figure 10 Essential Service Routes, Wales

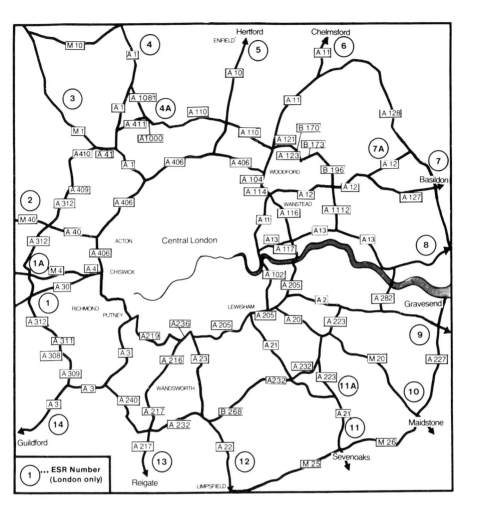

Figure 11 Essential Service Routes: London. The ESR scheme for London provides complex and detailed arrangements for controlling movement out of and within the capital. Sixteen major radial routes and three ring roads are designated as ESRs.

ESR 1	A30	ESR 5	A10	ESR 8	A13	ESR 12	A23
ESR 2	M4	ESR 6	A11	ESR 9	A2/M2	ESR 13	A24
ESR 3	A40	ESR 7	A12/A127	ESR 10	A20	ESR 14	A3
ESR 4	A1	ESR 7A	A1023	ESR 11	A21		

Ring Roads:
ESR Route 'A' Peacetime inner ring road (A406/A205)
ESR Route 'AA' Blackwall Tunnel and access roads
ESR Route 'B' Outer Ring Road as shown
ESR Route 'C' or Constabulary Ring Road: A25 and others as shown

Besides the ESRs, London civil and military Group Controllers have also drawn up a scheme of 'priority routes' within the central area for use in war or peacetime emergencies.

them. And at all times, they would be shepherded off the ESRS to keep these free for military and other 'essential' vehicles.

The ESR network neatly embraces the task of providing military logistic routes between major ports, airports, depots and bases, etc, with the task of sealing off the cities. Many cities are in the same situation as London; five out of nine major roads from Newcastle are ESRS, four major roads from Cardiff; and so on. The intention of preventing self-evacuation of the civil population by these means is quite explicit. At one recent Home Defence conference, for example, in Cambridge in December 1981, city councillors were astonished to hear military and police planners discuss the most efficacious methods – whether to put a 'ring of steel' around the cities to block movement; or whether merely to control the ESRS, and allow escapees to seal off minor roads themselves through traffic jams, fuel shortages, and breakdowns.

The original ESR circular, CDC 4/71, also succinctly implied that there wasn't much hope for those who didn't get past the city roadblocks. After nuclear attack, there wasn't much point in having ESRS that ran *through* cities:

The larger *conurbations* and other *potentially vulnerable areas* have been bypassed as far as possible, but suitable ring routes on the *outer perimeters of main cities* have been included. (CDC 4/71 para 2; author's emphases)

The army has another version of the ESR network, called the Military Road Route System. It is smaller, largely overlaps with ESRS, and is intended to provide the main routes for military convoys and other movements, in peace as well as war. Each of the routes has an inelegant zoological codename such as STAG, ELK or PIG. These roads would be the first choice for the movement of any reinforcements, or such hardware as cruise missiles (See map, pp. 198–9).

The MRRS is based on a relatively recent and comprehensive survey of British roads and other key facilities that the army undertook between 1972 and 1975, as part of an overall review of its Home Defence and intervention capabilities ordered by the Cabinet Office. The data available on each route includes engineering and military detail about key bridges and intersections, as well as the whereabouts of ammunition and fuel depots.

Enforcing ESRS and other measures to assist transition-to-war measures is the major job for the police. At the same time, they have to prepare themselves for war. So far as is known, war precautions to be taken at Force HQs are no more sophisticated than those planned for County Council bunkers. Existing or easily protected rooms have been chosen for war controls. At Divisional HQs, the precautions to be taken are of the 'Protect and Survive' sort – increasing the Protective Factor (PF) of buildings from fallout by sandbagging and re-inforcement. The police will naturally benefit, however, from priority access to supplies of suitable materials.

Apart from Police Support Units (PSUs), which will be dispersed, the police force are expected to take casualties at roughly the same level as the civil population. The PSUs are thirty-six man units with their own transport (police or re-quisitioned buses) which will be made up of, roughly, twenty per cent of a force's normal strength. (At the same time, police strength is expected to increase by about fifty per cent by taking in a war duty establishment of recent retirees, special constables, and volunteers.) The PSUs will disperse to police or requisitioned premises in safe areas, in order to provide a post-attack mobile force.

The PSUs replace a previous concept of huge Police Mobile Columns, which would have been placed under regional or sub-regional government command before attack. The for-mation of PSUs, and related plans for 'mutual aid' between different police forces now apply in peacetime also. The PSUs have, since 1981, become the focus for the development of police anti-riot forces – an example of the increasing congru-ence of wartime and peacetime emergency planning.

Before attack, police forces and PSUs are instructed to re-quisition and lay in their own food and fuel stocks – at least fourteen days' worth, and preferably rather more. PSUs may have to take their stores with them, although briefings con-cerning the earlier scheme for mobile columns note that 'arrangements have already been made with selected whole-salers to make available a fourteen day supply of food for individual police mobile columns.'

In the pre-attack period, the police will also test and pre-pare the attack warning system described in Chapter 9, with its 252 Carrier Control Points located at police premises. Radiac instruments, maroons, and other special equipment are stocked at Home Office Supply and Transport stores throughout the country (p. 211). Some may store arms and anti-riot equipment for police use, including CS gas. There are also stocks of materials to use in strengthening premises

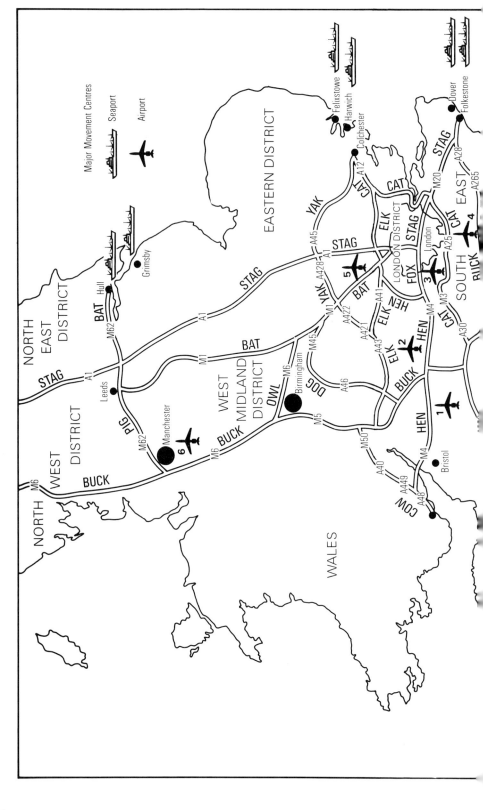

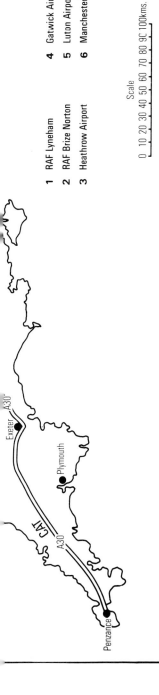

Figure 12 The Military Road Route System

1	RAF Lyneham
2	RAF Brize Norton
3	Heathrow Airport
4	Gatwick Airport
5	Luton Airport
6	Manchester(Ringway)Airport

Scale

0 10 20 30 40 50 60 70 80 9C 100kms.

BUCK Carlisle to Folkestone via M6, M5, Cirencester and A338, A345, A419, Winchester via A303, A34, then on A272, A265, A28 to link up with M20

STAG Edinburgh to Folkestone via A1 and A1M, North and South London Circulars A406 and A205, Dover via A20, M20

CAT Penzance to Colchester via A30, M3, Guildford via A322, A25, M25, A2 and Dartford Tunnel, Brentwood and Colchester on A128, A12

BAT London to Hull via M1, Leeds, M62

PIG Manchester (BUCK) to Leeds (BAT) via M62

OWL Birmingham M1 (BAT) to M5/M6 (BUCK) link via M6

COW Cardiff to M5 (BUCK) via A48, A449, A40, M50

HEN Cardiff to Hemel Hempstead (ELK) via A48, M4, A404

ELK Gloucester/M5 (BUCK) to Colchester via A40, A421, A41, and A414

YAK Bicester to Colchester via A421, A422, A428, A45, Cambridge, Colchester via A130, A120

DOG Cirencester (BUCK and ELK routes) to M1 (BAT) via A429, A46, A45

FOX Slough (HEN) to London North Circular (STAG) on M4/A4

pre-attack, and communications and other equipment for both the police and the 'green' (emergency) fire service. Many police and fire officers are also trained to carry out air reconnaissance from light aircraft after attack in order to survey bomb damage and refugee movements. Much of the coordination of police war planning is done not by the Home Office, but by the Police War Duties Committee, part of the Association of Chief Police Officers (to which Chief Constables and their deputies and assistants all belong). The committee was set up in 1949, and in 1952 recommended the novel appointment of wartime Regional Police Commanders. They are all either Chief Constables in the area concerned, or HM Inspectors of Constabulary.

Once appointed, Regional Police Commanders are in overall command of each force in the Region, through its own Chief Constable. The RPC, according to the *Police Manual of Home Defence*, will accompany the Regional Commissioner to regional dispersal locations. When Regional Seats of Government are set up some weeks or months after the attack, he would operate from there.

At each of the SRHQ bunkers, an Assistant Chief Constable from a suitable force would be in charge of a small police team as Sub-Regional Police Adviser. Similarly, Police Laison Officers are to be sent to each County, District or Borough War HQ. But except at regional level, the police – like the military – remain independent and autonomous. They do not have automatically to comply with the requests or plans of Sub-Regional Commissioners or Local Authority Controllers.

In order to link wartime HQS to police forces, the plan for *Communications in War* (mostly in ES 5/75) provides for police (speech) radio links from each SRHQ to force HQS in the Sub-Region, and for speech and teleprinter connections by landline and radio from each County wartime HQ to the appropriate police force. Most police forces, of course, already have major communications systems for vehicles and foot patrols in existence, and these would continue to be used as long as possible. But each police divisional HQ and mobile column would also have at least one motorcyclist available as a dispatch rider. The *Police Manual of Home Defence* explains that 'dormant vehicle hire contracts' will automatically augment police transport facilities in emergency, even without requisitioning powers.

Once the bomb has dropped, the full emergency system of government controls automatically comes into operation. In the early post-strike period, police and military home defence duties will not have changed very much – trying to control refugee movement and settlements, and guarding key points and installations. But gradually they will acquire a grim new range of tasks, which are seldom examined or discussed.

During *Square Leg*, for example, police and military *Post Strike Tasks* were enumerated as follows:

1. Maintenance of law and order – greatest problem urban areas
2. Control of selfish and disgruntled minorities
3. Support and protect special courts
4. Execution of sentences (military only)
5. Key points protection and reinforcement
6. Protection of convoys
7. Guards for controls
8. Personal protection for VIPS
9. Subjugation and elimination of hostile elements
10. Control of weapons
11. Bomb disposal (military only)
12. Supervision and control of operations involving the use of explosives, eg demolitions.
13. Guards on internment areas
14. Assisting in control at communal feeding centres
15. Enforcement of controls to prevent the spread of disease
16. Manning any pre planned pattern of military stations and posts . . .
23. Maintenance and control of Essential Service Routes
24. Control of movement. . .

The remainder of these twenty-seven military and twenty-two police tasks were concerned with training new personnel ('to compensate for wastage') or with general reconnaissance or advisory tasks.

The *Post Strike Tasks* offer a grim, but clearly accurate, picture of circumstances after attack – very much, in fact, the circumstances portrayed in Peter Watkins' suppressed film, *The War Game*. With few exceptions, the police and military monopoly of coercive power is used to maintain control of movement, of food supplies and their distribution and to guard the resources of government – Controls, VIPS, etc – against the survivors. Perhaps, in some parts of the country, resources will be not be completely overstretched, and the military and police will genuinely be able to help the community. However the military task in war is *Military Aid to the Civil Authority* (MACA); this contracts with peacetime military intervention either in cases of disaster (Military Aid to the Civil Community: MACC) or strikes (Military Aid to the Civil Ministries: MACM). As can be seen from the list, there is no intention that troops or police should assist in rescuing or caring for survivors. A grim comparison of *Post Strike Tasks*, which is classified, may be made with the somewhat diluted suggestions on the subject made publicly – for example by the Home Defence College in its courses for local councillors. These notes say nothing of internment or guards for VIPS and Controls, but suggests that MACA tasks could include 'route clearance', or the 'restoration of essential services' like water or sewerage. The classified list does not mention them. The Jobson paper reaches this conclusion:

(The police) do not have all the answers and the prospects are not bright. . . . Plans must be made for the worst possible situation. We can only prepare for the worst.

Facilities for the police and military to take refuge from bombs and fallout in war may be just as unpleasant as for most members of the public. The *Police Manual* outlines some features of life for officers taking refuge in a heavy fallout zone; the air in the refuge area must be sealed in, and candles used as little as possible to conserve oxygen. If the temperature rises too high, in spring or summer, outer clothing should be taken off to prevent water loss by perspiration. If fallout conditions and building damage do not permit using the normal lavatory facilities, 'a hole may well have to be pierced through the floor to form a pit' for urine and excreta. Moral, however, remains vital, since:

. . . when police emerge from refuge, they will have to lead and set an example to the public . . .

Once out of their refuges, the police would administer and operate the systems for advising the public when and if it was safe to emerge from their homes – if they had survived.

Official plans for post-attack administration invariably focus on law and order. It is an aspect of Home Defence planning which is paramount, but which is carefully screened from the local authorities who do the most public parts of the planning. Local authority Controllers never take on the responsibility for law and order, which remains exclusively with regional government officials, the police and the military. So their councils do not 'need to know' what it is going to be about.

It was, indeed, on the basis of 'need to know' that, in 1976, the Home Office distributed a closely guarded set of extracts from central government war plans as *Briefing Material for Wartime Controllers* (ES3/76; 'restricted' and 'not to be communicated directly or indirectly to the Press or any person not authorised to receive it'). It was concerned with law and order, surviving industrial and manpower resources, and economic planning. Only Controllers (designate) were supposed to see the material.

Under 'Law and Order', it explained the plans contained in the Home Office's draft Emergency Powers Bill. 'The maintenance of public order,' it said, 'would be one of the essential tasks of wartime regional government.' To adminster the judicial system, Commissioners of Justice would be appointed by Regional Government and they might hold court 'anywhere in a region where radiological conditions permitted movement'. Anyone with any kind of peacetime judicial office would be eligible to act as a Commissioner; normally, but not necessarily, two or three lay Commissioners would be expected to sit together. A court of three Commissioners, or a single Commissioner with a jury of 'not more than five' could impose summary sentences of execution. There would be no appeal.

Of course many peacetime 'crimes' would have ceased to matter, 'at a time when the paramount aim would be survival'. The problem of non-capital penalties after a nuclear attack is quite ticklish, and the Home Office suggests forced labour – 'communal labour'; starvation – 'restricted rations'; and the old, medieval stocks – 'exposure to public disapproval'. Firing squads are mentioned somewhat circuitously in paragraph 6 of *Briefing Material*:

Provision for appropriate penalties not normally available to courts might be made under emergency regulations and Regional Commissioners, acting through their Commissioners of Justice would be empowered to impose such penalties as they thought fit in the light of circumstances and conditions at the time.

After all:

In conditions in which death, destruction and injury were commonplace, such penalties as probation, fines or sentences of imprisonment would no longer be effective in dealing with anti-social offenders.

On other occasions more exotic solutions have been proposed. A series of Home Office seminars codenamed *Trent Beacon* was held by staff of Civil Defence Region 3 in the late 1960s; they suggested that:

For minor offences, many advocated chastisement by ridicule. . . .
In the absence of help from the armed services, special
punishment squads might have to be recuited or a marshal with
deputies appointed.

This suggestion came largely from a group of elected councillors interested in civil defence. They also argued that the
police should never become responsible, as far as possible,
for administering death sentences – a view with which the
Home Office apparently agrees. Their suggestion, however,
that judicial officials and special constables should be *elected*
by surviving communities unsurprisingly found no favour.

In practice, as has often been said, Commissioners and
Controllers and indeed any government official who acted in
good faith could do anything at all without reproach. The
Machinery of Government in War circular (ES7/73) explains
that, 'if necessary, Regional Commissioners would, by ordinance, sanction *post facto* the actions of the County Controller' if communications to the SRHQ were not functioning.
Martial law (where looters or other offenders might be shot
on sight) could not take effect unless the civil law could no
longer practicably be administered by the police – or if such
actions as shooting looters were decreed lawful by ordinance
of the Regional Commissioner (as indeed is highly likely).
Otherwise civil and common law would be maintained; a
policeman or soldier could not shoot someone unless there
was no other safe way of dealing with the situation.

Such niceties of principle are likely to be abandoned,
though, even before the bombs start falling. Early on in the
exercises like *Scrum Half*, for example, there were fairly
heavy preparations being made to deal with the civil population. Three days into the *pre*-strike phase, for example, this
message was sent from Aldershot to all the SRHQS and County
Military HQs in Region 6:

RESTRICTED   EX SCRUM HALF.
CS GAS. I. SCALE.
SCALE OF CS GAS EQUIPMENT AUTHORISED FOR ANY TYPE OF SUBUNIT
IS CANNISTERS 150, GRENADES 150, RIOT GUNS 25. ARRANGEMENTS
BEING MADE FOR ISSUE ASP TO ALL CGR* COMPANIES AND FOR STOCKS
AVAILABLE TO ALL OTHER SUBUNITS . . .

Such massive issues of CS can only be directed against the
public disorder about which the government is so concerned.

* Composite General Reserve

The same concern echoes through other exercises and plans. For example, the *Square Leg Pre-Strike Scenario* offers this appraisal under the heading 'Political'.

There has been continuous left and right wing political activity mainly in the urban areas from the beginning of September 1980. Pacifism as a front for subversion has been the main theme. Some demonstrations called for troops in support of the police (MACP), especially in the West Midlands and Stafford.

And under 'Industrial Unrest', the military scenario foresaw:

There has been unrest in the transport sector including intemittent bus strikes which have aggravated the manning situation in many factories and army depots, etc. . . .

In *Hard Rock* the theme is again picked up, though slightly diluted:

September 1982 was characterised by: . . . b. Peaceful rallies, urging the government/NATO alliance to reach a negotiated solution, cause problems with traffic disruption. Some isolated demonstrations cause some law and order problems. . .

The military and government view, as expressed in *Square Leg*, that pacifism equates to subversion, is quite prevalent in Home Defence plans, and there is little doubt that leading campaigners of any anti-war group would rapidly face internment. Despite this, Leon Brittain wrote in 1980 from the Home Office to an MP enquiring on behalf of his constituents that 'it is certainly not the policy of the government to seek to intimidate peace campaigners and pacifists, and we have no intention of interning pacifists during a build up to nuclear war'. This falsehood – for such it clearly is – may be ranked alongside the same Ministry's recent claim that the central government had nothing at all to do with the Arts Bunker at Manod (see p 283).

Whilst police forces will continue to operate on a fairly autonomous basis, at least until the outbreak of war, the opposite is true of the armed forces. The system for the military administration of the UK is comprehensive and has been in operation for more then thirty years. In its contemporary form, like the regional police system, it is entirely a product of the post Second World War era.

At the head of the British military administration is the United Kingdom Commanders-in-Chief Committee, UKCICC (pronounced UK-chick). Details of the formation of UKCICC,

once 'Top Secret', are now openly available at the Public
Records Office after thirty years of secrecy. The proposal for
establishing UKCICC was made and accepted in a February
1950 report entitled 'Joint Command for the Defence of the
United Kingdom in War'. (Paper JP (50)4 of the Joint Planning Staff at the Ministry of Defence; now in PRO file COSC
573).
The overall aim of UKCICC, within military strategy, was:

to defend the United Kingdom so that it can remain a main
offensive base for as long as possible, and an advanced air base in
all circumstances.

The paper was written only months after the Soviet Union
first tested an atomic bomb. The planners, basing themselves
on advice from the Joint Intelligence Committee, believed
that 'in the long term, although the Soviet (sic) might not be
able to mount attacks from the Channel coast, they would
make the maximum use of weapons of mass destruction and
guided missiles.' They anticipated that, possibly quite quickly,
'London would be so severely damaged that it would cease
to be the centre of administration.' It was therefore felt that
a new committee, subordinate to the Chiefs of Staff Committee, would be necessary to organise day to day operations
for the defence of the UK. At this time, in 1950, it was also
anticipated that the army's role, after providing anti-aircraft
and anti-invasion units, would be 'to assist in the Civil Defence of the United Kingdom'. This role did not survive the
decade.

Ukcicc was set up more or less as recommended, and a site
for its protected Joint Operational Headquarters bunker was
sought. Three sites were examined: Wilton Park, Beaconsfield, HQ of the army's C-IN-C Home Forces; Stanmore near
London, already equipped with a bunker from the war, as HQ
of Fighter Command; and Fort Southwick, Portsmouth, the
HQ of the Commander of Naval Home Forces. Eventually, it
seems, Stanmore was picked as the site for the 200–250 person
UKCICC HQ. Protected accomodation was also built at Wilton
Park however, probably for London's Army District HQ, and
it retains this role today as AFHQ5. Fort Southwick is still the
HQ of the Commander of Naval Home Forces.

The three commanders in UKCICC (HOME) (an overseas
UKCICC was later set up) are now:

Commander-in-Chief UK Land Forces (the Chairman); peacetime HQ, Wilton, near Salisbury

Air Commander Home Defence Forces (in peace, Air Officer Commanding RAF Support Command): peacetime HQ RAF Brampton, near Huntingdon

Commander-in-Chief, Naval Home Command: peacetime HQ, Fort Southwick, Portsmouth

The staff who are appointed to serve UKCICC in war are normally based with the UKLF commander at Salisbury. Most of the UK's Home Defence plans are drawn up by the Salisbury-based UKLF Home Defence Joint Emergency Planning Staff, in conjunction with the Home Office and the Ministry of Defence. A few naval and air support staff are

Plate 21   United Kingdom Land Forces peacetime headquarters at Wilton, near Salisbury. These offices house the UK Commanders-in-Chief Committee (UKCICC) and the Joint Emergency Planning Staff, responsible for military defence.

based at Brampton and Fort Southwick. Meetings of UKCICC (H) are attended by the Home Office, usually by the Assistant Secretary in charge of the F6 Home Defence division. Some UKCICC staff are detached to teach at the Easingwold Home Defence College; others work full time on exercises, including drafting the scenarios and attack plans for exercises such as *Hard Rock* and *Square Leg*.

On receipt of mobilisation orders, the HQ of UKLF will move from Wilton to a protected war location. The exact whereabouts of the UKLF war HQ is not certain, although it most probably moved from Stanmore at the same time as the decision was taken to move central government out of London to Hawthorn. The most likely site would be the former Tunnel and Hudswell quarries close by Hawthorn in the Corsham complex, which were emptied of their Second World War munition stocks by the early 50s. A breezy description of the place is given in *The Third World War* fiction by General Sir John Hackett and collaborators, who describe the UK situation as war began:

Delegation of power over military and civil defence resources had become the responsibility of the headquarters of UK Land Forces. Representatives of the Prime Minister, the naval, air and military commands were assembled there in well-defended underground bunkers, hardened against attack or interference to communications, containing all necessary equipment.

If the war HQ of UKLF, is not at Corsham, it will certainly be not far away. It is, as Hackett suggests, the central authority in the UK in the aftermath of an attack – and, if it survives, likely to be the only national communications centre still functioning, through the Defence Communications Network.

The 1950 planners discussed the appointment of a Supreme Commander to take charge in case of an extended battle for Britain, possibly also including American army units defending US airbases here. The proposal seems to have been left dormant, with the idea that the present-day C-IN-C of UKLF would get the job if need be.

In war, UKCICC places each of the armed services in Britain under a unified command. The same happens in the regions, as described earlier. The General Officer Commanding (GOC) each military district usually takes command from the Regional AFHQ. Also present on the staff of each AFHQ will be a Naval Regional Member, a senior naval officer, and the Air Officer Commanding the Region, who will have charge of the

RAF's allocation of helicopters and light aircraft. Later, more aircraft may be requisitioned to the squadron.

At lower levels in the command structure, Joint Services Liaison Officers of Lieutenant-Colonel rank are appointed to work with (and, in war, serve at the HQ of) each County Council, Scottish Regional Council or London Group. At the bottom level of District Councils and their equivalents, a single Military Liaison Officer may be given a similar role. These officers will normally be on the staff of the regional Military District, or come from permanent services establishments in the area.

Military briefings stress that civil authorities must leave the armed forces to operate without interference under their own commanders, once tasks have been allocated by Regional Commissioners. The JSLO at County Military HQs would 'not normally be in command of armed service units, but would report direct to his military commander'. (*Armed Forces in War*, ES 11/74).

Home Defence military units would be formed as platoons (twenty-five to thirty), or companies (100–120), with men being provided from the Regular Army, TAVR, the Composite General Reserve (including regular soldiers at training or administrative units in the UK), or 'ad hoc' (ie, wartime volunteers). Larger, battalion-level formations (400–600) would also be available at regional level from Regular Army or TAVR resources. The new Home Service Force announced in 1982, will increase the number of units available by taking over the duties of guarding Key Points.

According to the 1981 Defence Estimates, some thirty per cent of the army's mobilised strength would be available for Home Defence. This amounts to some 100,000 men and women, before the 1982 increases. The 1981 Estimates also described the introduction of a new and powerful VHF military radio system, now known by its codename MOULD, for the command of Home Defence forces in war.

The number and extent of Key Points in Britain is not known. Details, classified 'Secret', were circulated to Chief Constables in 1974 (*Protection of Key Points*, ES6/74). At the same time 'restricted' booklets on *Countersabotage Planning* (ES2/73) and *Key Point Protection* (ES7/74), both prepared by MI5, were issued to the police only. The accompanying letters explained that MI5 had redrafted the booklets so as to be more applicable to the British mainland situation; previous versions had been oriented towards colonial counterinsurgency campaigns.

Table 6   Key Points in Warwickshire*

Essential Industries	
Shipston Engineering Shipston on Stour	Compressed air equipment
Stratford on Avon Canners Stratford on Avon	Fruit and vegetable canners
Clarkson International Tools Nuneaton	Precision tools
Courtaulds Bedworth	Man-made fibres and chemicals
Automotive Products Ltd Leamington Spa	Auto components
Thwaites Engineering Ltd Cublington	Agricultural machinery
GEC Machines Ltd Mill Road, Rugby	Heavy machinery
GEC Turbine Generators Boughton Road, Rugby	Turbine generators

Buffer Depots	*Other Key Points*
Bidavon Industrial Estate Bidford on Avon	Kingsbury Oil Terminal Kingsbury, Near Coleshill
Eclipse Road Trading Estate Alcester	Hams Hall Power Station Coleshill
Kineton Road Industrial Estate Southam	Police Fuel Dump Council Depot, Wingfield Road, Coleshill
National Agricultural Centre Stoneleigh, Kenilworth	Police Fuel Dump Motorways Depot, Coleshill Heath Road, Coleshill
	British Home Stores Distributors, (food store) Riversdale Road, Atherstone

* This is *not* an exhaustive list of Warwichkire key points. The fuel
dumps would be set up in accordance with wartime plans for
requisitioning fuel supplies, and are not permanent.

Some idea of the extent of Key Points can be gleaned from
the details in Table 6 based on the war plan for Warwickshire
county. The county has seventeen general Key Points, ten
Food Stores, ten Industrial Key Points (Essential Industries)
and four Buffer Depots, which require to be guarded. The

Table 7 Home Office Supply and Transport Stores

Region	
1	Topcliffe, Thirsk, Cambois, Ashington, Aycliffe, Middlesborough
2	Pollington Airfield, Snaith, York Harrogate Road, Yeadon Portobello Road, Wakefield, Rudgate Lane, Tockwith (repair)
3	Desboro Airfield, Northampton Weedon, Northants North Willingham, Lincs Burton Road, Branston
4	RAF Watton, Gaydon Chilton Airfield, Sudbury, Colchester Bassingbourne Barracks, Royston RAF Rayden, Great Wenham
5	Southwold Road, Watford Royston Road, Caxton
6	Steventon, near Abingdon Kingsclere Woking (Brookwood) South Camp, Biggin Hill Shirburn Road, Watlington
7	Temple Cloud, Somerset Bishops Cleeve, Somerset Edinburgh Street, Swindon (repair) West Ashcroft, Taunton Dunkeswell Airfield, Honiton
8	Pencoed, Cardiff
9	Arbury Road, Nuneaton Meir Airfield, Stoke on Trent, Blythe Edge
10	Carlisle Burtonwood, Warrington
Scotland	Hayford Mill, Cambusbarron, Stirling (Scottish Home and Health Dept)
Northern Ireland	No information

list suggests that, overall, there may between two and four thousand general and industrial Key Points. In the later, post strike period, Key Point priorities would be changed, and it is obvious that food stores might well require the heaviest guards.

Defence Secretary John Nott's decision to create the Home Service Force precisely mirrors a decision taken by his predecessors exactly thirty years before to reintroduce the Home Guard in peacetime (they eventually became TAVR 3 and then disappeared altogether after 1968). The original recreation of the Home Guard followed a report of the Cabinet Office's Key Points Working Party during 1951. It recommended that 'anti-sabotage guard forces should be mobilised and positioned as soon as the threat of war develops.' A Key Points Sub-Committee in the Cabinet Office continues to operate under the overall control of the official Home Defence (HD) committee.

At regional level, there are now closely linked systems for dealing with peacetime contingencies as well as wartime Home Defence. As a former deputy commander of UKLF, Major General Hugh Beach, explained in a 1970 paper:

Although the function of (military) support for the local authority in the maintenance of law and order in peace is quite distinct from home defence, it would be disingenuous to overlook that in practice a close connection normally exists between them. (See *State Research*, 1978, p. 20)

Since those words were written, the links have immensely strengthened. On the Home Defence side, a Joint Services Planning Committee, chaired by the Regional Military Commander (Designate), meets at least twice yearly. Its meetings will normally be attended by Home Office F6 officials and other central government staff, including the designated Regional Fire and Police Commanders.

On the civil side, Regional Emergency Committees, usually chaired by Department of the Environment regional directors have been set up to work under the direction of the Civil Contingencies Unit to deal with major strikes. The revamped civil contingencies organisation is a product of the 1970–74 Heath Government, which declared five States of Emergency, and was deeply alarmed by its failure to beat the miners' strike of 1972. The CCU was set up that year, in place of the Cabinet's former Emergencies Committee – itself an historical successor to plans and organisations going back to the 1920s and the Organisation for the Maintenance of Supplies.

The Regional Emergency Committees are normally based on regional economic planning boards, and bring together officials from the Departments of Trade, Energy, Industry, Environment (including Transport), plus police and military liaison staff. Paralleling the wartime structure, they will then normally liase with Chief Constables, Fire Brigade Chiefs, and Chief Executives of local authorities to obtain information and coordinate official responses. Some councils, particularly Labour-controlled councils, may be reluctant to assist. Other councils will direct their Emergency Planning staff to put Home Defence duties aside to assist in countering strikes.

The Civil Contingencies Unit's chief official is a Cabinet Office Deputy Secretary, Richard Wade-Gery, a former diplomat. Its secretary is a seconded army officer, Brigadier Richard Bishop. It is normally chaired by the Home Secretary. Wade-Gery also heads the Home Defence and Civil Contingencies Secretariat within the Cabinet Office, which is responsible for all centralised planning for war measures.

In all emergencies calling for military aid to the civil power (MACP) or civil ministries (MACM), the CCU will normally convene in the Cabinet Office Briefing Room ('Cobra') – now well known to the public after the Iranian Embassy siege of 1980. Cobra is equipped with an extensive communications network, via the military TARE and TASS telex systems, and by direct speech links to police and military operations centres. Other departments have made similar arrangements for drastic civil emergencies; the Department of the Environment, for example, has a 'siege suite' at its Marsham Street headquarters in Victoria. The 'Federal' telephone network also provides ministers and senior civil servants with a telephone network not generally accessible to striking communications workers. (See Chapter 9; Federal was in fact ready to take on emergency work during the 1974 miners' strike.)

In case of widespread public unrest, Home Defence plans would go into operation through the formation of Regional Seats of Government broadly in accordance with wartime planning. There would be no need, however, for SRHQS and other protected accomodation to be staffed; RSGs would be set up in government or requisitioned offices, usually close to military command centres like York, Preston or Shrewsbury. This is the contingency plan for dealing with uprising or revolution. But an uprising sufficiently widespread to seriously threaten the overthrow of government by force seems possible only if the government or NATO was about to take Britain to nuclear war in the face of public opposition. This is a circumstance which further emphasises the congruence of peacetime and wartime emergency planning, harking back to the primary objective of Home Defence to 'maintain the internal security of the United Kingdom'.

Besides the now biennial series of military Home Defence exercises (the *Inside Right/Scrum Half/Square Leg/Hard Rock* series), there are also NATO-wide exercises with a similar theme. The most important of these also occur biennially, under the general title of *Wintex/Cimex*. ('Winter exercise'; 'Civil-military exercise'). A detailed military scenario for a Soviet attack pattern is drawn up (they are usually more innovative scenarios than the monotonous Soviet invasions of West Germany which are standard in UK plans) and NATO military commanders rehearse the moves towards war. The alliance's civilian command structure is then tested out – in principle, the critical decision to commence the use of nuclear weapons must be taken by the NATO Heads of State in Council, communicating from their dispersed national war headquarters like Hawthorn, via NATO satellite links or a number of other specialised communications networks. Separately, the US President must also agree to nuclear weapons release (or the Prime Minister for British weapons). Once that has happened, SACEUR (Supreme Allied Commander Europe) and the subordinate NATO commanders are free to wage the nuclear battle. As Lord Zuckerman and others have recorded, NATO has yet to hold a serious exercise in which the nuclear exchange stays limited.

Such War Room exercises are usually conducted by civil servants, who play ministers' roles in decision-taking. In a real emergency, the site of decision taking would move from the Whitehall Cabinet Offices to Hawthorn and other military and government command centres. *The Times* (26 February 1980) reported in 1980 that Mrs Thatcher had chosen to play her role personally in *Wintex 81*, and had asked other ministers to do the same.

Both the *Hard Rock* and *Wintex* series are essentially 'command post', paper exercises, in which headquarters communicate with each other but no actual military formations are engaged. The 8th Field Force has exercised (on army ranges) during the *Inside Right* series, mainly attempting to detect and counter infiltrated Soviet saboteurs and British 'fifth columnists'. Other exercises have had the same sort of theme as these pre-strike parts of the series. In 1975, for example, US and British troops parachuted onto Salisbury Plain to exercise putting down a rebellion in an 'imaginary country'. Two 1978 exercises, *Whisky Galore* in the Hebrides (June) and *Northern Wedding* in the Shetlands (December) both rehearsed counter-insurgency in a NATO, West European context. In *Whisky Galore*, over-enthusiastic Dutch marines began rounding up some local civilians at gunpoint, taking them to be the fifth columnists and saboteurs which were being played by British marines in mufti. In a more down-to-earth – and chilling – context, the 1980 BBC series on the army's Camberley Staff College, *War School*, showed young officers being instructed in dealing with 'subversion'. An exercise featured a deployment of Military Aid to the Civil Power in order to suppress a riot with armed force in the fictional city of 'Two Rivers'; the maps corresponded to Aberdeen.

The same sort of exercises are in fact conducted in all NATO countries, particularly in conjunction with the international *Wintex* series. Even the relatively liberal and open conscript-based armies of some northern European NATO members have broadly similar plans for suppressing refugee movement and public dissent. In the Netherlands, for instance, a raid by pacifist protesters in 1981 on the North Holland Provincial Military Command (analogous to a British military district) unearthed comprehensive plans for everything from press censorship to lists of individuals and organisations selected for surveillance or internment. The plans were exhibited and then published by part of the Dutch peace movement.

7
Going underground

The 1981 Home Office pamphlet *Civil Defence – Why We Need It* offered this rhetorical commentary on the government bunkers:

What about those deep bunkers we hear about to protect the privileged few? – Most senior ministers, government officials and service chiefs would have to remain at their desks if war threatened, and they would take their chance like anybody else if the UK were attacked. . .

This is deception at its most unashamed. The 'desks' referred to, for senior ministers, government officials and service chiefs are all some distance below the ground. Across Britain, there are twenty thousand or more desks in war headquarters; half are in relatively well-protected central or regional government HQs and half in less well protected district or county council HQs.

Since biblical times, people have taken to caves and underground sanctuaries for shelter from war. There is nothing new about that. Many British government shelters originated as industrial or warlike workings of a much earlier time; our predecessors excavated below Dover's medieval castle, hollowed out caverns in Berkshire, and pressed into service numerous slate and stone quarries. In fact, very few bunkers have been built since 1960, although many have been repeatedly refurbished or re-equipped, for the privileged 'few'.

There is no evidence that the 'few' of World War Three are an extraordinary class of citizens chosen by some Whitehall Strangelove for qualities of genetic merit. They are, rather, the same grey rulers familiar from peacetime: mostly civil servants, police and military officers, a few industrialists and bankers, some judges, academics and scientists, and a smattering of politicians. There is no profession, except cabinet minister or three star military officer, which guarantees a ticket for one of the government bunkers. Nor could they honestly be said to be taking sanctuary; some time, be it six days or six months after the holocaust, they will have to emerge from cramp and discomfort to face the exterior world. It will still be a better lot, however, than that of the population whom they had led to war.

Thus, in a limited sense, the Home Office's claim that the embunkered 'few' will 'take their chances' has some justice. There are no really deep bunkers. The main government citadel, Hawthorn, is only 80–100 feet (25–35m) below ground and very few are any deeper than this. No government, except the Soviet Union, has emulated the United States' policy of tunneling huge sanctuaries hundreds of feet below ground.

In May 1950, a 'Top Secret' report of the United States Joint Chiefs of Staff (now declassified) recommended the construction of an underground command headquarters six hundred feet below Raven Rock Mountain, seventy-five miles northwest of Washington. This level of protection would be truly incredible for an atomic bomb, and the Soviets had only just exploded their first, Hiroshima-sized weapon. In fact, the American planners were anticipating, correctly as it turned out, the much greater explosive power which would eventually be achieved – as one paper noted – by a 'so-called hydrogen bomb'. Planning continued on grim assumptions about a protracted war involving A and H bomb attacks on the national capital. The Raven Rock Mountain citadel, now known as the Alternate National Military Command Center, was constructed quickly at a cost, in 1951, of over $30 million.

Similar citadels were built at Mount Weather in the Blue Ridge Mountains of Virginia, forty-five miles west of Washington, and Mount Marshall. Mount Weather was to be the US President's sanctuary during nuclear war. The two centres would also house the 'uninterruptibles', as prominent US citizens with an allocated space at the centre came to be known.

Besides this, some 135,000 government staff were to be dispersed to locations and offices up to fifty miles from the city. A new motorway – the Beltway – around the outskirts of Washington was originally built to link these dispersed offices.

Now, however, the US has abandoned any belief that there can be sanctuary from the H bomb. In 1963, a new and massively blast- and shock-protected headquarters was built far below Cheyenne Mountain in Colorado, to house the US – Canadian North American Air Defence Command (NO-RAD). It was the last of its kind. In 1978, Mount Weather was abandoned as the Presidential citadel, and American policy is now to place all its commanders, including the President, in huge flying war rooms converted from Boeing 707 or 747 jets. No attempt is being made to protect other underground HQs in the style of the 1950s. The headquarters of the US Strategic Air Command in Omaha, Nebraska for example, are only fifty feet below the surface. In war, the SAC Generals would also be airborne, in converted Boeing 707s known as 'Looking Glass', and supported by an airborne network of communications relay aircraft.

The message is simple. Nothing can now be built hard enough to withstand an H bomb. Nor can a citadel be constructed in such assured secrecy that it will escape observation, and targetting. The only solution available lies in multiple, dispersed, and mildly protected sites, as the US debate over the deployment of the proposed MX missile has shown. And for targets as critical as enemy nuclear missiles, even this plan is insecure.

Hydrogen bombs with a yield estimated at over fifty megatons have been tested by the Soviet Union. Both the massive SS18, and older SS9 missiles are fitted (in some models; others are MIRVed), with a single massive warhead with an estimated yield in excess of twenty-five megatons. The government *Nuclear Weapons Effects Computer No 1* gives the immediate effect of this weapon as a crater about 250 feet (77m) feet deep and 3200 feet (1km) across, even in hard rock. The US has slightly less massive weapons available, as air-dropped bombs or on the fifty-two Titan missiles now in operation. These giant weapons can only be employed in three ways: as airburst 'city-busters' of the combatants' most widespread industrial areas; for exoatmospheric (above the atmosphere) detonation to disrupt communications and control systems through the electro-magnetic pulse (EMP); or as groundbursts to destroy underground citadels. As a former US Assistant Secretary of Defense put it, 'if you're in the crater, you're in the crater.' There is no escape.

British planners are aware of this. *Square Leg* anticipated three groundburst hydrogen bombs directed against High Wycombe in Buckinghamshire, the site of RAF Strike Command Headquarters and UK Regional Air Operations Centre.

Most NATO commands have war headquarters well below ground – but not as deep as the US citadels of the 50s. Perhaps the deepest is the NATO headquarters in Belgium, in a disused coal mine. But this is just as vulnerable as the others to shock and the destruction of communications and entrances and exits on the surface. The French government has its war headquarters in a former V2 factory well below ground, west of Paris. This is fairly typical.

While the US was burrowing deep into the hard rock of the Blue Grass, West Virginia and Maryland Mountains, British planners had no such expansive dreams. In 1950, most of our efforts and expenditure was directed towards the huge expense of building our own atom bomb. Protection against the consequences of atomic warfare came a poor second, though it was stimulated by news of the first Soviet explosion. Even after the Soviets rapidly closed in the nuclear race with their own H bomb, Britain's response was largely confined to the adaptation of the underground detritus of the Second World War.

There was not much digging, in Britain, during the First World War. Although a few Zeppelin raids between 1914 and 1917 caused deaths and huge panic, they threatened neither government nor property on any huge scale. For all practical purposes, the building of government citadels in Britain started in the 1930s. Late in 1929 the War Office department responsible for ordnance had begun to inspect possible caves and mines in which ammunition could be stored. Amongst the sites examined were the Box bathstone quarries near Corsham, four of which – Huddswell, Seven Shaft, Monks Park and the Ridge – had been requisitioned in 1914 for precisely this purpose (and later released). A 1934 tour concentrated on three groups of quarries as being suitable for munitions and explosives: Bathstone quarries at Box (Corsham) and Bradford on Avon; the slate quarries of Blaenau Ffestiniog, in North Wales; and the hard rock flagstone quarries in the Rossendale district of the Pennines, southwest of Blackburn. Seven quarries at Rossendale were examined, and eleven at Blaenau Ffestioniog. Another site examined was the Chislehurst caves in Kent, which had also been requisitioned for the 1914–18 war.

In 1936, the War Office was authorised to take over the Tunnel and Ridge quarries at Corsham, the former having been previously reserved for the growing of mushrooms. The purpose of the acquisition was to store three months' ammunition for the British Army Field Force in the event of war. At the time, almost all of Britain's ammunition was in a very vulnerable store at Bramley, Surrey or at a set of storehouses in Chilmark, west of Salisbury, another underground bathstone quarry site.

The Tunnel quarries, which had their own underground railway sidings, amounted to 650,000 square feet of storage (61,000 m²) – some fifteen acres. The entrance to the Tunnel Quarry sidings can still be seen at the northern entrance to Brunel's Box railway tunnel on the London-Bath railway. Auxiliary railway sidings for the growing complex were later built at Filton, Bristol, and at Thingley, where the sidings still serve the underground government complex.

By 1937, the War Office had taken over all the First World War quarries once again. The next year, two more distant quarries were added, at Eastlays and Monkton Farleigh, making over three million square feet (282,000 m²) of underground storage. At considerable expense, floors were levelled and walls repaired, and conveyors, lighting, generators, and ventilation plant installed. By December 1940, the requisitioning had extended to every quarry of any size in the Corsham district, including the huge one hundred acre Spring Quarry. Corsham became, as it remains today, the greatest underground complex in Britain. In any future war, Corsham will be the main seat of government for the embattled nation – if it survives. The War Office ordnance staff who visited it in 1935 wrote with foresight:

The quarries . . . form part of an immense ramification of underground workings. They extend over many square miles. In case of emergency the underground storage at Box . . . might be extended on a very great scale.*

In London at the same time, the problem of maintaining the machinery of government under aerial bombardment had received considerable attention. It is worth recalling (Chapter 3) that at this time the government was anticipating that a few weeks of bombing might produce casualties on a scale we would now only envisage in a nuclear attack. A sub-committee of the Committee of Imperial Defence had started work on the 'Evacuation of Government Departments' in wartime in 1937. On its recommendation three underground citadels

---

* On Public Records Office file WO32/3343

were constructed in the London suburbs, each designed to resist a 500lb bomb.

These first citadels were:
Admiralty: Cricklewood (in the grounds of the Admiralty Charts Depot, 403–5 Edgware Road NW2).
Air Ministry: Harrow (beside HMSO Factory, Headstone Drive, Wealdstone); 'STATION Z'.
Cabinet Office: Dollis Hill (In grounds of Post Office Research Station, Brook Road, NW2); 'PADDOCK'.

These citadels in the north west suburbs were built in anticipation of the centre of London becoming unuseable early in an air war. As the war drew closer, this assumption was revised, and in February 1939 the Cabinet decided that 'to enable essential services work to be carried on during a bombardment, deep bomb-proof quarters should be provided in the central area for the five war rooms of the Cabinet, service departments, and the Home Security organisation'. The Foreign Office, who wanted thirty of their staff to be placed in such a shelter, were promised further consideration.

In the summer of 1939, with war weeks away, the Cabinet decided to start to take the first steps in constructing what is now a huge network of twelve miles of tunnels and interconnected war rooms and citadels a hundred feet below London's streets. The London Underground's tunneling consultant, Sir Horace Dalrymple-Hay, was called in to advise on schemes which might, at most, house some three thousand staff deep below ground – in addition to six hundred in the suburban citadels.

Initially, Dalrymple-Hay proposed a three-tunnel system to run deep below Whitehall, with war rooms provided in parallel twenty-five-foot diameter tunnels, and Post Office cables and other services running in a twelve-foot diameter tunnel between them. To hold all three thousand staff would require four large parallel tunnels, however, which would cost £1.8 million, and take two and a half years to construct. Many officials had grave doubts about the value of the scheme; what was the point of the deep citadels for a 'nucleus' of staff, if London were being so heavily bombarded that life on the surface was impossible? In those circumstances, they argued, it was better to disperse Whitehall departments entirely to the provinces.

In the autumn of 1939, construction began on the most

modest of Dalrymple-Hay's schemes, which provided for a single, twelve-foot tunnel to run down the length of Whitehall to provide a protected run for telephone and telegraph cables to government departments and their war rooms. A shaft was dug just south of Trafalgar Square, and the tunnel ran to the Cenotaph in Whitehall. At its northern end, small tunnels ran from the main vertical shaft to the running tunnels of the Bakerloo line underground station at Trafalgar Square. The system is still used; cables may be seen disappearing under the platforms at the station, and into these connecting tunnels.

From the northern end a short eight-foot diameter shaft ran across to link up with Craigs Court, a Whitehall cul-de-sac housing the Whitehall Post Office exchange. The main access to the Post Office Whitehall tunnel scheme is (still) from the automatic lift just inside the entrance to this exchange; a special key is inserted by engineers who have access to the Whitehall 'Deep Level' system.

The Trafalgar Square – Whitehall tunnel was used to run cables into each of the government departments' war rooms, including the Cabinet War Rooms. The cables ran through twelve-inch bore steel tubes from the basement of the government offices in Whitehall, and then through narrow five-foot shafts into the main tunnel. Much of the tunnel itself was taken up with distribution frames, on which all the cables terminated and were interconnected. Long distance lines would be fitted with 'repeaters', an old term for amplifying or balancing a trunk line.

This wartime exchange is still the centre of all special or secret communications networks for the British government. It is known as Q Whitehall, more usually abbreviated QWHI – Q is a standard letter used by the Post Office to designate a secret or defence site. It is operated twenty-four hours a day, with engineers still gaining access from the apparently orthodox lift in the Craigs Court exchange.

Another measure to protect government communications in wartime had been the construction of the 'Federal' telephone exchange in the basement of the Old War Office building in Whitehall. Federal, although linked to the public telephone system, was a private exchange with extensions restricted to ministers and chief civil servants. This 'top peoples' exchange continued in existence throughout and after the war, and remained a mystery connection within the London telephone system. Callers 'in the know' dialled FED

0101 (or 333 0101) and asked, in a prearranged manner, for the official they wanted. During the 1960s, the exchange was transferred to another former citadel in Marsham Street. Its new number became 222 8080.

The Cabinet War Rooms are perhaps the most publicly known part of the Whitehall tunnel network. They are, ironically, the least protected. It emerged after the war that all the Cabinet's and Chiefs of Staff meeting places, including Churchill's sleeping quarters, could easily have been destroyed by a few large bombs. The War Rooms are in the basement of the former HM Office of Works (now the Cabinet Office), the huge Victorian government block which stands between Whitehall and St James Park. The walls were thickened externally by adding many feet of concrete, and inside the basement a steel frame was built to support, eventually, a three-foot thick concrete roof. The Cabinet War Rooms were partially ready by early 1938 and were used by Chamberlain during the Munich crisis. Dollis Hill was ready early in 1940, for use 'as soon as there are signs of the position in Whitehall getting too hot.'

Public tours of the Cabinet War Rooms are arranged by the Department of Environment twice daily, but are confined to a relatively small part of the complex, where maps and papers from the latter stages of the war are displayed.* Long after the war, doubts emerged that the war rooms had ever been bombproof – doubts confirmed by some civil service minutes, not entirely respectful, which have survived in declassified files: In November 1942, an official at the HQ wrote to a Mr Sheepshanks of the Ministry of Home Security:

Doubts are felt as to the adequacy of the Cabinet War Rooms 'slab' to resist more than a 500 lb bomb . . . the safety of the Cabinet War Room and its illustrious inhabitants *is* a matter of importance. . .

The prevailing Whitehall view was that seven feet of concrete and steel, not three feet, was the minimum necessary. Nothing was done, and Sheepshanks was asked to comply with a request for great secrecy:

May I ask that this enquiry should be kept confidential and the fewest possible people informed? I don't want to create either distrust in the lovely slab, or despondency at the possibility of further slabbing operations.

* Applications to No 41 Sub-Ground, Treasury Chambers, SW1.

Table 8   Second World War Government citadels in London

Citadel	World War II use	Current use
PADDOCK, at (former) PO Station, Dollis Hill NW2 (200 persons)	Originally reserved for War Cabinet HQ, but later allocated to the War Office	Derelict; was used as recreation and storage space by PO staff, and considered (in 1980) as London Region northern group control – plan rejected by Labour GLC.
Station Z, HMSO Factory Headstone Drive, Wealdstone, Harrow (200 persons)	Air Ministry, including intelligence staff	Home Office Central Communications Establishment; maintains and supervises government radio facilities in London area, and has been communications centre for regional home defence HQS.
Cricklewood Citadel Admiralty Chart Depot, 403–405 Edgware Road, NW2 (200 persons)	Admiralty staff	Disused; Health and Safety Executive laboratory on top.
Curzon Street House, Curzon Street, W1 (190 persons)	Royal family and King (in 1942), War Office and General Staff of Home Forces	Headquarters of the Security Service (MI5). Only the basement and ground floor are protected.
Faraday Citadel Building, Faraday Telephone Exchange, Carter Lane EC4 (A few persons)	Post Office trunk exchange, for long distance connections; some residential accomodation for ministers	Same as WW2; Faraday trunk telephone exchange.
Montague House, Whitehall SW1 (550 persons)	War Office staff	Montague House is the Ministry of Defence Main Building; basement citadels (north and south) include the Defence Communications Centre and government telephone exchanges.

Citadel	World War II use	Current use
Admiralty Citadel, Horseguards Parade sw1 (capacity unknown)	Admiralty staff and operations centre	Same as ww2; also includes the Whitehall Commcen, housing message switching equipment.
Horseferry Road sw1 (three sections) (820 persons)	North Rotunda; South Rotunda, and 'Steel Frame' section, housed Air Ministry staff, Home Security War Room, London District Army command.	The three citadels each support one tower block of the new Department of the Environment Offices, Marsham Street. Current uses: North Rotunda houses Federal, Horseferry Tandem (p. 234) and other government exchanges. South Rotunda is Civil Service Council sports centre; 'Steel Frame' section also houses government telephone exchanges.
Cabinet War Rooms, Treasury Chambers, Storeys Gate, sw1 (about 500 persons)	Cabinet War Rooms, including residential accomodation for Churchill. Military staff accomodation on other, less well-protected, floors.	Part is a museum section open to the public; part is closed, and probably includes the Cabinet Office Briefing Room (cobra) used in civil emergencies and strikes.
South Kensington War Room, Cromwell Road sw7 (capacity unknown)	London Regional Home Security (ie civil defence) War Room	Used as storage annexe by Geological Museum, to which it is adjacent.
4 Central Buildings, Matthew Parker Street, sw1; (entrance: bunker in Broad sanctuary) (capacity unknown)	Unknown; possibly used by intelligence service (sis).	New International Conference Centre being constructed on top. Citadel houses telephone exchange for House of Commons and several government departments; has been and may again be used for communications interception and 'sigint' (eg telephone tapping).

Whatever its safety, this was the only protected government accomodation available in central London at the start of the war. The Cabinet therefore ordered the construction of a host of further citadels, all of them due to be ready during 1941. These were: the Admiralty citadel on Horseguards Parade; Montague House (now the Ministry of Defence's main building); Citadel Building at the Faraday PO trunk exchange near St Paul's Cathedral; Curzon Street House in Mayfair; and the two Rotundas and a steel frame building in Marsham Street, off Horseferry Road, Victoria (See previous page).

By the end of 1941, the London citadels could hold over three thousand staff. At the same time, the whole network became linked up, not just by cable but by using the Post Office tunnel system to allow physical passage between different War Rooms without coming up to street level. Small lift shafts and stairwells were built to each of the citadels; at the same time the main Whitehall tunnel was extended southwards from the Cenotaph, and around Parliament Square, finishing up below the Horseferry Road citadels. An emergency exit into a basement of the Westminster Hospital marks the southernmost extension of this wartime scheme. The map (p. 227) shows the final result of the scheme; huge protected citadels linked by cable and passages a hundred feet below ground. Forty years later, this network still protects the critical core of government communications from interference or disruption. In one area, below Broad Sanctuary, the tunnels widened out to fourteen feet to accomodate a teleprinter centre. Nearer the surface, a system of 'Lamson' hydraulic tubes carried documents around between the different war rooms in the Whitehall complex.

The final Whitehall tunnel was nearly a mile and a half long, with six passenger lift shafts provided. All were operating by the end of 1943. Another, one-and-a-half-mile long, tunnel was built to the east of Whitehall, in order to link together what were then the Post Office's two major London trunk exchanges: Holborn, in High Holborn, and Faraday, standing between St Pauls Cathedral and the Thames. This

---

Figure 13 Planning for a deep network of Whitehall tunnels and War Rooms began before the Second World War. Each service ministry, the Cabinet War HQ and other civil and military administrators had protected accommodation in the 'citadels' (see Table 8). A deep level tunnel and lift shafts linked each citadel. In 1950–53, new bunkers were built under Whitehall.

KEY

☐ War Rooms, Citadels

▬ Tunnel

O S Shafts (all with lifts)

Original shaft gives access to Bakerloo line tube tunnels at Charing Cross station, Trafalgar Square.

Whitehall PO Telephone exchange

Admiralty Citadel

Q Whitehall (in tunnel)

Old War Office and 'Federal'

Montague House Citadels (South and North) Now Ministry of Defence

Cabinet War Rooms

Central Buildings Citadel

Rotundas

Horseferry Rd Bldg

tunnel was for Post Office use only, and completed the scheme for deep level protection of London's telephone cables. After the war, new schemes for atomic bomb protection were to weld the two together into a vast network.

The original Holborn-Faraday tunnel ran from four shafts in the Faraday complex (including one in its 'citadel') around the west of St Pauls, and then underneath Holborn for three-quarters of a mile to the Holborn exchange shaft. Each shaft was blast- and flood-proofed. At Faraday, there were cross tunnels into the Waterloo and City underground lines, and deep below the Post Office Headquarters in St Martins-Le-Grand other shafts connected into the Central Line tunnels, and those of the Post Office's own private underground line, used to carry mail bags between sorting offices. These London underground railway tunnels could provide secure cable runs between the two deep level tunnels, and out of London in all directions. Around London too, a circumferential cable network was constructed, with provision for re-routing any damaged cables around the outskirts of London. Some time before the war ended, the government had indeed completed, as a 1942 minute promised, 'a complete underground system of accomodation and protected communications'. At the same time the public campaign for the construction of deep air raid shelters resulted in the building of eight deep level tunnel shelters, each of which was supposed to provide eight thousand bunks in which Londoners could shelter from air raids. The resistance of the Ministry of Home Security, and Sir John Anderson, to allowing the public such excellent shelter had not abated however, and even though the shelters were ready by the spring of 1942, they were not opened for general public use until July 1944.

The general form of each of the shelters is broadly similar (see Figure 5, p. 105); two parallel tunnels, each a quarter mile (425m) long and sixteen feet (5m) in diameter. The tunnels are divided into two floors, and lined all the way along with bunks. Each shelter could accomodate eight thousand people overnight. All were built below existing Northern or Central Line underground stations, with the faint hope that after the war they might form stations on a new high speed tube network. The deep level shelters were constructed in secret, and places in them were denied until 1944 to the thousands who had, eventually, been allowed to use the ordinary London tube stations for shelter.

Shortly after the shelters were finished, in April 1942, it

was decided to remove the bunks from three of them, Clapham Common, Goodge Street, and Chancery Lane. At Goodge Street, a new high speed lift was installed and it became General Eisenhower's HQ as Chief of Staff, Supreme Allied Command ('COSSAC'), and it remained the war headquarters for Eisenhower and the US Army throughout the war. Chancery Lane and Clapham Common were taken over as citadels for additional staff in the event of an anticipated rocket bombardment, and code named 'BIG BEN'. In the five remaining shelters the government accomodated US and British troops passing through London, and billeted Ministry of Works staff doing essential urgent repairs to government buildings. Eventually, a protest campaign by, amongst others, the Communist Party in South London led to the opening of the shelters; some five thousand places in each were still reserved for troops. Thus, at this late stage in the war, some 37,000 of the planned 64,000 shelter places were at last available to Londoners.

The deep tube shelters remain in being today. Each is entered through two shafts at either end of the tunnels. At the head of each tunnel shaft is a pillbox-like structure housing the lift, stairwell and ventilation equipment. Some half–dozen of these pillboxes can easily be seen along Clapham Road in south London. There were also entrance shafts, gates and stairways from the ordinary tube stations overhead, although these have now been sealed off.

After the war, Goodge Street continued to be used as a transit home for troops, and was only abandoned after a fire swept through the tunnels in 1956. At a cost of some £4 million, seven of the shelters were maintained, empty, until 1975, when an advertisement placed by the Property Services Agency appeared in London and national papers: 'Former Tube Shelters in Central London: TO BE LET.' This offered leases on the seven remaining shelters, each with a floor space of ninety-four thousand square feet (8900 m²) for 'commercial or other uses' and with the 'highest security'. A clause in the proposed lease reserved the government's right 'to resume occupation if the need arises'.

In the event, lessors were apparently only found for three of the tunnel shelters. The major use of the others has been repeatedly to provide convenient film sets for *Doctor Who* programmes and other science fiction films.

The eighth shelter, at Chancery Lane, was taken over by the Post Office in November 1949. It was the first stage in a massive programme of new underground tunnels in London. This network is discussed in Chapter 8.

Outside London, the wartime emphasis on providing protected accomodation applied to safeguarding war materiel production rather than government staffs. Underground HQs were also built for many operational service headquarters – most of which still operate from the same sites today as they were dispersed to more than forty years ago.

Plans for underground factories began to be discussed in earnest in September 1940, after the effects of air raids had begun to make an impact on production, particularly aircraft production. Such proposals were strongly resisted by the Treasury, which claimed that as much as five per cent of the national income – some £250 million – would be soaked up if all aircraft production were to be moved underground. Nevertheless, largely at Lord Beaverbrook's insistence, a number of schemes went ahead. The largest of these was the Spring Quarry at Corsham, where some fifty-four acres (2.25 million square feet or 215,000 m²) was developed. In the nuclear era, Spring Quarry has continued to have the most important role. Of the other six underground factories built for the Ministry of Aircraft Production, two (Warren Row, near Maidenhead, and Drakelow, near Kidderminster) were to become RSGs in the H bomb era. (see Table 12). One of the Ministry of Supply's factories is still in use at Henley on Thames, whilst a fourth, in Central Line Tube tunnels in east London, reverted to London Transport after the war was over.

These were merely the largest items in a huge programme of construction of underground and protected works which went on across Britain, and at British bases abroad. In 1941, Churchill's War Cabinet received a series of reports from a specially appointed Sub–Committee on Underground Chambers, otherwise known as MISC* 21. They reported that, by December 1941, no less than fifty-two underground sites had been developed. These included twenty-five air raid shelters, two Ministry of Supply Factories, the seven Aircraft Factories, the RAF's bomb store at Chilmark, Wilts, army munitions stores in the four Corsham quarries, and sixteen Admiralty projects. Five of these were underground oil stores, and the

---

* For Miscellaneous (Cabinet) Committee.

remainder were for munitions. Most of these projects are listed in Appendix 4.

The Board of Trade reported that over one hundred other sites had been inspected, including disused mines, quarries and railway tunnels but many suffered from problems of humidity and poor access. Although many of the underground tunnels in use in 1941 were intended as air raid shelters, these had only been built in the face of considerable resistance to a 'universal policy of deep shelter'. As is clear from the list, almost all of the shelters were constructed in easily excavated chalk or sandstone, and no shelters were considered elsewhere except in already existing tunnels. The policy was 'not to make deep shelters, but only to provide them for certain essential workers who might otherwise leave their localities.'

Amongst the more spectacular schemes was the conversion of the Manod Slate Quarries, Blaenau Ffestiniog, into a deep underground store for the pictures of the National Gallery. Inside the caverns from which Welsh slates had been quarried in the nineteenth century, the Ministry of Works erected air-conditioned brick and concrete warehouses, which were fitted out with frames to hold the pictures. The entrance tunnel was widened to allow either lorries or narrow gauge rail trucks to carry goods inside the hill. In a remarkable display of bureaucratic inertia, the Manod Quarry has continued to be allocated to this purpose in the 1980s – clearly, without any review of the purpose of a policy of dispersing arts treasures in the nuclear age. The quarry is one of the most spectacular government sites in Britain, being approached only by four miles of private road which winds up into bleak moorland and mountain and abandoned quarry workings.

The government showed almost as much resistance to the construction of underground factories as they had to deep air raid shelters. The Treasury, which had opposed most of the proposals for siting factories underground, eventually won the day, as costs for most of the schemes turned out to be far in excess of original estimates. The principal offender in this respect was the Spring Quarry aircraft factory at Corsham, which by the end of the war, had cost over £19 million – including the construction of surface hostels for some eight thousand workers. The initial proposal to move some of the capacity of the Bristol Aeroplane Company into a smaller Corsham quarry, Monks Park, had been put at £1 million, and the Spring Quarry scheme at £2.3 million. This was later

Plates 22 & 23 At huge expense, the Corsham quarries were made habitable during the war. During the 1950s, the largest, Spring Quarry, became the Central Government War HQ. Plans and photographs of a neighbouring quarry show endless corridors and underground space divided into 'districts' of several acres each.

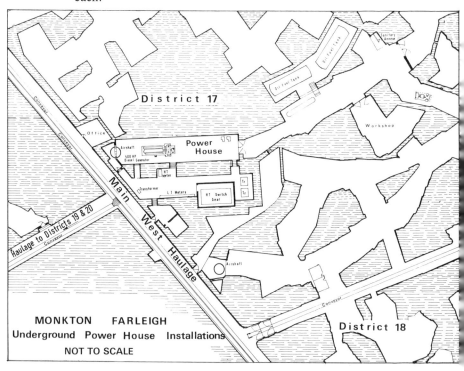

District 17

Power House

500 HP Diesel Generator

Office

Airshaft

Transformer

L.T. Meters

HT Switch Gear

Workshop

Oil Fuel Tank

Oil Fuel Tank

Sanitary Annex

Tr

Tr

Haulage to Districts 19 & 20

Conveyor

Main West Haulage

Airshaft

Conveyor

District 18

MONKTON   FARLEIGH
Underground Power House Installations
NOT TO SCALE

admitted by some of the scheme's proponents to have been a gross 'guesstimate'. In 1943, the Commons Public Accounts Committee held a special enquiry into the scheme, and were told that it was a product of the concern felt at the time of the blitz about protecting industrial production in the event of invasion. They were told that the scheme would have been turned down if it had been proposed later, in 1941 or 1942.

Corsham was not the only underground project to face difficulties. The Drakelow tunnels suffered from sandstone falls, and the Dudley Caverns were never put into productive use.

By the end of the war, the RAF had expanded from one to at least ten underground stores, most of which are now abandoned; but most of the navy's underground ammunition dumps and oil stores remain in use; several, such as Immingham, Harwich, and Invergordon, are the targets of Soviet bomb attacks in the *Hard Rock* exercise. Most of the air raid shelters and tunnels from the Second World War have long since been abandoned. In principle, the Home Office and Scottish Office were willing to provide grants for their upkeep until 1972; in practice, few councils took any interest in the preservation or maintenance of the shelters.

Military headquarters are in a different category. Almost all of the Second World War headquarters of the RAF and the Royal Navy are still in operation as NATO HQs in the nuclear age. The primary control centre for Polaris submarines, the Royal Navy and the Eastern Atlantic NATO command, is Northwood in Middlesex, the former HQ of RAF Coastal Command. Its two subordinate centres, at Pitreavie Castle, near Dunfermline in Fife, and Mount Batten near Plymouth, bear much the same relationship to Northwood as they did in the 1940s. Not all of the HQs concerned have been modernised since then. RAF High Wycombe, the wartime centre of Bomber Command, is now the RAF's principal wartime headquarters, coordinating both Strike Command and the UK's air defence. Only in 1982 was authority given to commence building a new 'Permanent Static War HQ' on an adjacent site. The nerve centre of Britain's nuclear deterrent in the 60s was thus the same underground space as controlled 'Bomber' Harris's attacks on German cities. Caught between tradition, inertia, and the inability of the British economy to finance underground schemes of the grandeur adopted by the US, civil defence and military planners have in fact been very conservative.

Just as the ideas of Regional Seats of Government, and

crown-appointed Commissioners was born of earlier eras, so the schemes to move the seat of government out of London to the west has always featured in the shadows; the ultimate Second World War scheme, many of its details still kept secret, was known glumly as the 'Black Move'. Some plans, such as those for the 'Maintenance of the machinery of government under rocket bombardment' will not be open for public inspection until the next century.

Many ministries were dispersed during 1940; the Royal Navy to Bath, for example (where it still occupies the requisitioned Empire Hotel and much else), and the Air Ministry to Harrogate. The basic government department evacuation scheme was for a move to a zone around Stratford upon Avon and Worcester. The BBC had already got an emergency control operating nearby at Wood Norton near Evesham. Each ministry had its own town with communications networks pre-installed; the Air Ministry, 'Longfellow', at Worcester; the War Office, 'Chaucer' at Droitwich; and the Royal Navy, 'Duke' at Malvern.

One major difference in today's plans is that the House of Commons membership is not included in any 'Black Moves'. The House of Commons continued to sit during the Second World War; in the Third, there will be neither place nor time for any anachronistic pretence at maintaining democratic structures. The 'machinery of government' will be all.

8
Nuclear citadels

The British government's response to the threat of nuclear warfare came in two massive waves during the 1950s. The first Soviet atomic bomb test of September 1949 sent a spasm through the establishment, and a range of projects for government and military protection were established. Because of changes in military technology, most of them were useless for their original purpose in rather less than ten years. Another spasm of military preparation greeted the less unexpected Soviet H bomb test of 1955. At the same time, Britain began expending huge sums on acquiring her own atomic weapons, and the means of their delivery. The two projects consumed a not insignificant part of the national income in the 1950s and 1960s. Most of the money, and all of the key decisions, for both programmes were taken in complete secrecy, a feature no less evident in recent developments – of the Polaris missile system, for instance.

In the first wave of military preparations, there were three major schemes. The first involved relocating all British radar stations and anti-aircraft gun control centres in well-protected accomodation, often deep underground. The second scheme involved greatly extending the protected communications networks in central London, in the hope that the wartime network of citadels would also prove resistant to an atomic attack. The third scheme provided for regional military and civil defence preparations, and protected War Rooms were built both for military commands and for civil defence regional offices.

The A bomb precautions of the early 1950s were derived, by way of extension, from what had been done in the Second World War. The second wave of 1950s citadel construction took on a quite different character. The H bomb had created real despair, from which the idea of civil defence on the Second World War pattern never recovered.

Regional Seats of Government were created and brought into operation, together with schemes like *Backbone*, to try and assure national telecommunications after an attack. (see Chapter 9). Standing at the centre of the new communications network was the Corsham complex. All the evidence suggests that by 1959 Hawthorn had been selected to be the wartime national seat of government, and such it fundamentally remains. Given the weight of nuclear fire power that can now be brought to bear on any kind of fixed national or military command and control site, there can be little doubt that Hawthorn will be destroyed if the Soviet Union so wishes. In such circumstances, British policy seems to be accept this, but to endeavour to disperse as many separate government and command centres as possible.

The postwar rundown of military preparedness began, in a dilatory way, to turn round in early 1947. In the summer of 1948, two US Air Force bomber groups came back for a 'temporary' stay, shortly after the Berlin blockade began. During 1948 and 1949, the Home Office, together with the Ministry of Defence, made a renewed survey of tunnels and caves, and the Ministry of Supply sought proposals for restoring the radar and anti-aircraft networks to working order. The Royal Observer Corps had been re-instituted in 1947. By 1949, the Home Office had also made an assessment of new civil defence requirements 'in the event of war'. War planning was back in business.

The most striking feature of the 1950–55 period was the construction of over one hundred bunkers, many of them some way (40–50 feet or 12–15m) underground, or with walls fourteen feet (4m) thick – the vast majority of which were redundant within five years of being built. The major scheme of this kind was the RAF's 'Rotor' plan, which involved seventy-one radar and control stations, six of them specially built. The Rotor plan began in 1951, and was supervised by the Marconi company. Almost all of the radar stations of the 1940s were given protected accomodation which was constructed to a small number of standard designs.

The overall map of the Rotor system as it stood in 1955 is shown in Figure 14. In February that year, Air Minister Lord de L'Isle told Parliament in the Air Estimates that:

Hundreds of new (radar) installations have been built and vital parts of the system have been put deep underground and

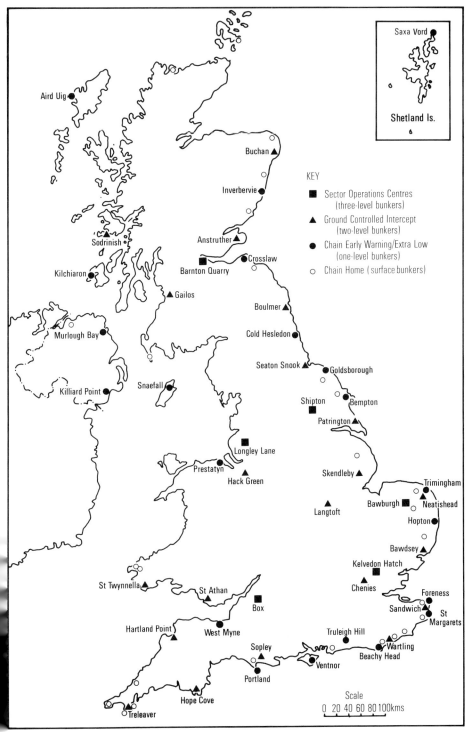

Figure 14 The Rotor Network.

Table 9　Rotor stations

Seventy-five stations went underground or were strengthened during the 1952–55 RAF *Rotor* plan for a new radar system. Three years later, three quarters of the system was obsolete. Rotor used a standard design of bungalow to conceal the entrances to a tunnel leading to the underground bunker. All major east coast sites were built in this way in case of A bomb attack (they could withstand a near miss with a Hiroshima–sized bomb). On the west coast, the bunkers were built more economically, on the surface, but using the same thicknesses (8–14 feet: 2.5–4m) of concrete. This table lists the current uses of the major stations shown in Figure 14. Each bunker cost between £¼ million and £1 million to build in the early 50s; an Air Ministry spokesman later explained that 'the advent of rockets caused a change in policy'.

Rotor station	*Current use*
Saxa Vord (Shetland)	RAF radar station
Buchan	RAF radar station
Inverbervie	Bunker disused; US Navy microwave station
Anstruther	Scottish Northern Zone HQ
Barnton Quarry (Edinburgh)	Scottish Central Control since 1964 (Scottish Regional Seat of Government, 1961–64)
Crosslaw	Bunker disused; Civil Aviation Authority (CAA) radio station
Boulmer	RAF radar station; sector operations centre
Cold Hesledon	Bunker derelict; communications relay
Seaton Snook	Bunker derelict
Bempton	Bunker derelict
Shipton	SRHQ 21
Patrington	RAF station; radar removed but site maintained
Skendelby	SRHQ 31
Trimingham	Guardhouse bungalow in private occupation
Neatishead	RAF radar station; sector operations centre
Bawburgh	SRHQ 41
Hopton	Bunker derelict; was civil defence centre in 60s

Rotor station	Current use
Bawdsey	RAF missile station
Foreness	Unknown
Sandwich	Civil Aviation Authority radar station (Ash)
St Margarets	Site demolished
Kelvedon Hatch	SRHQ 51
Chenies	RAF Strike Command radio station
Wartling	Site for sale (1982)
Beachy Head	Bunker dismantled; coastguard station
Truleigh Hill	Home Office radio station
Ventnor	CAA radar station; Isle of Wight War HQ
Sopley	Army War HQ for 2 Signal Group
Portland	Bunker maintained by Royal Navy
Box	HQ Defence Communications Network
Hope Cove	SRHQ 72 (Bunker at Bolt Head)
Treleaver	Bunker derelict; guardhouse bungalow in private occupation
Hartland Point	RAF radar station
St Athan	RAF airfield: bunker dismantled
West Myne	Unknown
St Twynells	Bunker derelict
Langtoft	Storehouse in private occupation
Hack Green	SRHQ 101 (under construction)
Prestatyn	Unknown
Longley Lane	UK Warning and Monitoring Organisation Western Sector HQ; wartime national HQ
Killiard Point	RAF radar station (RAF Bishopscourt)
Snaefell	Unknown
Murlough Bay	Unknown
Gailes	Radar station (CAA/RAF, Dundonald)
Scarinish	Unknown
Aird Uig	RAF signals unit

protected by massive thicknesses of concrete.

The extent of the work on any one underground installation is not much less than that involved in building a new Tube station.

Whilst his references to the number of stations involved may have been exaggerated, his appreciation of the thickness of concrete walls was not. When the Home Office asked for an extra floor to be constructed on top of the former RAF Sector Operations Centre at Shipton, north of York (now SRHQ 21), workers had first to cut access hatches through fourteen feet (4m) of concrete.

Besides Rotor, convoys of mobile radars were built. Their code name was 'Vast'.

The Rotor stations shown on the map are of seven types. The most important were the Sector Operations Centres (SOC) which coordinated fighters and radar plots across a wide area. Ground Controlled Intercept (GCI) stations were responsible for guiding fighters to their targets. Four sets of ordinary radars were responsible for detecting these targets: an eastern and western network of 'Chain Home' stations (CH(E) and CH(W)); a low level detection network, 'Chain Home Extra Low' (CHEL) and a specialised long range set of 'Chain Early Warning' radars (CEW).

Depending on the modernity of the equipment, the importance of the station, and its location, a one, two, or even

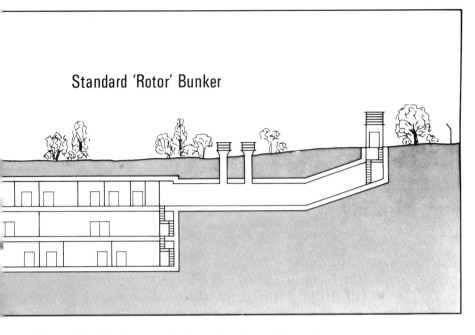

Figure 15 The layout of a Rotor bunker. Although the presence of radar scanners identified most of the stations, Sector Operations Centres such as this were extremely unobtrusive, with an innocent looking bungalow concealing the entrance.

three storey underground bunker was built. The more exotic station design was called an 'R3'; here, the bunker was completely underground, and access was obtained via an innocuous looking bungalow/guardhouse – built to a standard plan – at the entrance to each station.

In general, each of the six SOCs were equipped with three-level bunkers, deep underground. The GCI stations had two-level bunkers; on the east and south east coasts, these were completely underground, whilst on the west and southwest coasts they were of the same construction, but the concrete blockhouses were built above ground. The CHEL and CEW stations had similar, single-level bunkers, whilst the ageing Chain Home equipment used only refurbished high explosive bomb resistant accomodation that had been retained since the Second World War.

Almost as soon as the Rotor stations had gone underground the availability of a new British radar, Type 80, meant that, to start with, all the old Chain Home stations could be dispensed with; Type 80s, fitted at each GCI stations, more than covered the same range with much greater precision. In a

1955 exercise, it was also observed that it was much easier for a radar controller to guide an intercepting aircraft when directly watching the radar display. Within two years, all of the huge and massively protected underground Sector Operations Centres were dispensed with. The CHEL and CEW chains went too. By 1960, the radar control system had slimmed to just five major stations – Boulmer, Patrington, Neatishead, Bawdsey, and Wartling in Sussex. Six other radars, including Saxa Vord, Buchan, Gailes (also known as Dundonald), Staxton Wold, Killiard Point (now known as Bishopscourt) and Hartland Point in Devon reported to the new control centres, known as Master Radar Stations.

Thus at the end of the 1950s, as the Home Office was searching for new underground sites for their expanded regional HQs, a great deal of suitable property became available. Barnton Quarry in Edinburgh was released in 1961 to become the Scottish RSG, Hope Cove (actually located at Bolt Head, but the RAF living quarters had been at Hope Cove) became RSG7. The Box SOC, in the Hawthorn complex near Bath was developed (and renamed RAF Rudloe Manor after a country house some distance away) as the major communication centre in the new network. All the other former SOCs found new uses, together with many of the slightly smaller GCI type stations. Anstruther provides Scotland's Northern Zone HQ, Shipton (former SOC) is SRHQ21, Skendelby (former GCI), SRHQ31, Bawburgh (former SOC) SRHQ41, Kelvedon Hatch, a very deeply buried former SOC, is the London Region SRHQ51.

Protected accomodation was also built, or refurbished for other control centres involved in Britain's air defence. Fighter Command HQ and the Air Defence Operations Centre (ADOC) remained in its 1940s underground site, Bentley Priory, an estate on a high ridge overlooking northwestern London, near Stanmore in Middlesex. There were also protected HQs for the four main groups in Fighter Command; No. 10 Group was at Box, as it had been during the war – its accomodation is now used by the Defence Communications Network. No 11 Group was at Uxbridge, from where much of the Battle of Britain had been directed. The RAF station there remains in charge of the Military Air Traffic Organisation, and also accomodates, underground, a major United States telephone communications centre (the 'Autovon' system); but the old wartime operations centre has now been restored as a Battle of Britain museum. No 12 Group's protected HQ at Watnall, near Nottingham, now appears derelict, and only a regional forecasting centre of the Meteorological Office remains on the site. No 13 Group's former HQ at Ouston, east of New-castle has been passed to the army, and the site has become AFHQI. There were two other Group centres – No 9 was at Barton Hall, near Preston, now a Civil Aviation Authority training centre, and – for a short while, a No 14 Group was based at Inverness. No 15 Group (of Coastal Command) was given a protected headquarters in Liverpool.

The substantial late 1950s run down in RAF defensive organ-isation followed the new NATO 'tripwire' policy; the only re-sponse Britain was going to be able to make to aggression for many years to come was to launch a nuclear strike. The run down in fighter airfields and the radar system also affected the army, whose Royal Artillery anti-aircraft units, in some twenty-seven groups across Britain, had been equipped with automated 3·7 inch guns after the war. Each 'ack-ack' group had been given a protected headquarters located at a suitable army camp. These HQS, like the RAF's Rotor centres, were also built to a standard pattern – a one or two storey concrete blockhouse, above ground, whose most distinctive feature was two communications masts to carry HF and VHF aerials adjacent to the blockhouse. Like many emergency communi-cations installations, these masts were equipped with plat-forms at the top, in this case unique crossed walkways, so that inexperienced fitters and non-steeplejacks could install or repair aerials after bomb or blast damage. The capacity of these centres could vary from four thousand to fifteen thou-sand square feet (380–1400 m^2), depending on the importance and complexity of their work.

Table 10 (p. 244) shows the disposition of the various anti-aircraft groups around Britain, and the location of their headquarters (where known). In 1955, the predominance of high speed jet aircraft and the coming of missiles, which were then presumed to be likely to take over every military job, resulted in the scrapping of the entire anti-aircraft network and the disbandment of the gun units. That created a further pool of nuclear bunkers which were no longer needed for their original purpose. At least six became local authority bunkers, and one (Lansdown at Bath) was handed over to the Royal Observer Corps. On a more significant level, one (Ullenwood near Cheltenham) became an SRHQ (No 71) and the two which had been intended to control the northern and southern ack-ack batteries protecting London were passed to the Metropolitan police, and are now used as their nuclear war HQS.

Table 10 Anti-aircraft control rooms 1951–1955
The construction of nearly 30 surface concrete blockhouses for the army's anti-aircraft gun control centres was another defence preparation for atomic war that rapidly became redundant – and created a further abundant supply of bunkers.

Anti aircraft zone	Control centre	Current use
National HQ (2 AA Group)	Stanmore	RAF reserve air defence operations centre
London north	Lippettshill	Metropolitan Police War HQ
London south	Merstham	Metropolitan Police War HQ
Thames & Medway	Fort Bridgewood, Chatham	Former SRC for London
Dover	Unknown	
Nottingham & Derby	Unknown	
Sheffield	Conisbrough	Derelict
Humber	Wawne	Humberside CC War HQ
Liverpool & Manchester	Frodsham	Cheshire CC
Birmingham & Coventry	Wylde Green	West Midlands CC War HQ
Swansea	West Cross	West Glamorgan CC War HQ
Cardiff & Newport	Wenallt	South Glamorgan CC War HQ
Cheltenham & Brockworth	Ullenwood	SRHQ 71
Bristol & Bath	Lansdown	UKWMO Southern sector HQ
Plymouth	Unknown	
Southampton & Portsmouth	Fort Nelson, Portsmouth	Dismantled
Leeds	Birkenshaw	Fire Brigade HQ
Tyne	Unknown	
Tees	Unknown	
Clyde	Craigiehall	Army HQ Scotland
Forth	Torrance House, East Kilbride	Western Zone HQ (Scotland)
Shetlands & Scapa Flow	Unknown	
Belfast & Derry	Lisburn	Belfast UKWMO group HQ
Leighton Buzzard	Unknown	
Norwich	Unknown	
Barrow	Unknown	
Pembroke	Unknown	
Falmouth	Unknown	
Portland	Ridgeway Hill, Weymouth	Royal Navy HQ

As the list of Rotor sites (p. 238) shows, the final effect of the early 1950s boom in protected military accomodation was to leave so many nuclear bunkers surplus that many have passed into private hands. In 1981, for example, the former SOC at Wartling, Sussex, which had closed in 1964, came onto the property market for the second time. It had become a little bit run down, and was priced at £28,500 – an enthusiastic Sussex coast estate agent stressed in advertising literature that it was a 'perfect country retreat', adding that 'the deep underground shelter or tunnel, formerly part of the RAF radar station would provide excellent storage. Built of concrete it was constructed for active war usage.'

Although such installations as radar stations and AA gun control centres were of prime importance to air defence, they were by no means the only organisations to 'go underground' or disappear into bunkers. A War Office 'Secret' minute of November 1951 (now declassified) comments that 'the question of protected accomodation for (army) headquarters has been studied . . . the overall cost of the protection required is in excess of two million pounds.' The paper asked for urgent progress on four south-east England HQs: the three commands, East Anglia (Colchester), South Eastern (Aldershot) and London District, and 1 AA Group's HQ at Glenthorne, Stanmore, close to RAF Bentley Priory. These were to cost £182,000 – suggesting that the overall programme would have included about forty such sites.

Other massive steel–reinforced blockhouses were built, for example at Boddington, near Cheltenham, for a Tape Relay Centre for the army and now used in the Defence Communication Network for all three services. The site was presumably chosen because of the old wartime plan to disperse the War Office staff to the Cheltenham area – and the new move of the GCHQ intelligence centre to the town. At Rothwell Haigh, near the village of Robin Hood south of Leeds, a smaller but similarly massive blockhouse was built to house a switching centre for the RAF; it only recently closed. On the same site were built a new Post Office repeater station to interconnect to trunk cables, and a regional electricity Board emergency control room. This would be one of the Board's dispersed and protected regional emergency control centres (see Chapter 10).

*

The major communications project of the first half of the 50s, however, was the massive extension of the London deep level tunnel system and the construction of three large underground trunk exchanges: *Kingsway*, below Holborn in London, *Anchor*, below Colmore Lodge in Birmingham; and *Guardian*, below Piccadilly in Manchester. A plan for a fourth such exchange in Glasgow was apparently mooted but never proceded with.

The London Post Office deep level tunnel scheme was also accompanied by the construction of a new set of remotely controlled floodgates for the London underground. Both projects took until 1957–58 to complete, by which time the advent of the Soviet H bomb had made the protection they afforded a little futile. In the earlier A bomb era, however, a Hiroshima or Nagasaki type of weapon exploding at ground level would perhaps have left the deep level tunnel system intact; this at least was the hope. A postwar Home Office manual on civil defence protection suggested that 'shelters constructed to provide protection (against standard five hundred or one thousand lb bombs) . . . should normally be capable of being strengthened to provide protection against atomic attack.'

The digging of the Post Office London tunnels began in 1951, after some fifteen months of urgent planning. The first phase of the scheme was to construct the underground telephone exchange, *Kingsway*, in the citadel and shelter tunnels which had been built below the Chancery Lane tube station. At the same time, another shaft was dug in Whitehall Gardens, a street no longer in use immediately to the west of the present Ministry of Defence Headquarters. The MOD offices, then known as the New Government Offices, were still being completed, on top of two wartime citadels, Montague House south and north. This shaft was used for extending the Whitehall tunnel network both around Whitehall, and to link it directly to the Holborn tunnels and Kingsway telephone exchange. A map of the current system Figure 16 (p. 25) shows how this was done, by driving a shaft from Holborn through Covent Garden to link up with the Whitehall tunnel at Trafalgar Square.

By 1954, a basic network was near completion. The Whitehall network of bomb proof tunnels and citadels was linked to the major trunk exchanges at Faraday (Citadel), *Kingsway*, 'Trunk Control North' at Judd Street near Kings Cross, and the Museum telephone exchange (site of the present Post

Office Tower). *Kingsway* itself went into service in October 1954. With a permanent staff of one hundred and fifty, it connected over thirteen thousand long distance lines. It had its own 1·5 MW generator, and oil supplies for six weeks' operation (22,000 gallons) stored in the tunnels. All lines to and from the exchange ran via the deep level tunnels, and through them to the underground or Post Office railways. Four extra tunnels were dug under buildings to the south of High Holborn to accomodate automatic switching equipment. By the time *Kingsway* was in full operation, it was the major long distance exchange in the British telephone system, switching between 1·5 and 2 million calls a week. It has its own artesian well for water, food supplies, canteen and emergency accomodation.

The secrecy of the new government project did not last long – a report of the 'Secret network of tunnels' appeared on the front page of the *Daily Express* in September 1951. The article accurately listed four tunnels being dug for *Kingsway*. The four – two in Furnival Street, one behind Staple Inn Court, and others opposite Southampton Buildings in Holborn – are all still in use to provide goods lifts, ventilation, oil inlets and exhaust outlets for the underground exchange, leaving the area littered with a remarkable, but discreet, collection of clandestine technical workings well blended into their surroundings. The main entrance (plate 32) remains unmarked and unremarkable, as though it were a goods entrance for adjacent shops and offices.

The *Express* reported some official Post Office comments on the tunnels:

a depth of one hundred feet underground gives the maximum atom blast and radiation protection in the central London area.

The Post Office claimed that they were:

only concerned to a certain extent, because telephone lines would be required in the tunnels . . . I am not allowed to say much more. It is work in connection with defence.

Which was more than a slight misrepresentation of the Post Office's involvement.

The government was rather more concerned when a second article appeared three days later describing the second shaft being dug to build more tunnels under Whitehall. At 10.15 the same day, a secret meeting was called by the Cabinet Office, attended by two Commanders from the Security Service (MI5), together with Post Office and Ministry of Works officials. They discussed issuing a D Notice, or a confidential warning to editors, or merely a suitably misleading press release from the Post Office. The problem was particularly severe because the public might get the (correct) idea that the government was building deep shelters in Whitehall for itself whilst refusing the public any such protection. The minutes of the secret committee, known only as MISC 379 observed:

It would be embarrassing to the Government if the public got the impression that deep shelters were being constructed. Either the public would think that the Government were out to protect their own skins and those of their immediate servants; or the public would assume that the shelters were intended for public use in time of war and would be disappointed when they found they were not.

After experiences of government attitudes to public deep shelters in the Second World War, the 'public' might have a more cynical reaction. The minutes added:

The Home Office in particular would be embarrassed because Government policy generally was that no significant shelter construction could be undertaken at present because of lack of resources.

It was ever thus. There was also the problem that an enemy, knowing details of where 'the British government was constructing underground accomodation' could allocate 'his scientists . . . to constructing bombs especially designed to penetrate so far.' The prudent enemy might have imagined that such accomodation would be under Whitehall anyway.

An MI5 investigation of the journalist and his sources came up with no leads beyond a report that he had had drinks in a pub with a number of those working on the *Kingsway* site. Severe security precautions were therefore instituted to try and prevent leakage about another phase of the project known as 'Post Office Scheme 3245'. This involved the construction of another shaft in Horseguards Parade and the Mall (for which the Trooping the Colour ceremony had to be moved). The Scheme started in October 1951, and was to involve some four to five hundred workmen for several years. A second meeting of MISC 397 noted:

Details of the existing network of Post Office tunnels, with which the proposed new tunnels would be linked, had been published together with explanatory diagrams soon after the war. It would therefore be possible to guess with some accuracy at the possible direction of the new tunnels, even though they would not run (from A to B). But the information which it was most important to safeguard was the use to which some portions of these tunnels would be put, and this would not be obvious until the equipment engineers got to work . . . an astute journalist had only to ask one or two questions of different workmen to learn enough to piece together a fairly accurate picture of the tunneling system.

Only about a third of these tunnels were in fact to contain Post Office equipment, although 'this would lend authenticity to the official version of the purpose of the tunnels'. The Post Office prepared a press release, which falsely stated that the whole project was just a set of cable tunnels:

The shafts and tunnels being driven in several parts of London are being constructed for the Post Office. Experience has demonstrated the advantage of using deep tunnels for Post Office cables in congested street areas. . . A tunnel of this type was provided along Wood Street as long ago as 1925, and some years later another was constructed along Holborn.

A final sentence referred to the need to protect 'vital communications' in the 'present defence situation' and the installation of 'terminal equipment associated with the cables'.

Nothing further was published about the Whitehall tunnels through an article suggesting that the government was indeed building itself an atom bomb proof citadel appeared in the *Daily Worker* on 8 September 1951.

In 1980, I was personally able to explore much of the system of Post Office cable tunnels and see what in fact had been constructed. There has been much speculation about just what lay 'beneath the city streets', as Peter Laurie's book put it. My explorations were not authorised by the Post Office, who nevertheless took no action when they were reported* – save to suggest, untruthfully, that perhaps my trips had all taken place in a photographic studio.

There are more than ten miles of the basic cable tunnels and they are impressive. But, apart from the sections under the Whitehall area, they house only cables – with occasional large chambers in the vicinity of shafts or elsewhere, for 'repeater' boxes, amplifiers, and other interconnections. There are toilets and rest rooms, but no underground switch-rooms or dormitories (except *Kingsway*). The Post Office network, as such, is only for the cables.

Access to the network is via shafts inside the adjacent

* *New Statesman*, 18/25 December 1980.

exchanges, or via a very few shafts coming into subways below ordinary streets. Such subways are at Bethnal Green, Waterloo, the Mall and Maida Vale. Anyone going into the system is warned by notices that they should hold a 'deep level pass'. Large lifts at the major exchanges can carry drums of cables and other equipment down the necessary eighty to one hundred feet. At some sites, small, specially-built electric trucks wait to move the equipment around, plugged into their battery chargers. There is no permanent presence in the tunnels, only the day shift of staff installing new cables and maintaining the network. It is quiet and carefully ventilated; at some seven or eight points, there are frequent rumbles as tube trains pass some distance overhead. The Post Office tunnels are the deepest of any of London's underground networks.

The use of the deep level network has eventually proved a cost effective way of connecting tables where tunnels already existed. In the 1960s and 1970s, the Post Office made significant additions to the system, both in London and in Manchester. Some of the tunnels have been filled to capacity, such as the original wartime tunnel along Holborn, and other tunnels have provided new routes between exchanges. A general view of the tunnels is on p. 108.

It was not possible to explore south of Trafalgar Square, and consequently an exact contemporary description of the Whitehall part of the system after the war cannot be given. A function of the Whitehall shafts may simply have been to remove spoil as the Post Office tunnels went north from Trafalgar Square. There is today a ventilation plant built into the east wall of the Duke of York's Steps on the Mall, which appears to be associated with these postwar extensions; it does not however ventilate or connect to the short run of Post Office tunnel which goes to the Duke of Yorks Steps and finishes outside the Institute of Contemporary Arts. (As Peter Laurie has noted already, this ventilation plant may be inspected in operation from the men's toilet inside the ICA!).

The British government did not, it seems, try to follow the US example of constructing citadels below hundreds of feet of hard rock. As the previous chapter made clear, of course, the American predisposition for very deep shelters was based on

Figure 16   The Post Office (now British Telecom) network of deep level cable tunnels under central London. Most were built to give protection against A bombs during the 1950s.

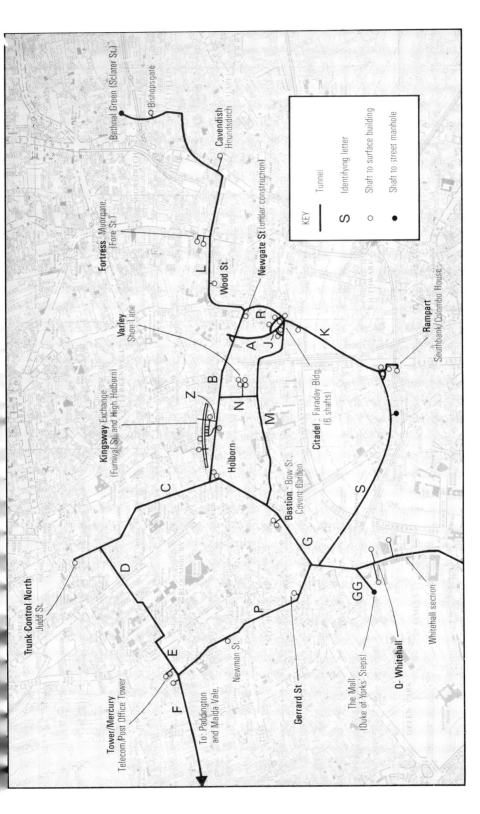

an (accurate) hypothesis that a hydrogen bomb might shortly be developed whose super explosive force might be sufficient to knock out, or even vaporise, shelters a mere hundred feet below ground. In this respect, the British government appears to have been completely deficient in intelligence and foresight, and as wasteful of public money as it had been in the air defence programmes described earlier. The United States was by 1950 already well known to be pressing on with the development of hydrogen bombs, whilst the unexpected 1949 Soviet test should have served notice that the 'gap' in military development of nuclear weaponry was much less than had been anticipated. Whether or not the US Chiefs of Staff communicated to their British counterparts their intention to build very deep shelters, it seems remarkable that the government should in 1950 have authorised the construction of an extended central London citadel which could not be expected to function securely in only a few years' time.

That was precisely what happened. The Soviet H bomb test of 1955 resulted in a second spasm of government defence preparations, and the early 1950s scheme for a London citadel was replaced by another (larger but not deeper) sanctuary ninety miles west at Hawthorn.

In the London scheme, the basic principle was to provide a Whitehall citadel which could accomodate several thousand essential staff (in the wartime citadels and some new tunnels); they would communicate with the outside world via the Post Office cable system to which they were interconnected at the northern end of Whitehall. If need be, the same tunnels, running several miles north, east (and eventually west) of Central London could provide emergency exit routes for the inhabitants, if London above their heads had been levelled by atomic bombs. In 1953–54, extensions ran out to Bethnal Green (tunnel L), Southbank exchange near Waterloo (tunnel K), and to Paddington and Maida Vale (tunnel H). A new series of tunnels, not this time primarily intended for civil defence purposes, began in 1960, when a new tunnel ran under Fleet Street to Trafalgar Square (tunnels M and N) and from Trafalgar Square to the newly constructed Post Office tower, providing a direct link to it from Q Whitehall.

A 1966 project (tunnel R) provided a bypass to the east of St Pauls; at the same time a new shaft was dug opposite St Pauls tube station, in anticipation of the new telecommunications centre now being built there. The last tunnel to be dug, tunnel S, provided a second connection from the South-bank exchange and the new Columbo House London Main Switching Centre. By 1980, over one thousand miles of cable ran in these twelve miles of seven-foot wide tunnels. In 1967, the tunnels were taken off the secret list and the D Notice list of prohibitions and a year later the press were briefly shown round part of the system. Overall, there are nearly forty shafts giving access to the system, a dozen of them with lifts.

The concept of the tunnel network as part of Fortress London seems to have been prevalent in Post Office thinking, and the names given to new trunk exchanges of the 60s and early 70s which were gradually connected to the tunnels reflected this medievally-inspired outlook. After *Citadel* and *Kingsway* came *Bastion* at Covent Garden, *Fortress* at Moorgate, and *Rampart* at Southbank (Waterloo). All were connected via the deep level tunnels, although built on the surface and without any form of bomb protection. However one of the London trunk exchanges, Colombo House in Blackfriars Road, was secretly strengthened by building massive steel girders into the building's framework in 1977. Despite the anachronistic nature of this precaution, the defence nature of the work was kept secret by getting different contractors to reinforce each separate floor of the building.

In the 1970s, the reorganisation and expansion of the London telephone system shifted many long distance connections to seven very large 'Sector Switching Centres' around the outskirts of the metropolis, and the key role of the central London tunnels and exchanges diminished. *Kingsway*, in particular, is apparently now no longer functioning as a trunk exchange.

The map of the Post Office tunnels (p. 251) shows the final development of the network, stretching from Bethnal Green in the east, to Maida Vale in the west, and from Euston to Waterloo. Its scale and resilience is an impressive reminder of the scope and secrecy of government planning.

As *Kingsway* was completed in 1954, work began on two other deep underground exchanges, Manchester *Guardian* and Birmingham *Anchor*. *Guardian*, one hundred and twelve feet (34m) below ground, cost £4 million to dig in the 1950s. There had been no previous workings there. The main tunnel, one thousand feet long and twenty-five feet wide (300m by 7m), lies below buildings in Back George Street, linking up to an anonymous and unmarked surface building containing the entrance lifts and ventilator shafts. There are also access shafts in the *Rutherford* telephone exchange in George Street. *Guardian* came off the secret list in 1968 at the same time as its London and Birmingham sisters. Its purpose, it was then explained, was to resist a Hiroshima-sized twenty kiloton atom bomb, and preserve essential communications links even if the centre of Manchester had been flattened. Manchester, too, has a deep level tunnel system, running east and west from *Guardian*. A mile long (1.3km) tunnel runs west to Salford, and a thousand-yard (700m) tunnel runs to Lockton Close in Ardwick, where a modernised ventilator building marks the south eastern extension of the Manchester deep level tunnels.

In the event of an attack warning, *Guardian*'s main entrance shaft was to be sealed by a thirty-five-ton concrete slab which could be positioned over the entrance. Staff could escape either by using built-in hydraulic jacks to lift the slab (if covered with debris) some weeks after attack, or via the deep level tunnels to Ardwick and Salford. Emergency stores contained six weeks' of food rations, and like *Kingsway*, *Guardian* had its own artesian well, generators, fuel tanks, and artificial windows and scenery painted on to rest room walls.

All the exchanges were built in complete secrecy, under Emergency Powers. After the leakages concerning the London tunnels, all building staff working on the Birmingham and Manchester projects were security vetted to prevent leaks.

Birmingham *Anchor* was built at the same time below the city's existing *Colmore Lodge* exchange, and is now beneath it and the Birmingham Post Office (Telecom) tower, close by. The extent of the Birmingham deep level tunnels, which are presumably some 2–3 miles in length as in Manchester, has not been revealed. All three exchanges were the subject of a special Act of Parliament in 1959, when the withdrawal of Emergency Powers made it necessary for the secret construction to be discretely revealed and vested in the Post Office. Had this not been done, it appears, the owners of the buildings above might have had a claim on the ex-

---

Figure 17　Government underground tunnels: Manchester *Guardian* telephone exchange.

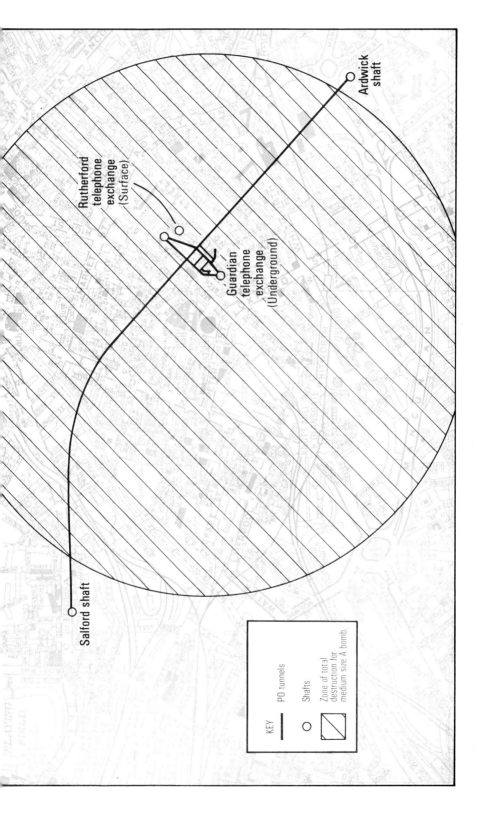

Rutherford
telephone
exchange
(Surface)

Guardian
telephone
exchange
(Underground)

Ardwick
shaft

Salford shaft

KEY

——— PO tunnels

○ Shafts

▨ Zone of total
destruction for
medium size A bomb.

changes as being on (or below) their land. The Act noted that:

in the exercise of emergency powers, the Postmaster General has constructed works in the City of Manchester and works in the City of Birmingham . . . and extended certain underground works (in London) . . . each consisting of a system of tunnels together with shafts and other means of access thereto from the surface and ancillary works.

The Act did not appear to excite any particular attention. Although the Post Office had just spent about £20 million building three exchanges which were to live even if the cities they served died, nothing more was to be heard of *Kingsway*, *Guardian* or *Anchor* until classification and D Notices were finally removed in 1967. The network seems once again to demonstrate the remarkable futility and repeated mistiming of British civil defence construction – even by government standards. By the time the network was complete, it was entirely vulnerable to Soviet H bombs.

In London, a related scheme by London Transport to protect the underground system suffered from the same defects. In 1951, LT decided, on government advice, to construct a ring of special floodgates within the deep tube lines (Piccadilly, Northern, and Central Lines) in the central London area. This network of floodgates is still supposed to be secret. D Notice No 7 on 'War Precautions and Civil Defence' was part of a new issue of D Notices distributed to the press in January 1982; it included a claim that:

it would be damaging to the national interest . . . to publish details of . . . (d) underground flood gates that are not in public view on the London underground railways.

Figure 18 London Underground A bomb protection. Eighteen special floodgates were built into the London tube system between 1953 and 1957. The aim was to create a 'ring' around possible bomb damage in the centre of the capital. The system was – and is – operated from an underground control beneath Hampstead. The exact purpose of the concealed complex is still mysterious, the mystery reinforced by a D Notice in 1982 requesting censorship of references to 'floodgates that are not in public view on the London underground railways.' Two new gates were added when the Victoria Line was built in 1968. The second set of gates at Liverpool Street would hold back water from the Lea Valley area. All the gates are sufficiently far from platforms to avoid public scrutiny.

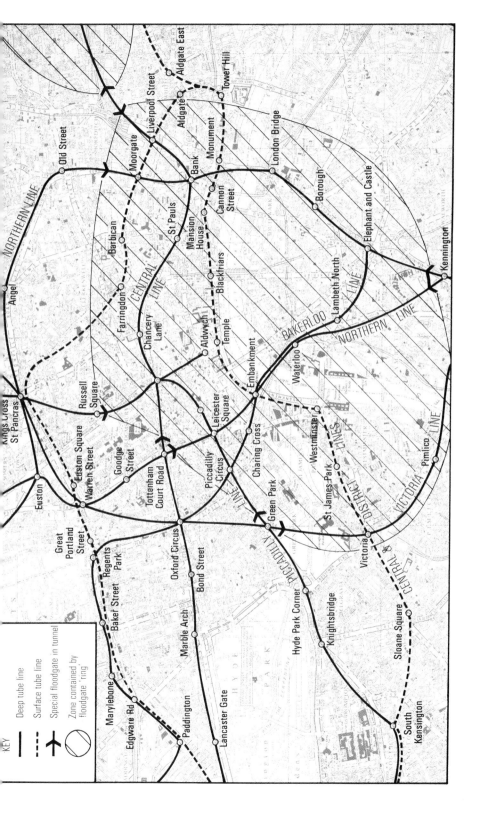

So far as they relate to any operational defence purpose, they relate to the A bomb era. All the details have in any case been published, in 1979.

The floodgates referred to, some twenty in all, were built into the tubes between 1953 and 1957. They are generally about one hundred and fifty feet (50m) down the tube tunnels from the stations concerned – and are thus 'not in public view' except to a very sharp-eyed passenger. Each gate is lowered from a recess at the top of the tunnel, and seals off water flow from the direction of central London.

The floodgate 'ring' is shown on p. 257; it forms a circle about three to four miles (5–6km) in diameter around the central area of London. The intention appears to be to prevent flood water entering the central London tubes from penetrating beyond the 'ring' thus enabling the deep tubes to continue in use for transport or air raid sheltering after, and perhaps during, an atomic bomb attack on London.

The control centre for the system is in a never completed station at Bull and Bush, in Hampstead Way near Hampstead Heath and the well known pub of the same name. Conversion work on the station began with the digging of a 110 foot (33m) shaft to connect the station tunnels with the surface (it had been abandoned before a shaft to the surface had been built). A blast-protected two storey control room was built underground adjacent to the station tunnels and panels installed to control all the London floodgates. Two panels may be seen in the photograph of the inside of the control centre on p. 259. The lefthand panel is the same as that used in the Second World War to supervise the closure of floodgates on stations threatened by flooding if the Thames embankment was badly damaged. It was taken from the former control centre at Leicester Square. The righthand panel controls the operation of the postwar A bomb gates. The gates can be operated individually or by a single master control. They are maintained ready to operate under full remote control at any time.

The surface works in Hampstead are unmarked save for an electricity substation for the underground control. Blast-proofed ventilator shafts provide fresh air to the control. Access is by a lift, whose entrance is itself two storeys below ground, its workings protected by a thick slab of concrete.

Such determination in making the Bull and Bush HQ survivable under heavy atomic bombing (the control centre is even sealed off from the underground tube tunnels by heavy

Plate 24 The control centre and switching unit for the special floodgates in the London Underground. The gates were installed in the A bomb era, and the control is positioned at the deepest part of the system in the uncompleted station beneath the *Bull and Bush*, north of Hampstead.

blast doors) speaks for either an excess of engineering zeal or an important purpose in creating the system. That purpose is hard to divine from the hardware which London Transport has installed. The controls certainly have some unusual features, such as the ability to open and close individual doors to allow trains to pass through the central area under supervision even after an attack warning – although the utility of such a procedure is difficult to imagine.

The gates are separated into 'entry' and 'exit' groups, however, suggesting that a likely procedure for isolating the area is to close the entry gates some time in advance. There is no provision for accomodation or shelter within the Bull and Bush control, which is packed out with batteries, relays and control panels. Only a toilet is provided, implying that once the attack had begun, there would be no further use for the control centres. Buried far below Hampstead, it is, nevertheless, (together with the Belsize Park shelter) the furthest below ground that London shelter accomodation goes.

It may be that part of the purpose of the system is to protect Post Office cables which run into London along the deep level tubes, although research within the Post Office system showed that there had been few new connections between the two networks since the war. (These were the links to the Bakerloo line from the Whitehall main shaft at Trafalgar Square, and to the Waterloo and City line, below Queen Victoria Street near the Faraday building.) In fact, few cables would have been run on these routes since the war. Nevertheless, the system was extended in 1968 after the construction of the Victoria Line, and a new pair of gates installed at Green Park station to protect the northern part of the line. The ring concept was not maintained insofar as the entire southern part of the Victoria Line, to Brixton, was left unprotected.

Although this system continues to be maintained at some expense, it does not appear to be the intention of London Transport to use the floodgate ring in the event of peacetime flooding of the Thames – even though it is ideal for providing a final line of defence for the deep tubes. The LT standing instructions on London flooding, issued in August 1979, make no mention at all of the Bull and Bush control centre or the special floodgates.

Besides Bull and Bush, several other disused stations of the London underground found wartime use. A former station at Down Street, near Green Park, accomodated an emergency headquarters for the Railway Emergency Committee, the predecessor of British Rail, during the Second World War. Brompton Road station, now owned by the Ministry of Defence, was also used during the war as an anti-aircraft control centre. The most interesting, however, is the former British Museum station on the Central Line, whose distinctive red brick surface buildings are at 4 Bloomsbury Court WC1, near the Museum. This building is also now in the hands of the Ministry of Defence, and the station tunnels, which closed in 1933, are sealed off from the tubes. The site is occupied by the administrative headquarters of the Scots Guards and other regiments in the Household Division; in the event of a peacetime flooding of London, the London District military command will operate from here rather than from the wartime AFHQ5, at Beaconsfield. Why it should be either necessary or desirable to site both the Greater London Council's Flood Control Centre and a London military HQ *below ground* (although above the flood level) is something of a mystery. One might note in passing that a sustained and serious Thames flood will be no small catastrophe. The Seat of Government will move from Whitehall to Holborn. The House of Commons will sit in banqueting rooms in Queensway; the Defence Staff and the MOD HQ will be in Lacon House, Theobalds Road, a few hundred yards away.

In a war emergency, the bunkers that will matter are those of the central government and military staff. In Chapter 4 we examined the development of more and more extensive control systems through the 1950s and 1960s. This chapter examines how the new citadels to accomodate them were developed after the advent of the Soviet H bomb required the previous generation to be abandoned.

The first stage in the 1950s civil defence buildup was the construction of War Rooms for each Regional Commissioner. The regional civil defence offices and staffs had been retained since the war had ended, and were located in hutted government buildings at suitable provincial centres. Each War Room provided for a minimal staff to work in blast and fallout protected conditions, and was built around a two storey Central Map Room. Most of the War Rooms were placed beside the existing regional centres. Each cost about £100,000 to build. Some papers later discovered at Reading show how the War Room there was to be laid out. Accomodation was provided for about fifty operational staff; besides offices for the Regional Commissioner, and a Scientific Adviser's Room, there was a Fire Control, Hospital Control and Police and military liaison staff. Most of the rest of each War Room's 7500 square feet of space (710 m^2) was allocated to the operations room or communications.

The War Rooms may easily be inspected at the regional government sites listed in Table 11 (p. 262). The concrete and brick blockhouse style is characteristic 1950s A bomb

Table 11 Regional Government in the 1950s: the War Rooms

Region	Regional War Room	Current use
1	Government Buildings, Ponteland Road, Kenton Bar, Newcastle upon Tyne	Disused; offered by HO to Tyne and Wear Council
2	Government Buildings, Otley Road, Lawnswood, Leeds	Leeds District Council Control
3	Government Buildings, Chalfont Drive, Nottingham	Extended as RSG3; current use may be AFHQ
4	Government Buildings, Brooklands Avenue, Cambridge	Extended as RSG4; current use may be AFHQ
5	London was divided into four separate Sub-Regions, each with its own War Room.	
	NW London: Partingdale Lane, Mill Hill, NW7	Barnet Borough Control
	NE London: Northumberland Avenue, Wanstead, E7	NE London Group Control
	SE London: Chislehurst, Kent	Disused
	SW London: Church Hill Road, Cheam, Surrey	SW London Group Control
6	Government Buildings, Whiteknights Park, Reading	Sold to Reading University, now physics laboratory
7	Government Buildings, Bath Road, Flowers Hill, Brislington, Bristol	Avon CC War HQ
8	Post Office Training Centre, Coryton, Cardiff	Mid-Glamorgan CC War HQ
9	Birmingham (site unknown)	–
10	Mill Lane, Cheadle, Manchester	Greater Manchester Council War HQ
11	Kirknewton, West Lothian (for Edinburgh)	Scottish Eastern Zone HQ (extended)
12	Government Buildings, Forest Road, Hawkenbury, Tunbridge Wells	Police communications centre
NI	Mount Eden Park, Malone Road, Belfast	Believed to be East Area HQ for Northern Ireland

architecture, with small chimneys housing ventilator intakes and exhausts, metal blastproof doors, and flat roofs. Few go any distance underground; at most, one storey is below ground.

The War Rooms scheme was designed to cope with what

would now be a rather genteel form of attack – some 10–20 Hiroshima-sized bombs airburst on the major cities, and a tiny level of radioactive fallout. In September 1955, the government decided to enormously strengthen the staffing and responsibilities of the civil defence regions, as a preliminary response to the H bomb. Very quickly, the citadels and communications schemes so expensively prepared in the previous five years were consigned to the scrapheap.

In place of the Regional War Rooms there were to be huge new provincial citadels to house the Regional Commissioners and greatly enlarged staffs. These were the RSGs – Regional Seats of Government. Although this term was administrative in origin it has come to be inextricably linked to the popular (and accurate) concept of the governments' 'deep bunkers' for officials' shelter. What had changed by 1958 was that, as the horror of the H bomb worked its way into official (and public) thinking, civil defence gradually lost its Second World War, ARP style. The dead of an H bomb attack were going to be measured in the tens of millions, and lethal belts of fallout would cover huge tracts of countryside for days. The government coordinators and administrators were going to have to be relocated as far as possible and well protected against blast and radiation. That applied with equal force to the Regional War Rooms, which had rapidly become insufficient both in scale and in protective standards, and also to the Whitehall tunnels in London which would be shattered, even vaporised, by an overhead thermonuclear explosion.

Thus came the RSGs, which thanks to the Committee of One Hundred and the Campaign for Nuclear Disarmament, have worked their way into a whole generation's consciousness as a symbol of the duplicity of civil defence measures. The RSGs were built in complete secrecy; at the Ministry of Works in London a special suite was set aside for drafting work, and the staff were vetted, isolated and locked in all day whilst they drafted the plans of the RSGs and the new Central War Headquarters. This secrecy did not prevent leaks in a not unfamiliar direction to encourage the patriotic readers of the *Daily Express*. This appeared in December 1959, entitled:

'Britain gets a chain of H-Forts':
A chain of underground fortresses from which the Government could control Britain and mount a counter-offensive in the event of an H bomb attack is being built far outside London.

It replaces ten miles of reinforced tunnels built under London after the last war at enormous cost. These tunnels which run below Whitehall, Leicester Square, Holborn and Victoria are not deep enough to withstand a near miss with an H bomb. The new forts which have already cost more than £10,000,000 are excavated so deep in rock that they would withstand anything but a direct hit. . .
The Cabinet, defence chiefs, the essential parts of the Whitehall machine and possibly some embassy staffs would be evacuated to the forts, the precise locations of which are being kept secret. (Chapman Pincher, 28 December 1959).

Three months later, Pincher announced that some of the Whitehall tunnels were being used as ordinary office accomodation by 'Whitehall Moles' (!) because of a shortage of offices. Reassuringly:

In the event of emergency, the key Moles would be evacuated to a much deeper underground HQ being hollowed out far away from London. . .

The *Daily Express* readers were reassured of a prompt revenge on the attacker, as the forts were to be linked directly to 'the deep pits housing the Blue Streak retaliatory rockets', the us-run Thor missiles then in eastern England, and the V bomber airfields.

A veil of secrecy descended on the sites which were being converted. Corsham, for example, was amply publicised after the war and the official wartime history of *Works and Buildings*, published in 1952, makes a specific reference to the construction of the underground aircraft factory at Spring Quarry, Hawthorn. By 1958, it was a secret again, and the official history of *Factories and Plant*, published that year, which should have given some space to this mammoth project, makes no mention at all of its whereabouts or features. The same was true of the other aircraft factories – two, Warren Row and Drakelow, were then being converted to RSGs.

The RSG system was comprehensively blown by activists of the Committee of One Hundred group in April 1963. A team of eight, who later took the title of *Spies for Peace*, had been part of a group who had heard rumours about the bunker system early in 1963. They looked for – and found – RSG6 at Warren Row. In a carefully planned raid during February 1963, four of them clandestinely entered the bunker by picking a boiler room lock, and examined, photographed and removed some of the RSG's contents. From this material they were able to prepare a pamphlet which, with considerable care that the real authors remained anonymous, was circulated during the 1963 Aldermaston march.

The pamphlet – *Danger–Official Secret!–RSG6* – attracted considerable controversy. It exposed the whereabouts, and function of RSG6 at Warren Row, together with details of its staff, and the telephone numbers and whereabouts of the other RSGs in the system. There were, it said, places for about four hundred people in RSG6, and five thousand altogether in the other Regional Seats of Government throughout Britain. RSG6, the Spies for Peace discovered, had been activated for two recent exercises, in particular *Fallex* 62, the then annual autumn home defence exercise which was the direct forerunner of *Square Leg* and *Hard Rock*.

The fifty offices in RSG6 included accomodation for every government department except the Board of Trade and the Foreign Office: there were Home Office staff, a BBC studio, HMSO and Central Office of Information teams, and staff from the Treasury and Ministries of Housing, Aviation, Power, Labour, Transport, Health, Agriculture, Fisheries and Food, the GPO, the National Assistance Board and National Insurance (now part of DHSS). There were police, fire brigade and senior military staff, including the Chief Constable of Hampshire (the Regional Police Commander) and the General Commanding Aldershot District (the Regional Military Commander). The Regional Commissioner had a secretariat, two Directors of Operations, and a Principal Officer. It was indeed a microcosm of all of Whitehall; and, as the *Spies for Peace* pointed out, citing the profusion of Oxford dons who were Scientific Advisors, it was also a microcosm of Britain's ruling elite.*

The pamphlet was available in time to steer many who were marching from the Aldermaston nuclear weapons research establishment to London to turn left as they marched down the A4, and walk a quarter mile to the gates of RSG6. After a short demonstration, most rejoined the march, but the point had been made and the RSG's secrets lost.

---

* The original *Spies for Peace* pamphlet was reproduced many thousands of times, but is no longer available. A copy is said to be in the British Museum. *Peace News* reproduced much of it on 11 March 1977. A detailed account of the episode was given in *Anarchy*, No 29. The true story of how it was done was revealed ten years later in *Inside Story* Nos 8 and 9 (March and May 1973).

Table 12 Regional Seats of Government (RSGs): 1957–63 scheme. These details of the RSG network were published in the original *Spies for Peace* pamphlet 'This was an official secret – why?' distributed first on the Aldermaston march of 1963. The pamphlet gave the location and telephone numbers of each of the RSGs. Not all the sites were located with precision, in particular RSGs 1–4. In Regions 3,4, and 6 the former Home Office Regional War Room was turned into a communications centre, and in at least one of these cases (Reading) the RSG site was quite remote. The same may be true of Nottingham and Cambridge, although both War Rooms have been considerable extended.

The London Region was not expected to survive as a region; instead, sectors of London would be administered by adjoining RSGs, through sub-regional controls on the outskirts of London, which were moved away from the former War Room locations to more remote sites around 1960.

RSG1	Catterick (Catterick Camp)
RSG2	York (Imphal Barracks)
RSG3	Nottingham (Chalfont Drive government buildings)
RSG4	Cambridge (Brooklands Avenue government buildings)
RSG6	Reading (Warren Row)
RSG7	Dartmouth (Bolt Head)
RSG8	Brecon (The Barracks)
RSG9	Kidderminster (Drakelow, Kinver)
RSG10	Preston (Fulford Barracks)
RSG11	Edinburgh (Barnton Quarry) (Scotland was Region 11)
RSG12	Dover (Dover Castle)
RSG-NI	Armagh (Gough Barracks)

A major row followed the leaks, and the police and MI5 hunted for the culprits. Chapman Pincher claimed to have, along with 'other defence correspondents', been taken into the government's confidence about the RSGs. But he had loyally 'agreed not to reveal the locations'. As for those not in the government's confidence, he demanded that the security authorities:

track down the Spies for Peace and (treat) them with the same vigour as spies for war.

Harold Macmillan told the House of Commons ten days later that:

Although the existence of these headquarters had long been widely known, the exact location and details of their organisation have not been publicised. . .

Nevertheless, the disclosure was embarrassing since, as with the public news of the digging under Whitehall, there was not, now or ever, any cash available for public shelters. As Macmillan continued:

There is no question of building deep air raid shelters. That has long ago been stated to be impossible on a large scale. (The RSGs) are merely an arrangement by which the Regional Commissioners will be placed in suitable locations. . .

In fact, the government had just been building one very large-scale deep air raid shelter. As Pincher explained, whilst asking that the *Spies for Peace* face the gallows:

There is a bomb proof underground citadel for the central government – including quarters for the Royal Family – 'somewhere in the west'.

His informants' vague hint of 'the west' was a reference to the Hawthorn Central Government War Headquarters, which had become the new wartime national seat of government to which the Cabinet, central government and defence staffs would retreat early in a crisis, leaving London to its fate as the H bombs fell.

The haul of material from RSG6 had given *Spies for Peace* some details of the staffs of other RSGs as well as their whereabouts. Almost all the staff were senior civil servants; the Principal Officer at Warren Row was a Treasury Under Secretary, S. L. Lees, MVO. *Danger–Official Secret!* also listed a London HQ for the RSG system called CHAPLIN and its telephone number – ABBey 1255, in the Westminster area. However this sort of use of a telephone number instead of a direct connection suggests that CHAPLIN was more concerned with controlling RSGs during exercises than in war. (The communications networks are described in more detail in Chapter 9).

Inside RSG6, the clocks operated on Zulu time, the standard NATO reference system (Zulu time is in GMT, with the date of the month preceding a twenty four-hour clock; thus 191155Z in any month means 11.55 am on the nineteenth). It was entirely self-contained with water supplies, generators, sewage disposal, food supplies and, claimed the *Spies* rather surprisingly, a bar.

Eventually, most of the details about the RSG system seeped into the press, although the Home Office and Ministry of Defence acted quickly in reminding most editors of the D

Notice self-censorship system, with which they were asked to comply. Coming shortly after journalists had been jailed by the Vassal tribunal for refusing an order to reveal sources, many newspapers saw the attempt to bottle up the RSG revelations as pointless. The *Daily Telegraph* eventually reprinted a large part of the text of the pamphlet – after it had been broadcast on Prague Radio! The point of official information controls emerged in sharp relief; the purpose was not so much to maintain real secrets, as to control public opinion and minimise the impact of such a revelation, if it could not be altogether suppressed.

The full list of RSGs is given in Table 12 (p. 266). The RSG system was based, like the War Rooms, on the existing twelve Regions. There was one exception to this; London Region was thought unlikely to survive an H bomb attack and stay intact as a viable Region; it was therefore split up into five Sub-Regions, each of which was annexed to adjoining RSGs at Cambridge, Warren Row and Dover, and their regions.

A 1957 pamphlet on civil defence explained that the

'regional headquarters' which were then being built would be 'specially equipped . . . and wherever possible will be a joint headquarters with the corresponding army district. An arrangement of this kind will be particularly desirable because of the increased importance of the part which the armed forces are to play in civil defence operations.

In the spirit of this, five of the RSGs were sited at military headquarters, presumably by extending existing protected military accomodation built in the early 1950s. The five concerned were York (Northern Command), Catterick (Catterick District), Brecon (Wales District), Preston (North West District) and Armagh (Northern Ireland Command). Two RSGS seem to have been based on extending existing Home Office War Rooms, at Cambridge and in Nottingham. The remainder were derived from a miscellany of sources, all described in this or the previous chapter: Warren Row and Drakelow had each been aircraft factories of the 1940s, whilst Bolt Head in Devon and Barnton Quarry in Edinburgh had been RAF Rotor stations. The tunnels below Dover Castle had housed a Combined Headquarters built for the D Day invasion of Normandy.

The RSG system did not long survive, however, and wholesale changes were prescribed in the Home Office Circular CDC 17/63. Whilst the RSGs were being built and connected in, another system of civil defence centres, called Sub-Regional Controls, had been proposed in 1956. These were required in 'certain densely populated industrial areas' because of the huge increase in 'the extent of damage and casualties and the need to impose restrictions on movement because of radioactive fallout' after the H bomb. By 1963, these had been introduced in a fairly ad hoc way. London, for instance had at least two operational: Kelvedon Hatch for the north east, and Fort Bridgewood, Chatham for the south east. These new, heavily protected Sub-Regional Controls gradually replaced the 1952–3 War Rooms. It is not certain whether suitably remote sites were found for the other three Sub-Regional Controls.

In July 1963 the Home Office circular prescribed that the whole country would henceforth be divided up into Sub-Regions, each with its own Control and Sub-Regional Commissioner. The lessons of exercises like *Fallex* 62 had been that, in a major H-bomb attack, the close level of coordination between different industrial counties which had previously been arranged by Sub-Regional Controls would be required everywhere.

At the same time, this rearrangement marked the beginning of the end of attempts at proper civil defence in Britain. Circular CDC 17/63 noted that:

a balance must be struck between the requirements of a control system solely designed to deal with the life-saving, operational stage and those of a system which could function effectively in the much longer (survival) period. . . . it is *no longer realistic to relate a control system to short term life-saving requirements* (author's emphasis).

Because of the 'considerable difficulties in the administrative sphere' that would follow from pursuing 'short term life-saving' activities, these were no longer the priority. Two or three of the new Sub-Regional Controls would be formed in each former Region, and the 'Regional Seat of Government' would once more become an administrative term, rather than a bunker. The 1963 plans laid down twenty-six Sub-Regions for England and Wales; Scotland already had three Zones (and a Central Control) on a similar model. The Regional Seats of Government then disappeared, and in July 1964 Warren Row became Sub-Regional Control 61 (SRC61). Its counterparts at Cambridge (SRC41), Bolt Head (SRC72), Nottingham (SRC33), Kidderminster (SRC91) were similarly renamed. In principle, some fourteen new underground or protected controls were then required. The shortfall was indeed rather greater, because the RSGs which had been sited at military HQs once more reverted to their service owners. Most of the SRCs needed were in fact never built, and when the SRC system was reorganised once again in 1972, only seventeen controls were then specified. Of even this reduced number, only thirteen were in fact in existence.

The *Spies for Peace* never discovered, for certain, the whereabouts of the national government in war. During the two years following their initial, successful and unpunished, *exposé*, they penetrated a number of other 'suspect' establishments: the Belsize Park tube shelter, civil defence controls in London and the Sub-Regional Control at Kelvedon Hatch. They tried to get into *Kingsway*, and made a number of forays into establishments in the Corsham area. They searched, in Surrey, for an establishment called 'Hawthorn' which had been identified in documents as the national seat of government – ironically, because 'Hawthorn' was one of the places that they had indeed searched at Corsham, but found it too dangerous to go far enough to confirm its nature.

Today, some two hundred white collar civil servants work full-time operating and maintaining the Hawthorn war headquarters and related establishments. Astonishingly, for government establishments as secret as Hawthorn and the Corsham complex, some details of their administration may be found in public documents of the Property Services Agency of the Department of the Environment, which supervises and maintains all government buildings.

The Central Government War HQ is entered from two sites in Westwells Road, Hawthorn, near Corsham. The main entrance (and former main entrance to the Spring Quarry factory) is – according to the sign over the police lodge – a PSA Supplies Division Depot. It is beyond doubt the only such purported warehouse in Britain which displays, immediately on entering, a defence 'Alert State' (normally, 'Black'). To the right of the entrance lodge is a large mound with two pedestrian entrances. Inside, there is a bizarre ressemblance to the London underground, as escalators provide the main means of access to the underground workings. Beyond the lodge, amongst a distant collection of air shafts and surface works are four high chimneys – exhausts from the headquarters' power station. The chimneys are adjacent to one of the former main entrances to Spring Quarry. When the quarry was requisitioned, there were about one hundred acres of underground space – over four million square feet (450,000m²) had been hewn out of the hard rock beds by the Corsham quarrymen; just over a half of this was converted to the wartime aircraft factory. Nevertheless, the space available in the whole complex is staggering; its underground area is sufficient to swallow up most of Whitehall.

All along Westwells Road are visible symbols of the well-prepared government nuclear sanctuary. At the northern end of the road, is a Post Office microwave station, the original westward extension of the 'Backbone' emergency defence communications network planned in 1954. This tower, known as 'Five Ways', came into operation in the early 1960s. Together with the numerous underground telephone cables which have been diverted through the Corsham complex since 1943, the Five Ways tower provides the headquarters with its vital lines of communications. Two microwave 'horns' on the high tower provide thousands of telephone, telegraph and computer data links to east and west.

The tower stands amongst the station buildings of RAF Rudloe Manor, previously known as RAF Box or RAF Hawthorn. The station is now the base for two RAF organisations, the major unit being the headquarters of the Defence Communications Network which provides and supervises strategic communications for the three armed services. (The other is the HQ of RAF Provost and Security Services). The office of the Controller of the DCN is not at this point, however, but in a field two hundred yards east. It is little more than a guardhouse and a lift shaft.

Sandbagged sites for machine gun nests are positioned around this entrance, and also around two other surface installations just south. One is a similar lift shaft which provides access to the underground space of the RAF's No 6 Signals Unit, which operates the underground telegraph and telephone switching unit for the Defence Communications Network. The Post Office's Five Way radio tower a few hundred yards away comes under the joint control of a Post Office (British Telecom) engineer and an RAF technical supervisor. Adjacent to this is a 'Surface Fuel Compound' through which fuel oil can be delivered for the underground oil stores. This too features a machine gun site. The oil fuel store is shared, according to a sign on the installation, by the RAF and the PSA's underground, civil government estate.

Adjacent to these on Westwells Road is the ordinary British Telecom exchange for Hawthorn. Many of its works are underground too, although it is on the public telephone network. Its construction was the subject of a special wartime project, associated with the Spring Quarry aircraft factory.

The whole complex is supervised by another PSA installation directly opposite the so-called 'Supplies Division' site. This is the Corsham Area Works Office of the Property Services Agency. Although such a title is normal in the PSA network, Corsham is not. Its real title is Headquarters Controlled Special Site and it is administered direct from Whitehall, and not from Bristol or any other local supervising centre. Under the 'Headquarters Controller Special Sites' come the proliferation of underground bunkers, stores and former surface hostels in the Corsham area, together with Post Office works in the vicinity and at Limpley Stoke and Bradford on Avon. It also controls the second Special Site allocated for use as a central government bunker. This is the huge complex of tunnels in limestone at Rhydymwyn which were carved out into the side of hills in the Alyn valley, near Mold (Clwyd, North Wales) to hold thousands of tons of poison gas in the Second World War (see pages 283 and 483).

Rhydymwyn was officially visited by journalists from Harlech TV early in 1982, and shown to be empty. It has never been converted to a modern bunker. Its function in the central government war plan is thus a little ambiguous. A geographical organisation chart for the Special Sites office at Corsham nevertheless shows it to be allocated specifically as a depot 'for Corsham'. In the absence of suitable funds to equip the site, it may perhaps be earmarked for emergency fitting out, if possible, in the early stages of a crisis.

Some official sources indicate that there may at one stage have been a third Special Site for use as a central government bunker, but there was no trace of it in 1974. It may, like Rhydymwyn, have been allocated but never fully converted.

The existence of the secret 'HQ Special Sites' is described in the annual reports issued by the Property Services Agency. The reports break down the numbers of white collar staff in each division. The fourth division listed is 'Home Regional HQ Special Sites'. In 1980 there were 208 such staff – implying that an overall total of four hundred staff work full-time on the supervision and maintenance of the Corsham area and its bunkers. In peacetime, the Special Sites are controlled by the Director of Home Regional Services of the PSA, Mr A. J.

Aveling, based in Croydon. His staff include engineers responsible for 'Railway Inspection – civil and defence sites' – confirming, it seems, longstanding rumours about the use of underground trains (as well as London Transport style escalators!) within the complex.

If anyone asks, unofficially, why the huge Corsham complex is run direct from London, and its costs concealed within the PSA's annual £1 billion expenditure, the answer can be fairly direct: 'If the balloon goes up, it will *be* London'. The accomodation available could house twenty thousand government staff; if one uses the wartime extreme minimum limit of bunker space required for one individual – forty square feet (3.6 m²) – then there could be space for fifty-five thousand. The technical standard of the installation is high; instead of using ordinary air filters, for example, the air coming into the complex is 'scrubbed' by high speed mixing with water sprays to literally wash all radioactive dust out of the atmosphere. Purified water supplies feed this system and the living areas. If it is not directly attacked, the selected civil servants and others with earmarked places at Hawthorn could expect several months of protection from the ravages to which the northern hemisphere may have been exposed in a major nuclear exchange.

The Corsham Area Works Office of the PSA, so called, is aptly located at Number 1, Old Shaft Road, Hawthorn. Old Shaft Road contains a collection of government hutted offices, most of them *not* used by the PSA. The main access from the police lodge at 1 Old Shaft Road is to a further, fenced-off compound, and inside is 'Seven Shaft' entrance to Spring Quarry. The Southern Electricity Board has its own office at the surface huts at Spring Quarry, as does the Womens' Royal Voluntary Service. Around all of these are a profusion of air shafts, and 'slope' shafts, which plunge fairly steeply into the ground, and were formerly used for hauling the worked-out stone from the ground.

Apart from the central government bunker, Corsham also seems likely to be the site of the UKCICC military command which would have primary control over United Kingdom defence and civil defence activities. (UKICC – the UK Commanders in Chief Committee – is described in Chapter 6). After 1945, all the Corsham quarries used as munitions stores remained in army hands, though none were used after the mid-1960s. In 1967, they were declared surplus to MOD requirements and eventually two quarries, at Monkton Farleigh and Eastlays,

Plate 25 A slope shaft leads into Sands Quarry, Hawthorn, part of the Spring Quarry complex, now used by the Royal Navy.

were sold off. The former Tunnel and Hudswell quarries were retained, however, and these are directly connected both to the Spring Quarry PSA Special Site and the Defence Communications Network centre. Five or six shafts connect the army workings to the surface; in addition, there is a direct railway access from the London-Bath railway through a nineteenth century side tunnel directly into Tunnel Quarry. The siding runs into a half-mile long platform area, and at least one further standard gauge siding ran north from it. The whole of the Hawthorn underground workings are crossed by the Box railway tunnel (on the London-Bath line) and although it is apparently not connected to any further sidings in the hillside, it is well protected to stop conventional bombs accidentally penetrating the railway tunnel's air shafts and exploding at deep level. Each air shaft has a thick concrete lid above it to avoid such a contingency. Down below, only about twenty feet (6m) of rock separates the government citadel from ordinary passengers on British Rail.

The original slope shaft entrance to Tunnel Quarry, when

it was used as a munitions store, is on a public road not far from the entrance of the Box railway tunnel. It was converted to become a loading bay for munitions in 1940, and has recently been refurbished with new metal doors. A story is reliably told about the refurbishment which apparently began in 1978. A group of military officers and PSA staff had come to the site to inspect the reported poor repair into which the UKCICC's war headquarters had fallen. Making their way to the selected shaft entrance, they were astonished to find that the other buildings around – a former workers and families hostel – was temporarily occupied by Vietnamese refugees, who were likely to take a keen and unwelcome interest. The inspection and works programme had to be held up until a more discreet means of entry could be found.

About this time too, the UK Land Forces Command at Salisbury were reported in a rail enthusiasts' magazine as advertising for underground trains for an unspecified establishment. This army command (UKLF) would staff the UKCICC headquarters, and the only likely site that they would need underground trains for would be Hawthorn. Since the total workings are several miles in extent, a train service would indeed be useful.

In 1981 the Department of the Environment re-emphasised the importance of the complex when directions were issued to staff to start 'privatising' contracts for maintaining government establishments. Two places in Britain were wholly exempt from the requirement; one was the Palace of Westminster (including the Commons and Lords); the other was the Corsham 'HQ Special Sites'. The detailed list of Special Sites, however, no longer appears in the DOE's internal directories.

Besides the two underground war HQs, the area also contains three underground Royal Naval Stores Depots, – Copenacre, Monks Park and Spring Quarry (an intentionally misleading title, it seems; it is actually sited on Sands Quarry) and surface camps used by the army, RAF and Royal Navy. It is worth noting in passing that Corsham is the only site, other than MOD headquarters, where the three services are normally stationed together, a further pointer to the area's clandestine significance.

The former ammunition sub-depots at Monkton Farleigh and Eastlays, both a few miles from the main sites, were advertised and sold off in 1975. National press advertisements announced:

VAST UNDERGROUND PREMISES: Wiltshire: Two properties offering underground clean, dry, level space.

It wasn't an unreasonable claim. The two depots together had a floor space of about two million square feet – almost as big as the Spring. In fact these underground dumps proved difficult to sell. Both were initially bought by a Shepton Mallet farmer; after various pieces of surface land were sold off, the Eastlays depot finished up in the hands of a Bristol-based consortium who, in 1980, attempted to develop a scheme to turn the place into a nuclear condominium, with bomb proof family lettings available and services including supermarkets and cinemas. Although sales caravans were installed around the slope shaft entrance, the scheme attracted a great deal of adverse publicity, and apparently not enough commercial interest. Eastlays is thus still abandoned, as is the Ridge Quarry nearby, still owned, however, by the Ministry of Defence. Monkton Farleigh, seven miles west, is also more or less disused and is now owned by a building firm.

The pictures on pages 157 and 232 show some of the features of the underground stores as they were sold. We may presume that the Spring Quarry workings were converted in similar fashion. One former very small munitions store at Goblins Pit, near Neston, has been in use since 1957 as a security archives and vault. It is run by Wansdyke Security Ltd, a subsidiary of the Bath and Portland Stone group who originally owned all the quarries. The company specialises in storing microfilms, and more recently computer tapes, for such major companies as Texaco and Esso. The A bomb-proof characteristics of the underground store were originally a strong selling point when it was set up in 1957; customers now might be more sceptical about the ultimate utility of a nuclear war-proof store for 'essential' records.

The stone quarries of Corsham are vastly less secure against direct nuclear attack than the citadels the United States carved into the Virginia and Maryland mountains. But they are all Britain seems to have. It is of course possible to accomodate a few key staff at some much smaller installation, which may escape public notice and Soviet nuclear targetting through relative (small) size and unimportance. In this way, the Queen or Prime Minister could perhaps be separated off from the Hawthorn HQ staffs. But there appear to be no plans to mimic the United States' *Air Force One* and its flying presidential war rooms. Britain has had airborne strategic command centres, but only briefly; in the 1960s, when the V bombers were the main nuclear force, they were accompanied into the air by converted Victor aircraft which could broadcast and confirm orders to attack. The RAF does not appear to have any such capacity now, although such aircraft as the long-range VC10s could be used as final airborne command or relay centres. But they are not equipped with the large amount of communications required for controlling a war.

The overall job of the Central War Headquarters is to direct all aspects of the war (and what officials describe as the 'recovery'), in conjunction with NATO allies, through the Defence Staff and the military commanders. The Foreign Office's conduct of wartime international relations would go on from Hawthorn, as would the Department of Trade's supervision of trade and shipping coming to and from Britain. Ministries like Energy, Transport, Environment, the Home Office and so on, who are also present in the Sub-Regional and Regional HQS would be present in greater numbers at Corsham, with a view towards 'recovery'.

The present plan for the dispersal of central government now rests on three discrete groups. The top level is the central national seat of government at Hawthorn – if it survives. There are then regional and national groups of staff sent to suitable, relatively safe, country locations – large hotels and country houses in Wales and the West Country being preferred – who have no operational function until well after an attack, but who are intended to sit out the attack, be guarded, supplied with fallout protection, and fed, and will eventually gather at suitable offices to re-establish national administration. On a regional level, plans are similar, and many of the staff for each ultimate 'Regional Seat of Government' will be dispersed at 'group locations' of relative safety. Once radioactivity levels have fallen sufficiently for free movement on the surface to be possible, and some form of communications and transport system is in operation, they will join with SRHQ staff to form each Regional administration.

The Sub-Regional HQS are the main level of attack and post-attack civil control within the UK. They are the direct successors to the Sub-Regional Controls, and the fifth phase of postwar development of the civil defence system. After the Civil Defence Corps had been disbanded in 1968, and all life-saving and rescue work abandoned, the SRCS were put onto a care and maintenance basis. Out of twenty-six planned in the SRC system in England and Wales, only about ten were then in existence, with three new sites under construction. In 1970, at the end of the decade in which the government had tried to cope with the problems of a missile attack with hydrogen bombs, and failed, there was nothing left of civil defence preparations on any level. The Civil Defence Corps had gone; and of the control centres for civil defence operations, barely over a third were in operation.

Warren Row itself continued to present a microcosm of the whole civil defence world. It was abandoned in 1970, after a new SRC became available in the specially constructed fortified concrete basement of the Civil Service Commission HQ in Alencon Link, Basingstoke. It continued, empty, through the 1970s and in 1978 my colleague Peter Laurie found it open and was able to film with the BBC a reflective interview on civil defence in its sombre, dank caverns. A friend who visited the place a number of times in the next year discovered its ultimate fate, as family tourist groups and couples were repeatedly encountered in the darkness – some of them, no doubt, in their younger days, had demonstrated around the centre in the 60s. On a subsequent visit, Warren Row was filled with choking smoke as scrap dealers equipped with welding equipment removed, wholesale and illegally, its pipes and fittings. But it is now back in use.

The civil defence reorganisation began in earnest in 1972, and military district commands and Home Defence Sub-Regions were adjusted to align with the new counties which were formed in 1974. The reorganisation of Sub-Regional HQs came at the same time. The seventeen Regions and Sub-Regions of England and Wales (Zones in Scotland) are shown in Figure 6; the SRHQs are listed in Table 13 (p. 280). The SRHQs are the final rump of the civil defence system, and are the focus of and control centre for the minimal civil defence to be carried out by local authorities. There are no rescue or fire service columns to direct any more, just the coordination of attempts to provide or restore essential services, and the control of the civil population – by police or military force, or the withholding of food supplies.

Only three SRHQ bunkers are of recent construction – Basingstoke, (SRHQ62), Hertford (SRHQ42) and Southport (SRHQ102). Each is the same design – a two storey concrete basement below government office blocks built in the late 1960s. Each cost about £200,000 at the time and has a staff of one hundred and eighty. The walls are 20–30 inches thick

(50-75cm) and each has its own borehole for water. Some one hundred and fifty thousand gallons of water are also stored in permanent tanks, and a generator room can power all the SRHQ's equipment for a month, with a ten thousand gallon fuel reserve. Two sets of filters are fitted to the air conditioning plant, one for peacetime exercise use, and the second for war. If the level of fallout dust becomes too high, the air conditioning can be switched to internal circulation for a considerable period. The bunkers were designed to have a radiation 'protective factor' of about 400, and to resist blast pressure of 1·5 psi. In contrast, the average house is unlikely, after attack, to offer a protective factor better than 5–10.

According to officials, no food supplies are normally stored in the bunkers. They fear that they would merely be consumed by the army during military exercises. When the press were shown round SRHQ62 in Basingstoke during the 1980 *Square Leg* exercise, they found that both dormitories and radio equipment rooms had been seriously damaged by water leaking in from a car park above – and that all of the centre's radio equipment had been dismantled for almost two years. Readiness had not improved much over ten years. The newly built SRHQ102, at Southport, suffers from regular flooding.

Some have considerably more protection from blast and fallout than others. Two former cold stores at Hexham and Loughborough have been converted to SRHQs; their brick walls, now being reinforced internally, will provide minimal protection. At the other end of the scale, the former RAF bunker at Shipton near York has ten-foot thick side walls and a fourteen-foot (4m) thick roof.

Each SRHQ has a strong radio mast to carry its link aerials to other bunkers, and a small BBC broadcasting studio with a somewhat vulnerable link to the nearest suitable medium wave or VHF transmitters.

To prevent a repeat of the *Spies for Peace* episode, each bunker is equipped with direct alarms to a local police station. Special Branch and official military patrols are called out each time the alarm sounds, according to a former policeman. Many authorised tours of the centres have however been arranged for local press and TV reporters, on condition they do not specify the exact addresses. Home Office officials say they fear 'vandalism', but do not regard the locations as 'secret'.

At Regional level there are bunkers for the military only – the AFHQs (Chapter 6). The additional staff for Regional

Table 13 Sub-Regional and Zone HQS
The contemporary arrangement of Sub Regional and Zone HQS
came into being in 1973, when the abandoned mid-60s plan for a
chain of over thirty such controls was scaled down and rationalised.
One SRHQ – No 81 for North Wales – remains to be built. During
1981 and 1982, many others such as Hexham, Loughborough, Shipton, Hack Green, Drakelow and Southport have undergone reconstruction, refurbishment, or remedial work.

Home Defence Sub Region or Zone (Scotland)	*Site*	*Origin*
11	Hexham, Northumberland (under construction)	ww2 Cold Store
21	New Parks, near Shipton, N Yorks	RAF Sector Control
31	Skendelby, Lincs	RAF Radar Station
32	Loughborough, Leics	ww2 Cold Store
41	Bawburgh, Norfolk	RAF Sector Control
42	Hertford, Herts (Sovereign House)	Purpose Built
51	Kelvedon Hatch, Essex	RAF Sector Control
61	Dover Castle, Kent	ww2 Military HQ
62	Basingstoke, Hants (Alençon Link)	Purpose Built
71	Ullenwood, near Cheltenham, Gloucs	Army Anti-Aircraft HQ
72	Bolt Head, Devon	RAF Radar Station
81	Not built (1982)	–
82	Bridgend, Mid Glamorgan	ww2 Ordnance Factory
91	Swynnerton, Staffs	ww2 Ordnance Factory
92	Drakelow, Kinver, Hereford & Worcs	ww2 Aircraft Factory
101	Southport, Merseyside (Dukes House)	Purpose Built
102	Hack Green, Cheshire (under construction)	RAF Radar Station
Scottish Central	Barnton Quarry, Edinburgh	RAF Sector Control
N Zone	Anstruther, Fife	RAF Radar Station
E Zone	Kirknewton, Lothian	Regional War Room
W Zone	Torrance House, East Kilbride	Army Anti-Aircraft HQ
NI Central HQ	Armagh, Co Armagh	Purpose Built

Plates 26 & 27 Many Sub-Regional Headquarters such as these were converted from the multitude of sites fortified as part of the RAF's Rotor system. SRHQ 21, Shipton (above) and SRHQ 41, Bawburgh (below).

Government will join up with the SRHQ staff to form the Regional administration between, the government hopes, one and three months after nuclear attack. The SRHQS will function, sealed off from the outside world, for a minimum of four weeks, and longer if fallout or devastation has been unusually severe.

Scotland and Northern Ireland are the exception to this rule. The Scottish Central Control at Barnton Quarry in Corstorphine Hill, amongst the well-to-do western suburbs of Edinburgh will function as the Scottish Seat of Government from the time war measures begin. It will control all the operations of its three subordinate Zone HQs. The Northern Ireland Central HQ at Armagh is similarly the Province's sole wartime centre of administration.

A perplexing question, which is never answered in Home Office circulars, concerns the whereabouts of the Regional Commissioner on pre-war 'dispersal'. The question is central to the maintenance of the civil authority, since military and police forces are under Regional command. It seems likely that the Regional Commissioner will be accomodated in one of the Region's bunkers, either AFHQ or SRHQ, depending on the Region concerned. this is certainly the case in Sub-Region 51 (Greater London) which, like Sub-Regions 11 and 21, has the same boundaries as the parent region. SRHQ51 at Kelvedon Hatch has offices for the Regional Commissioner, as well as the Sub-Regional Commissioner.

Until 1980, it was not intended that the Sub-Regional Commissioners would be ministers, and official pronouncements on this subject always evaded the truth – which was that the appointment would be held by an Under Secretary (the second highest civil service rank). To improve the public image of the system, the bunkers (in England and Wales) now come under the control of a junior minister instead. Regional Commissioners (designate) have always been said to be chosen from amongst ministers in the government of the day.

No space is provided in the SRHQS or other bunkers for dependents or spouses of the designated staff. Indeed, almost all of the staff nominated to operate the SRHQS are selected not on a personal basis, but on the basis of holding a particular government post, and may often not be aware that they are nominated to SRHQ or Regional Government staff. Nor have any of them received any training, or – until *Hard Rock* – participated, in however minimal a fashion, in any exercises. The Home Office plans to persuade any reluctant bunker nominee to do his or her duty by offering guaranteed and guarded billets to family members in the same area as the SRHQ.

By late 1982, one SRHQ for North Wales (SRHQ81) remained to be built. It was suggested in Parliament that they might use the Rhydymwyn caverns, but these were claimed to be 'liable to flooding'. One other Welsh site did attract considerable attention during 1981. This was not SRHQ81, but the Arts Bunker at the Manod slate quarry, near Blaenau Ffestiniog. Several MPs and a peer, Lord Jenkins, pressed the government to explain the purpose of the store and received most disingenuous and dishonest answers, a reminder of the government's unwillingness to be frank about nuclear war planning. Labour MP Frank Allaun asked the Home Secretary, William Whitelaw:

I am writing to enquire what is happening at Manod Quarry and for whom the facilities are intended. (1.9.81)

He described two concrete bunkers inside caverns, steel doors barring access, and the presence of a maintenance team on the site as well as other more exotic features a correspondent had claimed were there. Whitelaw replied:

I can assure you that the acitivities you describe have nothing at all to do with central government. I can only suggest that if you wish to pursue the matter you approach the mining operator at the quarry. (24.9.81)

No doubt the Home Secretary would not have approved such a mendacious reply if he had first been given the full facts about the store. They emerged a few months later, but not until after Lord Jenkins had pressed the point in the Lords:

Which works of art are to be selected for location in the Arts Bunker at Blaenau Ffestiniog in the event of nuclear war . . . and (I ask) whether provision is being made to house there any living artists or Arts Council officials?
The Earl of Avon: My Lords, it would not be in the public interest to disclose details of security arrangements. . .
(12.11.81)

Two weeks later, the government was suitably embarrassed when the owner of both Manod and the nearby Bwlch and Cwt-y-Bugail quarries, Mr Owen Glyn Williams, pointed out that the government were not only very much present inside the Manod quarry, but were squatting illegally as their lease had run out a year before. The government went into fast reverse, admitted that two PSA officials were employed on full-time maintenance at Manod, and said that the work was for the Office of Arts and Libraries 'who need protection for selected items of public interest'. A twenty-one year lease (which had run out) had been renewed on the Manod Quarry in 1959, during the second nuclear war planning wave. It had cost at least £250,000 to operate the caverns since the war as an emergency store for three galleries – the Tate, the British Museum and the National Gallery. The irony and absurdity of storing 'items of public interest' for circumstances in which no galleries and few members of the public would survive, with a strong likelihood of diminished public interest in fine arts, seems not have crossed Whitehall officials' minds during those thirty years. The House of Commons Education Committee elected to visit the site in April 1981, and found that the art galleries' directors had been there not very long beforehand, in order to revise their secret war plans. An embarrassed Department of the Environmental Minister, Sir George Young, meanwhile failed to find 'any discrepancies' in the government's earlier deception of Frank Allaun MP. He stressed that their letters describing Manod were 'confidential'.

The Arts Bunker has thus continued to be kept ready alongside the AFHQS, SRHQS and, of course, the voluminous Hawthorn complex. Through the many episodes of government shelter and citadel planning both in the 1930s and now, it is possible to see the same elements and hands at work. Firstly, an almost total unwillingness to provide protection for, or to care about, the civil population; and secondly, a high degree of incompetence in protecting even themselves. Sinister though the government bunkers and citadels may seem, they might well end up as much of a shambles as the irradiated world they are planned to administer.

9
Communications and warning

The most grand and fortified network of bunkers and controls would be of little value if they were not in operation in time, or if they could not function with lines of communication expected to be at least as invulnerable as they are themselves. Official priorities in home defence expenditure have always placed the installation of communications, warning and broadcasting systems a close second to the assembly of the protected wartime headquarters.

The 1968 dismantlement of civil defence meant only that the preparations which directly supported public welfare had gone. The axing of the Home Office CD budget did not, for instance, affect plans or preparations made by the Ministry of Defence or the armed forces, whose whole *raison d'etre*, a main wartime engagement in the Rhineland, would require the nuclear protection of headquarters, communications and warning systems in the UK and elsewhere. The main military headquarters in the United Kingdom and abroad are linked by the central Defence Communications Network (DCN) as well as by each armed service's own network and public communications systems. American forces in Britain also operate their own communications networks, including satellite communications, microwave radio relay stations, and similar, but longer-ranged, 'troposcatter' stations.

The national warning system is provided by the UK Warning and Monitoring Organisation (UKWMO), which did not suffer unduly from the 1968 cuts. Field work for UKWMO is done by the network of Royal Observer Corps (ROC) posts which are scattered throughout Britain, generally located on high points – some 872 in all. The first function of the UKWMO and associated organisations is, initially, to provide a communications system for passing the first warning of attack – probably by missile, but possibly by manned aircraft. The second task is to report the extent of bombardment to government and military headquarters. The third task is to report fallout, from the first few hours of attack, until radioactivity levels have decayed enough for ROC posts to stand down.

Most of the present national warning system was constructed between 1959 and 1963. During these years, the whole system of air raid warnings which had evolved since the Second World War was completely replaced, in order to match the speed and destruction of an H bomb attack. At first, two national centres were chosen to be the point of origin of the first warning of nuclear attack. It was no longer sufficient to rely on local links between radar stations and police or civil defence HQS; in the 1960s, the only source of warning for the first attack might come from the Ballistic Missile Early Warning Station, at Fylingdales, which was completed in early 1964. Although other radar stations would 'see' the missiles, they would probably be unable to identify them in time, and certainly too late to issue any warning. The function of the massive radars at Flyingdales was to look across the far horizon, three thousand miles distant, and see the missiles as they passed the top of the 'boost' phase of their ballistic trajectory. Early IBM computers would then observe the pattern of motion to see if it corresponded to that of an incoming missile; if so a 'threat' alarm would sound, and the computer would calculate the endpoint of the missile's course. The Fylingdales BMEWS system, although much modernised, still operates according to the same principles.

Fylingdales was linked to the Air Defence Operations Centre (ADOC) at RAF Bentley Priory, near Stanmore in Middlesex. This was at the time the headquarters of Fighter Command, and the centre for British defensive air operations. In a 1968 re-organisation, the RAF reformed its operational units into a single Strike Command, with its headquarters at High Wycombe (now called, in NATO parlance, the UK Regional Air Operations Centre). The Home Office now have a Warning Officer on permanent duty at High Wycombe, and at a second, reserve, centre. A warning of attack, now, will not in fact originate with BMEWS, but with US satellite warning systems. The main satellites involved are the Project 647, or Defence Support Program series which are located in fixed,

---

Figure 19   Britain's attack and fallout warning system relies on the High Wycombe base to pass out early warning of aircraft or missile attack. After attack, UKWMO Group and Sector controls would produce fallout warnings.

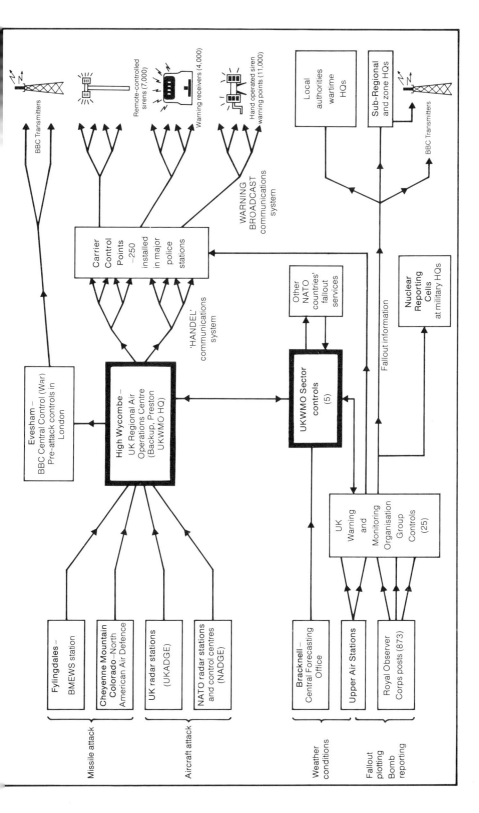

BBC Transmitters

Remote-controlled sirens (7,000)

Warning receivers (4,000)

Hand operated siren warning points (11,000)

WARNING BROADCAST communications system

Local authorities wartime HQs

Sub-Regional and zone HQs

BBC Transmitters

Carrier Control Points –250 installed in major police stations

Other NATO countries' fallout services

Nuclear Reporting Cells at military HQs

'HANDEL' communications system

Evesham – BBC Central Control (War) Pre-attack controls in London

High Wycombe – UK Regional Air Operations Centre (Backup, Preston UKWMO HQ)

UKWMO Sector controls (5)

Fallout information

UK Warning and Monitoring Organisation Group Controls (25)

Fylingdales – BMEWS station

Cheyenne Mountain Colorado – North American Air Defence

UK radar stations (UKADGE)

NATO radar stations and control centres (NADGE)

Bracknell – Central Forecasting Office

Upper Air Stations

Royal Observer Corps posts (873)

Missile attack

Aircraft attack

Weather conditions

Fallout plotting Bomb reporting

geostationary orbits 22,000 miles (32,200 km) high. These satellites, which were at first launched clandestinely in the early 1970s (disguised as 'failed' communications satellites), use infra red telescopes to detect hot spots on the face of the earth. In this way, they can see, and locate, missile launches. The alarm they raise would reach High Wycombe from NORAD headquarters in Colorado, where Project 647 satellites are controlled. After a nuclear exchange, the same satellites are also used to determine what targets have been destroyed, in both the west and the east. In the latter case, they enable the next stages of US nuclear bombardment to be matched to any surviving cities or bases.

The Fylingdales/Bentley Priory linkup was the origin of the famous 'four minute warning' and the source of a great deal of defence mythology. Firstly, it is not a four minute warning. The Scientific Advisers' *Training Manual* issued by the Home Office Scientific Advisory Branch has this to say:

No particular warning time can be guaranteed, but it is expected that the warning will be given not less than *three minutes* before an attack (Author's emphasis).

Secondly, many people who should know better – and this includes many of those critical of government plans – talk about the four minute warning as though it is likely to be the first and only notice of an impending nuclear attack. This is unwarranted criticism; there are more than enough deficiencies in *Protect and Survive* without also suggesting that it is a plan to be completed inside four minutes, or less. It is extremely hard to envisage the circumstances or rationale of a major pre-emptive strike without a military confrontation, conventional war, or extended crisis having taken place first. Indeed, were an attack to come out of the blue, it is quite likely that parts of the attack warning system would not work anyway – the *Hard Rock* scenarios, for example, include instructions for the police to fully test the system.

In some circumstances, even with war expected, there might be no warning. This could happen if submarine launched ballistic missiles were fired from close range – particularly from the west (from the Atlantic) – as such launches would be unlikely to be detected by Fylingdales (which would be looking the wrong way). These bombs would not explode unnoticed, however. Thirteen of the twenty-five UKWMO Group Controls are equipped with an instrument called AW-DREY, which was developed in the 1960s to detect nuclear explosions through the heat and electromagnetic pulses of energy from the explosion (AWDREY; Atomic Weapons Detection Recognition and Estimation of Yield). The AWDREY devices would then provide warning that an attack was under way – albeit too late in some cases. The AWDREYS can detect explosions at least seventy miles (120km) away.

In order to pass out the warning, a new nationwide communications network was constructed between 1960 and 1964. The network was constructed in two stages. The first stage was a signalling system for warning broadcasts – WB400, or *Handel* – which links the High Wycombe warning points to 252 police stations and headquarters throughout Britain. These police centres had previously been responsible for distributing air raid warnings. They were equipped now as Carrier Control Points (CCPS) and connected in to the *Handel* network.

Plate 28 Operating a Carrier Control Point in a police station. The warning of attack originates at a national warning centre, normally High Wycombe.

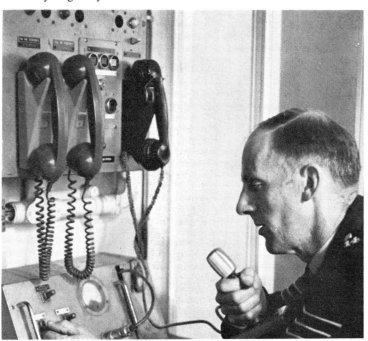

Handel consists of two separate networks throughout Britain whose lines are routed as far as possible to avoid target areas, but which connect to every major exchange. According to some Telecom engineers, the lines used are those which, in peacetime, carry the speaking clock.

Each police HQ and its CCP are connected to the sirens and warning broadcast receivers in its warning districts by two other networks called the WB400 and WB600 carrier systems. These use a system of 'carriers' which, by superimposing an extremely high frequency *onto ordinary telephone lines, enables sirens and warning receivers even in quite remote areas to be cheaply connected in. All the sirens in a warning district (and some 7,000 nationwide) can be automatically set to give the air raid warning (a falling and rising sound) or to give the all clear (continuous pitch). While controlling the sirens, the police operator can hear, on a telephone receiver, any detailed warning information, such as a list of missile targets, from the Home Office Warning Officer at High Wycombe. When the police operator speaks, however, his voice is heard not at High Wycombe but by the warning receivers in his area.

The signal for a nuclear attack is the Attack Warning – Red. It is the signal for the police operators at CCPs to operate their sirens. Many warning points, which include other local police stations, airports, factories, hospitals, power stations, TV and radio stations and transmitters, and so on, also have their own, hand-operated sirens which they can sound. In more remote areas, village Post Offices or even pubs have been fitted with warning receivers, and the landlord issued with a hand cranked siren. When not is use, the warning receivers are turned down but not switched off. Normally, they emit a quiet ticking sound, a sort of nuclear 'all's well'.

A loud wail is the signal for Attack Warning Red. A loud staccato sound alerts the warning recipient for a message from the police CCP. The warning receivers are also used to send out fallout warnings. But no siren signal has been devised to indicate 'fallout', and instead, police at surviving stations in fallout areas would be instructed over the WB400 network to give a signal with three loud maroons, warning the population to take shelter from fallout. Many ROC posts would also issue these warnings.

The BBC would also issue the Attack Warning Red through

* The carrier frequency is 72 kHz, far outside the audio range, although modulated by an audio signal.

Plate 29 The UK Warning and Monitoring Organisation's Western Sector HQ at Longley Lane, Goosnargh, near Preston. This HQ was extensively rebuilt in 1980–82 to be a national UKWMO reserve warning centre.

its broadcasting networks from the BBC Central Control. If the attack had come suddenly, this central control would be Broadcasting House in central London, where a red phone linked to High Wycombe sits beside the desk of the BBC's technical operations manager. If crisis measures had been adopted, the BBC would have moved its national control to the broadcasting bunker at Wood Norton, a training centre near Evesham used for the same purpose in the Second World War. Some BBC staff would also be at each SRHQ.

The UKWMO, in a publicity booklet, stress their job of warning the public. 'Ten million lives may have been saved' by early warnings, the booklet suggests.

If one adds together the various exaggerated claims of life-saving by different measures, the number of people saved appears to exceed the total population. Nonetheless the 'four minute warning' (ie, three minute warning) is of clear value in all circumstances, particularly in enabling those in the open to take cover and avoid burns from the thermal flash. But the UKWMO also has a task more closely connected with the conduct of nuclear war, which is not strongly featured in its publicity, and which is not well known to individual members of the ROC. Many military bunkers in Britain have attached to them UKWMO 'Nuclear Reporting Cells' (NRCS), which pass details of bomb bursts and fallout. This data is of relevance to 'war-fighting'. For example, the USAF and RAF commanders of nuclear bomber bases in Britain wish to know which military and civil airports have survived, to which dispersed or returning planes can go.

The UKWMO's twenty-five Group Controls also disseminate details of fallout and bomb bursts to SRHQS and County War HQS. Both SRHQS and the Group Controls have lines to BBC regional offices or their transmitters in order to provide fallout warnings direct to the public. Fallout warnings would be issued in any area where activity rose (or was expected to rise) above 0.3 Roentgens an hour; this would còver many thousands of square miles, even after just a few bombs.

After the attack, the UKWMO would probably also take over the job of providing a meteorological service. The Bracknell

---

Table 14   The UK Warning and Monitoring Organisation (UKWMO)

Sector Headquarters and groups	*Sector Headquarters and groups*
Metropolitan sector: HQ Horsham, Sussex	**Western sector: HQ Preston (Longley Lane, Goosnargh)**
1 Maidstone	(Also wartime national HQ for UKWMO, and alternative national warning centre)
2 Horsham	
3 Oxford (also peacetime headquarters of UKWMO)	16 Shrewsbury
4 Colchester	17 Wrexham (Borras)
14 Winchester	21 Preston (Longley Lane)
	22 Carlisle (RAF Carlisle)
Midlands sèctor: HQ Fiskerton, Lincoln	31 Belfast (Lisburn)
6 Norwich (Old Catton)	**Caledonian sector: HQ Dundee**
7 Bedford	24 Edinburgh (Turnhouse)
8 Coventry (Lawford Heath)	25 Ayr
15 Lincoln (Fiskerton)	28 Dundee (Craigiebarns)
20 York (Acomb)	29 Aberdeen (Northfield)
	30 Inverness (Raigmore)
Southern sector: HQ Lansdown, Bath	
9 Yeovil	
10 Exeter (Poltimore Park)	
12 Bristol (Lansdown)	
13 Carmarthen	

Plate 30 Plotting fallout and bomb bursts in a UKWMO HQ. Information comes in from ROC underground posts and is collated and plotted to show radiation levels over a wide area.

Weather Centre and Central Forecasting Office is closely involved in providing weather forecasts for military operations, and might be expected to be a target. In that event, ROC Group and Sector controls will provide Britain's weather service – a reasonable undertaking, since the most vital question about the weather will be the speed and direction of winds, not so much at the surface but at the high altitudes to which the fallout-laden nuclear fireballs will have risen. The ROC will get its information from Britain's eight Upper Air Stations, which periodically send radiosonde balloons to high altitudes, and from 80–90 ROC posts with simple meteorological instruments.

Each ROC post* can also measure the pressure from the blast wave of an explosion, and a simple pinhole camera is used to record the bomb's position. From inside their underground shelter, the operators can also monitor radioactivity levels on the surface, and pass them by phone or radio to their Group Controls. Five Sector controls are responsible for drawing up more extensive information on the pattern of nuclear attack on Britain, and passing this to NATO and overseas government headquarters. Table 14 lists the UKWMO Sector and Group HQs now in operation.

*The full list of the 872 ROC underground posts can be found as an appendix to *Attack Warning Red*, by Derek Wood, which is the ROC's official history (to 1975). (MacDonald and Janes, 1976).

The Observer Corps no longer has any function in relation to observing aircraft movements; that disappeared twenty years ago. Although the Home Office pays about ninety per cent of the costs of the system, the 11,000 ROC personnel come under the Royal Air Force. Some 370 warning and control staff are employed by the Home Office – they make up, in fact, ninety per cent of the Home Office staff working on Home Defence. Training warning point operators – and indeed the maintenance of the entire systems of sirens and carrier receivers – is a police responsibility.

Other than the Warning Broadcast Systems, a wide range of other special purpose communications have been installed for home defence or civil defence purposes. Some are merely special networks within the existing telecommunications system, such as 'private wire' direct links between the different bunkers in the government and local authority networks, or the UKWMO. These are backed up by the Home Office's own network of radio stations. Another more extensive network of this type, using all kinds of links including satellites, is run by the Ministry of Defence. There are also schemes for streamlining the public telephone scheme for emergency use, by cutting off most subscribers and allowing operators to retire to fallout protected switchboards. Many of the systems available were described to local authorities in the *Communications in War* circular from the Home Office (ES5/75), in particular the 'Government Control Network'.

As part of the increasingly frequent rehearsals of transition-to-war measures, British Telecom held an exercise to test their wartime activities for a week in late April 1982 – Operation *Fanfare*.

The main communications systems for civil defence are:

Government Control Network (GCN), recently renamed the Emergency Communications Network (ECN). This links all SRHQS, NICHQ, Scottish Zone and Central Controls, County Main and Standby Headquarters and subordinate bunkers by landline and radio.

Defence Communications Network (DCN) links central government HQ and all military bases by telex and telephone, with radio backup connections.

Telephone Preference Scheme is installed at all public exchanges, and will cut off 90–98 per cent of subscribers on government orders.

Emergency Manual Switching System (EMSS) is a network of manual telephone switchboards in protected basement accomodation in telephone exchanges. The EMSS operators provide a manual long distance service to priority users. Emergency Circuits can be connected from the ordinary network to provide extra civil and military links.

Both the Government Control Network and the links for the UK Warning and Monotoring Organisation use a backup system of radio and cable links. Each connection between sites goes both by Post Office underground cable, and by radio links through the Home Office's chain of 'hilltop' radio stations.

The Telephone Preference System has been built into all of Britain's twenty million telephones from the very start. When a new subscriber gets a phone, they are given a preference category, from 1 to 3. Only two in one hundred lines at most can be top category – category 1 – and never get disconnected, in any emergency. Category 2 lines can cover up to ten per cent of all lines – they will be cut off in war, but not in a peacetime civil or military emergency.

Although the basic intention of the preference scheme is to safeguard lines required by the authorities responsible for the fighting services and essential public services to retain control of their organisations during a war emergency, like all Home Defence measures, it is also oriented towards internal security 'civil contingences'. In the event of strikes causing serious disruption, or even insurgency or riot, the government's ability to disable most of the telephone system at the throw of a few switches is, obviously, a potent weapon.

This is spelt out in the British Telecom standing instruction for the preference service; lines given preference in a non-war emergency are those, not already in Category 1, which are:

required in a civil or military emergency for the maintenance of law and order, for the continuance of the various public services, for distribution of essential supplies, and generally to maintain the life of the community

(British Telecom instruction D I B0012, August 1980)

At each exchange, each telephone line is wired up to indicate its preference category. On older exchanges, an engineer has to visit the exchange and operate a row of switches. Modern electronic exchanges can however be put on electronic alert by turning a key in the equipment. A 'Prime' light goes on, and the preference scheme can then be remotely activated by dialling two numbers in sequence within three minutes at any future time.

Since the Second World War, the preference scheme has only been used once, in 1975, when a gas explosion badly damaged an exchange near Newcastle on Tyne. Once the preference scheme is activated, only Category 1 users (in war) or Categories 1 and 2 users (in a peacetime civil or military emergency) can make calls. Everyone else would find that their phones had suddenly gone 'dead' (although they could still *receive* calls from those connected to the service). Some people or organisations might find to their surprise that they still had telephone service after the mass disconnections; this would be bad news – because their premises had been earmarked to be used by some emergency government organisation. To avoid such arrangements being discovered, British Telecom staff are ordered not to tell anyone other than government departments whether they have been given telephone preference.

The preference system was started during the Second World War but only in an *ad hoc* and temporary fashion. The Post Office decided to standardise it in 1953 as part of its nuclear war plans then being made. By cutting off most of the subscribers, the amount of power used in the exchange is drastically reduced, and the exchange's battery power supply will last longer, if mains electricity is cut off as is inevitable. The preference scheme also means that the essential users will not encounter congestion – inevitable in a pre-war crisis as families and friends tried desperately to stay in touch. Indeed there will be no way to stay in touch, since the Post Office also plans to gradually withdraw all postal services as mobilisation starts in the run-up to an expected attack.

According to the official specification for telephone preference, even after it is used the public telephone network is not expected to last more than five days after an attack, if there is no outside electricity available. After this, the exchanges will stop working, and the only service available will be on direct lines like the GCN or DCN – or via the emergency manual operator network.

Appendix 5 lists the organisations and individuals who get preference service. The Category 1 lists cover mainly government organisations – the main exception (for obvious reasons) being the 'petroleum industry'. In Category 2, the system's orientation towards civil emergencies, including strikes, is clearer. The list of organisations covered (see p. 487) includes employers' associations, the CBI (Confederation of British Industry – the employers' central organisation) and the government's Advisory Conciliation and Arbitration Service. It does not include, curiously – and perhaps significantly – the Trades Union Congress, although Staff Associations and Trades Unions' local and national offices are mentioned.

Category 2 includes MP's private homes, and also the official and private residences of Lords Lieutenant, whose normally dormant role as the Queen's appointees is constitutionally and legally highly significant in civil emergency or crisis.

The exact sorts of civil emergency where the telephone preference scheme could be used on police, government or military request are still secret. A circular on the police use of the *PO Telephone Preference Scheme* in peacetime emergencies (ES6/75) was sent to Chief Constables only late in 1975. It was (and is) classified. The intention to use the system as one part of a series of extreme means to deal with strikes, etc, is indicated in the British Telecom instruction referred to earlier, which notes that new exchanges may have to start operations before the preference system there is complete. If this is done:

It will be necessary to balance service and economic considerations against *security risks* (of letting the exchange operate for *a few days or weeks* without preference) having regard to conditions at the particular exchange and current international *or industrial* tensions (Author's emphasis).

The provision of the scheme is quite costly, as most modern exchanges, designed for overseas sales, do not normally have this uniquely British requirement built in. As far as is known, the cost of the scheme is distributed onto ordinary telephone bills.

In most areas, rather less than the maximum number of preference scheme lines are allocated. In London for example, the GLC and London Boroughs have about 4,000 lines. In the construction industry, nationally, there are only 2–300 lines allocated at most, chiefly to the National Federation of Building Trades Employers and some seven other manufacturers associations, together with a handful of some nine large manufacturers of cement and building supplies. Like all non-government users, they are unaware of the telephone preference granted to them.

The British Telecom Emergency Manual Switching System (EMSS) is the main means of long term communications after a nuclear attack. The telephone preference scheme is useless once most of the public telephone system stops operating, which will almost certainly have happened within ten days of attack. At that stage, the system will revert, for a very long time, to manual operations. Emergency switchboards are installed in the basements of major trunk exchanges, and equipped with fallout protection, supplies, sleeping accomodations and so on. Like County Council Controls, the accomodation available may vary from the purpose-built to the makeshift, supplemented by a liberal supply of sandbags.

The EMSS switchboards are in most ways merely duplicates of the ordinary switchboards several storeys above ground in most exchanges, known as Auto-Manual Centres. During peacetime there is a skeleton network of long distance lines connected to the emergency switchboards only – before attack, they would be at least doubled in number by taking away trunk lines from the ordinary network.

EMSS is intended to serve only main 'key wartime installations', from where there are direct lines to the emergency switchboards. These include government and local authority Controls, police and fire HQS, and military establishments. These HQS are much more limited in number than even Category 1 preference subscribers. For a long time after nuclear attack, when electricity supplies and the public telephone service had failed altogether, the EMSS could continue operating from its fallout shelters, using human hands in place of automatic STD equipment, and an absolute minimum of battery stored electricity.

During and immediately after nuclear attack – when normal operators would have stopped working – telephone preference scheme users who could not get through would not be able to use EMSS – apart from a very restricted group given a special code. Once the attack had abated, however, they could all use EMSS by dialling the peacetime code, 100.

The EMSS network can also be used in peacetime emergencies, as all the lines to the emergency switchboards also go to the normal switchrooms. There, they are known as 'Trunk Subscribers', and can if need be have direct use of EMSS or other manual facilities if ordinary exchanges cease to function.

The postal service might be restored 'when radiological conditions permitted', according to *Communications in War*. It notes:

Initially . . . the Post Office would concentrate on the provision of an improvised point-to-point message courier system for official letters. For some time this may have to be operated without using fuel, for example by couriers travelling relatively short distances on foot or on bicycle to the next relay point and back.

Not surprisingly:

Parcels services are likely to be non existent . . .

After attack, the communications networks most likely still to be operating are the Emergency Communications Network (ECN) and the Defence Communications Network (discussed also in Chapter 12). The ECN is provided and paid for by the Home Office; as its former title – Government Control Network – suggests, it is the main means of communications between the government and local authority bunkers.

The Government Control Network (GCN) came into existence with the RSGs in the early 1960s. Prior to that the much smaller Regional War Rooms had relied only on the ordinary telephone network, enhanced with the schemes described above. In 1961, according to papers later found in Reading, the first direct lines were connected into the War Room at Whiteknights Park, Reading, which had become the communications centre for RSG6 some miles away at Warren Row. Thereafter, this network of links to other RSGs and local controls was rapidly and urgently built up. It was just reaching completion in April 1963 when, ironically, the existence and purpose of the whole system was revealed by the *Spies for Peace*.

The main part of the network was its set of connections to other RSGs, county council and county borough headquarters and police and military sites. The majority of these connections used an ingenious system whereby a telephone call could be made over a single line at the same time as it was being used for telegraph signals in each direction. This is called Speech and Duplex, or s+DX for short. Further reliability was provided by wiring in at least two independent routes to each destination. One connection went through ordinary Post Office telephone cables, which run along the sides of main roads. The other links went from a radio mast at the RSG (or its communications centre) via the Home Office hilltop stations, to other masts at the destination bunker.

In this way, the Warren Row RSG was linked to neighbouring RSGs at Cambridge, Nottingham, Kidderminster, Dover, and Kingsbridge (Bolt Head). It was linked to council HQs in its area – Hampshire, Oxfordshire and Oxford Borough, Berkshire and Reading, Buckinghamshire and Dorset. Since London was then partitioned up between the adjoining regions in the control scheme, RSG6's territory extended as far as Westminster. It also had lines to RAF Uxbridge, the naval HQ at Fort Southwick, Portsmouth, and the army HQs at Aldershot and Warminster. There was a broadcasting connection to BBC transmitters via the BBC regional HQ in Bristol.

The GCN links also extended to a few more important central government HQs – Hawthorn itself, and also the North Rotunda in London, through which the Home Office, under the code-name 'CHAPLIN', controlled the RSGs, at least whilst on exercise.

In July 1963, almost as soon as the communications network was complete, the Sub-Regional Control scheme began to replace the RSGs (see p. 266). Lines to the newer and more extensive network of SRCs were installed; at the same time, the centre of the SRC communications net moved from the North Rotunda in Westminster to the rather less vulnerable former wartime 'citadel' in Harrow. This citadel, formerly the Air Ministry's emergency 'Station X' wartime HQ, lies underneath what is now the Home Office's Central Communications Establishment, behind an HMSO factory in Wealdstone, Harrow.

When civil defence was revamped in the 1970s, the controls and their communications were restored and reconnected much as their predecessors had been. Each SRHQ (see Figure 20) is connected to adjacent SRHQs, and to all the county (or Scottish region) main and standby war headquarters that its area covers (in London, Group Controls).

The connections between SRHQs and lower controls go both by British Telecom cable connection, and by radio through the Home Office 'hilltop' radio station system. The British Telecom lines are routed to avoid likely target areas, but some may be damaged. The ability of the Home Office radio system to withstand the effects of EMP is somewhat in question; although aerials at SRHQs and manned controls could be disconnected if an attack was expected, the same could not be done at remote stations. In short, it might be some time before the network became operational. Indeed, much of the network was not even installed by 1982.

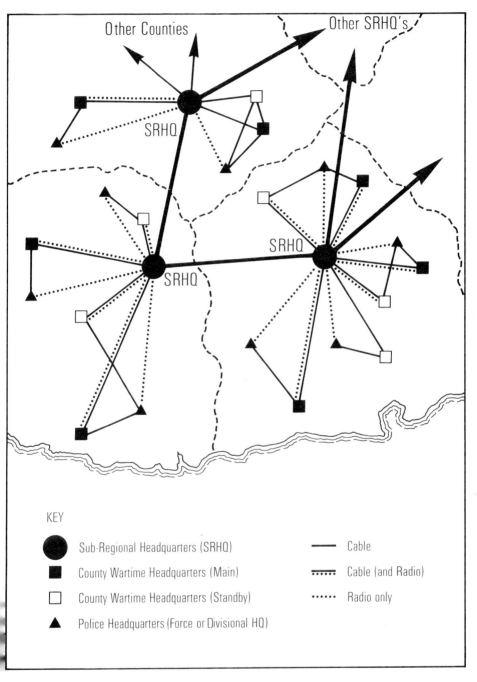

Figure 20 The Emergency Communications Network (ECN) provides links between neighbouring SRHQs and other controls, using British Telecom cables and the 'hilltop' radio stations.

Figure 20 shows the final planned network, and the state it had reached at the beginning of 1981. Even where bunkers had been built, or converted, such as SRHQ32 at Loughborough, communications were not installed – and at that time, three bunkers had yet to be built. By 1982, no location had been found for the (North Wales) SRHQ81, and it was apparent that large parts of the Home Office radio link network were far from operational. Despite public claims made by Home Office ministers for civil defence it has been apparent that the tiny amount of money available for capital expenditure has resulted in extremely slow progress – even on schemes of such high priority as the SRHQS. The Home Office acquired the Loughborough site in 1974, yet it was not complete even eight years later; an extension scheme for SRHQ21 (Yorks) at Shipton took five years, from 1976 to 1981. The Liverpool/ Manchester SRHQ 102 at Hack Green was acquired in the late 70s, but it was two years before construction work had gone further than erecting a fence.

Each SRHQ has a civil 'tape relay centre' to exchange messages, and a separate military communications centre. Most of the twenty SRHQ military staff are concerned in operating the military 'commcen' (communications centre). Through military telex networks – 'TASS' and 'TARE' – and through mobile radio links the army signals staff are able to pass messages to AFHQS, military bases in the Sub-Region, and other HQS, including national civil or military headquarters. The AFHQS also control the new £7 million MOULD VHF radio network which is being installed exclusively for home defence purposes in 1982 and 1983. These systems are likely to be substantially more resilient to EMP and other effects of attack than the Home Office's. Many home defence communications systems are run by TAVR Signals Regiments; for example, squadrons to operate AFHQ and SRHQ communications in the North of England are provided by 38 Signals Regiment (V), based in Sheffield. They form part of the army's 2 Signal Group, which appears to have its own war HQ in a former RAF underground bunker at Sopley, near Bournemouth.

British Telecom also keeps records of other radio communications systems in private hands, of which there are many – including nationwide networks run by organisations like the AA, RAC or Securicor. Records of these systems can be inspected by county council EPOS (although 'normally not more frequently than every five years,' according to *Communications in War*), who can then prepare plans for equip-

Plate 31 Hilltop home defence radio station: Cairn-mon-Earn, Grampian Region, Scotland.

ment to be requisitioned after attack. Within British Telecom, an 'Area War Group' in each telephone managers' office plans for the incorporation of these and other systems into post-attack communications. British Telecom also has its own national wartime HQ, at Broggyntyn Hall, Oswestry, where the national network control centre is located.

Radio amateurs also have a scheme for helping in civil defence operations, through the Radio Amateur Emergency Network, *Raynet*. No central government organisation has sought their cooperation, but the use of Raynet stations is a feature of many county council War Plans and is also suggested for peacetime emergencies. Raynet stations would be used in the event of tidal flooding in London.

A list of Home Office 'hilltop' radio stations is given in Table 15 (p. 304). Although incomplete, this gives some impression of the amount of work that has been done. The stations are generally used for four types of communications – Home Defence, police, fire and ROC/UKWMO. Each set of

Table 15 Hill-top Radio Stations: the Home Office and Scottish Office network

Sub-Region	Station Sites	Sub-Region	Station Sites
11	Walthwaite Moor Harras Dyke Scar Quarry Beacon Fell Gt. Dun Fell Hazelshaw Hill Ottercops Moss Marley Hill (depot) Trimdon Collier Law Richmond Moor Cleave Dike	42	Kelvedon Hatch Seward's End High Garrett Bushy Hill Throcking Bedmond Oakley Streatley
		51	Harrow (Central Communications Establishment) Cranbrook (depot)
21	Kippax (depot) Ilkley Moor Golcar Pateley Moor Dunhazles Skipton Moor Weedley Cot Nab	61	Knockholt Pound Fairlight Beddingham Hill West Hoathly Gravelly Hill Guildford Burton Down Race Hill Stoke D'Abernon
31	Idle Robin Hood's Hills Kirkby-in-Ashfield Alport Height Sir William Hill Hutchinson's Holt Kirkby Underwood Normanby-le-Wold Grange Farm Fulletby Stanston (depot)	62	Lockinge Down Quainton Amen Corner Lark Stoke Hannington (depot) Alton St Boniface Down East Meon
32	Potcote Old Poor's Gorse Bardon Hill Glebe Farm	71	Shapwick (depot) Morgan's Hill Cleeve Hill Stoford Cinderford Thorney Hill Bulbarrow Hill West Compton East Harptree
41	Chevely (depot) Gt. Gidding Reed Tacolneston Brink Hill Bodham Hill	72	St Just Four Lancs Kensbarrow Downs Trewassa Quiter Common Waddles Down Stockland Hill Tavistock (depot)

Sub-Region	Station Sites	Sub-Region	Station Sites
81	Gwaenysgoer	101	Billinge (depot)
	The Catch/Halkyn		Winter Hill
	Cefn Du		Hameldon Hill
	The Graig		Heaton Park
	Holyhead		New Hey
	Llandonna		Darnacre
	Capel Garmon		Dunhazles
	Rhiw		Snaefell
	Colwyn Bay (depot)	102	Old Palace
82	Werfa		Idle Hill
	Crickhowell		Sutton Common
	Bridgend (depot)	Scotland	Cairn–mon Earn
91	Brown Edge		Montreathmont
	Ridge Lane		Craigowl Hill
	Cannock Chase		Hill of Foudland
	The Wrekin		Millstone Hill
92	Romsley (depot)		Green Lowther
	Redmarley D'Abilot		
	Dinmore		
	Lark Stoke		
	Brown Clee		

links is provided separately. The police and fire links provide one or more channels from each force's operations room to vehicles; a more extensive network connects divisional stations to pocket 'personal radio' receivers usually carried by beat police officers. Similar services are provided for local fire brigades. (Local and health authorities are responsible for ambulance services, which use different stations and different frequencies). All Home Defence radio links are provided using UHF frequencies, and provide the backup links for the connections shown on Figure 19 (p. 287). Another, grid type network using VHF frequencies links ROC Group Controls. There are also special connections to offshore islands, including the Isle of Man and the Channel Islands.

At the strategic level, communications plans are more striking. Extensive plans were made during the 1950s for a 'survivable' communications system. By 1960, two separate developments – the underground exchanges of *Kingsway, Anchor* and *Guardian* – and the *Backbone* microwave system – were nearing completion. The extensive cable and government tunnel network under London itself had been completed in the early 1950s. In general, these systems do not appear to have been oriented towards any specific network of controls,

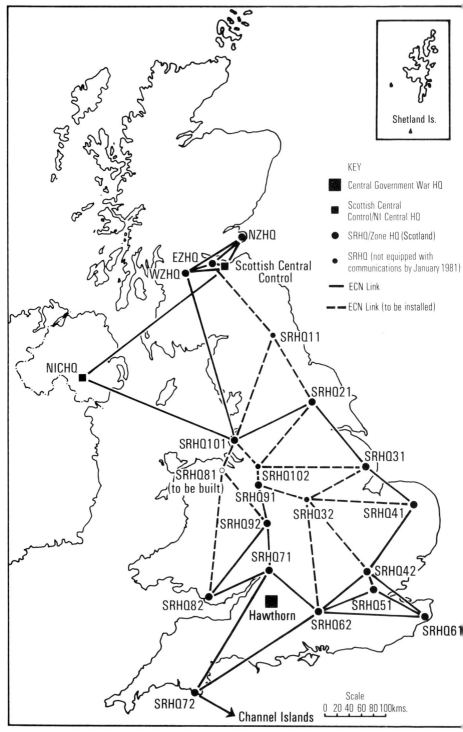

Figure 21 Each SRHQ contains a communications centre for the Sub-Region. Telex messages are sent via a Tape Relay Centre within the SRHQ.

but instead intended to provide a strategic reserve communications system. While they operated, the three underground exchanges provided connections to virtually every major exchange in Britain, most of which ran through the microwave system or specially routed cables. With the exception of direct connections to the Hawthorn central government HQ, emergency connections on the microwave network and special cables appear to have been provided in a generalised way. The head at the top of *Backbone*'s spine and nervous sytem was, in effect, Hawthorn. The microwave tower at Five Ways was built directly over the underground quarries and is a conspicuous local landmark. Shortly before this, a £1 million underground cable had been laid from London, through Hawthorn, to south west England.

Communications in War explains the ultimate post-nuclear attack requirement:

As soon as conditions permitted after an attack and decisions are taken on the location of regional government facilities, the Post Office, aided perhaps by the mobilisation of surviving engineers from the private sector, would concentrate on developing an improvised public telephone service. This telephone system . . . would have to rely for several months on the surviving elements of the peacetime systems and a considerable degree of cannibalisation. . . .

It appears to have been originally intended (in 1954) that *Backbone* should enable a bomb-blasted Britain to carry on functioning throughout a prolonged nuclear battle as an airbase and support base. After the war was over, the 'improvised' communications networks could be tacked onto *Backbone*,

Figure 22 shows the contemporary state of the British Telecom microwave system. Prominently marked is the set of connections which form the emergency *Backbone*, its 'spurs' and western and northern extensions. (Although not all links on each route shown are for *Backbone*, some east coast RAF radar stations are also connected into the network, but they use separate links, which were only installed in the late 1960s after *Backbone* was complete.)

Originally, all the *Backbone* stations were to have been extremely strong, concrete towers with perspex shields for the aerial galleries (which would, incidentally, have made the layout of the network difficult to discover by observation). Eventually, the high cost of constructing the network

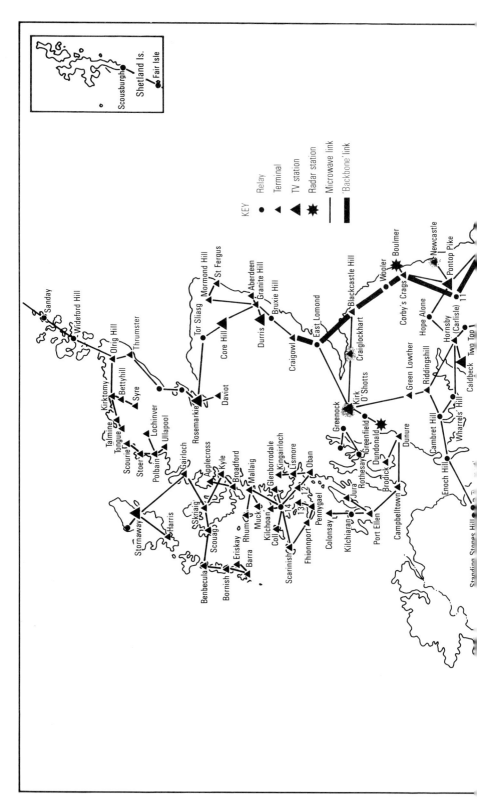

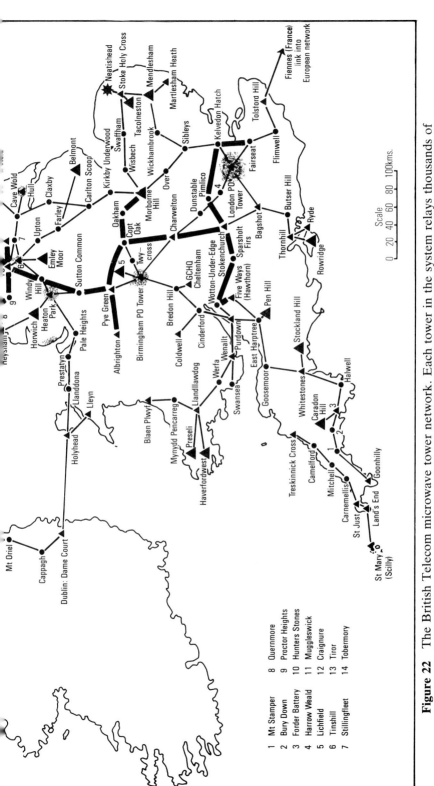

Figure 22 The British Telecom microwave tower network. Each tower in the system relays thousands of telephone channels, telex or data links, or TV connections by means of radio beams. The parabolic dish aerials generally used to transmit the signals are the towers' most distinctive feature.

Plate 32 The entrance to *Kingsway* underground trunk exchange is discreetly sited in London's High Holborn. Nearby buildings house goods lifts and exhaust extractors.

entirely out of concrete towers, and some unexplained technical difficulties, ruled out the use of reinforced concrete at every location.

The first part of *Backbone* was the straightforward London-Birmingham-Manchester-Leeds route. This provided the underground exchanges in the first three cities with alternatives to underground cables, which could not be so easily protected against sabotage or restored after attack. Only three relay towers were needed between London and Birmingham; two between Birmingham and Manchester; and one between Manchester and Leeds.

Many of the towers in this section of *Backbone* were built of concrete. Apart from the towers inside the cities (and Heaton Park on the outskirts of Manchester), these towers were at Charwelton, Pye Green on Cannock Chase, and Sutton Common. Three other towers, low down on high sites at Dunstable and Harrow Weald, and in the central Pennines at Windy Hill, away from targets, were made of steel latticework.

The second part of *Backbone* included bypasses for the four main cities, and the provision of two new hubs for the emergency links. The most important was a concrete tower at Stokenchurch on the Chiltern Hills, which linked *Backbone*'s western extension to bypass routes around London, and south to Southampton. The *Northern Backbone* system was built in 1962, starting at the second new hub of the emergency network, the Hunters' Stones tower near Harrogate. *Northern Backbone* ran all the way to Dundee; a bypass around the Tyneside conurbation was later provided at Muggleswick in moorland west of the area.

Spurs run out from *Backbone* to Lancaster, York, Shrewsbury and Peterborough, north to Dundee, east to Maidstone, and west to Hawthorn and then on to Plymouth and the transatlantic satellite and cable terminals in Cornwall. The whole system was explicitly designed only for nuclear war, save its use in peacetime for providing eavesdropping 'sigint' (signals intelligence) links to the us National Security Agency base at Menwith Hill, near the Hunters Stones tower.

The wartime purpose of the network was fully explained by Mr J. H. H. Merriman, then an engineer and later the Post Office's technology director, when a planning inquiry was held in 1962 over the building of a tower at Wotton-under-Edge, near Stroud in Gloucestershire. Merriman explained in written testimony:

The Post Office is responsible for ensuring that in the event of an attack on this country adequate communications for the administration of the country are available up to the time of the attack and as far as possible to assist in the work of restoration afterwards. This means that communications services must be provided in advance, routed in diverse ways, for the operational needs of the Fighting Services and of Civil Defence and for the dissemination of essential information.

He explained the general problem with cables; since they linked city centres, and for the most part ran along major roads, they were generally too near to too many targets.

The terminal points in the existing network . . . are in the more populous areas. . . . The Post Office cannot rely on any of these major telecommunications centres escaping damage from attack.

But radio relay stations require no physical connection to each other, and only a few key relay sites need to be protected, they are therefore 'less vulnerable' than cable systems:

As a safeguard in the case of possible attack the Post Office has been obliged to supplement its cable network by a radio relay network. This network must do two things. First, it must avoid the main centres of population; second, it must provide a service to those centres that may not be knocked out nevertheless whose cable communications may have been cut.

The 1955 and 1956 Defence White Papers had indeed promised such a network, designed to meet an atomic attack, and the 1956 White Paper had reported Post Office 'progress' on 'a cable and ultra high frequency radio network outside the main towns designed to ensure the maintenance of vital communications in the event of a nuclear attack'. Both the Post Office evidence and the White Paper stress the need to avoid major towns, despite advice given to the public then and now, to stay put in the selfsame towns. The Post Office's radio network was to cost over £20 million.

The Wotton-under-Edge planning enquiry was told that the Post Office had been easily able to provide 'comparatively safe' cable routes, but wanted to keep the number of radio stations built to a minimum. The new station, they said, was required to link from *Backbone* in the east to Wales, and to the west (a route not in fact provided), to Bristol and the southwest (and to Hawthorn). Mr. Merriman explained:

> The primary need for this radio station . . . is to maintain essential defence telephone and telegraph communications. Once established such a station would permit the further development of the normal peacetime network for public trunk and television services (such as 625 line and colour TV). . . . All the new stations are in process of development. . . .

The rest of the network was nearly complete, the inquiry was told, and Wotton-under-Edge was 'urgently needed' if the 'radio network as a whole' was not to be delayed.

Wotton-under-Edge was indeed critical, since it provided the direct, high capacity connection to the Hawthorn complex. The western extension of *Backbone* had not been specifically planned in 1956 – *Backbone* then ran from central London to and around Manchester and Birmingham, and then north through Yorkshire. However the provision of the new links to what is now publicly identified as the centre of the Defence Communications Network meant that relatively 'survivable' lines of communication were available, through the special links, to control military operations during nuclear war, and link up regional governments after attack.

The Post Office, in public statements on the history of the microwave system, invariably sets out to deceive the public with suggestions that the system was built to provide colour television; a 1974 article in the *Guardian* by the PO's Director of Research, for example, suggested that 'an important stimulus came from the need to provide a nationwide network for distributing television signals. . . . Having created a micro-wave trunk network it was natural and economic to deploy it further to provide for the future growth of trunk telephony.' Every account of the network's history the Post Office (or BT) now gives carefully omits to discuss the period in which the network was actually constructed, between 1956 and 1965, in order to avoid discussing the way it bypasses the targets of a nuclear strike.

Notwithstanding this, the government sought in the 1978 ABC Official Secrets Acts trial to criminalise research on this system, and Post Office and other witnesses attempted to establish that the Post Office towers might be 'prohibited places' on the grounds that they carried 'traffic forming part of the United Kingdom network of defence communications'. Taking pictures of Post Office towers, it was suggested, might be unlawful and a selection of such pictures, including several of the Post Office Tower in central London, were, ludicrously, produced in evidence. Only one tower, in Aberdeen, was exempt from the suggestion that examining it was illegal.

In the event, this allegation collapsed, and the prosecution in the ABC case rapidly withdrew its charges as being based on an insufficient appreciation by security officials of how much information was already available to the public. The judge in the case later declared the use of such charges (under the first, 'espionage' section of the Act) to be 'oppressive' and 'unjustified'.

By the start of 1964, some 1200 miles (1900 km) of links had been provided, each carrying 600 telephone channels. A new, separate, and defence–only network was added to the system in the mid 60s to support the *Linesman* air defence plotting and computer system then being constructed. The principle of *Linesman* was to integrate all British radar signal inputs and produce a national radar 'picture' at the Air Defence Data Centre at West Drayton near Heathrow (also the Civil London Air Traffic Control Centre). Three master radar stations – Boulmer, Staxton Wold, and Neatishead, were linked together on a microwave ring, taking in West Drayton. New Post Office towers were built at RAF radar stations and elsewhere, particularly in south Lincolnshire and Yorkshire, to provide these connections. The southernmost connection went to the Post Office Tower in London from which another aerial, said to have been concealed behind perspex shrouds on the upper part of the tower, linked to West Drayton.

Besides the ring around Boulmer, Staxton Wold, Neatis-

Plates 33 & 34 British Telecom microwave towers: Proctor Heights, between Lancaster and Harrogate, part of a *Backbone* spur (above) and Forder Battery, Plymouth (right).

head and London, there were separate spurs to connect in other radar stations. A small chain ran west of Edinburgh to link Boulmer to the radar station at Dundonald, and another link in Northern Ireland connected in Bishopscourt radar station.

In the late 60s, finally, the system began to be used more and more extensively for colour TV and telephone signals.

They are now the major users of the system, and with the
capital cost of the towers having been largely met by the
decision to provide a nuclear defence network, providing new
routes by radio is often cheaper than cable.

Similar uses of microwave have been made in most European NATO countries and in the United States. At the same
time as the British Post Office network was built, the US
Western Union constructed a $80 million, 267-station system
across the United States for 'both military and commercial
needs'. It, too, bypassed cities – 'for reasons of national
defence . . . stations are routed to bypass critical target areas.'

The links did not run *through* any city. Like the Post Office system, a primary purpose of the network was the control of forces during a nuclear war, for example by sending launch data and instructions to missile control centres.

In the mid 60s, the Post Office constructed three further trunk exchanges designed to provide reliable communications in war. These were *Granta* in Cambridge, *Kennet* in Reading, and a third at Tunbridge Wells. These new 'zone' centres were intended to lessen the peacetime load on London, and in war to substitute for the possible destruction or disablement of the capital's extensive systems. The cities they were in were not expected to be targets, and the exchanges were not particularly hardened or placed underground. It does appear more than a coincidence that the three cities selected were then the sites of Regional Civil Defence HQs, and leading candidates for sites of postwar regional government.

Some special cable systems also formed part of *Backbone*. A striking example is a chain of cables running from Heysham, Lancs, undersea to Colwyn Bay, and thence to Shrewsbury. These cables join together two *Backbone* spurs, at Lancaster and Shrewsbury. The provision of an undersea cable was an extremely expensive way of bypassing Liverpool and Manchester, and was later strangely augmented by further cables and links in this part of the Irish sea between Colwyn Bay, Douglas (Isle of Man), Heysham, and Dalton-in-Furness.

The cable route south from Colwyn Bay directly passed the large underground tunnel complex at Rhydymwyn near Mold in North Wales, which is earmarked as a 'Special Site' for wartime central government. It may have been the intention to use the Shrewsbury/Colwyn Bay/Heysham links to connect this centre of emergency government to the rest of the country. In the event, and like many other plans, it clearly has not yet come to pass; the Rhydymwyn caverns, although maintained, are not converted for any wartime use. (Railway sidings into the site were kept in being after the 60s closures, and the track was only finally lifted in 1977).

Since the last war, the Post Office (British Telecom) has, clearly, spent considerable sums on digging tunnels, laying networks, constructing the towers and converting exchanges so as to be able to disconnect most of their customers – as well as providing a national telephone tapping centre disguised as an 'Equipment Development Divison' and arranging

Plate 35 British Telecom bunker at Sennen, Cornwall. It protects terminal equipment for transatlantic and other submarine cables.

the monitoring of international communications for the US at their Menwith Hill base. Their public statements tend to be, if anything, more directly misleading on the subjects covered in this book than, for example, statements of the Defence Ministry or Home Office. The provision of the national communications system has given the PO/BT an unprecedented grip on the hard core of national emergency planning. It was the PO which prepared a press release claiming, untruthfully, that the deep level tunnels under Whitehall were theirs, and were being dug to avoid congestion. Such a lie was needed to avoid the unwelcome public conclusion that the government might be building deep shelters to 'protect their own skins' (as they were). In 1965, a senior Post Office official was part of the group who made it clear that Whitehall would like the BBC to ban the *War Game*. Nowadays, British Telecom officials invariably claim that their tower network was built 'for television', although, as the evidence of their former technology director makes clear, that was the last thing on the Post Office's mind in 1962.

The BBC have had an equally important and little-advertised role to play. During the Second World War, the Corporation constructed many new short, medium and long wave transmitters to maintain broadcasting services to Britain, the Empire and overseas. The closest possible links were made with the military services – a particularly important requirement being to turn off transmitters in each area to avoid them being used for homing purposes by approaching bombers. During the war the main studios and network were considerably diversified, with country houses in Bangor, Evesham, Bedford, and Elstree as well as many different sites in London acting as emergency controls or studios. The BBC also got its own reinforced concrete London control centre a hundred yards behind Broadcasting House, through which main programme links were connected. During the war, most broadcasting was done on a single channel combining the pre-war National Service (on 1500m from Droitwich) with Regional Services. This network is now Radio 4 (previously the Home Service). Its most powerful transmissions are still on long wave from Droitwich, and Westerglen and Burghead in Scotland. But like all BBC services, it is now provided nationwide on VHF (save that Radios 1 and 2 share a single VHF allocation).

The BBC's broadcasting networks would be used nationally to transmit the attack warning, and after an attack various transmitters would be linked to SRHQs to provide the Wartime Broadcasting Service (WTBS). *Information Services in War* (ES2/72) explained:

The BBC's plans for broadcasting in war provide for a network of transmitters throughout the country, equipped with generators to supply power and providing fallout protection for the staff. In addition to providing facilities for national broadcasts, the system (WTBS) is linked to the Sub-Regional Headquarters. Each SRHQ will be equipped with studio facilities enabling broadcasts to be transmitted simultaneously throughout the region simultaneously with, and independent of, similar activities in other regions. A small team of BBC personnel is included in the complement of each SRHQ. Official news items would be broadcast on the WTBS and printed in local sheets. . . .

The BBC's national role in boosting wartime public 'morale' is one which strikes a responsive note inside government. The regional broadcasting system is a newer idea; it arrived with the Regional Seats of Government, when it was apparent that broadcasting arrangements would have to be linked to the regional plans during the 'survival' phase. Each RSG, and later the SRCs and SRHQs were provided with small studios and linked to regional BBC transmitters. In the case of RSG6 (later SRC61) at Warren Row, this linkage was nothing more exceptional than a good sound quality telephone line to the BBC's Whiteladies Road, Bristol offices, from where southern and south western Radio Four transmissions were controlled.

During the early 1960s, the BBC was said to be building a new chain of 'self-supporting transmitters' – in addition, apparently, to the transmitters and fallout protection which were available or would be installed at major existing stations. An autobiography of the late Sir Charles Curran also mentions them as a network of 'secret' medium wave transmitters which were later taken over to complement local radio broadcasting, at a time when they were in decay as a result of civil defence 'care and maintenance' policies. One such transmitter centre was built in 1966 at Brinklow Heath, on a fruit farm between Coventry and Birmingham. The transmitter units were in a purpose built concrete building, complete with generators and oil fuel store. By 1975, however, the site had become more or less derelict – never inspected or tested; and in 1976, the aerials were removed, and the generator taken out. The BBC's war planners seemed nevertheless reluctant to give up anything, however apparently little needed, and the lease on the site was extended from twelve to twenty years in 1978. The announcement in 1980 that part of the money added to the Home Defence budget would be spent on improving WTBS suggests that, by then, it had fallen into a state of some considerable decay.

It seems likely that the revamping of WTBS will centre on the BBC (and possibly IBA) local radio transmitters, both medium wave and VHF (VHF is received better inside structures). However the exact wavebands and frequencies to be used for WTBS remain secret; *Information Services in War* merely says that:

Normal peacetime television and sound broadcasting would continue until the Government decided to introduce the special wartime broadcasting service (WTBS). Before the changeover took place, special announcements would be broadcast on radio and television, telling the public about the new system, the actual time when it would start, and the various frequencies to which radio receivers should be tuned.

The circular also explained that WTBS would at first be a single programme consisting of official announcements, official news, and official advice on increasing 'prospects of survival';

'there would, for morale purposes, be an entertainment element'. On careful examination, it seems unlikely that the government would wish to switch off the television networks until the last possible moment. Public calm and the 'stay-at-home' plans could well be encouraged by keeping everything as 'normal' as possible, until normality was no longer possible. There would seem few more effective ways of doing that than keeping TV on the air – even increasing, rather than reducing, TV programming.

That might be one reason why, according to engineers who have been able to visit the emergency Central Control at Evesham, the centre was equipped for television as well as radio (although an alternative explanation is suggested; that some floors of the emergency centre found peacetime use as a training studio). The 'Broadcasting Bunker' at Evesham was apparently completed, structurally, around 1970 and power supplies and air conditioning installed. But this was at the time when CD generally received no cash, certainly not for capital spending, and the full installation of equipment was not then completed. Little is said in the BBC about its emergency plans, whether for the earmarking of staff to serve in SRHQs or the emergency transmitter networks. Engineers who have seen the emergency systems say that most major

Plate 36   The BBC Central Control bunker at Wood Norton, the Corporation's Engineering Training Centre near Evesham.

transmitters are provided with extra lines to reorganise the network in emergency – 'deferred services'. The Post Office have arrangements to provide 'emergency circuit' switching for these. There also used to be 200 watt medium wave transmitters in caravan convoys which could, in emergency, be used for dispersed regional broadcasting. BBC engineers, during the 50s, also went on special government civil defence courses in anticipation of their war roles. One engineer recalled how they were all issued with the *Advising the House-holder* guide, shown films and taught that:

the Government doesn't expect the whole population to be killed and regards its biggest threat to be from the civilian population rioting for food. The police and army's job would be to 'keep civil order' and the films I saw showed armed police fighting back hungry mobs.

(private correspondence, 1975).

Most of the 'deferred services' lines appear to originate at the Wood Norton HQ. Wood Norton had also initially been the home of the BBC Monitoring Service, which obtains both intelligence for the government and news for the media by listening to open overseas broadcasts.

Both the BBC Monitoring Service and the External Broadcasting networks would be of considerable importance to the government nationally during nuclear war. There is evidence that some of the more modern External Service transmitters may have been installed with thoughts of emergency use – the Skelton transmitters in Cumbria, for example, are separated in two duplicate sites – and presumably these, like the Monitoring Service HQ at Caversham Park near Reading, are provided with fallout protection and emergency supplies.

In the later stages of the 'survival' phase, the government might open up a full Regional Broadcasting System using WTBS in conjunction with a chain of local informations centres and, possibly, news sheets being issued *ad hoc*. These services would be arranged by Central Office of Information personnel, assisted by the BBC. Orthodox journalists might be used as part of the local authority staffs, and the *Information Services* circular suggested that county councils should 'explore discreetly the local availability of suitable persons in private employment ' – but 'not at this stage approach' them, unless there was a 'rapidly deteriorating international situation'.

The circular also suggests that 'local nominal rolls of survivors' could be built up at information centres, and that radio stations might lates find time to transmit 'personal messages, indicating the death or injury or good health of the person named'. It was stressed however, that it would be unwise to start drawing up lists of survivors too soon:

For as long as the death toll from injuries and radiation effects continued at a high level, the effort in compiling nominal rolls would not be justified. Until national postal services were restored . . . (that might take a year or two) there would be no way, except on a very limited territorial basis, of helping to allay grave public anxiety as to the fate of relatives.

The major question mark hanging over the provision of communications, warning and broadcasting systems in war is the problem of electromagnetic pulse (EMP). Government departments in Britain have generally proceeded with their plans in a state of almost total ignorance of EMP, and no studies have been done by the Home Office of which county emergency planners are aware. Many of them, who share the Home Office's enthusiasm for emergency planning, but not its self-satisfaction with miniscule measures of preparedness, fear that the lack of interest in EMP effects could ultimately destroy even the inadequate and fragile systems of administration which they are planning. Some might think this no great loss. But no one is certain what precisely will occur.

Part of the problem with EMP is that the bomb designers became aware of its effects only relatively late in the day (in the late 1950s), when it became apparent that this was the cause of many unexpected failures in monitoring equipment during test explosions. EMP is a blast of radio energy which is very efficiently gathered up by metal structures and in particular by many of the elements of communications systems – aerials, aerial masts and telephone lines. The energy comes from the ionisation of the atmosphere around the nuclear detonation; as the ions move and recombine, the surge is generated. There are two sorts of threat; firstly, EMP is a consequence of all nuclear explosions, and equipment and systems within, say, eight to ten miles of a one megaton burst would be very likely to be damaged by electric fields of the order of tens of thousands of volts per metre.

Secondly, a few – probably just two – large yield thermonuclear weapons detonated outside the atmosphere over Britain would eventually release most of their energy in the form of EMP. Such bombs would blanket Britain in very high energy EMP; starting an attack in such a fashion by attempting to disable a country almost cleanly (there would be no fallout, and very few immediate casualties related to the EMP) seems a potentially rewarding strategy for an aggressor. The EMP surges would not only destroy communications systems and equipment but the control networks of essential services would also be affected – in particular the national electricity grid. At an official briefing at the MOD in 1980, I was told that all the RAF's bunkers were constructed as 'Faraday cages' – a fairly effective form of shielding against EMP, and similar precautions have been taken with major military communications systems. But the whole phenomena has sometimes attracted studied disinterest from other sections of the British government; during the 1970s it was made clear to Emergency Planning Officers that the Home Office disapproved of them attempting to obtain research information and materials direct from the United States. By 1980, the Association of Civil Defence and Emergency Planning Officers had set up their own research project on EMP to supplement the official guidance – or lack of it.

The effect of EMP is particularly marked on transistors, and even more so on integrated circuits. One of the best protection methods is to ensure that aerial systems are disconnected during attack, but close in to an explosion, or in an EMP oriented attack, that may not be sufficient. (Hence the *Protect and Survive* suggestion – second edition, the first contained nonsense – to take *two* radios and keep aerials pushed in). During storms very mild EMP can be heard on the radio as a crackle of static which accompanies a lightning flash (not the thunder, which is a shock wave). The EMP from a bomb would be sufficient to produce many thousands of volts at the input to electronic devices, and burn out or destroy many parts. Despite the recently increased level of concern about EMP, there has been no government advice beyond that which was contained in the *Communications in War* circular:

All radio communications sytems must be considered vulnerable to the effects of EMP. . . . All telephone systems must also be regarded as vulnerable; present knowledge, although limited, indicates that EMP might be expected to do extensive damage to the Post Office network. . . . Interruptions of public electricity supplies are likely to be widespread . . . distribution systems, especially overhead systems – are much more vulnerable. It should be assumed for planning purposes that in the event of a nuclear attack interruption of mains power supplies could be both widespread and prolonged, even in areas where no damage had occurred. Damage may also be sustained by mains operated equipment. . . .

Despite all this:

No financial provision (is) being made for protection to be installed in respect of the Home Office telecommunications in existing local authority wartime headquarters.

'Theoretical' advice was, nonetheless, offered free of charge.

From the point of view of those who believe in a purpose for civil defence, the official failure to pay any heed to EMP suggests that nothing may work on the day. For those of more sanguine disposition, it is merely a reminder than even Armageddon will not proceed according to the plans of central committees.

For civil non-nuclear 'contingencies', the government also has a further communications network, much of which is built into the central London wartime 'citadels'. This is the Government Telecommunications Network (GTN), the purpose of which is to provide a central exchange linking all government buildings together, all over Britain, independently from the public telephone network. Since it uses 'private wires' the GTN would not be affected by the operation of the Telephone Preference Scheme.

The central exchange in the GTN system is the *Horseferry Tandem** which is housed within the bombproof Rotunda citadel below the Department of the Environment's offices in Marsham Street, off Horseferry Road in Victoria. All Whitehall offices' exchanges are connected to *Horseferry*, generally via the deep level tunnels. Many of the departmental exchanges have also been housed in underground citadel accommodation. The Ministry of Defence exchanges are in the Admiralty and Montagu House (main building) citadels; the Palace of Westminster, Foreign Office, Cabinet Office, and Home Office exchanges are all buried deep below the new government international Conference Centre, in the Broad Sanctuary citadel. GTN provides the government with a useful degree of invulnerability to disruption of the ordinary telephone network.

Beyond GTN there is the top people's exchange, Federal, inauguarated in 1938 and still in being. (It, too, is now in the bowels of the Department of the Environment, and has been automated.) Federal is intended to provide special secure communications for ministers and the top echelons of the civil service; it forms an additional network to which they would

---

*Also known as YTAN.

be connected. The precise purpose for which it continues to be provided is unclear; it is in twenty-four hour operation and its GTN number and Westminster public telephone number are in the House of Commons telephone directory, although MPS are not told what – or whom – the system is for. It is important in civil emergencies; the only occasion on which specific telephone numbers within the Federal system were given a wide circulation was in 1974, shortly after the Heath Government had declared a State of Emergency. Instructions on how to contact ministers and senior civil servants through Federal in case the ordinary systems were 'disrupted' were circulated to middle rank civil servants and outsiders with a 'need to know'. However, the contingency which the government feared was developing – an all-out confrontation – was averted at the polls. Home Defence precautions then reverted to their normal state of quiescence.

10
Essential services

It is considerably easier for the government to provide bunkers, radios, and armed squadrons of troops than it is to plan for the 'survival' and 'recovery' which are piously held out as the goal of post-attack administration. They may be as unachievable as the Holy Grail.

The government suggests ('for the purposes of survival planning') in *Home Defence Planning Assumptions* (ES3/73) that 'loss of essential services, . . . loss of power supplies, and lack of raw materials could be as high as eighty per cent.' At the same time it is suggested that about seventy-five per cent of the population will survive a 'postulated' two hundred megaton strike. The fact that this latter claim is a gross overestimate can only be helpful to those responsible for the post-strike subsistence economy, in that there will be fewer mouths to be fed.

Compounding the problem of the certain destruction of energy supplies is the expectation that imports will cease, certainly for a month, perhaps for the foreseeable future. It is not possible to rely on the arrival of the United Nations or Oxfam. The realistic expectation is that no outside help of any consequence will come once ocean shipping at sea has reached its destination (and many ships' masters will turn away from the war zone). As the several global studies of nuclear war have made clear, one of its consequences will be widespread famine in third world countries not directly involved in the conflict. There will be little stimulus for southern hemisphere countries to supply the north; certainly not until the surviving society seemed reasonably well established. They might choose not to assist, on the ground that the northern hemisphere protagonists deserved their fate, and had themselves long been willing to turn a blind eye to famine and deprivation in the south.

They might choose not to supply because there would be

no goods produced to trade for, and no system of international debts with which to finance trade. New Zealand and the Falklands might send some sheep out of Commonwealth fellow-feeling. South Africa and Australia might feel less inclined than other nations to let the UK meet its fate alone. But whatever came would have to be shared with NATO partners under the notion of the 'equalisation of misery'; and it would be a drop in the ocean compared to pre-war supplies.

The prospects for any kind of 'survival' are grim, as the government well knows. During the first few weeks after attack, circumstances might not seem terminal; gross shortage might not necessarily appear quickly. Everyone would be living on borrowed time – time paid for out of the stockpile of surviving pre-war supplies. There would be little prospect of more oil once supplies ran out. Almost all the refining capacity would be gone, and the rest short of power, making it difficult to utilise stocks of crude which may be held in offshore tankers.

Construction work could cannibalise the remains of towns and cities, and food supplies would be eked out. The problem will come when there is assessed to be insufficient food to go round until the harvest arrives – and any harvest will be one of enormously reduced yield. The situation then is essentially Malthusian; the survivors will fight over remaining supplies, with conflict, starvation, and disease taking their toll. In a stable environment (which the post-nuclear attack world will not be) the population should (in years rather than months) stabilise at or below subsistence level.

In such a situation, all the Commissioners and Controllers can do is to use the armed forces to ensure that their group is predominant. If the point has been reached where, whatever lies may be told, groups of people are being deliberately starved to death, they will have clearly lost their legitimacy as providers of welfare and have become just one more power base. In some areas, particularly the south west, with plentiful agriculture, stocks, and a mild climate, the key 'survival' problem will be to prevent the ingress of refugees and the egress of food stockpiles. In a ravaged Britain, it is very easy to envisage the Commissioner (or other government) of the south west declaring boundaries closed to all except those who could offer essential skills or services.

As with the local authorities' home defence plans, central government plans for key industries – energy, transport, food and water – are rudimentary and simplistic, merely means of coordinating, hopefully, whatever may survive. Wartime Controllers have been advised about the labour and industrial situation after an attack in *Briefing Material for Wartime Controllers*: (ES3/76):

In spite of heavy casualties among the able-bodied population, there should be no general shortage of manpower, since industry as it existed before the attack would be virtually at a standstill. The problem would be to make the best use of manpower resources available. In the immediate aftermath of a nuclear attack one aim would be to provide as many people as possible with some form of useful work to sustain morale.

Idle hands are always a problem for rulers:

The main demand would be for heavy manual labour, for such immediate tasks as the clearance of roads, emergency sanitation, and the burial of the dead. With insufficient food and no balanced diet available, there would be an added reluctance to undertake heavy or unpleasant work.

Each Regional Commissioner would have statutory powers to direct labour, which would be coordinated by Department of Employment officials on the RGHQ staff. He could, in any case, make any emergency laws he liked. The circular implies that effective sanctions to get unwilling workers to work might include 'summary execution' for those who failed to 'comply with directions'. (Curiously, although this blunt phrase is readily used in connection with unwilling workers, a much more restrained description is given concerning the use of firing squads for punishing offenders sentenced by the courts.) If workers were not coerced by the execution of the less enthusiastic, the circular suggests, then 'incentives' would be needed, as well as the 'community's acceptance of the need and their voluntary cooperation'. What would be the incentives?:

Money would have no value, and initial rewards for labour might be a meal or extra food for the family. Fortunately most of the tasks would be seen to relate to a local improvement in living conditions.

Like everything else, the industrial civil defence service was axed in 1968 and was soon cut off from such government training facilities as remained. After the 1972 revival, a conference was held at Easingwold in 1974, when the Society of Industrial Emergency Services Officers met with county council EPOS and asked for increasing planning and new arrangements. The Home Office was asked to issue an ES circular for industry, to set up regional planning boards, and provide liason with local authorities. Eight years later, nothing had been done to meet these recommendations. Policy then, as now, stressed that anything done should be at 'no additional cost' to the government and 'no expenditure should be incurred in creating new physical assets'.

In general, government plans for industry are to take it all over, in a generalised and ill-coordinated way. Many managers and executives have been incorporated into the emergency Regional and SRHQ staffs, or in central government war organisations, such as the Emergency Works Organisation. Most of this planning is done, not by the Home Office, but by the Departments of Industry, Energy or Environment. There was to have been a general war organisation for industry, and until the early 1970s, 'shadow nominees' were selected, most of whom, according to a Home Office briefing, 'held (secret) letters of appointment'. But the organisation did not exist by 1978.

The energy industries are, except for oil, nationalised and under government control in peace. The oil industry has a unique place in government planning, since the oligarchy which controls the British market – chiefly Shell, BP, Mobil, Texaco and Esso – have been given a unique degree of control over their own emergency arrangements. 'Senior oil executives' will supervise Regional Goverment and SRHQ oil and petrol arrangements. Petroleum Officers, who with police support will freeze many petrol filling stations, come from industry. There are oil industry emergency arrangements, headquarters and executives at every level – national, regional, sub-regional and county, and the oil industry is more involved than any other in government planning. Through the Oil Industry Emergency Committee (OIEC), the big five have access to the government's real expectations of nuclear attack, so that their plans are 'consistent with (the government's) nuclear scenario'. The OIEC is supported by, and works with, the Oil Policy (Home) Division of the Department of Energy; its secretary is a Shell official.

Shell, BP and other oil companies also jointly own the British Pipeline Agency Ltd, which runs almost all of the extensive network of oil pipelines in Britain. Some were built in the Second World War and, more recently, many have been constructed as part of NATO 'infrastructure'. The pipelines themselves provide useful storage capacity, as well as a protected route to major air bases from distribution centres. The major companies in peacetime generally operate as a cartel, and 'swap' arrangements, whereby the retail supplies of one company are for convenience supplied from another's refinery, are common. The highly integrated distribution arrangements of the companies, as the Home Defence College briefing explains, 'allows a number of companies to compete for the available market' in a less than free market manner; in war it means that the whole system of refineries, storages, pipelines, distribution and retail outlets is easily convertible to a single organisation.

On the outset of war, a national Oil Mobilisation Control would provide national executive coordination of the industry, based on OIEC plans. Each Home Defence Region will have a Regional Oil HQ which will run oil industry assets in its areas. The HQS will be run by Regional Oil Managers (probably Department of Energy officials) but the staff would be drawn entirely from the industry. Sites have been chosen for these headquarters. In addition, a few senior oil executives would work at the SRHQ and be dispersed as part of regional government. The job of the Regional Oil Managers would be to 'improve supplies and availability'.

At each SRHQ, and later if Regional Government was established according to plan at RGHQS, the energy industries would be supervised by Department of Industry officials, but coordinated, in the post-war mini civil service, by Department of Energy officials, together with a cell of representatives from each industry.

The first stage in oil emergency planning is the 'freezing' of petrol filling stations. The *Energy Supplies in War* (ES 5/76) circular explains:

> The stocks at a limited number of retail filling stations would be topped up and 'frozen' for use after attack by local essential services under release arrangements made by the Petroleum Officer. The pre-attack 'freezing' of these stocks would be executed by police forces, acting on government instructions.

At the same time, the remaining 'unfrozen' stations would be asked to limit supplies to each customer, and to give priority to 'people who had essential needs' (it does not explain how filling station operators would make such judgments). Few stations would have stocks to last more than a day or two at the increased levels of demand which would surely exist and:

'At some stage, these stations would not receive any further supplies.'

The supply depots would probably be frozen at the same time as conservation was required. In some scenarios, such as *Square Leg*, the conservation measures started four weeks before attack. There could be a considerable period in which only a trickle of supplies, if any, was let through for sale to non-official users. Petrol rationing coupon forms exist (the last available stock was distributed to vehicle owners, but not in the event used, in the 1972 crisis) but it is not currently planned to use rationing either before an attack or in the foreseeable aftermath. The logic is simple; fuel supplies are such a critical element of post-attack survival that any non-official use seems wasteful, once war is judged imminent; furthermore, allowing people to have petrol supplies would only encourage self-evacuation and disobedience to the 'stay-put' instructions.

Official plans also provide for a large number of emergency oil stockpiles to be dispersed along with fire appliances and other supplies. Many of these stocks would be in such places as minor airfields, Home Office Supply and Transport stores, or local authority highway or stores depots in the countryside. Other stocks might be safeguarded by bunkering ships, and mooring them in remote inlets.

Nevertheless, it is expected that most major storages will be lost, and the all out attack on oil resources which was a strong and realistic feature of *Hard Rock* will mean that no indigenous supplies would be available, nor refining capacity to meet demand with available crude. Planning assumptions made by the Home Defence College anticipate 'a large proportion' of stocks being lost and the distribution system becoming disabled through lack of electricity; no new supplies are expected for a minimum of three months; and they note:

stocks will scarcely meet competing essential service needs, amongst which should be included the prominent part played by oil and oil products in agriculture

Like every other essential resource, fuel supplies would be under the control of regional government officials, and depots would be guarded (though perhaps less stringently than food depots). The Petroleum Officer in each local authority bunker would supervise the use of the 'frozen' prewar stocks.

The main pipeline network is still that built in the Second World War. In Scotland there is one major pipeline, for crude, which runs from the NATO deep water anchorage in Loch Long (where there is also an ammunition depot in Glen Douglas) and BP's Finnart oil terminal, past a naval store at Garelochhead, and thence to the Grangemouth refinery complex on the Forth. This pipeline generally carries crude oil.

In England, there is a grid network; the central square of this runs between Stanlow and Ellesmere Port on Merseyside, Avonmouth at Bristol, Misterton near Gainsborough in Lincolnshire, and, of all places, Aldermaston (an old airfield). Aldermaston was the central connection point in the wartime network (it would have been prudent to have bypassed it by now), with spurs running to the Fawley refinery at Southampton, the Isle of Grain refineries, and Rye, Dungeness and Wye in Kent. Another network extends east from Sandy in Bedfordshire, to the Shellhaven refinery and depots at Hethersett, Thetford and Saffron Walden. This network feeds most of the major air bases in East Anglia. Many of the depots and intermediate pumping stations on the pipeline network are also protected railheads, paid for jointly by the government and the oil companies. Fuel is the government's major priority, after communications.

The pipeline network is accorded high priority. Under the 1962 Pipelines Act, private companies can get compulsory purchase orders to build the pipelines. More and more military bases, chiefly airfields, are being connected into the pipelines system. In 1978, a multi-million pound pipeline was laid between the Swanvale depot in Cornwall and RAF St Mawgan; a year later, another £2.5 million project was announced to connect the RAF stations at Scampton, Waddington and Coningsby to the pipeline network at Misterton. The army also has a considerable supply at its Petroleum Depot at West Moors, north of Bournemouth.

According to D Notice No 7, the NATO Wartime Civil Agency for Oil also has its headquarters in Britain; a site has been earmarked for its operations.

Although the big five oil companies more or less run emergency arrangements for the government, some emergency planners have doubts about the abilities of the Regional Oil Manager's staff – mostly salesmen and marketing managers – to be effective in a crisis, as they lack the necessary technical knowledge of storage and pumping systems. Moreover, the 'big five's' control of the market is now less than complete.

The National Coal Board has, in its emergency plans, designated thirteen emergency area headquarters, one for each deep coal mining area, generally in existing premises. There would be NCB officials at all SRHQS, and also at county HQS in mining areas. But there might not be much for them to do at first, except supervise the distribution of what might be several weeks' of stockpiled supply. A basic problem for all the energy industries is their interdependence; coal production requires electric power, which is unlikely to be available, and oil for transport; electricity requires both coal and oil or gas; oil refining and distribution require electricity and refined oil; and so on.

Few collieries have standby power supplies, and many would consequently be at risk through flooding or lack of ventilation. Although repairs and rescues could be carried out, little could be done to restore production until electricity became available.

In the longer term, coal would be critical and the major indigenous energy resource, North Sea oil and gas would be unavailable through the destruction of installations, at least for many years; whilst nuclear power stations, if not all destroyed or damaged (which is likely), would be unlikely to remain in reliable operation without a base of high technology industry to support maintenance and repair.

Energy Supplies in War warns:

Pits, particularly those liable to flooding, which are left unworked and without adequate maintenance would soon deteriorate to a point where working faces would collapse and equipment would be lost.

Such coal supplies as did not go to surviving power stations would be used only for commercial heating or similar purposes. There would be no private supplies available. The lack of transport would 'at least in the short term' restrict the movement of coal, even to priority users.

British Gas, like the NCB, is unlikely to be able to keep up any supplies. Almost all the gas now in use is natural gas from the North Sea, piped ashore either in East Anglia or in north east Scotland. Most storage is above ground in low pressure gasholders, which are very vulnerable to attack, although two depots – Glenmavis and Partington – store liquified methane under high pressure. There are also similar stores at Canvey Island and Ambergate, where liquid methane is imported from Algeria. These stores are thought likely to be wholly destroyed if at all damaged in an attack.

The *Hard Rock* 82 scenarios stressed an attack on oil and gas resources; indeed the first conventional bombs fell on the St Fergus gas terminal near Peterheard, and many related sites like Canvey Island were also attacked. If any of the North Sea terminals survive, British Gas hopes that much of the underground gas pipeline network will be intact, estimating that even overpressures of 30psi, (say, only 1¼ miles from a one megaton airburst) will not destroy them. Each of the twelve British Gas regions has set up an emergency HQ 'as near as they can be to a Sub-Regional Headquarters.'*

The British Gas peacetime national production and distribution headquarters is at Hinckley in Leicestershire, which is not a prime target area. The Corporation, like the CEGB, runs its own extensive microwave and radio communications system. But it is unlikely that many of the sophisticated controls and electronic systems used to monitor and control supplies would survive the EMP effects of a major nuclear attack.

The electricity industry is the only one for which extensive blast proof accommodations has been provided. The provision of emergency grid control centres was part of the 1950–55 wave of bunker building. In the Second World War, after fears that the National Grid Control Centre (at Bankside in London, on the south bank of the Thames opposite the City of London) might be destroyed by bombing, an underground grid control centre was built, using two disused lift shafts for the Central Line underground station at St Pauls. Although the National Grid Control returned to Bankside House after the war, it was thought necessary, in 1950, to provide alternative dispersed headquarters both for the national and regional controls. An Emergency National Grid Control Centre was built some distance from London in the Midland generating region. It is thought to be sited at the Drakelow power station near Burton on Trent.

There are eight peacetime regional control centres for the CEGB and the Scottish generating boards: Bankside (south east), Bedminster, Bristol (south west); Birmingham and Nottingham (Midlands); Aberford, Leeds (north east); Bramhall, Stockport (north west); Kirkintilloch (south Scotland); Pitlochry (north Scotland). The Northern Ireland electricity

*This is what a digest from the Home Defence College suggests. The only gas emergency control presently known is at Washwood Heath, Birmingham, which is (a) remote from the SRHQ for the area and, (b) somewhat vulnerable, lying well within the Birmingham conurbation.

Plate 37 A CEGB Emergency Grid Control Centre, at Rothwell Haigh, near Leeds (foreground).

supply has its HQ in south Belfast. Each of the seven mainland regions has a duplicated control bunker; at the same time as these were being built, strong protective walls were built around switchgear and generators thought to be vulnerable.

One such CEGB Emergency Control Centre was discovered by Leeds journalists near a small hamlet south of Leeds, called Rothwell Haigh. Here, built as part of the 1950s plans, there were, in fact, several bunkers – a Post Office (cable) repeater station and an 'emergency control centre' constructed in 1953 for the then British Electricity Authority (set up to nationalise the industry in 1948). The BEA's control centre was a concrete blockhouse, a hundred feet (30m) long and twenty-five feet (8m) wide. It was shown on Ordnance Survey maps as a 'warehouse', and the CEGB's transmission office claimed to enquirers that it had been built as an emergency control centre 'during the war' and since then had merely stored 'telecommunications equipment'. The Rothwell Haigh buildings formed a small emergency complex, including 'RAF Rothwell Haigh', which were unprotected offices adjacent to the Post Office bunker. The Post Office bunker housed a telephone switching centre for the RAF – now disused. Despite the misleading suggestion, the centre – and presumably six others like it – would provide wartime duplicate control centres for regional grid controls.

After the attack, the CEGB expects 'widespread damage to the grid and electricity distribution systems'. Apart from the disruption caused by the effects of EMP (which might not be too difficult to remedy), many power stations would have been targets themselves, or in target areas, and EMP or surges resulting from other damage might have destroyed sub-station equipment.

The quasi-autonomous area electricity boards, which sell electricity to consumers, would have their representatives alongside the CEGB's in each SRHQ and regional government staff. Electricity liason staff would not be posted to local authority HQs. Briefing notes on electricity supply issued by the Home Defence College suggest that: 'The cumulative weight of EMP effects makes likely widespread power failure on a national scale at the very beginning of a nuclear attack.' (Even though much of this might be caused by the tripping of safety equipment.) It also suggests that the loss of generating capacity might not be disproportionate:

It would appear from the scale of attack postulated that the generating capacity surviving would be theoretically sufficient to meet remaining demands . . . so long as the grid remains and damaged power plants can be bypassed.

It does not say, however, what the 'postulated' scale of attack actually is, or what level of demand the Home Office planners think will remain. The peacetime installed capacity is about 60,000 megawatts, against a peak demand of 40–42,000 megawatts. Increasingly, the supply is concentrated in huge units generating a thousand megawatts or more. Many of these – nuclear powers stations – are certain targets in their own right. Many more are located for convenience close to refineries or other sources of energy supply, such as at Fawley or the Isle of Grain. Others are in urban areas. A few (in Lincolnshire) are near strategic targets. Some Soviet writings suggest that electricity supply in general would be a key target, implying that many large conventionally fuelled power stations might be nuclear targets.

Other problems would affect the early restoration of generation. Fallout would particularly restrict operations because of its effect on cooling water supplies. Fallout particles, drawn into cooling systems, could built up 'severe radiation hazards' if stations continued to operate. Ultimately, electricity production would face a critical problem of interdependence, not being a primary source of energy. It would be foolish to waste oil on electricity generation (given the inefficiency of conversion) and once existing coal stocks were burnt in power stations there might be a much diminished supply from working or restored mines – which would first have to be supplied with electricity.

After many months, it might be possible to operate a rudimentary grid to distribute power from surviving coal-fired stations. Most electricity users would be disconnected; priority would go to essential services, communications, government and industrial facilities. It might happen that more generating plant would survive an attack than could in fact be used.

Overall, the destruction of energy facilities would do more than anything else to destroy social organisation after the attack. The Home Defence College *Digest* suggests that, although much 'non-essential' activity would have ceased, and demand would be much reduced, there is little prospect of easy 'recovery':

A full scale nuclear attack on this country would have a devastating effect on our fuel and power industries and the means of distribution.

Power shortage will probably be worst immediately after attack, and again feature as reconstruction is attempted. Gas supplies, if any remain, will considerably assist in survival. Some coal production will be available; oil may, however, be limited to a permanently declining reserve.

Only in the field of ports and shipping are the transport industries as prepared for nuclear attack as those concerned with energy. Under the direction of NATO's Planning Board for Ocean Shipping, the alliance plans to requisition 600 merchant ships to start with, to operate reinforcement convoys across the Atlantic. Later, all shipping under allied flags, and perhaps any other in the North Atlantic or Mediterranean, would be directed by NATO to surviving ports where supplies are required. This would be overseen by the NATO Wartime Civil Agency for Ocean Shipping, with its headquarters in the UK – probably at Northwood.

On a national level, the Royal Navy would take over British shipping from an early stage in the crisis, through another dormant agency, the Naval Control of Shipping Organisation. It will work with the Central Port and Shipping HQ, which will have a subordinate national network of Regional Port and Shipping Control HQs for which protected premises have been selected, if not purpose built. Each group of sea ports has a shadow Port Group Manager, selected by the Department of the Environment, who would run a wartime Port Group HQ, located away from major ports likely to be nuclear targets. 'Some staff from larger ports' might also be dispersed to smaller ports before an attack, according to the *Ports and Shipping in War* circular (ES4/76).

Scotland, although a single home defence region, would have two Port and Shipping Control HQs; East, for the Forth estuary and northwards; and West, for the Clyde and the western Highlands. A large number of NATO anchorages, including POL (Petrol Oil and Lubricant) depots and boom defence depots have been pre-positioned in the Scottish lochs, in particular in Loch Striven and Loch Ewe. Emergency anchorages on the Clyde are in western waters near Arran, in order to avoid the devastation expected on the upper Clyde after the Holy Loch and Faslane bases are attacked.

A Scottish version of ES4/76 (ES (SCOT)10/76) suggests that the national HQ might not ride out the attack – indicating that it is probably located at a major government HQ such as Hawthorn or Northwood.:

National decisions on shipping would be taken by the Central Port and Shipping Headquarters *if it survived*, but if it became a casualty, port and shipping controllers would be expected to act in the national interest . . . until such time as central government control could be re-established.

Each regional Port and Shipping HQ would be run by Department of the Environment officials. The Department has a full-time 'Defence Planning and Emergencies Division', which works on 'inland transport aspects of home defence' and 'policy in relation to NATO planning for ports and inland surface transport'. Although the government has denied that its home defence plans are structured according to NATO decisions, officials from the DOE, Home Office, MAFF and the Environment, Energy and Defence Ministries all sit on subcommittees of the NATO Civil Emergency Planning Committee, and such critical aspects of policy as 'stay-put' and the doctrine of the 'survival period' are common NATO policy.

Although the chances of food deliveries from overseas are very slender even months after attack, the DOE has set up a system of emergency port facilities in the expectation of most major ports being destroyed. These include 'stockpiles of specialised port operating equipment', but not heavy cranes – which would have to come from the Emergency Works Organisation. The DOE has appointed a group of 5–6 Regional Emergency Transport Planning Officers, who hold 'briefing sessions and occasional exercises' for port and shipping industry executives who have 'wartime appointments in the port and shipping organisation'. The emergency ports are minor ports with mooring buoys and, preferably, a convenient railhead. At one time, the port control bunkers were said to have their own radio links to regional Port and Shipping Control HQ's; this no longer seems to be the case.

Regional Commissioners would not generally control shipping movements unless central goverment control had broken down; and shipping, once at sea, would be under the control of the NATO navies. In the *Hard Rock* 82 plans, for the first time, the Royal Navy was to carry out a home defence exercise with the civil authorities. Plans included the use of Port HQS on the Medway and at Portsmouth, the Northwood command centre and minesweeping and landing craft HQS. Many ships were also earmarked, including 'selected HM Ships,' RFAS (Royal Fleet Auxiliaries), LSLS (Landing Ships Logistic – five ships like the *Sir Galahad*, destroyed in the Falklands war), RMAS craft and merchant shipping.

Each Home Defence Region, except London, has regional DOE offices, responsible for a wide range of (peacetime) services including Controllers of Housing, Planning, and Roads and Transportation. Regional Chairmen of Traffic Commissioners are appointed by the Department of Transport. The latter Department also designates the wartime Regional Inland Transport Administrator (RITA) who would generally be the Regional Chairman of the Traffic Commissioners. These officials also have significant powers in a state of (civil) emergency, and (in England and Wales only) can requisition transport to distribute essential commodities. The powers – which originate in measures to deal with a general strike – would be used in cases of prolonged industrial dispute.

Briefing Material gave a grim picture of post-attack transport facilities:

The railway system would be badly disrupted, not only because of the destruction of track, signalling equipment and rolling stock, but also due to a shortage of electricity and diesel fuel. There would be little fuel for road vehicles, and spare parts would have to be obtained through cannibalisation. The use of inland waterways would be restricted through damage to locks, embankments and aqueducts, although short stretches might be navigable by barges and some use might be made of small boats and rafts propelled manually.

Despite this classified assessment of transport prospects envisaging teams of survivors pulling rafts of supplies along canals the more widely distributed *Inland Transport in War* circular (ES2/77) envisages huge, 500–1000 strong, fleets of requisitioned goods and passenger vehicles being amassed out of existing fleets and put under the control of county council and sub-regional coordinators and administrators.

Surviving operators of inland transport would be expected to continue functioning from their normal place of business or alternative nearby premises.

The civil defence plans of the 1960s had featured extensive lists of vehicles to be requisitioned and distributed to various dispersed depots, civil defence mobile columns, or evacuation convoys. Now, the Home Office advises that, 'it is impractical to prepare specific transport requirements for a post-nuclear situation,' and suggests that local authorities would require few vehicles that they did not already own or could not place 'dormant' hire contracts for.

This view implies that there would be little purpose in local authorities or others making any attempt to conserve vehicles – certainly not cars (there will be gross oversupply, post-attack) and not even more useful goods and passenger vehicles. The shortage of fuel will restrict transport far more than the physical destruction of vehicles or rolling stock. Liquid bulk carriers – such as petrol tankers – are likely to be first employed carrying not fuel but drinking water supplies from reservoirs and supply points to rest centres and surviving centres of population. There will be more than enough vehicles for 'cannibalisation'.

The RITA staff, and their local authority equivalents, the County Inland Transport Coordinators, will include goods and passenger vehicle liason officials (from local bus and road haulage companies or undertakings), a British Rail liason official, and, if appropriate, a fourth official from the British Waterways Board who will be able to coordinate the movement of the human powered rafts. Aircraft in private hands will have no fuel, (unless private owners have conserved a private stockpile) and would be grounded. Some light aircraft or helicopters would be used for reconnaissance of damaged areas or refugee movements, under control of the Regional Air Squadrons formed by the RAF. But *Inland Transport in War* states, no doubt correctly, that 'it is unlikely that air transport could make a significant contribution to the solution of internal transport problems after a nuclear attack.'

The RAF plan, nonetheless, to set up a postwar Air Despatch Wing, of short and medium range transport aircraft. Its utility in home defence – except for military operations to which the services would continue to give priority – is questionable. The Air Despatch Wing would be part of the RAF's physical contribution to the home defence organisation, and would comprise whatever remained of the pre-war RAF No 38 Group, operating vc10s, Hercules transports, and Wessex and Puma helicopters – plus whatever civilian transports were taken over. NATO also has a Civil Aviation Planning Committee, although its activities apparently do not extend beyond the requisitioning of a planned eighty-five cargo aircraft to support European reinforcement manoeuvres in a crisis. The Air Despatch Wing and its squadrons were also planning to 'play' in *Hard Rock*. (In *Square Leg*, some Air Despatch Squadron helicopters were used, notionally, to ferry troops to deal with refugees attacking the GCHQ government building in Cheltenham.)

The critical problem for the railway network will also be fuel. British Rail scrapped steam locomotives entirely in the late 60s, and their fleet now consists of roughly 3300 diesel and 300 electric units. Many of these would survive attack if dispersed; track and heavy locomotives have also a high degree of resistance to blast damage. British Rail has, according to D Notice 7, a network of Mobile Emergency Control of Railways HQs, which would be moved around safe, surviving parts of the rail network. The D Notice asking for 'no discussion' of the 'identity or purpose' of these units, re-issued in 1982, is, as so often, out of touch with reality. The Department of Transport authorised British Rail to sell off the Mobile Emergency Controls in July 1979. Railway enthusiastis were then already aware of the locations of the mobile controls. The emergency trains were sold off in 1979 and 1980. Some eleven coaches had been stored at a depot at Craven Arms, in Shropshire, for this purpose, in a stock shed with bricked up windows and modern security alarms. These belonged to BR's Western Region; others were at Springs Branch, Wigan (London Midland Region); Carstairs (Scottish

Region); Retford, then Hitchin and Ely (Eastern Region); Newcastle (Heaton) and York (Clifon) for the former North Eastern Region; Faversham and Maidstone East (Southern Region). The Mobile Emergency Controls each consisted of three or four coaches – a personnel and office coach, a generator coach, and a telecommunications equipment coach. In war, the emergency trains would have been positioned at preselected sites; in the northeast, for example, Hebden Bridge and Darlington were selected.

The Home Defence College *Digest* on inland transport describes contemporary BR wartime plans:

The peacetime Divisional control will be the effective railway operating unit, and in each control the Divisional Operating Superintendent will be responsible for keeping rail movement going within his Division.

There do not appear to be extensive plans for railway operations post-attack. During the war, the pre-nationalisation Railway Executive Committee had an underground HQ in Down Street, a disused tube station near Picadilly. An extensive suite of executive and clerical offices were built there, with space chiefly obtained by bricking up the platform tunnels. A special halt enabled passengers to and from the control centre to get in and out, by travelling in the drivers cab, using a special pass. Down Street is now disused and derelict however; and although a London underground emergency floodgate control was built deep under Hampstead Heath in 1952, it is only a control centre for the floodgates.

For many years, there were rumours that a Strategic Steam Reserve of mothballed steam engines had been put secretly aside by British Rail, as the most expeditious way of keeping railways going after attack. This story seems unlikely now, and is denied by British Rail – who point out, reasonably enough, that the pre-existing infrastructure of water and coaling towers and troughs necessary to keep steam going nationwide had long since been dismantled. British Rail say they now have only three steam engines on an isolated track, and if steam engines were to be of value post-attack, they would presumably be requisitioned from the many private railways that now operate them.

During the buildup to war, and before nuclear attack, there would be extensive railway movement in and out of more than forty Ministry of Defence railway connected depots throughout Britain, particularly such vast centres as the US depots at Caerwsent and Burtonwood. At some twenty-three depots, the army's Royal Corps of Transport railway staff operate engines and Ministry-owned rolling stock (mostly for carrying light vehicles and ammunition). The Army Railway Staff, with headquarters at Andover, does however have a strategic reserve of main line diesel engines for 'emergency use'. Since there would probably be more than enough BR engines left after nuclear attack, this reserve is probably aimed more at countering a major rail strike than assisting the country after attack. The depots most likely to be used to store emergency locomotives are Longtown, near Carlisle (the sub-HQ to Andover), Long Marston, near Stratford on Avon, and, possibly Marchwood, a military port on the Solent estuary. Unlike Sweden and some other countries, which have specifically created a strategic steam reserve as a wartime survival measure, it appears that no such precautions have been taken in Britain, wise as they may seem.

The overall post-attack official view of the transport situation is extremely gloomy, reflecting the wholesale destruction of industry that would have taken place:

The overriding factor in the operation of any form of transport would be the availability of fuel and power. With the most stringent economy in the use of fuel and power even for priority purposes, some essential movement could be organised. With the resumption of energy production, these movements would be extended progressively until some simple national network connecting all regions would be operating.

Overall:

The availability or non-availability of oil and its derivatives is likely to be the deciding factor in any plans for the use of wheeled transport.

The circulars do not mention the use of bicycles or load-carrying tricycles, although both would be highly appropriate technologies. Short distance courier and postal services are likely to rely exclusively on bicycles. Useful supply carriers could be obtained by using converted tricycles or bike trailers, and might be more flexible than having teams of survivors haul rafts along canals, as the *Briefing Material* circular suggested. Road movement would also depend on the early clearing of the Essential Service Routes and, as the Home Defence College *Digest* notes, on most occasions 'it may be necessary to ensure the security of movement by the provision of guards.'

The Department of the Environment is also responsible for wartime water supplies and building services. The plan for the unitary national and regional Emergency Works Organisation is similar to those described for the control of other essential services. Emergency powers, according to the *Construction Work and Building Materials in War* (ES4/75) circular:

would enable the various Ministers or Commissioners to recruit and direct labour, to control all building and civil engineering undertakings, and to bring them all under a single Emergency Works Organisation (EWO) in war.

If, however, any employees or firms were engaged on 'vital military defence tasks', the Commissioner could only obtain their services after 'consultation' with the military commander concerned. Regional Directors of Works, and subordinates in the SRHQS, would come from the government Property Services Agency; at local authority level, the County Works Officer would usually become the local head of the EWO in war. 'Advisers' and 'representatives' in the form of construction or engineering managers would also have posts in regional government, SRHQS, and the local authority bunkers.

As with every other resource, control over the direction of labour, and the use of building materials or equipment would be in the hands of SRHQS. Local authorities are required under the 1974 Civil Defence Regulations to plan for a service of clearing highways and repairing or demolishing property in war. But they would not create or disperse emergency construction units, as had previously been planned. Once again official policy is no further advanced than to let the bombs fall, then look around and see what remains. Initially, building firms 'would retain their identity' and be gradually augmented by self-employed and directed workers.

Most able bodied survivors would probably be conscripted into the EWO as soon as fallout levels had declined sufficiently to permit movement; at first there would be mass graves to be dug and roads to be cleared; then emergency sanitary arrangements and simple repairs to be done to rest centres and other communal government property; according to *Construction Work. . .*, 'it is recognised that substantial reinforcement (of the EWO) would be required in the worst hit areas.' As the survival phase drew on, EWO teams would be directed – by the inducement of proper feeding, or by coercion and military dragoonment – to assist the restoration of energy industries, and water or transport services. Later, large numbers might be directed as auxiliary farm labour to assist in the creation of subsistence agricultural.

Building repairs would rely on salvaged materials, and ignore the target cities altogether. These cities would have to be abandoned to their dead, according to the secret appreciation in *Briefing Material*:

The repair of damaged houses would be restricted by the scarcity of all building materials. . . .Such work as patching and weather proofing, done by self-help or perhaps by teams of volunteers . . . would be dependent on the use of salvaged materials. Repairs would have to be confined to the more lightly damaged areas; any attempt to restore the more badly damaged towns and cities would be totally beyond the resources available, and the main activity in these areas, when radiological levels permitted movement into them, would be the salvaging of usable building materials.

The dead cities too would be cannibalised.

Providing water after a nuclear attack is the responsibility of ten Regional Water Boards in England and Wales, (in Scotland, the local regional authorities, equivalent to English counties, also supply water as part of their services.) The government plan is to make no provision for any water supplies during the first two weeks – *Water Services in War* (ES6/76) asserts that:

Human survivors should, for planning purposes, be deemed to have access to sufficient water to keep them alive for at least fourteen days after attack. . . .this would not necessarily apply to farm animals.

After an attack, each water authority would have to improvise whatever system of water supply seemed feasible. Although no specific plans exist (because official policy is, as ever, to wait and see where the bombs strike, then patch up and improvise afterwards) there are more convincing plans and preparations for emergency water supplies than in some other areas of civil defence.

Water supplies are thought 'less vulnerable than other utilities' and reservoirs and other installations are generally located away from target areas. Water mains would be unlikely to suffer extensive damage. Nevertheless 'a fracture of even one sizeable main would result in serious loss of water . . .and might cause flooding too'. A more serious problem would be the loss of electricity supply and changes in pattern of demand caused by refugee movements.

The minimum level of water to support life is estimated at about two pints (roughly 1 litre) per day. After attack, only stored water is recommended for use, but if mains supplies continued, they could be initially used for fire fighting and decontamination purposes. In areas where the supply failed, official suggestions include the use of water in central heating circuits (it would first need to be sterilised or boiled); if survivors grew really short, the Home Defence College *Digest* warns that:

> Water which under normal circumstances would never be touched would be eagerly collected and taken to shelters for consumption . . . such action would introduce a risk of serious infection. . .

After an attack, it is claimed, the problem of radioactive contamination of water supplies would not 'add significantly to the dangers' of other radioactive sources in the environment. There used to be 'emergency tolerance levels' of radioactivity in water; it now seems that most survivors will take such high doses anyway that the threat of ingestion of water possibly contaminated by radioactive material sufficient to cause extra, irreparable damage is 'not expected to last for very long'.

Post-attack supplies might initially start at a ration of a litre a day per person, though availability of supplies would vary widely. The ultimate goal would be about ten litres a day per person 'as soon as possible'. *Water Services in War* warns:

> It should be assumed that in all areas there would be prolonged disruption of piped drinking water supplies and even longer disruptions of industrial water systems and of sewerage systems.

Somewhat contradictorily, the same note asserts that:

> The provision after attack of minimum amounts of water to sustain the life of human beings and indeed most other animals would be of the highest priority. . . .Water services would themselves be competing for scarce resources against the needs of other public utilities and essential services.

Two sets of preparations made during the 1960s will help. In England and Wales (though not apparently in Scotland or Northern Ireland), there was a national survey of all wells and boreholes which might be used for civil defence emergency water supplies. The results of the survey were given to the then River Authorities, and are now lodged with each Regional Water Board. Secondly, the Ministry of Housing and Local Government built a chain of twenty-eight special depots for emergency equipment, (one each for all but one of the then twenty-nine River Authorities), and has also stockpiled emergency equipment at many water supply depots. In Scotland, the Scottish Development Department has a 'small stockpile'. These stockpiles consist of pumps, generators, piping, sterilising equipment, and tanks, (portable and fixed). Water authorities now pay for the upkeep of the Home Defence Emergency Water Supply Equipment stockpiles – in return, they have the use of them during civil emergencies. There are also arrangements to swap and interchange equipment and piping with the Home Office's Fire Service Reserve equipment (in Supply and Transport stores), and with some reserves held by the Department of Energy.

Some interconnection of different water catchments and river sources in the 60s and early 70s was done partly for Home Defence purposes. The full programme was, in 1976, nevertheless only 'partly carried out'.

The srhqs and regional governments-to-be would have Regional and Sub-Regional Water Coordinators (two per sub-region) appointed by the Department of the Environment from the appropriate Regional Water Authority. The Authority's Director of Operations is normally the Regional Water Coordinator, while deputies and assistants would join the srhq staffs or liaise with local authorities. Most of the water authorities have been approximately matched with Home Defence regions; Northumbrian for Region 1; Yorkshire – Region 2; Severn-Trent – Regions 3 and 9; Anglian – Region 4; Thames – Region 5 (and in 4, 6 and 7 for coordination); Wessex – Region 7; South West – Sub-Region 72; North West – Region 10. The Welsh National Water Development Authority provides supplies for Region 8, Wales.

The authorities would also be responsible for sewage disposal, which is no small problem. The majority of systems which work by gravity flow only would continue to operate if not blocked or damaged by attack. But those which relied on pumps to lift the sewage or surface water from storms for disposal might create backwashes of sewage once power supplies failed. Some have standby routes to nearby rivers.

The failure of water supplies would also prevent the normal use of wcs or other sanitary facilities. A Home Defence

College briefing on 'Water Supply and Sewage Disposal' explains official plans for such a situation:

Families would need to make their own arrangements for sewage disposal relying in the main on pails and chemical closets. As soon as possible they would seek to make temporary arrangements in their gardens or in the streets.

The survivor emerging from his or her *Protect and Survive* shelter might be forgiven for thinking that official advice and planning on the matter of leaving excrement in the street was superfluous. It is nonetheless there. The briefing continues to stress that communal latrines would be desirable 'as soon as conditions permitted'. The real danger to public health would develop if sewage and wastes began to contaminate water supplies, for instance through fractured pipes. Boiling would be the only practical safeguard against bacterial (but not, of course, radiological) contamination of water supplies.

The war plans for the fire service, unlike the construction or transport organisations, do envisage dispersal of 'approximately 50% of manpower and appliances' which should be 'withdrawn from certain home cover stations and redeployed elsewhere', according to the *War Emergency Planning for the Fire Service* circular (ES5/1974). This means removing most fire brigade personnel from the centres of cities before an attack, and is a notable exception to the government's 'no dispersal' and stay-put policies (The other exceptions being military personnel, police support units, and 4–5,000 officials with regional government or SRHQ posts).

The Auxiliary Fire Service was scrapped with the rest of civil defence in 1968. It had been intended to be equipped with reserve 'Green Goddess' fire pumps, and formed, together with regular units, into large mobile fire-fighting columns which would put out fires at least on the urban periphery of target areas. Besides the direct life-saving effect of such fire-fighting operations, the early extinction of a proportion of fires would determine whether or not large, joined-up, conflagrations – or even firestorms – developed. No such fire-fighting is now intended.

In the period immediately following nuclear attack, it is envisaged that fire–fighting would be undertaken only when:

the return is judged worthwhile and the survival of organised fire service resources would not be prejudiced. Planning should be directed towards the preservation of the fire service for its role in the longer survival period.

Plate 38 The entrance to the Arts Bunker, Manod Quarry, Blaenau Ffestiniog. In Scotland, art treasures would go to Newbattle Abbey, Midlothian.

The equipment for the fire service reserve (the former AFS) has been kept – over a thousand 'Green Goddess' pumps, bought between 1952 and 1957, and dispersed in small groups to Home Office Supply and Transport Stores up and down the country (in Scotland, a Home Defence store at Cambusbarron). They will be joined, pre-attack, by most of the 'red' engines, and every fireman who can be evacuated. Since there is no auxiliary service, both the red (regular) and green (auxiliary) companies which would be formed after an attack will rely on the normal peacetime strength of the fire service.

The 'Green Goddesses', which had been forgotten for many years, emerged from the Home Office stores in 1977, and were overhauled again in 1980, to deal with fire service strikes. The Home Office in its 1974 circular announced that the 'Green Goddesses' would be retained. However by April 1977, it was decided that the 'expenditure necessary to store and maintain (the fire reserve stockpile) can no longer be justified'. (This comment appeared, later, in the Scottish circular on the fire service (ES(SCOT)7/77)). The policy was rapidly reversed seven months later; only bureaucratic interia held up the disposal of the appliances.

Each Region would have a Regional Fire Adviser who would be selected from Firemasters in the region. Unlike most other staffs, the Advisers would not be in total command. Each brigade would answer direct to its local County Controllers, and Regional or Sub-Regional Advisers could merely give guidance or supervision on the redeployment of resources.

The new war role of the fire service does not include plans for brigades to assist in the emergency water supply. The value of the fire service conservation policy is not entirely clear, since the operation of fire appliances will be critically hindered by the lack of fuel – and, in many cases, water. Many fires starting in either the attack or survival period would or could have to be left to burn out, and the presence of trapped people might – in general conditions of 'death and destruction' – not make a great deal of difference.

Food will be the final criterion of survival. In the first few days after an attack, most people will have some of their own supplies. For a few weeks, emergency feeding arrangements may be adequate – once restrictions on movement imposed by fallout have been lifted. Then there will come the point at which the government's food controllers – *if* they remain in control – have to choose between the feeding of the many, at declining, sub-subsistence levels – or the feeding of a chosen few. Inevitably, because of the coercive power of the labour force, and simple necessity, obedient workers, police and military will get the food. The ill and insane will already have been left to die; the old and infirm and insane were early on to be abandoned to their fate, deserted in homes and evacuated hospitals. The ultimate horror of the British government's civil defence planners is that a nuclear attack *will not kill enough*. It will not be unduly difficult to decide to remove food supplies from 'useless' sections of the population; it will be much harder to do the same to useful workers and their families (noting that women and children over twelve may equally be regarded as labourers) if the only options are slow death for the whole society if no-one gets enough food to work, or deliberate starvation for some.

No detailed assessments of the long term prospects for the United Kingdom post-attack food and agriculture industries appears to have been carried out. The Home Office has prepared an economic model to predict the shortfall of requirements for a surviving population, but the model is based on existing and deficient assessments of the effects of attack, and uses extremely crude assumptions and a highly questionable methodology.

The Ministry of Agriculture, Fisheries and Food has an Emergencies Divisions responsible for emergency planning (and also fertilisers and feeding stuffs legislation); its director, Assistant Secretary Mr Leo Hanson (in 1982) also chairs the NATO Civil Defence Food and Agriculture Planning Committee. Although his department is responsible for the provision of the network of more than a hundred Buffer Depots in which the Strategic and Emergency Food Stockpile is stored, its position – muddled in with agricultural fertilisers and feeding stuffs – does not suggest that its officials are well placed to carry out detailed long term assessments of the effects of attack.*

The government's strategy may be simply expressed; first take control of all food supplies (dispersing as much bulk supply as may be feasible in the pre-attack period); thereafter, hang on and keep control through whatever comes next (and they know not what).

In the early stages of crisis or conventional war, the government would intervene in food and agricultural supply in a three-stage plan, according to the time available. The first phase would be confined to identifying large stocks of basic commodities such as cereals, soya and animal feeds, oils and fats, and sugar. These stocks would be earmarked – if emergency powers were available they would be requisitioned and those stocks located at ports or in other vulnerable areas would be dispersed elsewhere. Other 'major stock earmarked for regional control' such as major retail and wholesale distribution depots, would be identified. Traders would be asked to maintain normal stocks and prices.

In the second phase, MAFF would take over all imports and supplies of raw materials, and control major distribution chains. Specific or general emergency regulations would be passed. Statutory maximum food prices would be fixed. The third phase would involve consumer rationing and total con-

---

*A study of 'Feeding the United Kingdom after nuclear attack – a preliminary review' was carried out in 1980 by Dr A. A. Jackson of St Andrews University (*Journal of the Institute of Civil Defence*. October 1980). It compares detailed US studies with the unplanned situation in the UK, and suggests that the government – even within its own terms – is far from a 'credible home defence posture'.

trol of distribution. The *Food and Agriculture in War* circular (ES1/79) advises:

Any action, including rationing, that might be necessary to ensure the orderly supply of food to the public would have to be taken nationally by central government.

When the war was judged imminent, MAFF staff, trading executives and 'experts from the food industry' would go to SRHQS or regional government 'group locations of safety'. Regional and Sub-Regional Food and Agriculture Officers from MAFF would direct all food and agriculture activities after the attack. Most of the administrative work would however be done by MAFF's normal regional and district staffs working from or near to their peacetime offices.

For most of the public, the pre-war period would be increasingly fraught with difficulties in getting food supplies. It is not thought likely that there would be a sufficiently long period to get a formal public rationing scheme introduced, and only traders' informal controls on 'hoarding' would be available. Real problems start when the *Protect and Survive* advice is issued, and householders are advised to lay in fourteen days stocks of food. Circular ES1/79 is quite blunt about what happens next:

Food would be scarce and no arrangements could ensure that every surviving household would have, say, fourteen days, supply of food after attack.

Most households would be unable to obtain these supplies. The government anticipates this, but has no solutions. In *Hard Rock*, one household in three was unable to get food three days before the projected nuclear attack. Two days after the war started, there would be no further non-perishable bulk supplies coming through the major distribution outlets. Some planners are well aware of this problem. One of the most experienced British civil defence officers, and the EPO for Humberside Council), (in 1982), Eric Alley, wrote in a 1980 booklet*

Modern supermarkets only keep about three days' supply of food on the premises. A sudden surge in demand – such as people stocking up for a fourteen day period – would quickly empty their shelves. They would not be restocked.

In 1967, civil defence staff in York experimented in carrying out the 'fourteen day stocks' advice. They found that few

How to Survive the Nuclear Age, published by the Ecology Party.

people knew how much food was needed for fourteen days, or which foodstuffs to choose that would keep and could be prepared without fuel. And food suppliers and traders, as well as shoppers, would be unable to cope with such a surge in demand – especially if, at the same time, bulk stocks were being dispersed or stockpiled.

A significant part of the population would thus enter the immediate post-strike period without adequate supplies. This, too, is part of the official plan: circular ES1/79 suggests:

Even without food many would survive for quite long periods provided they were not too long without water.

As a description of the theoretical position of, say, a hunger striker or fasting zealot, this statement is quite interesting. It is surely worthless in the context of sheltering survivors. Those survivors without food in areas of no fallout will seek out emergency feeding services, which could, in such areas, be operating earlier than two weeks after attack. But for those in areas of heavy fallout faced with personal and family starvation, the immediate crisis of food supply will quickly overrun official advice about maintaining shelter. They will leave shelter, and suffer and die for it. They will not be waiting for a meals on wheels service after a 'quite long period' during which they had not died from lack of food, nor yet from the complicating circumstances of sub-lethal radiation damage, poor sanitation, and extreme psychological stress.

As for those who found the stay-at-home policy less than convincing on grounds of personal prospects, there would certainly be no food from the government. Circular ES1/79 instructs:

There would be no question of implementing emergency feeding arrangements during the pre-attack period for those who chose to ignore the government's advice to stay in their own homes.

This ill-tempered vengeance on the disobedient is a relatively recent feature of the policy. Notes on emergency feeding circulated in 1974 and 1976 included those who left home, *before or after attack*, in the first category of those to be fed (although the notes mentioned an ill-defined category of 'entitled persons' for food).

Once the radioactivity levels had declined sufficiently, emergency feeding arrangements would begin. For the foreseeable future, the long daily food queue at the local emergency feeding centre would be the main feature of each survivor's life, as long as it lasted. Planning to provide the emergency feeding service is one of the local authority's principal emergency planning duties. Providing the food is not.

Before the attack, all major stockpiles would be requisitioned and guarded by the government. Local authorities' only food stocks would be for their own bunkers, and central government would release supplies to the bunkers if need be. They would also earmark for themselves the school meals service stocks – although any 'residue' could be kept for general emergency feeding.

In preparing their emergency feeding plans, many local authorities have followed Home Office advice with slavish obedience and cooked up the most absurd sorts of plans. The school meals service and its officials and cooks are generally charged with providing the emergency feeding service, using their own equipment and other emergency equipment from MAFF and Home Office depots. Moreover, 'local authorities might also look to education departments for most of the emergency feeding staff.' The plans the Home Office asks local authorities to make are based on feeding the 'maximum peacetime population including tourists, visitors and the military', in three daily rounds.

Through thirty years of civil defence planning, one of the repeated and supreme absurdities has been the preparation of elaborate feeding plans based on menus wholly unrelated to foodstuffs likely to be available after an attack. The WRVS (Women's Royal Voluntary Service) were noted during the 1960s exercises for their surreal adherence to 'emergency' menus that comprised not less than five groups of cooked foods (soup, meat and two veg, desert), and tea, the overall standard of which would not have disgraced a seaside hotel. The MAFF circular on emergency feeding, issued in 1974 (MAFF E1/74) was shamefacedly admitted to have been just as absurd five years later, in the replacement circular from the Home Office. This confessed:

The Appendix to E1/74 on estimated food requirements for emergency meals has been proved to be misleading because the wide range of food items shown was unlikely to be available after attack. It has been discarded.

The new late 1970s realism in Whitehall did not extend to many local authorities. Some of the most elaborate and detailed Home Defence plans of all have been prepared, in more than a hundred neat volumes, by the emergency planners of the Greater London Council. There is a volume on emergency feeding for each of the thirty-two London boroughs. They are stunning fantasies. All are based on the assumption that the entire population stays put in its peacetime homes, wherever in London they are. And there is no explanation, amongst all the meticulous details, of where the food comes from; that is something that local authorities are not permitted to plan for. Such assumptions are ludicrous, as there will inevitably have been major population movements, and there will be refugees without homes, whether the authorities like it or not.

In a typical plan, for the Borough of Bexley in south London, there is discussion of providing special meals to be taken to the consumer, including 'the infirm, injured and seriously ill'; the inadvisability of using shellfish or crustaceans in immediate post-attack cooking; plans for emergency week-long training courses for food centre supervisors, and assessments of cooking needs for a typical 'menu' including stew, potatoes, greens and tea. (By the stage this was written, incidentally, the government view was quite clear – one 'stew–type' meal a day, and no side dishes.) The Bexley plan, in one paragraph, explains that 'the fuel normally used in meals kitchens will be gas' and twice, elsewhere, points out that 'no reliance can be placed on the availability of gas', and then glibly refers, without detail, to 'improvised cooking techniques'.

Such detailed and elaborate plans are wholly undermined by the fallacy of a fundamental assumption that the population would not have moved and that food would be available in sufficient quantity from the central government stockpile. In peacetime emergency, such a comprehensive plan would be extremely useful – people would not have moved, there would be food and energy. As a wartime plan, it is absurd; it is planning in the abstract.

Equally abstract is the plan to supply emergency cooking equipment from MAFF Buffer Depots. The Depots hold an estimated 400,000 cooking items, and 1.4 million plastic bowls and spoons, all stockpiled during the 1950s. There are also mobile bakeries (left over from the war), tarpaulins and tents, hurricane lamps and small stocks of other items. They are a highly dubious emergency cooking asset. The government (in MAFF advice) have claimed that there is sufficient equipment to feed twenty million survivors in the stockpile. However the allocation of equipment made, in the London area at least, suggests that the equipment is only enough to feed between five and ten per cent of the population (ie, less than five million people). For each 100,000 people (pre-attack), there are:

Soyer boilers	35	No 4 Field Cookers	10
Baking trays	50	Camp kettles ('dixies')	70
Plastic bowls	2500	Spoons	2575
		Food containers	480

Each boiler cooks about sixty gallons of food or drink at once. London planners estimate that thirty Soyer boilers or ninety dixies would be required for continuous feeding of 2–3000 people, suggesting that the scale of MAFF supplies are sufficient only for at most 8000 people out of the 100,000. The scale of provision of spoons, bowls and cutlery suggests a similar figure.

Operating the unfamiliar equipment successfully in post-attack conditions might be more difficult than is apparent; most of the staff earmarked for the service are the auxiliaries of the school meals service. The equipment is unlikely to be in good condition either, as was made clear in the circular on peacetime emergencies (ES7/75):

Local authorities may draw on the 'mothballed' wartime stocks of emergency feeding equipment which (MAFF) holds . . . . Much of the equipment needs cleaning and stripping before it can be used.

Instructions on cleaning and stripping do not appear in advice on wartime plans. This might be discovered after local authorities collected their allocation of equipment and saw its condition.

The consequence of the failure of ill-thought out emergency feeding plans do not bear thinking about in large metropolitan areas, especially if they are *not* attacked. The Home Office has repeatedly been challenged by local authority planners and executives, on its 'lack of consideration' for the problems of feeding a city population of millions. There is no answer to the problem, of course; the official reply is merely that the final plan for the location of food stocks will be worked out by MAFF officials 'the week before crisis', a scarcely helpful reply. They dare not admit that the cities are all written off.

The major stocks in the MAFF Buffer Depots are now flour, sugar, margarine and fats, special hard glucose sweets, sweet biscuits, and a little yeast. Corned beef (and also cake mix) was held up to the late 1960s (and the turnover of the stocks led to the Aberdeen typhus outbreak). Circular ES1/79 on food and agriculture says that: 'These foods have been chosen for their value in providing energy and nutrition;' . . . 'they do not constitute a balanced diet nor are the quantities held related to the needs of the population for a particular period.' The Buffer Depot network was set up during the Second World War, and most of the buildings still in use and the principles of the stockpile date from the same period. There were also forty special cold stores, for meat—now abandoned.

The Depots are all run by private companies on behalf of MAFF and their general locations have not been secret; some are marked by signs, and most used to be listed in telephone directories (under the entry for the warehousing or wharfingers' firm concerned) – some still are. There are probably about 100–150 such depots in all. A smaller network in Scotland is run by the Scottish Home and Health Department, including a major store at Montrose. Although Northern Ireland has been divided into eight 'food areas', it is not known whether any emergency food stockpiles are maintained there.

Plate 39 Sugar in huge sacks was released from the MAFF stockpile during the 1975 shortage.

The emergency foods are ordered in special bulk packages from major suppliers: sugar from Tate and Lyle (this stock was released during the 1975 shortage); sweets from Mars; biscuits from Huntley and Palmer; flour from RHM, Spillers and the Co-op; margarine from van den Berghs. Orders and deliveries are carried out by contractors, in conditions of some secrecy. Many of the foods have had particular problems – the cases of the margarine containers tend to mould, and stacks collapse. Sugar and flour sacks are polythene cased to prevent moisture ingress and rodent damage. However, this measure is negated – with the expected consequences – the moment the sacks are stored, as the warehouse workmen almost invariably puncture the bags with a finger to make them easier to stack. Pilferage is another, if less serious, problem according to a former manager of a chain of Buffer Depots.

The Depots also hold mobile bakeries, but those who have seen them are scathing about their value. The entire such stock for the south east appears to be six bakeries in the Redhill Buffer Depot – all untouched in almost forty years. There are also hammer mills for simple flour making (probably using grain stocks held as animal feed on farms), and emergency grain elevators and dischargers for use at the emergency ports. A list of most Buffer Depots is given in Table 16.

In carrying out dispersal plans before attack, new 'Buffer Depots' would be added to the MAFF network. In *Hard Rock*, there were estimated to be about 250 in operation, the network having 'doubled'. MAFF refuses to identify the amounts held or how long stocks would last. However, simple calculations, based on some information about a group of ten Depots, suggests that the total stock, on an optimal view, might last forty million survivors two weeks – or a more realistic twenty million survivors for a month, assuming a dietary level of 2000 food calories a day.* This assumes equity of distribution and that the depots themselves do not become damaged, which is unlikely. The dispersal pattern was based on Second Word War requirements, and most depots would be badly damaged by very slight overpressures, being built of brick with asbestos roofs.

---

*A crude estimate is that the Buffer Depots contain 4–5 million square feet (4–500,000 m²) of storage and mostly hold flour – say, 300,000 tons of flour, 20,000 tons of fat, 1.2m cases of biscuits and 30,000 tons of sugar. This yields about $1 \cdot 3.10^{12}$ calories sufficient for forty million people for sixteen days.

Table 16 Ministry of Agriculture, Fisheries and Food (MAFF) Buffer Depots
The information in this table is mostly extracted from telephone directories, over a period of years. It is therefore necessarily both incomplete and out of date. MAFF refuse to supply a list of Buffer Depots, or to say how extensive their emergency stockpile may be. It would certainly be less than two weeks' supply for the peacetime population, possibly far less.

Region	Depot Number	Address	Operator
1	322	Wooler, Northumbria	1
2	104T	Melbourne Avenue, Topcliffe Road, Thirsk, Yorks	2
	104V	Station Road, Kirkdale, Yorks	3
	104Z	Easingwold, Yorks	3
	351B	Rothwell, Leeds, Yorks	3
	351H	Drighlington, Bradford, Yorks	3
	464	Whitley Bridge, Leeds	5
	464E	Churchill Road, Doncaster	5
	464F	Full Sutton Airfield, Great Driffield, Yorks	5
	464G	Planet Road, Adwick-le-Street, Yorks	5
	337	Doncaster	4
	337L	Harleston Road, Old Mill Lane, Barnsley	4
	906G	Selby, Yorks	5
	87	Gamston Airfield, Nottingham	4
3	336	Main Road, Smalley Gate, Notts	7
	336H,J	New Street, Earl Shilton, Leics	8
	336K	Little Glen Road, Glen Parva, Leics	6
	336M	Humberstone Lane, Thurmaston, Leics	6
	336N	Harleston Road, New Dunston, Northants	6
	336T	Coxmoor Road, Sutton-in-Ashfield, Notts	6
	559A	Crick Road, Hillmorton, Northants	9
		Memory Lane, Belgrave Gate, Leicester	7
	–	Mackin Street, Derby	7
	–	Fiskerton Airfield, Lincoln	6
	–	Station Road, Castle Donington, Leics	7
	336P	New Unit 70, 10 Romany Way, Market Harborough, Leics	7

Region	Depot Number	Address	Operator
4	–	The Drift, Royston, Herts	10
	–	Tempsford Airfield, Sandy, Beds	10
	–	Royston Road, Godmanchester, Cambs	10
	19	Hoddesdon, Herts	16
	4F	Hertford Road, Hoddesdon, Herts	3
	4L	Huggins Lane, Marshmoor Sidings, Hatfield	3
	4M	New Ground, Tring, Herts	3
	36	Goodwyns Halt, Hemel Hempstead, Herts	17
	90	Manor Way, Borehamwood, Herts	–
4	–	Station Road, Thetford	27
	379W	Kings Lynn	27
	–	Heath Road, Burwell, Cantab	27
	521G	Elsenham Station, Stanstead, Essex	7
	521J	Station Road, Marks Tey, Essex	7
	–	St Peters Road, Huntingdon	7
5	111	Bath Road, Harmondsworth, Middlesex	18
	1002D	Walthamstow	4
	325	Windmill Road, Sunbury on Thames	9
	325E	Commerce Road, Brentford	9
	16B	Hounslow	15
	–	Rotherhithe Street, Bermondsey	–
6	339	Station Road, Betchworth, Surrey	13
	339	Westerham, Kent	13
	528A	Forstal Road, Aylesford, Kent	14
	528E	Lamberhurst Quarter, Tunbridge Wells	14
	–	Pattenden Lane, Marden, Tonbridge	–
	124	Frenches Road, Redhill	13
	139B	Hook (Daneshill Works), Surrey	13
	347	The Broyle, Ringmer, Sussex	13
	366	Quainton, Bucks	11
	366C	Saunderton, High Wycombe, Bucks	11
	450	Freeland, Oxon	12
	450F	Kidlington, Oxon	12
	357	South Leigh, Witney, Oxon	12
	450G	Culham, Oxon	12
	450H	Kennington, Oxon	12
	450J	Grimsbury Road, Banbury	12
	–	Eastlee, Deal	13
	–	Liphook	13
	–	Old Woking	13
7	68	Exeter	20
	361	West Pennard, Street, Somerset	20
	361	Halatrow, Temple Cloud, Somerset	21
	362A,S	Badminton, Avon	19

Region	Depot Number	Address	Operator
	363T	Gorlands Road, Chipping Sodbury, Avon	19
	96QQ	Hawthorn	10
	96QR	Coped Hall, Wootton Basset, Wilts	10
	397	Keynsham, Avon	22
8	–	Rheola Works, Neath, Glamorgan	11
	–	Hirwaun Industrial Estate, Hirwaun	11
9	99	Station Approach, Tewkesbury	–
	469	Badsey, Evesham, Hereford and Worcs	17
	4N	Stratford on Avon, Warwicks	17
	137AB	Stone, Stoke on Trent	24
	137AK,AL	Uttoxeter	24
	137AG	Newport, Salop	24
	137AP,AQ	Barton under Needwood, Staffs	24
	558A	Lichfield, Staffs	23
	558C	Cannock, Staffs	23
	–	Bidavon Industrial Estate, Warwicks	–
	–	Eclipse Road Trading Estate, Alcester, Warwicks	–
	–	Kineton Road Industrial Estate, Southam, Warwicks	–
	–	National Agricultural Centre, Stoneleigh, Kenilworth	–
10	314E	Brownedge Lane, Tardy Gate, Preston	28
	314QR	Railway Station, Grimsargh, Preston	28
	475Q	Orrell lane, Burscough, Lancs	28
	395D	Stanley Street, Blackburn	26
	395K	Taylor St, Clitheroe, Lancs	26
	395L	Feniscowles, Blackburn, Lancs	26
	395N	Broadway, Haslingden, Lancs	26
	562	London Road, Adlington, Lancs	25
	–	Gregson Lane, Hoghton	28
	544CD	Marston Sheds, Hornby Road, Claughton	29
	562C	School Bridge, Dunham Town, Cheshire	25
	–	Knutsford Road, Clelford, Cheshire	25
	562E	Raglan Road, Sale	26
	344B	Tattenhall	25
	344CD	Tarporley	25
	344E	Dunham Hill, Thornton-le-Moor	25
	344F	Mickle Trafford	25
	344G	Waverton	25
Scotland	–	Home Defence Store, Hayford Mill, Cambusbarron, Stirling	SHHD
	–	Montrose Airfield, Tayside	SHHD

	Operators		*Operators*
1	Newcastle Warehousing Co. Ltd	16	J. W. Cook and Co. Ltd.
2	R Steenberg and Sons Ltd. (Newcastle)	17	Hay's Wharf Ltd.
		18	Trinity Wharf Co. Ltd.
3	Free Trade Wharf Co. Ltd	19	Lovell C. Shaw and Sons Ltd.
4	New Fresh Wharf Co. Ltd.	20	MacLaines (Travel and Forwarding) Ltd.
5	Inland Warehousing Ltd.		
6	Brooks Wharf and Bull Wharf Ltd.	21	J. Warriner Ltd.
7	Co-ordinated Traffic Services Ltd.	22	Ford and Canning (1947) Ltd.
8	Robert Warner Ltd.	23	E. E. Roper and Co. Ltd.
9	Weber, Smith and Hoare Ltd.	24	Longton Storage and Warehouses Ltd.
10	Sterling Wharfage Co. Ltd.	25	Cheshire Storage Co. Ltd.
11	J. Spurling Ltd.	26	North Western Storage Co. Ltd
12	British and Foreign Wharf Co. Ltd	27	Cory Associated Wharves Ltd.
13	Butlers Wharf Ltd.	28	Lancashire Storage Co. Ltd.
14	J. Leete and Sons Ltd.	29	LUWKA Storage Ltd.
15	Ceylon Wharf Ltd.		

As the stockpiled food and personal reserves ran out, the only sources of supply would be farm stocks and whatever agricultural production could be restored to 'improvise a subsistence economy', according to official plans. The *Briefing Material* circular reminded Controllers that:

The highly mechanised agriculture industry would have to revert to more primitive methods of working for some time to come.

Food and Agriculture in War warns

After nuclear attack food would be scarce, lacking in variety and unevenly distributed throughout the country. It would be prudent to plan on the assumption that no significant food imports would be received for some time.

The MAFF regional government staff plan (although without great detail) to directly control all agriculture, and would appoint Farm Wardens – perhaps one for every twenty farms – to supervise all activities. Support staff at divisional offices would include radioactivity and veterinary specialists.

Like all western economies, the United Kingdom makes grossly inefficient use of plant calories, by using the bulk of indigenous cereal production to feed livestock. Were cereal production to be sustained at pre-war levels, survivors could certainly all subsist, given adequate distribution. But the agriculture industry is dependent on fertilisers and insecticides which will not be available, as well as high levels of mechanisation. Yields will fall, perhaps by more than fifty per cent depending on the time of year of the attack.

In the first year, the stocks of cereals and other grains held as animal feeding stuffs on farms might tide survivors over. Each harvest, about twelve million tons of grains are stored on the farms. In this respect, there could be no better time to have a nuclear war than the *Hard Rock* date of early October. The harvest would be fully in and stored and supplies would be at maximum levels. By the time the next year's harvest was at a vulnerable stage, radioactivity would be at 0.01 per cent of its original level. Processing and eating these supplies (as well as the livestock which could not be fed from them) for the first year might just sustain survivors until the next harvest. But the next harvest would be drastically smaller than before the war. And an attack at any other time of year would leave an inadequacy of stocks, certainly for forty million survivors; by March, there would only be 3–5 million tons in store. In any case, some grain will have to be withheld;

Agriculture officers will need to balance demands in the immediate post-attack period against the requirement for a greater agricultural yield in the recovery period.

The problem of the direct effects of nuclear weapons is severe. The 'standard' two hundred megaton attack in Home Office plans would, according to the Home Office (see Chapter 11), include some sixty per cent of the land area within at least the outer zone of 'minor' blast damage. A MAFF analysis* suggests that seventy per cent of the surface area of the UK would receive aggregate radiation doses greater than two Roentgen; and some 27,000 square miles ($70,000$ km^2) would receive doses greater than 700 R – lethal for most humans without protection, and at the level at which crop production could begin to be seriously affected. The vulnerability of crops depends on the stage at which they are irradiated, greatest vulnerability occurring during periods of maximum growth. One measure is the YD_{50} radiation level, at which fifty per cent of the crop will be lost. During the growing season for Britain's main crops, wheat and barley, the YD_{50} varies between

*'United Kingdom Considerations in Agricultural Defence Planning.' by W. T. S. Neal of MAFF, in *Survival of Food Crops and Livestock in the Event of Nuclear War*, symposium held at Brookhaven National Laboratory, New York, September 1970. Published by the US Atomic Energy Commission in December 1971.

Plates 40 & 41 A network of thirty-foot-wide (10m) tunnels in the Welsh hills at Rhydymwyn has been reserved as a Special Site or central government war citadel. The entrance is wide enough to admit large vehicles and three tunnels run directly into the mountainside. Although not fully developed, the site was allocated as a Depot subordinate to the Hawthorn complex. (right) Ventilation towers on a hillside overlooking the site.

600 and 2500 R (for barley) and 100 and 3500 R (for wheat), according to a MAFF circular (E1/77). It is apparent that the exact effects depend very much on the time of year. Vulnerability will also be increased by beta irradiation – caused by fallout particles alighting on exposed crops – a hazard which does not threaten humans or animals in all but primitive shelter conditions.

On a rough estimate, the postulated attack would destroy one quarter to one half of the cereal harvest, and a fifth of pasture and potato yields. The effects would be at their worst

in early summer, when stocks were lowest, and the crops most vulnerable. The next winter would see many millions starve, unless the number of survivors was already tiny.

The strategic stockpile is acknowledged officially to hold 'quantities . . . insufficient to meet the needs of the surviving population over a protracted period' (and this is certainly true). Farm stocks and the early slaughter of fallout afflicted and surplus animals (particularly poultry and pigs) will provide rather more food than the 2–4 weeks in the emergency stockpile – if the dead animals can be got quickly to feeding centres. Milk, if available, would have to be turned into butter or cheese and stored until the concentration of radioisotopes declined.

The government's declared longterm aim would be to promote a 'reorientation towards subsistence agriculture growing more food crops, particularly cereals.' All foodstuffs would contain, for a long period, levels of radioactivity which would brand them as untouchable in peacetime.

The MAFF assessment by Neal, which discounts the loss of fertilisers and production aids, claims that, in principle, sufficient food resources may be available. It is not a robust conclusion however. As in many other official assessments of the effects of attack, cumulative and unknown effects are dealt with simply by being set aside.

The Home Office's survival model is even cruder. It takes general damage assessments for each district and converts these to assess the surviving resource levels in each of forty-two economic sectors, from barley and cereals to transport, labour and 'essential imports'. The survivors' final demand for each commodity is estimated, and the necessary economic inputs can then be calculated, and compared with surviving resources. The model is deficient in at least one major respect – it assumes implicitly that a survival economy will use resources in the same way as in peacetime – an assumption which renders the study of little value. Even so, the results may have been disturbing and politically unwelcome, since no account of the results of such studies have been released, or made available to researchers such as Jackson (see footnote, p. 351). He commented later in *Protect and Survive Monthly* that:

Government guidelines gloss over problems which without extensive preparation could prove intractable.

Glossing over unwelcome difficulties of public behaviour or the effects of war is, of course, endemic in Home Defence planning.

11
Death and life

The direct and immediate effects of nuclear weapons, if not their long term effects, are not much in doubt. In principle, the physics and medicine should be the same for everyone, everywhere. In fact, there are significant differences between Home Office estimates of bomb effects (physical damage and casualty levels) and those made by all other, authoritative, sources.

Many seperate factors, from the likely weight and pattern of attack, to the level of building destruction and individual vulnerability to radiation, are all assessed by the Home Office in a way that remarkably diminishes the death and injury toll claimed to result from nuclear war.

In 1981, the government required each of the fourteen Regional Health Authorities in England and Wales (and similar groups in Scotland) to appoint War Planning teams, and provided nearly £½ million for the purpose. Yet no amount of planning can conceal the impossibility of a medical response to nuclear war.

In Britain, war planning for the Health Service began late in the day. The circular on the *Preparation and Organisation of the Health Services for War* (Home Office ES1/77; DHSS circular HDC(1) 77) was issued after almost every other major subject had already been discussed. Health services have not been given high priority. There are (small) reserve stockpiles of drugs and supplies held by the DHSS. There are no emergency hospital facilities, and now only the most rudimentary schemes for dispersal of stocks and supplies. The war planning effort – against a significant background of internal resistance within the National Health Service – is perhaps the most cynical of all the civil defence preparations. No money is spent on stockpiles or special facilities; on the contrary, the swingeing cuts in the Health Service in the 80s have resulted in the closure of hospitals, cuts in staff, and an overall diminution of resources. Against this background, the preparation of war plans is indeed a cruel deception; in a situation of overwhelming casualties and insufficient doctors or supplies, all a plan can do is to redistribute the misery. Supplies will run out quickly, in a very few days. Palliative paper plans will save no one's suffering or death.

In order to understand the specific medical problems, and the assessment of the ultimate casualty rate, it is worthwhile to summarise, in some detail, the immediate and delayed effects of a nuclear attack. Earlier chapters have dealt with the government's overall preparations, and the development of British civil defence policy. It is now worthwhile to examine the scientific and medical consequences of nuclear war.

The major source of nuclear weapons information, highly commended and repeatedly relied on by the Home Office (and also their critics), is the US standard work, *The Effects of Nuclear Weapons*, by Samuel Glasstone and Philip Dolan published by the US Department of Defense. The first edition was in 1952, and the book has been repeatedly revised since; the third edition being prepared in 1977 (published in the UK by Castle House Publishing Ltd, Tunbridge Wells). In 1980, the US Congressional Office of Technology Assessment (OTA) published another study, *The Effects of Nuclear War* (published in the UK by Croom Helm Ltd). A Home Office booklet, *Nuclear Weapons* is on sale at HMSO, and like two other publications, not distributed to the public – the *Operational Handbook*, and the *Training Manual for Scientific Advisers*, – it acknowledges that the 'most important' source of information on weapons effects is Glasstone and Dolan.

However, different Home Office publications and papers quite often contradict each other; sometimes figures are given from Glasstone and Dolan, sometimes from the Home Office's own (unspecified) sources. On more than one occasion, totally contradictory figures are contained in the same book (in the *Operational Handbook* and *Domestic Nuclear Shelters – Technical Guidance*). Although there is scope for disagreement and re-interpretation of evidence, particularly about radiological effects, Glasstone and Dolan appears to be the premier and definitive source, and is so treated here.

Enough nuclear weapons were detonated in the atmosphere before the partial test ban treaty for most of the effects to be well documented; the obvious exception is the effect of high and rapid (acute) doses of radioactivity on human beings, for which there are only the studies of Hiroshima and Nagasaki victims, and a scattering of other cases.

The following details of bomb effects (pages 369–375) are based on observing the action of a one megaton groundburst weapon from a distance of about nine miles (14 km). At this sort of range – between areas of total devastation and areas affected only by fallout – it is easiest to see the more marginal effects of nuclear destruction, and the effects of civil defence measures – or the lack of them. If anyone is sheltering in the central area they will not survive – unless accommodated in an unusually hardened (ie, military) facility. Further away, each different weapons effect provides a different hazard. The effects can be scaled up or down according to the power of the bomb. The blast effects, as they spread out into the volume of air around the centre of the explosion, go down in power with the cube of the distance. So the distance at which each weapon has a given blast varies only as the cube root of the bomb power. A ten megaton weapon will produce a given blast only ten times further away than will a ten kiloton weapon, even though it is a thousand times more powerful. This physical principle subjects weapons designers to a law of diminishing returns. Improving the accuracy of a missile by a factor of ten is more worthwhile than providing a warhead five hundred times larger. Against cities, however, this kind of distinction does not much matter.

When the bomb detonates, the nuclear explosion is over within a microsecond; and the energy has been released. The first energy from the bomb goes out as neutrons, gamma and X rays from the nuclear reaction. These create a hazard in themselves, and in ionising the air create the electromagnetic pulse (EMP). But for an observer on the periphery of the area of a thermonuclear detonation, the initial nuclear radiation is inconsequential; it is absorbed and dispersed before it reaches beyond the killing distance for blast effects.

Most of the radiation is absorbed in the air around the centre of the explosion, heating up a huge, rapidly expanding, incandescent ball of air. As the fireball touches the ground, a crater is scooped out as the earth and debris are vaporised.

The first sign of the detonation, from a remote viewpoint, might be the reflected flash and shine of the explosion. The first effect would be the heat pulse – infra red radiation from the heat of the fireball. About one third of the bomb's energy is distributed this way. The heat pulse will last 10–20 seconds; it will start fires where the heat is absorbed by combustible material, and char black the skins of those who are exposed in the open, up to a distance of five miles (8 km) or so, on a

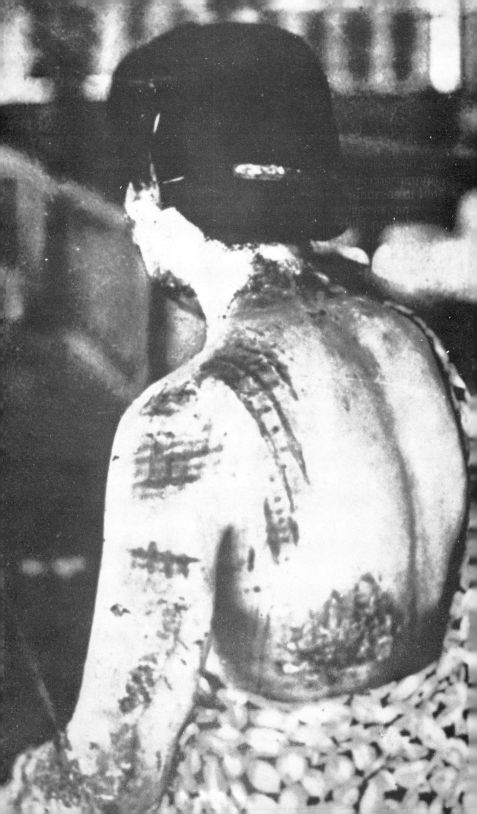

Plate 42   Hiroshima: the heat flash burnt clothing textures onto
the skin of victims.

---

a clear day. Even at nine miles (14 km), those caught in the
open will suffer burns and blistering of their skin. Towards
the centre of the explosion from one to five miles (1·5–8 km)
out, fires begin to burn. But despite the passing of the flash
and the heat pulse, the distant observer will have neither
heard the explosion nor felt its blast effects yet. The electricity
supply might just have failed, responding to the effects of EMP
and perhaps to direct damage. For half a minute, if one was
safely able to view the scene, the fireball would slowly be
coalescing at a diameter of about 7000 feet (650 m) and
beginning its rise up to form the characteristic mushroom
cloud. The sudden heating of the thousands of tons of air
creates a tremendous shockwave, or blast, which moves outwards at a rate of over 1000 feet per second (300m/s). It still
takes over forty seconds to reach a position nine miles from
the centre.

When the blast comes, it has already lost much of the
power and effect that it had near the centre. After the initial,
crashing shock wave, there is a phase of sustained pressure,
accompanying a wind away from the direction of the explosion. The high pressure will last for 3–4 seconds. At the
distance of nine miles the pressure will not do any direct harm
to anyone in the open. In this region the maximum pressure
created by the shock wave would be under a pound per square
inch (psi)*. Although the Home Office suggests that there
would be few if any casualties at this distance from the centre
of the explosion, US figures suggest injuries will affect 25 per
cent of those present. The pressure created by the blast wave
would blow in windows and seriously damage roof tiles; it
might blow in doors and partitions inside the house. Windows
would continue to be broken even twenty miles (32 km) out
from the centre, although without much other damage.

The combined effects of the blast and sustained 'overpressure' from a nuclear weapon detonation can be far more
severe than a comparable short, sharp blast from a conventional high explosive bomb. Buildings and their components
are first pushed back by the blow of the shock wave; then as
it passes, and parts of the wave are reflected from the building
and other structures, new, high and uneven pressures add to

---

*The metric measure is kiloPascal (kPa); roughly, 1 psi = 7 kPa.

the risk of damage. The 'wind' following the blast wave may create a drag (pull) on the building and cause more damage. The few seconds of overpressure may cause considerable internal damage, and move occupants and goods around. As the pressure outside declines, if the building does not have many doors or windows, the pressure outside may fall back to normal much more quickly than that inside the building. Its walls and roof are pushed apart. It explodes.

Up to a range of eight miles (13 km) from the centre of the explosion, fires are now alight in one house in thirty, according to the Home Office estimate in *Nuclear Weapons*. The fires will spread into conflagrations or firestorms.

The fireball has seared out a crater, perhaps 100 feet (30m) deep and 1000 feet (300m) wide. It is the earth and other material scoured from the crater which will make all the difference to radioactive fallout. The debris of the nuclear explosion includes the creation of a wide range of more than ninety different radioisotopes, each formed by the fission of the original bomb fuel of uranium or plutonium. The relatively 'clean' fusion part of the bomb's yield will create fallout material only through the neutron bombardment of material in the soil, or bomb components. In an airburst explosion, the surviving residual isotopes eventually condense as very small particles, so small that most of their activity has decayed before they eventually fall from the atmosphere, across wide areas of the globe.

In a groundburst, the massive tonnage of (eventually) solid material scooped up by the fireball provides a mass of thick particles on which the explosion residue can condense. The particles which rise up in the mushroom cloud can be 1mm (1/30th of inch) across, or even larger. Once the cloud has stabilised, the particles begin to fall, being transported by the wind as they do so.

The very top of the cloud from a one megaton bomb will rise to perhaps thirteen miles (20 km), and its diameter will extend beyond ten miles (16 km), more than covering all the areas initially damaged by blast and fire.

The heaviest, most dangerous fallout will reach the ground in these areas, near to the centre of the explosion. As the particles drop to earth, they are carried along the ground by winds, which may vary at different height levels. The first fallout will build up to a peak within 30–40 minutes of the explosion. It will arrive early, and be extremely radioactive. Over the course of an hour or so, particles will continue to fall until the rest of the dust cloud in the atmosphere has been blown downwind, to fall over the next few hours.

A long plume of fallout will begin to fall downwind of the explosion. The people most at risk, however, will be those in the target area, who may have already been injured from blast or fire, or have been caught in the open. There will be many who, if they are following the advice of *Protect and Survive* to shelter in their own homes, now face the prospect of trying to repair, in minutes, some of the damaged or broken windows and demolished doors and roofs. The situation of almost everyone across a 300 square mile (750 km²) tract of land is now fairly desperate. There are those trapped or injured by the initial blast, or burned by the heat pulse. They will die, quite soon, while they are trapped, or trying to escape the damaged area. Those who are uninjured, but whose houses are irretrievably damaged or threatened by fire, face the problem of either improvising shelter against the heaviest levels of fallout, or attempting to get out of the area. But over everyone's head is the thirteen-mile-high cloud, slowly dispersing its fallout. Within the course of 30–60 minutes radiation levels in most areas near the centre of the explosion will have risen to an initial rate of thousands of Roentgen per hour. To spend more than thirty minutes absorbing such levels of radiation will quickly be lethal. Yet roads will be blocked with debris, there are no civil defence rescue troops, and to stay or to go may be fatal.

The same risks are shared by most of those ten miles (16 km) or more from the centre. There may only be lesser injuries from direct effects – flying glass or debris. But unless the houses can be quickly weatherproofed, even the minimal protection factor that they offer against radiation will be useless; those in the main fallout area, or in 'hotspots', will get a lethal dose. Throughout the post explosion period, strong winds will be blowing, caused by fires and the updraught from the epicentre of the explosion. These will not only impede self–help repair work, but will also ensure that, as the fallout comes to earth, it does penetrate the damaged roof and window apertures, and so on. This is a principal objection to the *Protect and Survive* advice; in areas where fallout protection is most needed, near the centre of an explosion, blast effects are likely to fatally degrade the protection available.

The casualty toll will be huge and increasing. American studies of a single one megaton attack on an urban area give immediate casualties of 800,000 dead and 900,000 injured for a population of four million; 420,000 killed and 330,000 injured for a population of one million. These exclude later radiation casualties.

Each of Britain's urban areas – except London and the West Midlands – would thus be more or less wiped out by these effects of a single one megaton weapon. The initial survival rate, citywide, might be more than fifty per cent. But with current civil defence policies, all the trapped will also die; most of the injured will face death through non-treatment, if they cannot evacuate themselves, and face lethal radiation exposure if they do try to evacuate. The direct, lethal effects of blast cover a much smaller area than marginal effects which nevertheless may destroy the possibility of taking effective shelter, either from the original bomb, or from the overlapping fallout plumes of bombs used in a multiple, large scale attack.

Downwind of the main explosion, fallout builds up as successively smaller particles reach the ground. The extent of the plume depends on wind speeds at different heights and distances; a range of 250 miles (400 km) would be typical for a one megaton weapon (for a radiation level of a few rads per day). Later fallout will be less dangerous than that coming down early, since it will have lost much of its activity.

All radioactivity follows an exponential decay law – its level falls by the same factor in each time period. Each radioactive substance in the fallout has its own rate of decay, but, overall it has been found that the mixture, for the first few weeks, obeys a fairly simple equation:

Dose rate = Initial dose rate $\times$ $T^{-1.2}$. (T represents time)

Initially radioactivity declines sharply. Later, the decline is much more gradual. The convenient rule for radioactivity levels over the course of time is that the level declines by a factor of ten when the time increases by a factor of seven. Thus a dose rate of 1000 Roentgens per hour, one hour after the explosion, would fall to 100 Roentgens an hour at seven hours; and after forty-nine hours (or, roughly, two days) it would be 10 Roentgens an hour – one hundred times less. The dose rate after an hour is (in Britain) usually called the DR1; that after seven hours, the DR7. It is apparent that the initial, relatively rapid decline in radiation levels helps those who may wish to make brief trips out from a secure shelter after a few days; equally, it works against those near the point of explosion whose maximum vulnerability (in trying to repair buildings, put out fires, get free, or flee to a safer area) comes soon after the explosion.

For a one megaton bomb, the area covered with a DR1

radiation intensity greater than 1000 Roentgens per hour may be ninety square miles (225 km²). Three hundred more square miles (750 km²) would have an initial dose rate of 300 Roentgens per hour. Within a day, without protection, anyone in such a zone would have received more than double the lethal dose of radiation; even with some protection and a lesser dose they would be crippled beyond recovery.

In the sort of attack that the government expects, more than half the land area of the country will sustain 'superficial damage' from blast. Everywhere is at risk of serious levels of fallout. From the hour of attack on, there will be millions of injured; within days, a huge toll of radiation casualties will join them. They will get no treatment.

The reference books mentioned above provide details of the effects of other types of weapons and other patterns of use. The example above, however, provides a simple basis on which to examine government health plans and casualty estimates.

The 1977 advice to health authorities on planning for war noted that many changes in the Health Service over the previous decade had made earlier plans quite obsolete. In keeping with the stay-put policy, health authorities everywhere had to 'plan to meet the consequences of an attack on *any* part of the country.'

The principles of the new policy were harsh. Rescue and succour – principles of 1960s civil defence – were also abandoned in health planning. Doctors, medical staff, and medical supplies were to be treated as a national commodity of particular value, to be dispersed and stockpiled for the future. Anything they might do to relieve pain, suffering and death for the victims of the stay-put policy seemed entirely peripheral. The circular explained:

Certain built up areas may be regarded as potential targets . . . .
If the total destruction or isolation of health service resources is to
be avoided, some redeployment of medical and nursing staff,
medical supplies, ambulances and equipment would be essential.
The major concentration of hospitals lies in the centres of large
cities and towns . . . The redeployment of resources could reduce
the possibility of total destruction. . .

This is perhaps as close as the government has come (in an unclassified document) to acknowledging the writing-off of the cities as an act of policy. The circular contrasts the fate of the public with that of doctors:

The government do not propose to arrange for any official evacuation of the public and through press, television and radio would advise against any random movement. . . . The public would be better protected by remaining in their own homes . . .

On the other hand,:

Trained staff are the most valuable asset possessed by the Health Service and could be replaced only in the very long term. . .all staff not required to operate an emergency service should themselves be sent home or dispersed within the Area or Region . . . . Arrangements should be made to provide as wide a dispersion as possible. When the greater part of a (Health Area) lies within a built up area, the dispersal arrangements should be made on a regional basis.

A clearer statement about the expendability of the general public has seldom been made, although some health authorities' plans go further. The North East Thames Regional Health Authority (RHA) War Plan, is one of many Health Service War Plans which have been leaked. It sets out, in terms, the dispensability of the ordinary citizen:

If all the great trees and much of the brushwood are felled, a forest may not regenerate for centuries. If a sufficient number of the great trees (sic) is left, however, *if felling is to some extent selective and controlled*, recovery is swift.

In its way, a nation is like a forest and the aim of war planning is to secure the survival of the great trees. (Author's emphasis).

As for the survivors, the North East Thames RHA has a clear view:

There will remain brushwood enough, if thirty million survivors can be so described. The planning policy is clearly elitist and is so because no wider policy is possible.

After a nuclear attack, according to the 1977 DHSS circular, there would be no question of 'wasting' medical staff by allowing them to work in fallout areas.

Immediate medical care for survivors might not be possible and medical staff . . . should not be wasted by allowing them to enter highly radioactive areas to help assist casualties. . . .

The spread and intensity of fallout would depend on many factors . . . but it may be assumed that the greater part of the country would be covered, in varying degrees, by plumes of highly radioactive dust, in many cases over-lapping. The intensity of this fallout would prevent, in most areas, any outside movement during at least the first forty-eight hours after an attack . . . in any case the whole of the United Kingdom would be under a RED attack warning against the possibility of further attacks during this period. For the first forty-eight hours after an attack, therefore, little or no life saving activity would be possible, except on the most limited self-help basis. . .

General life saving operations in areas of fallout might not be possible . . . until days or even weeks after a nuclear attack.

After a nuclear attack, radioactive fallout might be at lethal or near lethal levels. It would be essential that staff, vital to the long term recovery of the country, should not be wasted . . . and staff should not leave shelter until authorised to do so by the district controller.

Under the suggested 'release procedures' for the 'control of the public under fallout conditions', people could emerge for one hour a day once the exposure rate was down to 1–4 Roentgens per hour; and for nine hours when it had fallen to 0.5 to 1 Rph. This restriction is based on the (questionable) assumption that the average person could continue to absorb a dose of 10 Roentgens per day without being injured, in the short term.

Since the 'recovery' rate of radiation exposure is both injurious and hazardous, medical staff would effectively be prohibited from working, except under cover, for three weeks or more in areas of heavy fallout.

The first stage of preparation for war would be to empty hospitals and nursing homes, as far as possible. The DHSS suggested to hospitals that they would be able to rid themselves of all convalescing patients, 70 per cent of maternity and sick children cases, 60 per cent of acute cases, 50 per cent of chest cases and non-active infections, and 15 per cent of psychiatric patients. Other advice notes have made it clear that the old, infirm and mentally ill were relatively dispensable at an early stage. Circular HDC(77)1 says:

Discharge should not however be held up merely because home conditions were not ideal or could not be checked and it must be accepted that the crisis would entail hardship.

Remaining patients and staff should then move to the best parts of the hospital building for protection against fallout radiation.

In a 1978 circular on *Medical Supplies in War* (HDC(78)1) the DHSS spelt out in considerable detail the suggestions it had made in 1977 for the emergency dispersal of stocks. Simple supplies of dressings would be dispersed to the planned locations of first aid posts, most of which would be run by groups like the Red Cross or the St John Ambulance

Brigade. Larger stocks would be moved to pre-planned casualty collecting centres (cccs) and to anticipated 'surviving hospitals' where only emergency surgery would be carried out.

The DHSS stressed that all supplies – whether belonging to Health Authority stores, central government, or medical manufacturers and wholesalers – should be 'dispersed as widely as possible'. The DHSS's own medical stockpile, it revealed, was:

mainly held in central government stores, (and contained) items such as dressings, surgical and nursing equipment, camp beds blankets and linen essential to the establishment of cccs . . . The total quantities held are insufficient however . . .

A slightly more precise view of the situation is given in the blunt prose of the confidential North East Thames RHA War Plan:

It is improbable that supplies will last more than two days after the opening of cccs. There is a possibility that dumps in mental illness hospitals would be inaccessible or forgotten for months or years. When located they will be eked out to use for training purposes and treating from time to time a few of the normally occurring illnesses among survivors.

The circular on *Medical Supplies* suggested that health authorities might get powers to requisition drugs from manufacturers and wholesalers but held out little hope that there would be time to put such plans into practice. Moreover:

Health Directors with requisitioned medical equipment and supplies in their area should bear in mind that these are national assets . . . It may be a very long time after attack before any significant quantity of medical equipment or supplies could be manufactured or imported, and all items, however plentiful locally, would have to be treated as scarce nationally.

Control of stocks would be exercised at the 'highest practicable level'. Once an attack had taken place, the government would take over all stocks in chemists and pharmacies, according to the 1977 circular:

All supplies held by pharmacies (etc) . . . would be requisitioned for the health services and made available to the public only in the course of medical treatment through general practitioners and domiciliary teams.

The supplies to be dispersed before attack included some forty-five items, ranging from anaesthetics, antibiotics, antitoxins, vaccines and sera to enema syringes, insulin, cortisone, adrenalin and water supplies. The list also included 'tie-on labels' which would be used for grading casualties in *triage* (see below). There would be little point in labelling corpses, burials (or other means of disposal) would not require marking graves, or even keeping records.

The list also includes analgesics, sedatives, and opiates. The mention of opiates – that is, morphine and heroin – raises an interesting point. The DHSS advice makes no secret of the million-fold scale of casualties that nuclear war will create. But in these circulars, and elsewhere, it tries to disguise in sacharine sick prose the brutal and almost inhuman nature of the post-attack 'health service', in which many will be left on one side to die. If government planners were even prepared—in honesty and self respect – to admit to themselves, and in their writings, the implications of their policies, they might recognise that the greatest humanitarian health need of all after an attack (given that many casualties of burns, radiation and serious multiple injuries could never be given life, no matter how lavish a provision was made) would be to provide the dying and sick with a painless and comfortable passage out of existence. The United States authorities and other countries have made such preparations, which may seem brutal but are more honest than make-believe paper plans. The US government stockpile of heroin stood, in 1981, at some fifty tons, distributed across the country – increased from twenty-three tons held during the 1970s. It is repugnant, but more useful than recruiting boy scouts and girl guides to help out at first aid centres which will soon be drained of any medical supplies.

It would also be more useful than homilies on leadership qualities, such as appear in the East Anglian RHA War Plan:

In the unlikely event of war it will be necessary to rediscover a true sense of family and community discipline which over the years has markedly disintegrated in the face of changing attitudes and a differing sense of values. . . . We shall have to call upon . . . the ability of the nation as a whole to expend their energies on their own protection and not look upwards for others to do it for them. . .

This sort of sanctimonious piffle appears to feature particularly strongly in health authorities' War Plans. It is sometimes hard to escape the impression that some war planners, at least, would regard the aftermath of nuclear war as the achievement of an ambition, with great potential for some kind of national spiritual regeneration in its wake. The DHSS itself is not exempt from issuing moral strictures as an alternative to useful forms of activity like stockpiling drugs. In a 'confidential' set of *Guidance Notes for Doctors Teaching Mass Casualty Care* – issued in 1979* (and 'not for publication'), the final conclusion was that:

the civilian population would be stunned and under very great stress. This requires above all firm and sympathetic leadership. After people have overcome the initial phase, they need outlets for their emotions in the way of useful work

However, nothing could equal the efforts of the North East Thames RHA, who added to their War Plan's thesis on the survival of great trees amongst brushwood, an appendix listing major historical disasters in which, from the plague of Justinian in AD540 to Hulaga Khan invading Mesopotamia in 1258, leaders' survival had determined national survival, with an observation that 'we have warning now of the modern equivalent of plague. That is why isolation points (ie, presumably, bunkers for 'great trees' also known as 'leaders') have already been equipped.'

Somewhat more sane and hardheaded is the view in the Croydon Area Health Authority War Plan:

It is difficult to believe that a potential agressor invoking the use of nuclear weapons would not set out from the beginning to inflict the maximum disruption and disorganisation upon the nation.
    Conventional planning would normally prepare for a range of options . . . but the sheer scale of some of the more pessimistic assumptions challenges the very value of planning at all.
    A major nuclear attack on central or south London would create a scenario in which the whole population would have to remain under cover for up to fourteen days. . . . Each hospital would have to survive on its pre-existing stocks. . . .The problems at long stay hospitals hardly bear consideration. . . .Most of the casualties who manage to reach hospital or first aid stations during this period would probably die anyway from the effects of radioactive fallout.

The wartime organisation of the Health Service provides for each Regional Health Authority to appoint its Regional Medi-

_____
*In fact, the notes were twenty years old, and had only been slightly altered: 'civil defence' now reads 'home defence'.

cal Officer as wartime Regional Health Director. The boundaries of the fourteen Health Regions in England and Wales do not correspond with the Home Defence Regions, and appointments of Regional Health Advisers to the different SRHQS and wartime Regional Governments have been made on a more or less *ad hoc* basis. For example, the North West Thames RHD would be in overall charge of London (Region 5); the North East Thames RHD would be in charge of Region 4, including East Anglia. Area Health Authorities were scrapped after the circular was written, and the Regional Authorities now directly control the various hospital, community health, and general practice groups.

A summary of casualty policy in the 1977 circular repeated the warning about not wasting medical staff on 'organised life saving operations' (for the third time in the document), and defined a three tier system of casualty control, consisting of First Aid Posts (FAP), Casualty Collecting Centres (CCC) and hospitals. The function of the system is to limit medical treatment to prevent resources being overwhelmed. People would have to get themselves to a First Aid Post or Casualty Collecting Centre; there, they might get some treatment – or not. The FAPs would give first aid while resources lasted, and direct those with severe injuries on to a CCC:

The number of casualties may be expected greatly to exceed surviving hospital resources and Directors would have to impose strict admission priorities. Casualty Collecting Centres would therefore be established between the FAPs and the hospitals to treat, sort and hold casualties until they could be accepted by a hospital. Cccs should be set up in each neighbourhood . . . separate from FAPs.

The centres are supposed to come together on an *ad hoc* basis with general practitioners working in teams of 4–6 and local authorities supposed to supply food and other resources, including 'kitchen and unskilled staff, and the removal and burial of the dead'.

Although the 1977 *Health Services in War* circular noted that it was not worthwhile to disperse electric powered medical equipment (except for a few X ray machines), it offers no comments on the difficulties of running a health service centre in premises which may well be without water and electricity, as well as having negligible food or medical stocks. No CCC would have an emergency generator. Many hospitals do have emergency power, but the problems of operating these (or whether Regional Commissioners would allow priority use of fuel at hospitals) is not discussed.

In Scotland, plans drawn up by the Scottish Home and Health Department are similar, based on fourteen Area Health Boards. The Scottish circular (ES(SCOT)4/77 'restricted') also suggests that National Service Officers would be appointed to direct labour in the medical and nursing professions. The objectives of Health Service War Plans are the same as in England and Wales:

– to create a firm base from which the remaining staff (of the NHS) could work, and to raise morale of both public and staff by demonstrating a determination to rebuild the Health Service, albeit in modified form.

There is no objective of offering hope of medical treatment to anyone; on the contrary, 'the number of casualties might be quite beyond the resources of the existing health services'.

The *Guidance Notes* on mass casualty care explain, often disingenuously, how the problem is to be appproached. A 'Mass Casualty Situation' is defined as

one in which the total medical resources of an area are already overwhelmed or are about to be overwhelmed, with no prospect of early outside assistance. This condition would undoubtedly obtain following a thermonuclear attack. It is all too commonly thought that a thermonuclear attack would be so devastating that planning to deal with it is a waste of time.

This, it says 'is not so'. The DHSS claims that 'even in a very heavy attack considerable areas would be undamaged'. This is scarcely true; most of the country would be badly damaged, even if all that a country hospital suffered was the breaking of all its windows from remote airbursts and fallout drifting in. But the DHSS is concerned, again, with the *nation*:

It is therefore worthwhile to plan for the survival of the nation rather than to do nothing and achieve nothing.

The CCC's main function is sorting, or *triage*. Casualties are sorted into three categories: those who will survive without further attention, who are sent home or to rest centres; those who would need major surgery or medical attention to survive, who are discarded into a 'holding unit' to die; and those who might go to hospital for treatment if after 'limited surgical procedures' they 'would be likely to be alive after seven days', with a fair chance of eventual recovery. The public would not be admitted directly to hospital, and would only be sent on from CCC as space and resources permitted.

The nature of a CCC a few days after attack really does not bear thinking about. As the only centres at which casualties could have any hope of medical attention from a doctor or nurse, they would quickly become swamped. Each CCC might have a team of 4–6 GPs with a similar number of nurses, plus voluntary assistants. With staff working under intolerable, continuous pressure, it is easy to envisage the state of the holding units in which the dead and dying would lie together after a few days. As radiation sickness set in for those with early injuries, and the later, radiation–only, casualties came in, the holding unit rooms in the CCC would be filled with untreated dying people suffering from incessant vomiting, diahorrea, and nausea. The local authority Controller might have decided to provide no rations for them beyond a derisory biscuit or two. Volunteers would have to wade in periodically to pull out those who had died. Everyone working or waiting for treatment would have to work against a perpetual background of the pain and cries of the sick and dying. To maintain the most basic health precautions without sanitation, water, electricity, without painkilling drugs or antibiotics to spare, amongst seas of people dying in their own wastes, would be next to impossible. The psychological effect on staff and patients alike would be grim. It does not even have to be imagined what such a place would be like; John Hersey vividly described the Red Cross Hospital in Hiroshima after the bomb had been dropped:

Plaster, dust, blood and vomit were everywhere. Patients were dying by the hundred, but there was nobody to carry away the corpses. Some of the hospital staff distributed biscuits and rice balls, but the charnel house smell was so strong that few were hungry. By three o' clock the next morning, after nineteen straight hours of his gruesome work, Dr Sasaki was incapable of dressing another wound. He and some other survivors of the hospital staff got straw mats and went outdoors – thousands of patients and hundreds of dead were in the yard and on the driveway – and hurried round behind the hospital and lay down in hiding to snatch some sleep. But within an hour wounded people had found them; a complaining circle formed around them: 'Doctors! Help us! How can you sleep?'.

According to DHSS plans, one Casualty Collecting Centre should be set up for every 10,000 people. Some could expect to have to cater for more than a thousand casualties. The *Guidance Notes* notes explained how to sort them:

Sorting should be done by a doctor (if one is available) . . . .
Sorting would be necessary on arrival at the ccc. . . . Sorting
(must) be repeated and continuous, it must be ruthless if it is to
be effective; it would often be necessary to give priority to the less
severely injured casualties and have regard to the nation's need in
the phase of recovery.

A particularly difficult problem for staff might be to explain
the nation's need to a group of friends or relatives of a
casualty. Those who get no treatment and do not get selected
for evacuation become one of 'many problems':

This and similar problems are not created by the process of
sorting. . . . Casualties would naturally be made as *comfortable as
possible* while waiting: the point is that sorting, far from creating
additional problems, would be the best way of dealing with the
problems created by the overwhelming numbers (Author's
emphasis).

The DHSS note then goes on to explain the dishonesty and
self-deception in which the Holding Unit is to be enveloped.
Although the group consists of the severely injured who
would be unlikely to survive even if unlimited facilities were
available, staff are told that:

There is no room for a hopeless attitude . . . . It would be
important to the morale of all concerned that it should be clearly
understood that these patients too would receive hospital
treatment as soon as possible, ie when road transport was easier
and pressure on the hospitals was less severe. Any tendency to
refer to such cases as are admitted to the Holding Unit of the ccc
as 'moribund' is to be deplored.

In other words, they *are* all dying, but do not let on. One
may imagine that patients would have little difficulty in seeing
through the DHSS's contrived fictions – if medical staff were
to use them. The word to use is not moribund – expecting to
die – but 'expectant' meaning expecting to get away to hospital just as soon as possible, and there to hope for recovery
and life:

They (the moribund) are sometimes called the 'expectant'
category and must be dealt with as though expected to live

No-one would get any treatment for radiation sickness, beyond 'nursing care . . . in the community'. Those with serious
third degree burns, large penetrating wounds or multiple injuries would also be withheld from hospital treatment. The
cccs could expect 'vast numbers of burns cases with an injury

exceeding eighteen per cent of the body surface . . . all would need intravenous therapy if they were to have a reasonable chance of recovery.' Such therapy would be very unlikely to be available. It is interesting to note that while the DHSS expects 'vast numbers' of burn casualties, the Home Office's assessments of nationwide casualty levels (see below) include none. Major burns would provide a 'perfect culture' for infection, and in the absence of plentiful antibiotics, CCCs could experience an 'uncontrollable spread of infection'.

Only those cases which could benefit from not more than thirty minutes surgery would go to hospitals – long bone fractures, haemorrages, crush wounds on the extremities, and extensive muscle wounds.

There would be no treatment at all for radiation casualties: they would become a large scale problem 2–3 weeks after an attack, by which time 'hospital services would predominantly be occupied with cases of trauma and burns'. After the third week, radiation casualties might accumulate in the 'Holding Unit'; others would be nursed in suitable houses. Nursing in the CCCs or other centres would not be without difficulty:

Management of the uncontrollable and often explosive vomiting and diarrhoea would be difficult and would call for much improvisation, particularly in matters of hygiene and sanitation.

The chief effects of radiation sickness—at levels which are not quickly lethal – starts with nausea, fever and anorexia (loss of appetite). At doses of about 150 rads, most people will also experience diarrhoea and vomiting. The most damaging effect of the radiation is on cells in the gut and in the bone marrow, which are normally rapidly dividing.

Confusion about the measurement and other principles of radiation biology is rife in some civil defence writings, and has led to errors. Radiation levels are measured by their effects on matter. Any biologically damaging radiation leaves behind a trail of ionised particles and some of its own energy, in any medium through which it passes. The old radioactivity unit, the *Roentgen* (in which Home Office radiac instruments and dosimeters are calibrated) is a measure of *exposure*, based on how much ionisation the radiation causes in air. The *rad* is a measure of the *dose* and is based on how much energy the radiation releases in a given weight of matter – whether body tissue or air. The *rem* is also a measure of radiation dosage, but is adjusted to allow for the fact that some types of radiation – such as neutrons – have a more powerful and damaging biological effect than their simple energy release would suggest. If someone experiences only gamma radiation, then the two measures rad and rem are the same.

The Home Office booklet *Nuclear Weapons* refers vaguely to 'exposure dose', and measures everything in Roentgens. For human exposure, the numerical values, however, are nearly the same (one rad being equivalent to 1.04 Roentgen, which is an insignificant difference given the general imprecision of the measurement of the biological effects of radiation).*

Various estimates have been made, from studies of animals and the victims of Hiroshima, Nagasaki, or radiation accidents, of the radiation levels at which people die. In almost all sources – British, us, German and others – the so-called LD_{50} dose, at which fifty per cent of the population exposed are expected to die is put at about 450 rads. This is also the figure given in *Nuclear Weapons*, the Home Office *Training Manual*, Glasstone and Dolan, and other sources – often more vaguely put as 'between 350 and 550'. The critical factor, at this level of exposure, is damage to the bone marrow, which makes blood cells. At higher levels death is caused by the damage to the stomach and gut; at even higher levels, by direct damage to the nervous system. Because the body screens the bone marrow to some extent, the actual dosage which reaches it (at the LD_{50} level) is about 240 rads. These figures only apply to healthy adults receiving full care and medical treatment for any other conditions – not a probable state of affairs in nuclear war.

For those who receive a dose at or near the LD_{50} level, the first symptoms – of nausea, vomiting and diarrhoea – may vanish in days and reappear two weeks later. Within about two weeks, hair falls out, fever rises and blood spots – petecriae – form on the skin, together with haemorrageing. The most severe effect of the radiation, and the damage caused to bone marrow cells, would be (for a dose approaching the 450 rads, LD_{50} level) the destruction of lymphocytes in the bloodstream, together with white and red blood cells, leading to severe anaemia. Some of those having received an LD_{50} dose, or even more, will survive, if cared for; the greatly reduced blood cell counts will lead to weakness, fever, and above all an immensely increased susceptibility to infection.

*A new, modern (si) unit is the Gray, which is 100 rads. I have converted references given here into rads, to avoid unnecessary confusion.

Identifying likely survivors amongst radiation casualties depends very much on knowing when the first radiation sickness symptoms began. A rapid dose of 500–1000 rads will bring sickness on quickly, and implies a high probability of death. If sickness does not start for a few days, then illness may not recur (except in the long term) after the first phase has passed. The *Guidance Notes* suggest that early and violent vomiting would be a bad sign; on the other hand, the loss of hair after the third week since the attack would be, relatively, a good sign.

Distinguishing casualties who are moribund from those who might be nursed and fed would be a wholly new form of *triage*, as Professor Patricia Lindop has explained:

It will not be question of *triage* as in conventional disasters – that will have been done by nature . . . . It will be a question, however, when the fallout radiation has decreased of . . . selecting those cases for care who are known *not* to have received a high sub-lethal radiation dose, and who carry no contamination. . .

The *Guidance Notes* suggest that anyone who has had a probable dose higher than 350 rads should have 'a low priority . . . and be treated expectantly'. This would be despite the fact that 'only a very arbitrary estimate of the dose received could be made.'

The effect of different radiation dosages can be shown graphically, giving the probability of death at a given dose. It is a very steep graph. Between about 200 and 700 rad, the death rate rises very steeply – roughly from 10 per cent to 90 per cent. Thus, casualties in a nuclear war will increase dramatically in proportion to the average exposure to radiation.

In order to plan for working under heavy radiation conditions, the Home Office, like most other civil defence authorities, have defined a measure called the Operational Evaluation Dose (OED). Until recently, this was defined as:

OED = Actual dose – 150 – 10 D (D being the number of days since exposure started).

The OED was constructed on the basis of advice from a special committee on Protection Against Ionising Radiation (PIRC) set up by the Medical Research Council. This body is also responsible for reporting to the government about radiation hazards involved in civil nuclear power and other industrial activity involving radiation. The idea of the OED, when it was defined in the late 1950s, was to provide a standard for the dose which civil defence workers and other could be expected to take whilst working out of shelter, and survive. The OED had the great psychological advantage of being near zero – or negative – for those who were not expected to face immediate death.

Some 150 rads was deducted from the original dose to start with, because it was only a little above this level that the risk of death from radiation began to increase significantly. Nevertheless, a dose of 150 rads might be expected to be lethal in the short term even for as many as one in twelve healthy young adults. Forty per cent of those exposed at this level would suffer radiation malaise, and at least one in five would have full radiation sickness.

The deduction of ten rads a day is supposed to denote the rate at which the body can recover from radiation effects, as cells repair themselves. Although the probability of long term disease, such as leukaeima and cancer, will steadily increase with the accumulated dose of radiation, the short term effects are eventually repaired (though not always without damage to vital organs). The scientific advisers' *Training Manual* says that 'extrapolation from experimental results suggests that the human body can recover cellular radiation damage at an overall rate of about ten rads equivalent of whole body gamma radiation per day.'

Thus, according to current home defence instructions, staff may be exposed to 'War Emergency Doses' of up to 75 rads for essential work – and if need be, a second similar dose within a day. In addition they could be exposed to 10 rads a day into the indefinite future – at least for three months. Many radiation biologists of distinction regard this level as absurdly optimistic, and indeed the *Training Manual* observes:

Experimental data on these factors are so incomplete where man is concerned that most of the alternative expressions which have been proposed for the calculation of the biologically effective dose in long term exposure situations remain somewhat speculative.

Professor Patricia Lindop observes:

From limited clinical experience and animal data I would expect that (the ten rad/day) rate given after an acute dose of 150 rad would result in severe bone marrow damage. No data show that 10 rad or more per day can be repaired indefinitely.*

*Nuclear War in Europe' (Proceedings of April 1981 Conference). Polemological Institute of the State University of Groningen, Netherlands 1982.

Indeed, according to the chairman of the PIRC committee which advised the Home Office, Dr J. Vennart of the Harwell MRC Radiobiology Unit, keeping the OED to near zero merely means that the individual concerned 'wasn't going to die in a few weeks'.

The British standards are far more optimistic than those used in Germany or the US. The US recovery rate is 6 rads per day; the Germans use five. The normal German maximum dose is 25 rads; the absolute maximum dose is 100 rad, not 150 as in Britain. Both countries place limits on the ultimate total dose – two months' exposure in the US; in Germany, a total measured exposure of 500 rads.*

Undaunted, the Home Office have not only used the OED as a basis, unjustifiably, for calculating casualties in their computer model, but have recently revised all their figures *upwards* by one third. The reason for the revision was a report from the PIRC committee, which the Home Office had commissioned in 1975. PIRC's new advice, issued in 1977, suggested that the LD_{50} level for complete exposure to radiation should be 600 rad. This figure has not been accepted by any other country; specialists at the US centre which has advised on many of their casualty studies, the Oak Ridge National Laboratory in Tennessee, have not revised their figure of 450 rad (or rem, if appropriate). Their view was that 'most studies indicate' it would take 'somewhat less' to kill someone, perhaps 350 or even 300 rads 'taking account of the probable state of health of the survivors of an attack'.

The same view is expressed by Professor Joseph Rotblat in a comprehensive SIPRI study on *Nuclear Radiation in Warfare*. Rotblat suggested in this account that:

The analysis of death rates at different doses applies to whole body exposure of adults who – although not receiving special treatment – would be under care, particularly to avoid infection after the exposure. In conditions of nuclear war this is unlikely to be the case. Many of the persons exposed would also suffer from burns or mechanical injuries . . . these circumstances make infection more probable. . . the whole curve would shift to an

*The German standards were reported in the Home Office scientific advisers' own magazine, *Fission Fragments, 29,* June 1981. The reviewer commented that they merit 'study in the light of UK findings'.

extent impossible to predict but any exposure above 190 rads in air might result in death under these circumstances.*

In addition, children, the young and the old would suffer far more from radiation. Death rates from radiation amongst babies and infants would be significantly higher, since their smaller bodies and thin bones provide less shielding for the critical bone marrow.

The new Home Office figures are based on a two-year PIRC study finishing in 1977. The results were passed on to the Home Office as confidential, although the PIRC committee chairman has said that they would be eager to have them published. The information and results on which the new figure is based are acknowledged to be 'tenuous, of course', by the chairman. They accepted evidence from three studies, involving thirty people and only one death, on which to base their analysis. They rejected the results from Hiroshima and Nagasaki – which are in any case being re-evaluated by the US Lawrence Livermore Laboratory, which wishes to find out more about the effects of neutron radiation (to determine in more detail the effects of the neutron bomb).

At the time of writing (1982) a heated scientific debate about the validity of the new Home Office figures seemed likely. As a science, radiation biology has had more experience of politically biased analysis and experimentation than most, since public acceptance of civil nuclear power in no small measure depends on the perception of hazards of radioactivity emissions, routinely or in an accident, as not posing a severe threat. Authorities committed to nuclear power have a strong incentive to minimise the effects of radiation from nuclear power. It is clearly of advantage, in presenting a civil defence programme to the public, for the effects of the much higher levels of radioactive hazard prevalent in war to be similarly minimised. Given that the Pentagon shares that interest with the Home Office, it seems prudent not to accept the new British figure for LD_{50} until and unless it has been examined and tested by the scientific community at large. Indeed, Dr Vennart has suggested** that a higher rather than a lower level of LD_{50} was chosen because its 'its purpose was to see whether rescue was worthwhile'; a high estimate would

*SIPRI *Nuclear Radiation in Warfare*, written by Professor Joseph Rotblat; published by Taylor and Francis, London, 1981 (paraphrased).
**To the author.

therefore 'save lives'. If the Home Office sought a figure for LD$_{50}$ on that basis, as has been suggested, then they would appear to have been both anachronistic and misleading. Rescue schemes based on getting people out from fallout areas were abandoned with the closure of civil defence in 1968. Using a figure selected to err on the high side both signally increases the risk for workers whose radiation dosage is rationed by the OED, and usefully helps to minimise post-attack casualty assessments.

The unilateral raising of the LD$_{50}$ level by the Home Office does not justify consequent alterations to the OED formula, or the adoption and use of a long term recovery rate 150 per cent greater than used anywhere else.

After nuclear war, besides the immediate casualties, there will be millions who have absorbed high sub-lethal doses of radiation, up to several hundred rads. The entire population will continue to absorb high levels of radioactivity, well in excess of previous permissible peacetime doses, for months. For those who thus 'survive' there will be a significantly increased likelihood of dying of cancer. There will also be genetic mutations affecting childbirth, although early fears of enormous mutagenesis – and the birth of a generation of 'atomic mutants' – seem to have been based on an overestimate of this effect. Both cancer and mutation originate in the damage that radiation does to the cell DNA – the fundamental genetic and reproductive material in each cell. The International Commission on Radiological Protection, which has produced figures for radiation-induced cancer rates, suggests that for every million people who receive a dose of one rad, 125 will die of cancer, including leukaemia. Other estimates go a little bit higher, but as always, the calculation is thought to be potentially in error by a factor of up to ten. Using the ICRP estimate, if the whole surviving UK population received an average dose of 100 rads (probably a high estimate for *survivors*) then one to two per cent would die of cancer – say 2–400,000 of a surviving population of twenty million. Given the slaughter and devastation in general, the delayed cancer level seems to be of lesser significance than other threats to life, such as food shortages or disease. The cancer toll would only appear over one to two decades following the war; leukaemia would strike earliest, and hardest. For the same average exposure levels, there would be an estimated two children per thousand born with visible and adverse mutations. Again this figure is a very rough estimate.

Additional radiation hazards, which are not normally forgotten in studies of the effects of nuclear war, come from the risk of more intense, but localised exposure through contamination with fallout particles, or ingesting particles or radioisotopes in contaminated food. In these circumstances, other short range radiation – from alpha and beta particles – have a direct effect (clothing will otherwise often provide sufficient shielding).

The DHSS *Guidance Notes* also deal – extremely briefly – with psychiatric casualties. Comments are limited to two pages, and suggestions do not go beyond providing work and leadership to keep idle hands and wandering minds busy.

A final section deals with problems of public and environmental health; this has recently been reinforced by a Home Office circular on *Environmental Health in War* (ES8/76) which warns:

The breakdown of services on which most of the public rely . . . would be inevitable. Water would not flow from the tap or into sewerage systems. Electricity would be cut off. Refuse collection would cease. Large numbers of casualties would lie where they died. In such conditions, certain diseases could spread rapidly . . . the rapid improvisation of additional public emergency sanitary measures would be of paramount importance.

A DHSS commentary on the same subject notes that:

Two or three weeks after nuclear attack a situation might arise in which hundreds of thousands of people were living in grossly overcrowded and often temporary accommodation on a dull and barely adequate diet, on an inadequate and potentially contaminated water supply and in insanitary conditions worse than those found in the poorest and most crowded areas of the underdeveloped countries.

This view was presented to an Emergency Planning Officers' seminar in Cardiff in early 1981 by Dr S. L. Lees who runs the DHSS's war planning section. Dr Lees added that threat from the spread of food-borne infections was 'obvious' given that 'communal feeding under primitive conditions' was necessary:

Outbreaks of dysentery and other gastrointestinal infections would be almost inevitable and diagnosis would be complicated by the presence of individuals suffering from diarrhoea due to radiation . . . contamination of food and water supplies by intestinal organisms would be likely and outbreaks of respiratory infections and meningitis would also occur.

Such blunt views, contained in a classified briefing prepared by the DHSS, do not appear with the same clarity in the open circular, although it comments that 'labour-intensive emergency measures' would be necessary to maintain even primitive sanitation, with communal facilities 'in all areas', since 'living conditions would not be conducive to bowel control and regular habits.' The danger of infection is immense; bacteria and micro organisms are virtually immune to radiation, and flies and other disease carriers would be far less affected by radiation than humans. Other problems, and potential disease carriers, would be feral cats and dogs. Typhus is particularly effectively spread by both rats and insects (fleas and lice). A Home Defence College briefing on the subject of environmental health explains first that:

A nuclear attack would change the environment and radically alter the way of life of millions of people.

That seems fairly uncontentious. Further:

There would be overcrowing in the remaining habitable accommodation with a rapid increase in fleas, lice, bedbugs and the diseases they spread and an increase in airborne respiratory diseases. (These might be prevented by reducing) the risk of droplet infection through coughing, spitting, sneezing, talking (and, presumably, vomitting). . . . Diseases such as influenza, smallpox, measles, tuberculosis and the common cold are spread in this way.

As is the case in most areas of British home defence, there are only paper plans, and no equipment stockpiled. Authorities would be expected to manage with what local resources had happened to be available. The *Guidance Notes* suggests that:

a most valuable service which everyone could render would be the control of flies, by such means as . . . fly sprays and vigorous swatting campaigns (which would be) useful work for as many as possible. . .

Once disease had inevitably taken hold, there would be enormous difficulties in controlling its spread in prevailing post-nuclear war conditions. The DHSS is, in public, vague about this. Military planners are well aware that one of their post-strike tasks is the 'enforcement of control to prevent the spread of disease.' Special Rest Centres – in effect concentration and death camps – are planned in which suspected and confirmed disease carriers would be controlled, penned up to die. Such measures might now appear criminally harsh; no doubt Controllers will find them justifiable given that there could be no circumstances more conducive to a total epidemic than the kind of post-attack world envisaged in British home defence plans. Survivors, their personal hygiene and cleanliness degraded by loss of morale, sickness, diahorrea and vomiting and poor living conditions, their resistance to infection weakened by mild radiation illness and inadequate feeding, would gather daily, in close proximity at emergency feeding centres, sharing the same space, perhaps crowding together for warmth in winter, using the same utensils briefly washed and cleaned in a minimal supply of water. Typhus and other diseases could become quite unstoppable. The Home Defence College *Briefing* explains the counter-measures:

Isolating people suffering from an infectious disease, control of people who have been in contact with a case, and if possible detection and control of 'carriers'.

Once a disease was prevalent, medical staff might have to condemn anyone about whose health there was the slightest suspicion to a 'Special Rest Centre'.

The *Environmental Health in War* circular suggested, bluntly, that there would be no alternative to the clearance of human remains without any ceremony or attempt at identification.

The unpalatable fact of a nuclear war involving large numbers of civilian casualties is that the religious rites and personal wishes, previously expressed by the deceased or now by the next-of-kin, would have to be ignored.

Remains would be collected and cremated or put into mass graves 'when radiological conditions permitted movement'. It would not be a top priority, since the presence of unburied corpses would be have ' a more serious effect on morale than public health'. The corpses would attract bluebottle flies 'not potent disease carriers'; rats would feed off them too, but 'without reservoirs of plague', even that would not cause epidemics. After several weeks, burials might begin in 'permanent burial facilities' rather than in *ad hoc* tips, and the names of the dead would start to be recorded. But: 'there would still be a problem for several weeks of an above average rate of dying from disease and radiation effects'.

Not all those enjoined to plan for war by the DHSS or the Scottish Office have responded with enthusiasm. Some authorities have raised some of the issues the government is determined to fudge; the Croydon planning, and recent studies by professional medical bodies, have raised the question of euthanasia which would be part of any humane programme in the conditions the government expects. The Croydon AHA plan commented:

Ethical issues such as whether individual patients should be left to die, or encouraged to die, particularly if painkilling drugs were being conserved, would inevitably be raised. . . . Training in advance . . . creates formidable problems . . . there are no easy solutions. . .

The East Cumbria District Health Authority, in its War Plan, refused to believe that anyone would turn up to run the Casualty Collecting Centres or that they would even get set up at the end of the day – a view shared by other Health Authorities:

Casualty collecting centres on their own are unlikely to be staffed or have any resources. . . all survivors would be required to care for each other. . . The survivors who were well would be able to offer care to those who were sick or injured.

A further problem for the British population is that many hospital places in some regions – particularly in those dispersed hospitals which would be best placed to survive a nuclear attack – would be filled up by military casualties from conventional or nuclear war in Europe. This is revealed in the Manchester AHA plan:

Manchester Health Service . . . will need to support those areas in the North Western Region which are to receive military casualties from the European theatre.

The Manchester plans also refer to a general intention that hospitals would 'remain closed to the public until the All Clear'. Cambridge AHA, like many others, was in little doubt about the tiny size of drug stockpiles and noted that although first aid posts would get a 'pro-rata share of available medical supplies . . . such is the state of casualties which should be expected that those stocks will soon be exhausted, probably within hours.' For the first two weeks, in any case, they suggest casualties will be left to die, or just possibly survive. Their parent Regional Health Authority for East Anglia has prepared a twenty page list of natural or herbal cures and remedies which might be used instead of nineteenth and twentieth century techniques. Foxglove could be harvested to help heart failures, and powdered mistletoe was suggested for hypertension.

One Health Authority – for South Western Region – resisted DHSS blandishments, and an offer of £35,000 a year, to plan for war for eight months. An effort to try and persuade the Authority to continue its resistance failed in January 1982, despite a campaign led by a distinguished Bristol radiologist, Professor Sir Howard Middlemiss. He argued that planning was futile in the face of the overwhelming casualties: 'If the government has got money to throw away, they should . . . help start running the National Health Service properly.'

Statements on the medical consequences of nuclear war have been made by several distinguished gatherings, including the special Pugwash Conference of doctors and medical scientists in 1980:

A nuclear war would result in human death, injury and disease on a scale that has no precedent in history, dwarfing all previous plagues and wars. There is no possible effective medical response after nuclear attack. . . . Most of those requiring medical attention would die.

They rejected the idea of 'effective civil defence against a nuclear attack' as 'impossible' because of the effects of the bomb and the post-attack environment.:

There are no defences against the lethal effects of nuclear weapons, and there is no effective treatment for those who initially survive a nuclear attack. . . .Prevention of nuclear war offers the only possibility for protecting people from its medical consequences. There is no alternative.

No level of planning by the DHSS affects this outcome; as its own advice admits, the overwhelming part of the Health Service and its assets will be destroyed during the attack. In the postulated *Square Leg* attack on London, for example, which was unusual in omitting an attack on the city centre, 35,000 out of the city's 59,000 hospital beds were immediately destroyed. There would be 1.1 million immediate fatalities (out of a population of 7 million or so). There would be at least 2.5 – 3 million casualties from blast, and if many more were caught in the open trying to flee the capital the severely injured (including from burns) could amount (on a worst case basis – twenty-five per cent caught in the open) to 3.7 million.* Assuming London's doctors survived in the same ratio to the population of the capital as in peacetime, each doctor would have between four hundred and nine hundred patients to see. Even working at the rate of Hiroshima's Dr Sasaki – nineteen hours a day and twenty minutes on average for each patient – it would take more than a week to see each survivor once. It wouldn't happen of course; fallout levels across most of seventeen boroughs would make movement outside impossible for some time; *triage* and evacuation to hospital would be frustrated by unclearable debris everywhere and the destruction of facilities. Stocks would be exhausted before the first day was out.

If the government wanted greater readiness to deal with such medical contingencies, they could ensure that there were more and better trained staff in the National Health Service, new hospitals in the countryside, and similar resources, the provision of which would be equally worthwhile in peacetime. No amount of paper planning by DHSS will save every Casualty Collecting Centre from turning into a charnel house, every hospital from being beseiged by thousands of desperate sufferers, or make up for the supplies that first aid posts won't have. The dimensions of the problems are such that planning could not make even the slightest, short term, marginal difference. Planning will only make a difference if better administration could genuinely save lives during the aftermath, through more efficient allocation of the resources available. Without the resources – indeed, with *declining* NHS resources – medical war planning is a cynical confidence trick.

The Home Office has tried to put the effects of a nuclear war onto a quantitative basis, by measuring the survival rates which could be expected after a given level of attack. This exercise has been done on the ministry's computers since about 1971; before then, 'desk' methods were used. The calculations depend strongly on scientific and medical advice, which the Home Office gets from its own Scientific Advisory Branch (retitled and merged with other groups in 1982 to become the Scientific Research and Development Branch),

*From an initial analysis of the effects of nuclear weapons on London, by Dr Andy Haines, Medical Campaign against Nuclear Weapons. See *Radical Statistics Group*, 'The Nuclear numbers game', 1982 (pp 62–67), and *Nuclear War in Europe* (pp. 273–287). Further details are in *London After the Bomb*, by Owen Greene *et al*; Oxford University Press, 1982.

and from some of the scientists who are Regional Scientific Advisers with wartime appointments to SRHQS and Regional Government HQS. The same exercise has also been carried out, using similar models, by Scientists Against Nuclear Arms (SANA), who have obtained widely differing results, and much higher casualties.

The estimation of civilian casualty rates in war has gone on since the 1920s, as described in Chapter 3. No information is available about planning during the 1950s, but in the 1963 civil defence recruiting campaign, the Home Office spoke warmly of its scientists' skills:

The government has made detailed scientific studies of the probable effects if a nuclear attack was made on Britain. The picture is a grim one. The actual number of casualties would depend upon the weight and distribution of the attack, and other unpredictable factors such as the weather. But it is the firm conclusion of leading scientists that large areas would escape devastation. And millions of people would survive.

Neither at that time nor during the subsequent sixteen years has the Home Office made any public suggestions as to what survival level it thought likely. Considerable information is now available about the basic Home Office computer model, which has been in use since 1971. As discussed in Chapter 10, it has been used to study the demand for, and surviving supply of, various resources in a post-attack British economy, including houses for the homeless. It has also been used to study the effects of various assumptions about civil defence measures, plans or resources. In a descriptive leaflet, the Scientific Advisory Branch of the Home Office notes that:

best asssessments of (the precise pattern of attack) are made from time to time. It is the responsibility of the Branch to assess what would be the likely effect on life in this country of different patterns of attack.

The first scientific data on which to analyse casualty levels after a nuclear attack became available in the late 50s. The first Medical Research Council analysis of the effects of high radiation dosages became public in 1956; and in 1957, an analysis of the effects of blast from Second World War explosions in British cities was published to show the percentages of people who would variously be killed, trapped or injured at set distances from a nuclear explosion. The resulting graph was called 'exercise ARC'. Since then, these and similar studies of the effects of bombing and fire-raising in

British, German and Japanese cities have been used to analyse the effects of nuclear weapons.

As well as the civil defence exercises some of whose bomb plots are shown in Chapter 2, there have been various public or semi-public pronouncements about the effects of a nuclear attack in Britain. The *Home Defence Planning Assumptions* circular suggested that a survival rate of 60 per cent in the worst affected areas could be used 'for *planning purposes*' and 95 per cent in other areas. On this basis, the worst affected area would be the zone within 2–2½ miles (3–4 km) from the ground zero of a one megaton groundburst bomb. However both the wording of the suggestion and its high survival rate suggest that this was a notional, rather than calculated, assessment. In the Scientific Advisers' *Training Manual* a 205 megaton attack pattern is suggested, and the total area covered by blast effects is calculated. But none of these estimates appear to be based on computer analysis.

At a NATO civil defence committee conference in May 1977, Sir Leslie Mavor with other UK Home Office staff presented a paper on the 'Post-Strike Scene: UK' in which a more detailed assessment was given. (See pps 80–81). The postulated 80 target, 180 megaton attack was said to cause immediate casualties of 3–4 million dead and leave 5–9 million seriously injured (who are all assumed to die fairly quickly) – an initial survival rate, therefore, of 75 to 85 per cent. A year after attack, it is estimated that only two thirds will have survived, the rest having died from 'radiation, exposure, starvation and disease'. But if the government Home Defence plans were not put into action, it was claimed, then two thirds might die, leaving only fifteen million survivors.

The first part of this estimate is clearly derived from the Home Office computer model, as a target list was described but not enumerated. It is not clear whether the claims about the level of survivors after a year is based on the Home Office economic analysis. But the self-satisfied suggestion that the value of the government's Home Defence plans is such as to double the number of people alive after a year can only be based on the most gross, smug assumptions—particularly since the Home Office refuses to analyse elsewhere the likely long term effects of a major nuclear attack.

Notwithstanding that, the 1977 NATO paper has been used as the basis of many (private) addresses to emergency planning staff and others, particularly by Mr George Harrison, the Deputy Director of the Easingwold Home Defence College. In 1980, the same figures were used for the first time in a public speech by Lord Belstead. This appears to have been the first public ministerial statement quantifying the Home Office's expected death toll. A figure of 75 per cent survival is now quoted very often by government home defence lobbyists; sometimes, even 85 per cent. These figures often then appear in local authority or other plans, or in public claims about the effects of nuclear war – with none of the assumptions stated. Since the estimate was made in the context of a long term survival rate said to amount to only 66 per cent of the original survivors, it would be more honest if that were always said at the same time.

Generally, the use of these figures by second and third hand parties is justified by reference to scientific expertise. When, for example, Professor Michael Pentz of the Open University challenged claims made by the local county (Buckinghamshire) Chief Executive that 85 per cent would survive a nuclear war and only 10 per cent of the country would be damaged, he was eventually told that the destruction area related to an 'unspecified attack' and that the origin of the 85 per cent survival figure 'remains a complete mystery'.

Of course neither figure is mysterious; they originate from a specific set of Home Office computer studies. More to the point, are they in any way accurate? Examination of the basis of the Home Office techniques suggests that the casualty levels they have calculated are far too small. The models incorporate errors and omissions all of which work to reduce casualties. Although there is no evidence that this bias was built in deliberately, it is clear that those who have constructed policy papers and public pronouncements on the basis of its computations have been reckless in ignoring many casualty–causing features which are known to be left out altogether.

It is extremely important that such calculations be made as correctly as possible, and that their assumptions, methods and conclusions should be published. There is, understandably, a common interest in knowing what the effects of nuclear war on the United Kingdom are likely to be. At the annual meeting of the British Association for the Advancement of Science in York in September 1981, Mr Sid Butler, the then Deputy Director of the Home Office Scientific Advisory Branch, responded to the growing scientific criticisms of the Home fice's vague and unqualified utterances about the effects of nuclear war by presenting a paper on 'Scientific Advice in Home Defence'. The paper provided novel insight into the basis of Home Office planning, although it was highly self-justificatory. It provoked intense criticism from Professor Rotblat and others who said that the Home Office plans might only be of value if there were to be a limited nuclear war, which he did not accept was possible.

The 80 target, 200 megaton scenario is one which appears widely in recent Home Office documents and speeches. Butler explained to the BA meeting how the estimated attacks were converted into casualty levels. A Home Office computer was programmed with details (from the 1971 census) of everyone living in each one kilometer grid square throughout Britain. If an attack occurred whilst people were obeying the stay at home policy, then this would be as accurate a population distribution as would be possible. For each square, the computer works out the maximum blast overpressure to which the area is subject; then, for slightly larger squares, it works out the maximum radiation dosage which would be received by someone in the open.

The computer can then calculate how many in the whole population will have experienced what blast levels and over-pressure levels. The actual radiation someone receives depends on the protective factor of the building they are in. The theoretical radiation dose received is calculated from the out-of-doors radiation dose by dividing it by the protection factor.

The computer is fed with assumptions about how many people have what levels of protection factor. This is a very critical feature; relatively small changes in the average protection factor of the population can change overall casualty levels by millions. The Home Office use a 'spectrum' to indicate varying standards of protection. The computer then calculates the total trapped, injured or dead from blast effects, and the numbers dead or seriously injured from radiation effects.

The programme makes two assumptions:–

(i) Everyone who is trapped dies (because there is no civil defence rescue force); and

(ii) Someone who is 'seriously injured' from both blast and radiation dies too (this seems reasonable).

The casualty totals are added; and the final result produced. Butler reported:

For a representative attack of 200 megatons including city targets, at least half and possibly seventy per cent of the population would be expected to survive, given warning and general adherence to 'Protect and Survive' measures. Even with attacks an order of magnitude higher, indefensible in military terms, millions would survive and require assistance. . . national revival would be improved substantially by sensible home defence preparations, including the provision of sound scientific advice.

This kind of science is different from the (theoretically) value free research carried out (say) in universities. Home defence science may produce advice on which policy is based, but as Butler's introduction makes clear, it is also there to justify and publicly promote a politically predetermined policy. That is part of a civil servant's job. Butler, as the scientific Deputy Director, is a member of the Home Defence (Policy) Committee of the Cabinet Office, and consequently closely involved in making the policies which are then justified by the Home Office computer models.

The assumptions which are fed into such casualty models – for instance about the effectiveness of 'Protect and Survive' measures – partially predetermine the output. They do *not* prove that the measures work. But aside from the careful political control exercised over the way that the model is used, it has ten important defects or errors. All reduce the apparent casualty levels, some significantly, and, combined, certainly challenge the validity of *any* Home Office results. Independent analysis tends to provide much higher casualty levels.

The major errors or omissions in the model are:

1. It does not include any casualties from direct burns.
2. It does not include any casualties from fire, still less allow for the possibility of large scale conflagrations or firestorms.
3. In assessing the range of blast, the Home Office uses extremely low estimates for the range of airburst bomb effects.
4. The analysis of blast casualties has not been revised since 1959, was known to be in error in 1960, and does not accurately reflect the 'much greater house damage' which nuclear weapons would cause.
5. The protective factors are assessed extremely optimistically.
6. The level of radiation casualties is reduced by a 'ground roughness' factor of thirty per cent, is a gross simplification (although used by other authorities).
7. The lethal effects of radiation are further reduced by thirty per cent through the improper use of the Operational Evaluation Dose instead of the real radiation dose.

8. There is no increase in the lethal effects of radiation, despite poor feeding, insanitary conditions, or the lack of medical care.
9. No one dies of disease or starvation.
10. The model does not take account of special types of attacks such as those on nuclear reactors or underwater explosions.

In his paper, Mr Butler presented various graphs showing protection factors, radiation casualty rates, and various suggested attacks. But none of the key graphs were calibrated, and exact details of the target list were not given. So no-one could check or criticise the assumptions which were being used.

The use of 'more severe blast criteria' was shown to increase casualties in one attack from twenty-five per cent to fifty per cent yet Mr Butler did not say what the two blast criteria were, or which was more plausible. The difference between the two, nonetheless, would be 14 million deaths (or lives) – one quarter of the population. The talk was a most unscientific public relations and political exercise rather than a scientific paper, as it contained none of the data that other scientists could check results from. He did give one reference to an internal Home Office paper by a colleague, P. R. Bentley, which described in detail how the computer programme worked. The Home Office subsequently received many requests from scientists for this paper and hastily reproduced a slightly bowdlerised edition, from which some remarks about the uncertainty of method had been removed.*

Butler's public talk identified the survival level from the standard 'SAB unclassified attack' – 179 bombs, 193 megatons – as being 42 million, or 28 million with a 'more severe blast criterion'. For an 84 bomb, 181 megaton attack similar to that described to the May 1977 NATO seminar, over 50 million would survive if the attack was primarily on military targets. Some 49 million (or nearly ninety per cent) would survive an *attack primarily on civilian targets* if *Protect and Survive* was ignored, and people dispersed; otherwise only 36 million would survive. Thus, even according to this official estimate, *Protect and Survive*'s 'stay-put' advice will kill a quarter of the population.

The claim that ninety per cent of the British population could survive an attack with eighty hydrogen bombs each with a power 12,000 times Hiroshima and mostly *aimed at civilian*

Blast overpressure and fallout radiation dose models for casualty assessment and other purposes, by P. R. Bentley; Home Office, 1981.

targets is quite beyond belief. 'Science' so blatantly and absurdly distorted to support an ideological and political case rightly attracted considerable derision at the BA meeting. Mr Butler's paper even produced a 'worst case scenario' in which the UK was attacked by 3000 megatons of nuclear weapons (presumably, 300 ten megaton bombs) aimed *primarily at civilian targets* – and still 6–7 million survived. This 'proved' that the Home Office's home defence plans were valuable even in such an inconceivable level of attack. An attack with 500 megatons aimed primarily at civilians was said to leave about 17 million survivors; if aimed at military targets there would be 43 million survivors. On no occasion were assumptions or target lists provided so that others might check the validity of the Home Office case. A review carried out for the *Political Geography Quarterly** by Steadman and Openshaw (with assumptions published) analysed the worst case of an attack on civilian targets, assuming the enemy was thereby (as is reasonable to suppose) trying *inter alia* to kill the maximum number of people. If so, an attack with 150 one megaton airburst bombs would kill nearly seventy-five per cent of the population *from blast effects alone* (there would be no significant fallout).

Butler's assertion that an attack on the UK with 300 ten megaton bombs would leave anyone alive is staggering. The UK could be pattern bombed, with weapons spaced roughly every twenty-two miles. Three-quarters of the population would immediately be killed or seriously injured. There would be no surviving undamaged buildings, and all houses would be at least 'moderately to severely' damaged. With the bombs groundburst, their sixty mile wide mushroom clouds would merge to form a continuous fallout blanket over the whole country. The absolute minimum initial radiation exposure, would be about 3000 Roentgens per hour; most areas would be much higher. Every part of the country would be in the main fire zone. It would be two months before anyone would be able to move freely in the open. To survive, it would be necessary to have a shelter or house which stayed intact in the heavy damage zone' and provided a protective factor rather better than one hundred, and at least a month's food supply. The Home Office thinks that six million people

*'On the geography of a worst case nuclear attack on the population of Britain', S. Openshaw and P. Steadman, *Political Geography Quarterly*, 13, July 1982.

would survive such a bombardment.

Various objections to the Home Office calculations may be detailed. The original author, Bentley, makes no claim to include fire or burns data in the calculation and suggests that it might 'ultimately' be included. But 'following the philosophy of earlier work', it is ignored in the model. There *would* be casualties from burns – those unable to reach shelter, those who were travelling. There would also be the likelihood that after the first attack or attacks, the warning system might cease to operate; Butler observes that 'it is important to recognise potential effects (of EMP) on attack and fallout warning procedures.' If the warning system failed, hundreds of thousands of people could unnecessarily be caught in the open. It is certain that some – perhaps many – casualties would result.

There would also be fire zones expected around the target points and isolated fires beyond a certain distance. The Home Office and other civil defence experts in the US have gone to considerable lengths to dismiss the possibilities of firestorms which would be utterly devastating across a wide area. It is claimed that a lower building density, modern materials, and the style of construction would make fire storms unlikely in British cities. The truth is that no-one really knows what would happen. There would certainly be many large fires – the Home Office Scientific Advisers' *Operational Handbook* suggests that one house in fifteen will, in general, burn out in a main fire zone – which could cover an area of 180 square miles around a single one megaton explosion. Fires could take a week to burn out. The Home Office view is that whatever the state of property and personal damage, or the fallout threat, people will have to put out fires for themselves or face the consequences of having to flee through the heaviest fallout zones at the worst times: 'the possibility of widespread fires could be greatly reduced by suitable precautions and by the control of incipient fires by survivors of the attack.' This might not be very easy for those who had been injured or whose fire fighting bucket of water had been lost in the blast wave. It also overlooks the fact that many properties are joined together and, particularly in central districts, may be uninhabited, and could provide an easy starting point for mass fires, if not full firestorms.

The DHSS *Guidance Notes* have also suggested that casualties in general (based on Second World War data) might occur on the basis of one burn injury for every two mechanical

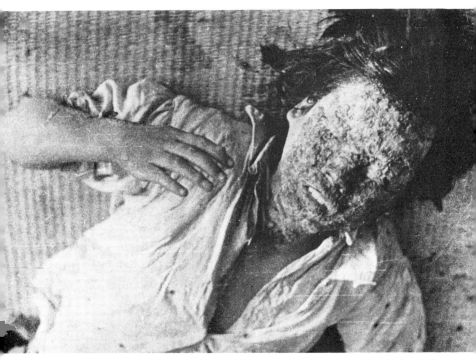

Plates 43 & 44 Hiroshima victims suffered hideously from full-body, third degree burns caused by the heat flash of the explosion. Skin is burnt irreparably deeply, and hangs off in shreds. The Home Office disregards all such burn casualties in its assessments of the effects of a nuclear attack.

(blast) injuries. If this were so then the Home Office estimates of blast casualties should be fifty per cent higher at least. The Home Office has in fact suggested in some documents that there might indeed be areas of firestorm within 3–5 miles of a ten megaton explosion. There would be no fire service to help stop the fires.

In assessing the comparative effects of airburst and ground-bursts bombs, the Home Office suggests (in *Nuclear Weapons*) that the range of effects 'would be increased by thirty per cent if the same sized bomb were airburst near the optimum height.' This simply isn't true, as may be seen by comparing the two, contradictory tables giving airburst weapons effects in their *Domestic Nuclear Shelters – Technical Guidance* booklet. The Home Office suggests that the outer

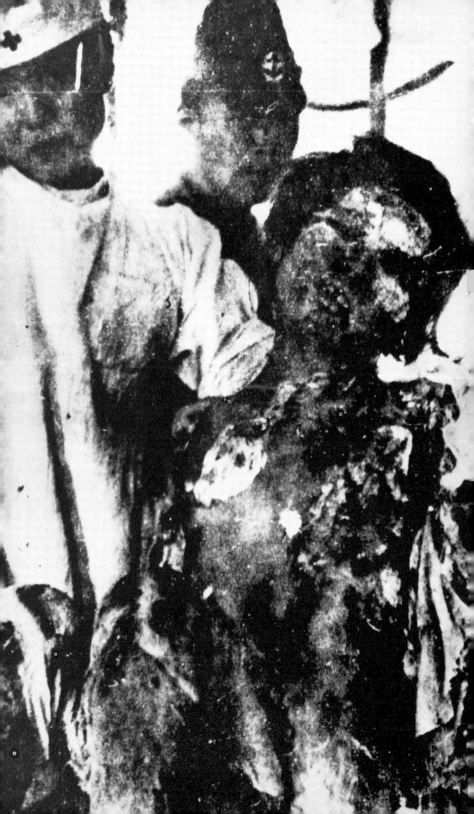

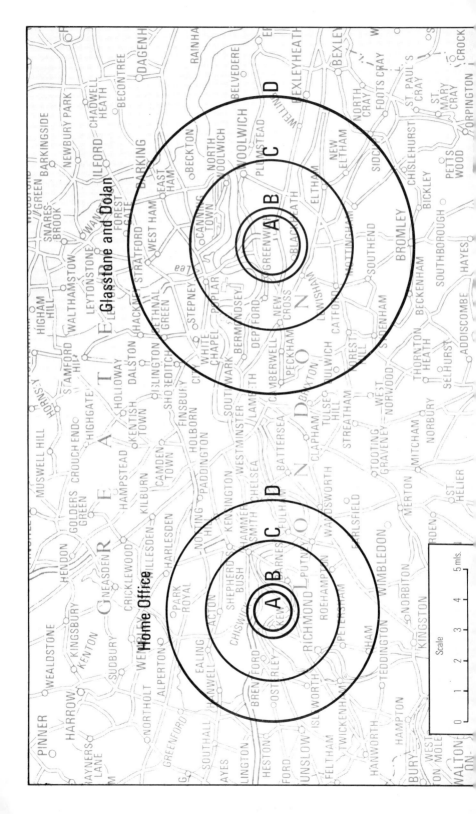

ring of blast damage for a one megaton bomb would be nine miles (14 km); the comparable figure for an airburst (thirty per cent larger) would be about twelve miles (19km). But a chart copied from the US text (Glasstone and Dolan) on the effects of a one megaton nuclear optimum height airburst blast , shows that the range would actually be sixteen miles. It is not thirty per cent greater but, on this occasion, over seventy per cent greater. There appears to be no explanation for the original error unless it results from a mistaken reading of the US sources.

This playing down of the effects of the air blast makes a vast difference to the areas which are calculated to have been damaged by a nuclear explosion. Figure 23 shows how the two different estimates relate to a 20 Kiloton bomb dropped on London.

The way in which the casualties are measured after the blast levels are known is based on data that is much more optimistic than that used in the US Office of Technology Assessment survey. The Home Office are now urgently revising their figures, still based on the graph called 'exercise ARC', which was circulated in a 1959 civil defence training memorandum. They show the killed, trapped and injured at various distances from the centre of the explosion, based on Second World War blast bombs. A remarkable feature of this graph is that it contains a glaring mistake, uncorrected for nearly twenty-five years; at a distance of about one mile (from a megaton bomb), if one adds killed, trapped and injured totals, it comes to 115 per cent of the population! This error was noticed by many in 1959. Nothing was apparently done about it; the graph was incorporated, error and all, into the Home Office Nuclear Weapons Effect Computer No 1, a small circular hand held slide rule device for rapidly checking bomb effects. Such calculators are still given to most students attending training courses at Easingwold; the instruction notes make no mention of the error.

Beyond this clumsy error, there is a fundamental problem

Figure 23 Bomb damage: Juggling the figures. The Home Office estimates of damaged areas for airburst weapons cover significantly less than the true area. Effects (blast damage 'rings') are shown for an airburst weapon of approximately 20 kilotons; the ratio of areas covered would, however, be the same for all bomb powers. (After a paper by Philip Steadman).

in that it is clear that the 'exercise ARC' grossly underestimates the power of nuclear weapons to damage houses. This arises because the pressure waves from nuclear weapons last much longer than those from conventional bombs. The Bentley report notes this problem:

> Some of the assumptions made in the model should now be re-examined, eg the longer positive pressure phase of the blast from nuclear weapons seems certain to result in much greater house damage, and therefore more casualties than reference to maximum peak overpressure. . . . Most casualties are likely to be directly attributable to blast. . .

Curiously enough, the government has also circulated contradictory sources of information about blast casualty levels. The figures given in exercise ARC (on which *Nuclear Weapons* is based) can be compared with those in the MAFF circular on the effect of radioactive fallout on food, agriculture and fisheries (MAFF E1/77). Two charts in the MAFF circular, based on US OTA figures show the contrast very clearly, for a five megaton bomb. The 'ARC' figures show roughly 100 per cent casualties out to only 1.6 miles; the US suggests that, within a three mile ring, there will be 98 per cent casualties. At three miles, the Home Office says that only 10 per cent will be killed and 35 per cent injured. The US says that there will be 50 per cent killed and 45 per cent injured out to five miles. At this distance, the Home Office says that no one will be killed or trapped and only 6 per cent injured; the US book says that there will be 5 per cent deaths and 45 per cent injuries out to eight miles. Beyond eight miles (up to about thirteen miles) the US suggests that 25 per cent will be injured; for the Home Office, it is about 3 per cent. The Home Office has not tried to defend their continued use of the Second World War data, and planned, in 1982, to hold joint meetings with the United States experts to adjust their figures. The wide discrepancy between the two sets of death rates suggests that the Home Office will have to considerably scale up its casualty rates.

The level of fallout protection which the Home Office expects everyone to have implies an average PF over 20. The range of protective factors written into the radiation casualty calculations has not been disclosed; Butler referred to 'a spectrum of protective factors (which) must be assumed, with due allowance for . . . enhancement'. The enhancement in question was to come from people doing their 'Protective and

Survive' precautions and remaining within their inner refuges (presumably the 'enhancement' referred to) for the eight day period of the calculation. This presupposed that everyone will have been able to get supplies and help to carry out the advice (which the Home Office does *not* expect will happen), that people do not self-evacuate (which the Home Office expects *will* happen); that they will stay inside their refuges and not expose themselves, having obtained in advance all the food and other supplies they need (which the Home Office does *not* expect). The model also assumes that shelters are undamaged even by minor blast effects; whereas everyone sheltering within many miles of any target will at least have their windows broken. As discussed earlier, some sixty per cent of the land area of the country will experience at least mild blast overpressures greater than 0.75 psi, more than sufficient to damage windows and roofs.

The Scientific Advisers' *Operational Handbook* suggests that all modern, lightweight one or two storey houses, and all detached houses, have a PF less than 10 and sometimes as low as 2. Only two storey terraced or concrete floored houses have anything near the assumed average PF of 10–15. The *Handbook* also notes that 'a well constructed core shelter may triple the PF values given.' It would seem that the Home Office assumes that everyone has time to construct a good core shelter and stay there, and that all bomb damage threatening the ingress of fallout particles just after the explosion can be immediately repaired despite damage, fire or even personal injury.

These figures are in distinct contrast to those used in US studies, which assume that much of the population finishes up with PFS around 3–5. They also provide for a small number of purpose built shelters with very high PFS, which do not exist in Britain. The death rate is in fact extremely sensitive to changes of PF. On occasion, changing the average PF from 3 to 10 can reduce the number of casualties to ten per cent of what it would otherwise have been.

This is clearly a good argument for getting the best possible radiation protection after the event. However such protection cannot just be assumed to happen, as the Home Office does.

Another factor which distorts the effect of radiation is the use of a 'ground roughness factor' in the calculation. This is supposed to allow for the fact that if you are sheltering above ground, not all the gamma rays travelling towards you will reach their destination because they will be absorbed or dissipated by passing through surface features (such as rubble) at low angles.

The final major distortion in the model is the extremely careless use of the Operational Evaluation Dose instead of the actual dose in order to assess the likely lethality of given radiation levels. The Home Office model runs over eight days so that someone who absorbed a total dose of 450 rads – the normal LD_{50} – would be recorded as having an OED of only 130, below the level for the onset of injury. The OED calculation, according to the PIRC committee who devised it, is 'merely an indication that (the person) won't die in a few weeks'. Since it starts off by making a fixed deduction of 200 rads, then 15 rads per day, this factor alone can quite significantly shift the radiation casualties downwards. The factors which are deducted from the real dose to make up the OED are based on the fact that the body can recover (in the short term) from repeated, lower level doses of radiation. Thus a higher LD_{50} level will apply if the radiation dosage is *even* and *gradual*. But the fast decay of fallout means that most of it is received very early, and quickly, and the body repair mechanisms will be overwhelmed. Some seventy-five per cent of the ultimate radiation dosage received by a person from fallout is received during the first day; by the second day it is eighty-three per cent.

The effect of the new Home Office formula is to create an effective LD_{50} dose of about 800 – 900 rads when, everywhere else, 450 is accepted as the right definition. The fact that the last ten or twenty per cent of the radiation will be delayed does permit a slight increase in the LD_{50} level. But it makes the levels used in Britain effectively double what they are elsewhere. The Home Office's particular error lies in using a figure which, even in their own internal documents, is said only to refer to 'relative radiological states'. It cannot be used, unmodified, to analyse absolute effects like death rates.

Taken together, all the errors and omissions in the Home Office's computer analysis of bomb casualties, go the same way – they reduce the casualty levels. It would not be unreasonable to suppose that some of the factors outlined might, put together, at least double the casualties from blast effects and radiation, and add in more from burns, multiple or interactive injuries, and so on. The overall level of casualties would be double what the government suggests; perhaps worse, even, than that. Whilst the Home Office analysis is valid, within limits, as a means of understanding the nature of nuclear war, it is (in itself) clearly of no value for public, educational use. It is quite unacceptable that public official statements and policies should be based on such a flimsy foundation. All that can be said about figures produced by this method is that they define a low *minimum* casualty level for a particular kind of attack, on a generally optimistic basis.

The more rigorous analyses which have been done by using fully disclosed assumptions suggest that, for attacks in excess of 200 megatons, the death and injury rate for the population as a whole could exceed eighty per cent – leaving perhaps 10–15 million survivors after an attack, instead of the 40 million or more in Home Office fiction. That outcome is a very big difference in the effects of a war.

In order to develop a more likely estimate of the effects of a major Soviet nuclear attack on the UK, scientists from the SANA group devised a new scenario – entitled, satirically, *Hard Luck* – as a counterpoise to the considerably understated *Hard Rock* 82 nuclear attack. The selection of targets and weapons was carried out on a similar basis to that discussed in the next chapter. The effects were calculated using the programmes developed by Steadman and Openshaw.

Whatever attack pattern is used in the event, however, any survivor is going to realise the considerable difference between *biological* survival – which will not be ruled out on a small scale, even for large attacks – and *social* survival. A failure to achieve viability by the surviving population would result in many additional deaths through social and economic deterioration. A major nuclear attack would not destroy every life, immediately. But it would utterly destroy society and civilisation and value in remaining alive.

12
Targets and forces

Even though extensive studies may be made of the consequences of 'postulated' attacks, public official policy still has to adhere to the fiction that there can be no telling where the bombs will land. 'No place in the United Kingdom is safer than anywhere else,' says the 'Protect and Survive' film, *Stay-at-home*. At the same time, real policy-making includes plans for the careful dispersal of some resources. Groups of officials for regional government have been found locations which are anticipated to be unusually safe. Food stocks, fire equipment and firemen, police and military units will withdraw from 'vulnerable' areas. Other stocks are already well dispersed, in depots built in the Second World War.

In Chapter 2, there was a brief review of some of the generalised attack patterns expected by the Home Office. Chapter 11 analysed the way these were converted into damage and casualty estimates. This chapter summarises what is known of Soviet targets and weaponry, and nuclear war doctrine. These weapons can be matched to the specific categories of sites in Britain which would be attacked, given Soviet targetting policies. I do not attempt to draw up a full personal scenario, and assess its consequences, for two reasons: firstly, it is easy to describe how, and where, the target list *starts*. Where it *stops* depends on decisions that may be taken on the day, depending on the level of reserve nuclear forces the Soviet Union wishes to retain. Secondly, the Soviet Union may not have the option of using all the weapons in its arsenal and strategic targetting plan. There may have been a US/NATO pre-emptive nuclear strike. There may be failures of equipment, and of command and control.

Some popular conceptions about the intended use of strategic nuclear stockpiles are in error. Critical though Britain's role as an unsinkable aircraft carrier may be, and certain target for major nuclear attack though the country is, it is less in the front line than some parts of the US mid-West, the Moscow *Oblast*, or the central fronts of the two Germanies. Some installations in Britain, although supporting military operations of some importance, are nevertheless far too low in the order of priorities to merit any attack. Of the one hundred plus US bases or facilities in the UK*, for example, at least one third to one half will not be targets.

The concept of overkill, as popularly discussed, does not exist in the sense normally implied, of there being far too many nuclear weapons for the available targets. (Few would dispute that there are, in general, far too many nuclear weapons.) But the opposite is true. Available nuclear warheads would only destroy *a fraction* of the preplanned target lists. This can be illustrated with respect to both US and Soviet planning.

American strategic forces, whether bombers or missiles from land or sea, are targetted together in the Single Integrated Operational Plan, or SIOP. The most recent SIOP editions are stated to have about 40,000 targets. American missiles carry about 9,000 warheads (more are planned). B52 and FB111 bombers assigned to the SIOP could deliver 5–6000 more (each B52 can carry twenty Short Range Attack Missiles). It is clearly not enough to cover all the 'options'.

In the *New Statesman* article and joint *Thames TV* programme on US bases – 'Target Britain' – we referred to a somewhat intriguing assessment of British 'geography, government, economy and elements of . . . infrastructure', published in a limited circulation Russian military journal in 1977.** Although some way from an official target list, it was a useful indication of Soviet thinking. Its author, Colonel V. Leskov, identified areas of chemical and oil production, transport and power, civil and military airfields and ports, and a 'ramified network of bases' for the Pentagon. A map displayed various command and control centres and ammunitions dumps, and over a hundred airfields, chosen in a somewhat haphazard way (and many of them far from useful to military aircraft). The Leskov map has been given undue prominence in circulation since then. But the huge number of airfields shown is suggestive of the problem facing the

*'Target Britain', *New Statesman* 31 October 1980. Reprinted in *Britain and the Bomb* (NS Report 3), *New Statesman*, 1981.
**Colonel V. Leskov, in *Zarybezhnoe Voennoe Obozrenie 5*, 1980. I am indebted to Professor John Erickson for unearthing this recondite item.

Soviet Union. If the US Air Force's F111 and FB111 aircraft were scattered to minor air strips all over Britain, it is extremely unlikely that sufficient nuclear weapons would exist to attack them all. Leskov refers to 336 civil and military airfields, notes that 180 have major runways, and that many have been preserved since 1943 and could still be used.

Thus, although 'overkill' exists in the sense of each side possessing weapons sufficient to destroy major population centres, several times over, that has not been the strategy of either side – for decades. The emphasis given in the 1960s to assured destruction of cities was a gross distortion of US nuclear plans, even then. For example, even as talk of 'MAD' was at its height in 1962, the US SIOP plans, revealed in the 1970s in leaked documents, spelt out these priorities:

The general war plans . . . will provide for the execution by SIOP forces, when directed by competent authority, of two pre-emptive US Attack Options. They are:

Attack Option I, in which the objective is the destruction or neutralisation of the Sino-Soviet Bloc strategic nuclear delivery forces posing a threat to the US and its allies and to US and allied forces overseas; and

Attack Option II, in which the objective is that of Option I, plus the destruction or neutralisation of other elements of Sino-Soviet Bloc military forces and military resources in being.

There was little new in the much discussed Presidential Directive (PD59) issued by President Carter in August 1980. Limited nuclear war 'options' had in fact been openly discussed by the US since the early 60s, together with the need to give priority to military targets – starting with the nuclear threat. In subsequent categories come various industrial targets, often generically known as 'urban-industrial'. What PD59 did do was to introduce a new precision into the target 'packages' that make up the SIOP, by selecting DGZs (Desired Ground Zeroes) and types of weapons which would most neatly destroy a specific airfield or a chosen steelworks, while allegedly 'minimising' population casualties.

The Russian targetting priorities, as developed below, are much the same as the American. They do not, however, espouse the ideas of 'limited war'. Shortly after PD59 was announced, Lieutenant General Mikhail Milshtein (in an interview with the *Herald Tribune*) reiterated the Soviet view that the concept was 'absolute fantasy. . . . There will be plenty of what those exponents of limited nuclear war call collateral casualties. . . . There are people around'. (General

Milshtein was the director of the political-military section of the USSR's Institute for USA and Canada studies).

The Soviet view of nuclear war is centred on an all-out battle and exchange of weapons. Attacks would be massive, and aimed at military, industrial, economic and population targets. In public, the British government's official view is:

If Britain is attacked by nuclear bombs or by missiles, we do not know what targets will be chosen or how severe the assault will be. If nuclear weapons are used on a large scale, those of us living in country areas might be exposed to as great a risk as those in the towns.

(*Protect and Survive*, 1980)

Home Defence Planning Assumptions (ES3/73) suggests:

Solely for the purpose of survival planning, it can be assumed that the population survival rate would range from 60% in the worst affected areas to 95% in the least damaged areas.

The *Training Manual for Scientific Advisers* (1977), however, gives a unique and frank summary of what the government expects:

It . . . seems likely that any initial nuclear strike would be a massive one aimed at making the country attacked totally ineffective militarily, politically and industrially. In particular, the means of nuclear retaliation would be primary targets.

The *Training Manual* then asserts, sensibly:

The home defence assumption is that nuclear war poses the greatest threat. To determine the scale of a nuclear attack, it is therefore important to consider the aims of a potential enemy. Taking an extreme view, these might be to render the United Kingdom ineffective militarily, politically and industrially. There is little doubt that Russia has the nuclear weapons to achieve this aim, but scentific research with varying patterns and weights of attack indicate that notwithstanding the immense loss of life, there would be many millions of survivors. . . . It is likely that the main force of attack by missiles and aircraft would be simultaneous and last no more than 48 hours.

It appears from preceding paragraphs that the 'extreme' view is the view regarded as 'likely' by the British government. The *Manual* then assesses targetting requirements:

The first priority in Russian targetting would almost certainly be the bases from which our retaliatory effort can be mounted. Next would probably come our ports and industry and lastly, perhaps, large centres of population with the aim of destroying the administration and economy of the country and the morale of the people. . . . After a major attack, the United Kingdom could present a scene of enormous destruction and havoc.

That is the official view. Nonetheless, a fair amount of propaganda on behalf of civil defence has made great play of the possibility of limited nuclear strikes. This reached an undue level of foolishness in documents circulated by the British Atlantic Committee, as part of their anti–CND 'Operation Alliance' propaganda campaign, which is financed by an annual grant of some £50,000 (in 1982/83) from the Foreign Office. The author of Operation Alliance's briefing notes, Mr Hugh Hanning, wrote:

Civil defence (could save lives). . . . If the deterrent ever broke down – which it shows no signs at all of doing – *the most likely form of nuclear exchange would be* that envisaged in Sir John Hackett's book 'The Third World War' – namely *a single missile on each side.* (In the book, it was one on Birmingham, answered by one on Minsk.) In such a situation, civil defence would be invaluable.* (author's emphasis)

This novel school of strategic nuclear thought appears to be unique to Mr Hanning and the British Atlantic Committee writers; their NATO sponsors would, one suspects, be ill at ease with this (and indeed many other errors and ill-informed nonsense about defence matters circulated in the same campaign). Defence analysts at the International Institute for Strategic Studies have a rather different view.

Evidence that Soviet military doctrine now incorporates the possibility of control, selectivity and restraint in a nuclear exchange is actually very fragmentary. It derives principally from some statements that stand aside from the overwhelming thrust of Soviet military literature – and even these particular statements fall far short of suggesting a Soviet willingness to engage in controlled escalation. . . . Soviet strategic policy and targeting doctrine, together with some quite explicit pronouncements, is to the effect that any nuclear exchange would involve simultaneous and unconstrained attacks on a wide range of targets, certainly not excluding C^3 (command, control and communications) systems. (Desmond Ball, *Can Nuclear War be Controlled?* IISS Adelphi Paper 169, 1981).

*In any event, Hackett's account was scarcely cheering about the 'invaluable' successes of civil defence: 'resources . . . were hopelessly inadequate to begin to attempt rescue operations in what remained of the city of Birmingham itself', and the city was 'cordoned off' inside motorways, rivers and canals – with *ingress* prohibited. The population within the cordon was abandoned.

The primary source for many western analyses of Soviet intentions is the compendious *Soviet Military Strategy* by the late Marshal of the Soviet Union, V. D. Sokolovskiy. The latest, revised edition was published in 1968. In addition, there are available a host of writings in other Soviet military publications and journals – although secretive, far more information is available from Soviet open sources than many suppose, although these sources generally say little in detail about Soviet capabilities, and – endemically – place their assessments of western capabilities in the mouths of western 'observers' or suchlike.

Soviet sources generally aver that they will not start a nuclear exchange (and in 1982 this became firm Soviet declaratory policy in a speech to the UN Special Session on Disarmament) but promise massive retaliation 'if (war) is unleashed by the imperialists'. The concept of victory in a nuclear battle does appear, including in Sokolovskiy, although more recent writings regard the concept as 'obsolete', the product of an earlier era at the dawn of the age of nuclear weapons.

Sokolovskiy provides a detailed and explicit account of Soviet nuclear policy:

Mass nuclear attacks on the strategic nuclear weapons of the enemy, on his economy, and government control system, with simultaneous defeat of the armed forces . . . will make it possible to attain the political aims of a war. . . . This type of strategic operation has been forced on our armed forces in the event of war. The aggressive imperialist bloc is preparing for a war for the total destruction of cities, industrial regions and objectives. . . .

The Soviet armed forces and the armed forces of the other socialist countries must be prepared to deliver massive retaliatory nuclear strikes by strategic means against the military-economic foundations, the system of government and military control, strategic nuclear devices and groups of armed forces of the imperialist bloc. Such strikes can destroy . . . the strategic means for nuclear attack – strategic aviation, ICBMs, IRBMs, tactical bomber aviation, naval forces – . . . the basic stockpiles of nuclear ammunition and material for conducting a war . . . regions where troop units and large units are formed and the main groups of armed forces and strategic reserves . . . and the main centres of governmental and military control.

The basic aim of this type of fighting is to undermine the military power of the enemy by eliminating the nuclear means of fighting and formations of armed forces, and eliminating the military-economic potential by destroying the economic foundation for war. . . . The most powerful attack may be the first massed nuclear rocket strike with which our armed forces will

retaliate against the actions of the imperialist aggressors who
unleash a nuclear war.

In making nuclear rocket and nuclear aviation strikes, military
bases (air, missile and naval), industrial objects primarily atomic,
aircraft, missile, power and machine-construction plants, etc, can
be destroyed.

The prime objectives of the strikes will be strategic air bases.

(3rd edition, pps 288–290)

Identifying specific countries in order of industrial potential,
Sokolovskiy lists the US, then Germany, then the UK. One
passage is particularly chilling for Britons:

> Those countries on whose territory are located military bases of
> the US, NATO and other military blocks, as well . . . would also be
> subject to shattering attacks in such a war. . . .
>
> According to the calculations of scientists, up to 1.5 million
> people can be annihilated immediately and approximately 400,000
> more people may perish in the subsequent radiation as a result of
> the explosion of one thermonuclear bomb in an industrial region.
> Even a thermonuclear bomb of average power would suffice to
> wipe a large city from the face of the earth.
>
> British scientists have concluded that four megaton bombs, one
> each on London, Birmingham, Lancashire, and Yorkshire would
> annihilate a minimum of twenty million people.
>
> Soviet and foreign specialists have calculated that approximately
> 100 nuclear weapons in the two megaton range dropped within a
> short space of time on a country with a developed industry and
> territory of approximately 300–500,000 square kilometres would
> suffice to transform all of its industrial regions and administrative-
> political centres into a mass of ruins and its territory into
> wasteland contaminated with death-dealing radioactive materials

Other writers have singled out special categories of targets.
In a compilation prepared by an anti-Soviet research group*,
there are a number of such examples, drawn from Soviet
military journals. A 1968 article in the limited circulation
journal, *Military Thought*, included:

mobile command posts, and automatic information processing
centres, the communication lines . . . underground and
underwater cable, radio relay, ionospheric and tropospheric
communications links; communications centres. . . . Especially
effective could be attacks against the electric power and oil
refining industries, since electric power is required in large

---

***They mean what they say*, by Ian Greig. Foreign Affairs Research
Institute, London 1981.

amounts by all branches of the national economy, including the defence industries.

Power stations, particularly large ones, are also advantageous targets because power-consuming and very important defence industry enterprises (chemical, aluminium, and magnesium plants and others) are frequently situated near them . . . under modern conditions it is difficult to underrate the (electricity supply's) importance.

Of all other branches of heavy industry, the chemical industry should be singled out in particular. . . . The disruption of transport operations will have an enormous effect on the economic and military capability of a country

Another article in the same journal commends the use of medium range missiles as a means of early strike against air defence bases and anti-aircraft missile sites 'to deprive the state subjected to attack of the capability of defence'.

These sources, and many more in similar vein, bear out and confirm the secret Home Office view of the likely weight and distribution of attack. If the Soviet writers mean what they say (and everything they say makes sense on *a priori* grounds), then we can – contrary to what the Home Office says publicly – indeed produce useful assessments of the major targets on the Soviet list and their priority.

Any actual attack will not, of course, merely start at the top of such a list, and proceed down the list as far as resources allow. A lot will depend on the detailed deployment of military forces at the time, so far as this may be discoverable by hostile intelligence. Following the priorities outlined above, we can examine what British targets would be covered by the different 'packages' of objectives which would make up a Soviet attack. The urgency of each category would depend very much on where forces were and their readiness. Disabling a major airfield which B52s had left would obviously rate a much lower priority than attacking while bombers remained on runways.

Table 17 (p. 424) lists the British sites in each category likely to be Soviet targets. Figures 24 and 25 (pp. 430 and 434) show the locations of the major military targets.

There is, then, harmony (if that is the word) between the expectations of the Home Office, the general statements of policy by Soviet writers, and the *a priori* expectations that one might form. The general circumstances leading up to a nuclear conflict may determine the way in which the first battle begins, but the way the war will finish seems clear. The

British expectation – reflected, *inter alia*, in Home Office circulars – is 'massive' destruction.

The customary western distinction between 'tactical' and 'strategic' nuclear weapons does not generally appear in Soviet military thought. The public position of the United States, after PD59 in particular, is increasingly close to what the Soviet view of nuclear weapons always has been – they are viewed as an adjunct to the fighting capacity of each arm of service, at each level of warfare. Once nuclear war is 'unleashed' the Soviets' declared intention is to respond, not by a restrained tactical strike, or a 'demonstration' salvo, but to take the initiative and achieve as much as may be possible in the way of a surprise attack against all western forces.

In some ways, the NATO and Soviet nuclear postures seem dangerously complementary. The Soviet Union promises no first use of nuclear weapons (and may or may not mean it), but will engage massively when so attacked. NATO military plans and preparations envisage the use of tactical nuclear weapons on a widespread, but geographically limited, basis within 'theatre' warfare. That is what the neutron bombs, nuclear artillery, and short range strike aircraft are for. But there has been no indication that the Soviet forces would play the nuclear game the way it is played at NATO staff colleges or according to the rules of NATO field manuals. If the Soviet central front forces were attacked by a salvo of 'small' (kiloton yield) weapons, they might respond, *in that theatre*, by pattern-bombing NATO armies with high yield thermonuclear weapons. They would also expect to attack the NATO rear – logistics, transport, reserve units and ammunition – and the means of further nuclear delivery. It is then necessary rapidly to eliminate the industrial and administrative base from which a prolonged and continued war might be conducted. So a nuclear exchange becomes all out.

Much western literature discusses theories of strategic deterrence at greater or lesser levels of abstraction, and tremendous attention is paid to the possible outcomes of initial nuclear exchanges; what level of one side or the other's missile silos would remain after a 'surprise' attack. But very little writing from official or defence circles seeks to follow this through in detail to the eventual outcome. That task is generally left to the critics of nuclear weapons, or independent scientists and analysts.

The reluctance to engage in public debate over prospective ultimate nuclear outcomes is understandable in the logic of deterrent theory. A nuclear exchange and its consequences imply the *total failure* of deterrence, and of nuclear weapons as a means of 'defence'; the protagonists would each have been better without. There is general reference to the 'second strike', in which deterrence is played out by responding to an initial, but incomplete, attack, by destroying the cities and military bases of the aggressor.

The manner in which these discussions take place has created a version of public theory which is quite at odds with actual practice. There are necessarily extensive plans maintained and updated by both sides, which deal, in terms, with the annihilation of the population and industry of the enemy. The military logic of such plans is to destroy war-making capacity; to ensure that nothing survives of the enemy society or nation state which could continue the war.

To this end, the thousands of targets which each side have selected are mapped out in considerable detail. The target areas are photographed, from space, if by no other means, the specific vulnerability of the structures assessed, and their locations plotted. From this information, the nuclear target planners compute a 'Desired Ground Zero' (DGZ), the point at or above which the bomb should burst. The size of the bomb has to be chosen, bearing in mind the likely 'Circular Error Probable' (CEP) of the delivery system being used. This describes the probability that the actual ground zero will be within a certain distance of the DGZ; normally, the figure given for the CEP is the maximum error or 'miss' distance for fifty per cent of the weapons in a given attack or trial.

The yield of the bomb will determine the distance from ground zero at which different levels of blast pressure will occur. The normal means of targetting is to select either a groundburst weapon or an 'optimal' airburst weapon. Against very hard targets, or if the 'bonus' of fallout is desired, a ground burst would be used. Against most targets, vulnerability to blast is such that an airburst will be more effective (because the blast reaches the target directly, rather than being diffused and diffracted as it propagates over the ground). As in the Home Office studies, the bomb burst heights are usually optimised in order to cover the maximum area with a peak pressure wave of a given value.

Table 17   *Target Britain – the Soviet view*

---

1   Nuclear strategic forces

(a) *Submarines and bases*
Holy Loch; Faslane; Rosyth; Chatham; Devonport (Plymouth)

(b) *Airfields (assuming US reinforcement, and some dispersal)*
Lossiemouth; Kinloss; Machrihanish; Stornoway; Scampton;
Waddington; Finningley; Cottesmore; Wittering; Greenham
Common; Fairford; Leeming; Marham; Cottesmore; Upper
Heyford; Lakenheath; Abingdon; Brize Norton; Boscombe Down;
Benson; Honington; Woodbridge; Coningsby; Farnborough;
Wethersfield; Molesworth

(c) *Stockpiles: at many of the sites above, and assumed at:*
Donnington; Chilmark; Coulport; St Mawgan; Machrihanish
In war, many conventional stores (*5d*) may also hold nuclear
weapons

(d) *Nuclear artillery units, short range missiles, and stockpiles*
All believed to be in Germany

2   Command, control communications and intelligence

(a) *Strategic command centres*
Hawthorn; Northwood; London (Whitehall); Bentley Priory/
Stanmore; Northwood; Mildenhall; High Wycombe (RAF) High
Wycombe (USAF) Pitreavie Castle (Dunfermline); Mountbatten
(Plymouth); Fort Southwick (Portsmouth); London (US Navy)

(b) *Other command centres*
Bawtry; Uxbridge; West Drayton; Brampton; Wilton (Salisbury);
Upavon

(c) *Vulnerable communications links*
Anthorn; Criggion; Rugby; Croughton; Defford; Thurso;
Oakhanger; Hawthorn

(d) *Other communications links*
Boddington; Stanbridge; Eddlesborough; Forest Moor; Inskip;
Bampton castle; Milltown; Greatworth; Eddlesborough;
Stanbridge; Sennen (Cornwall); Martlesham Heath (Ipswich);
Swingate (Dover); St Margarets Bay; Mormond Hill; Cioldblow
Lane (Maidstone); Barford St John; Daventry; Leafield (BT);
Bearley (BT); Rampisham (BT); Burnham (BT); Hanslope Park
(FCO); Goonhilly (BT); Madley (Hereford) (BT); Devizes.

(e) *Intelligence*
Irton Moor (Scarborough); Cheltenham (GCHQ); Brampton;
Alconbury; Wyton; Menwith Hill; Edzell; Chicksands; Cheadle
(Staffs); Morwenstow; Brawdy; Digby; Culmhead; Bracknell
(Meteororology); Croughton; Mildenhall.

3   Air Defence

(a) *Missile warning radar*
Fylingdales

(b) *Long range radar*
Saxa Vord; Benbecula; Buchan; Boulmer; Neatishead; Staxton
Wold; Bishopscourt (NI); Hartland Point; Dundonald; Ash;
Ventnor; Clee Hill; Burrington; Mobile stations

(c) *Air defence operations centres*
High Wycombe; Bentley Priory; West Drayton; Portreath.

(d) *Air defence missile bases*
Bawdsey; West Raynham; North Coates; Wattisham

(e) *Air defence interceptor bases*
Leuchars; Binbrook; Wattisham.

4 Industrial
(a) *Means of nuclear production*
Aldermaston; Burghfield (Royal Ordnance Factory); Chapelcross;
Cardiff (Royal Ordnance factory);
Components, plutonium or fissile material sources
Dounreay; Derby (Rolls Royce); Windscale; Bristol (British
Aerospace); Capenhurst; Springfields

(b) *Means of war production*
Royal Ordnance factories; and agency factories; Birtley, Durham;
Blackburn, Lancs; Chorley, Lancs; Glascoed, Gwent; Nottingham;
Radway Green, Crewe; Powfoot, Dumfries; Bishopton;
Bridgewater, Somerset; Enfield, Middlesex; Leeds; Patricroft,
Manchester; Featherstone, Staffs
The location of plants of major defence contractors is shown in the
1981 Defence Estimates, Vol 1, p.44. The main groupings of
defence industries are in the following areas:
Glasgow; Renfrew district; Birmingham; Coventry;
Wolverhampton; Southampton; Essex; Chelmsford; Tyneside;
Manchester; Lancashire; Cheshire; Bristol; Portsmouth; Surrey;
Barrow in Furness; Merseyside; Leeds; Leicester; Cardiff;
Newport; Greater London; Hatfield; Luton; Hitchin; Porton
Down and Winterbourne Gunner (CBW research)

(c) *Power stations*
Nuclear power stations
Dungeness; Heysham; Oldbury; Berkeley; Hunterston; Winfrith
Heath; Hartlepool; Trawsfynydd; Sizewell; Douuneray; Hinckley
Point; Wylfa; Bradwell; Chapelcross (Torness); Calder Hall

Conventional sets of (approx) 1000MW or more
Aberthaw; Ballylumford (NI)
Drakelow; Inverkip (Scot); Kingsnorth; Ratcliffe-on-Sour;
Rugeley; Blyth; Drax; Fawley; Ferrybridge; Longannet (Scot);
Thorpe Marsh; West Burton; Cockenzie (Scot); Didcot;
Eggborough; FiddlersFerry; Pembroke; Tilbury; West Thurrock;
Cottam; Ironbridge; Kingsforth.

(d) *Oil and gas terminals and depots*
Milford Haven; Grangemouth; Killingholme; Pembroke; Old
Kilpatrick; Stanlow; Llandarcy; North Teeside; Ellesmere Port;
Falmouth; Teesport; Isle of Grain; Fawley; Coryton (Thames);
Shellhaven; Kingsnorth; Bacton; St Fergus; Sullom Voe; Flotta;
Theddlethorpe; Easington; Cruden Bay; Flotta (Orkneys); Angle
Bay; Avonmouth; Eastham; Easington.
All North Sea oil and gas production platforms.

(e) *Chemical industry*
Runcorn; Immingham; Avonmouth; Birkenhead; Fenton; Beeston;
Barry; Redcar; Aycliffe; Tynemouth; Stockton

5   Conventional forces

(a) Airfields – military, logistic or dispersal
Heathrow; Brize Norton; Prestwick; East Midlands; Gatwick;
Lyneham; Newcastle; Luton; Ringway (Manchester); Norwich;
Dyce; Biggin Hill; Birmingham; Hurn (Bournemouth); Filton
(Bristol); Lulsgate (Bristol); Carlisle; Coventry; Dunsfold;
Turnhouse; Abbotsinch; Exeter; Glamorgan (Rhoose); Teeside;
Dalcross; Inverness; Liverpool; Woodford (Manchester); Bedford;
Aldergrove; Sydenham (Belfast); Benbecula; Bentwaters; Brawdy;
Church Fenton; Cranwell (2); Culdrose; Dishforth; Elvington;
Linton on Ouse; Lanbedr; Manston; Mildenhall; Valley; St Athan;
Shawbury; Sculthorpe; West Freugh; Yeovilton; Odiham;
Bankston Heath; Middle Wallop; Kemble; Pershore; Lindholme;
Swinderby; Leeds/Bradford; Topcliffe; Aberporth.

(b) Ports – naval or logistic
Harwich; Felixstowe; Liverpool; Glasgow/Greenock; Teesport;
Hull; Grimsby; Barry; Newcastle; Southampton; Marchwood;
Dover; Folkestone; Grangemouth; Portsmouth; Portland;
Ramsgate; Chatham; Rosyth; Devonport (Plymouth); Swansea.

(c) Troop concentrations
Catterick; Salisbury; Aldershot; Bordon; Colchester; Bulford
and at logistic centres

(d) Ammunition or materiel stocks
Donington; Chilwell; Rudington; Bicester; Hendon; Bramley;
Caerwent; Welford; Burtonwood; Trecwyn Dean Hill (Hants);
Ernesettle; Chilmark; Carlisle (Longtown); Sealand; Devizes;
(supply computer centre); Copenacre (Corsham); Eaglescliffe;
Aschurch; Quedgeley; Kemble; Crombie; Quainton; Stafford;
Stirling; Hilsea; Moreton-on-Luggcourt; Hessay; Kineton;
Ludgershall; Ashford; Yardley Chase; Long Marston; Poole; Glen
Douglas; Broughton Moor.

(e) Fuel depots (military)
West Moors; Milfo.:d Haven; Killingholme; Invergordon; Loch
Striven; Loch Ewe; Garelochhead

(f) Other logistic
Severn Bridge; Humber Bridge; Forth Bridge; Crewe; Motorway
intersections (M4/M5; M1/M6; M6/M62; M5/M6)

6   Administration, industrial and population

(a) Government centres
London (central); Cardiff; Edinburgh; Belfast; Manchester;
Newcastle; Birmingham.

(b) Major urban/industrial centres
Greater London; Manchester; Birmingham; Leeds; Bradford;
Glasgow; Bristol; Liverpool; Cardiff; Sheffield; Southampton;
Swansea; Nottingham; Edinburgh; Dundee; Aberdeen; Newcastle;
Teesside; Leicester; Coventry; Wolverhampton; Portsmouth; Hull;
Derby; Wolverhampton; Huddersfield.

This approach can be seen in detail in a leaked manual *Nuclear Yield Requirements**, which was produced for the US Air Force in Europe in 1962. Some thousands of potential 'tactical' targets from Finland to Egypt and from West Germany to the Soviet Union were listed in considerable detail. The targets included airfields, bridges, railway facilities and stockyards, air control centres and headquarters, ports, waterways, missile sites, road intersections, troop concentrations, and ammunition and nuclear weapons storage sites. For each target, a precise position was available, together with the dimensions of the vulnerable target area – such as the runway of an airfield. The exactitude of such plans, whether US or Soviet, demonstrates the detailed way in which attacks on the UK, like other targets, will have been planned.

Thus target 0163A and 0164A covered two airfields at Leningrad; 0256N was the port and city itself; Gdansk was 0265N; a road and rail bridge in Lauenberg in West Germany was 1256BD; a railway bridge and sidings, and a road bridge in Zagreb, Yugoslavia, merited three separate target plans: Zadar, a Yugoslavian port, was target 5567N. For all of these sites, target folders with photographs and charts were prepared, showing how the area would appear on a bombardier's aiming radar.

Weapons could be selected from sixteen available yields from 2.5 kilotons to 1.4 megatons, and fuzed to detonate at a 'height of burst' (HOB) which would have a high probability of creating necessary destruction, taking into account the error in ground zero. The heights of burst usually appear selected to 'optimise' three levels of overpressure: roughly. 6psi, 15psi and 40psi. (The Home Office casualty assessment model described in Chapter 11 used five such overpressure levels: 2, 4, 6, 10 and 20psi). *Nuclear Yield Requirements* suggested that attacks on airfields to destroy aircraft would require 6psi overpressure; bridges would require 40psi; other targets would be best attacked using the intermediate level of 15psi. Dams and other waterway structures could only be attacked by a groundburst. For other targets, this was an

---

Nuclear Yield Requirements was one of a series of documents circulated anonymously to eight British MPs and newspapers in early 1980. It is still classified 'Top Secret' by the United States. The source of the document was, clearly, ultimately the Soviet Union, as it would have formed part of an extensive haul of such information which they obtained through an American sergeant who was a spy in the early 1960s. The documents are nonetheless genuine.

option which provided a 'bonus of cratering and contamination'.

These targets were exclusive of 'city-busting' or other strategic strikes – these would be the province of the US Strategic Air Command, whose plans are equally comprehensive. For example, recently declassified US reports include some records of briefings on SAC's war tasks. One, in 1954, explained how objectives of destroying Soviet nuclear and war-making capacity were to be met, using 600–750 bombs in a two-hour long attack.

Heavy lines, one representing each wing, were shown progressively converging on the heart of Russia with pretty stars to indicate the many bombs dropped on DGZs. The final impressions was that virtually all of Russia would be nothing but a smoking, radiating ruin at the end of two hours.

Figure 24:   Target Britain–1   (*overleaf*) Strategic nuclear forces, air defence organisation, major ports and airfields.

The map shows the majority of places in Britain which might be destroyed in an attack aimed primarily at military targets.

It includes those nuclear strategic forces which would be of major concern to the Soviet Union – the submarine missile bases and other ports supporting them (Faslane, Coulport, Holy Loch, Devonport, Chatham, Portland, Rosyth and Portsmouth) and the nuclear bomber bases. These latter would include US FIII bomber bases at Upper Heyford and Lakenheath, and British bomber bases such as Lossiemouth (Buccaneers) and Scampton whose aircraft directly threaten Soviet territory with nuclear attack. But in a crisis, four new British Forward Operating Bases (Fairford, Marham, Boscombe Down and Brize Norton) would also house US Strategic Air Command bombers. There are a further eight Colocated Operating Bases for the US Air Force at Abingdon, Benson, Odiham, Leeming, Finningley, Coltishall, Waddington and Wittering. Britain would have other nuclear-capable aircraft, such as Tornados, at Cottesmore, Coltishall, Honington, and (for anti-submarine warfare) at Kinloss, St Mawgan, Machrihanish and Stornoway. Cruise missiles may soon be sited at Greenham Common and Molesworth, also US main bases.

The Soviet Union would wish to destroy all these bases with considerable speed. They would be likely to use either SS20 missiles, or some ICBMs which are targeted on Europe, and have a heavier yield.

In the hours or days before nuclear attack, US and NATO commanders would wish to disperse these aircraft. Dozens of minor military airfields and civil airports would be used to spread the targets as widely as possible across Britain. Typically, those living near civil airports such as Newcastle or East Midlands, near Nottingham, would find a few military planes and a support team had arrived shortly before nuclear war started. The map shows most such airfields with runway lengths of about 6000 feet (1840m) or more. These would be suitable for heavier aircraft, and are generally better equipped.

Such dispersal bases would be very likely targets. If Soviet intelligence sources were good enough to learn which civil and small military airports had been used to disperse American and British aircraft, then only these might be targets. One purpose of the US Colocated Operating Bases, according to the Commander in Chief of the US Air Force in Europe, is to 'provide additional high value targets around which the enemy must plan.' Unless the Soviet Union had lost many of its weapons in a US or NATO first strike, then many of these bases would be destroyed.

At the same time, other nuclear strikes might be aimed at preventing Britain and the United States moving more military forces into Europe. Many targets in exercise *Square Leg* were of this kind. They include the six major airports earmarked for troop movements (Heathrow, Gatwick, Luton, Lyneham, Brize Norton and Ringway at Manchester) and the seven major ports for troopships to Europe (Hull, Grimsby, Felixstowe, Harwich, Dover, Folkestone and Southampton). Liverpool and Barry would be the main ports used for bringing US troops and supplies in to Britain.

In order to use aircraft as effectively as possible to drop nuclear weapons on British targets, a Soviet commander would first wish to destroy the headquarters and radar stations of the air defence organisation (UKADGE—UK air defence ground environment). The major radar stations at Saxa Vord, Buchan, Benbecula, Bishopscourt, Dundonald, Boulmer, Staxton Wold, Neatishead and Hartland Point provide the first sources of such information. They are coordinated by the Regional Air Operations Centre at High Wycombe, the Air Defence Group HQ at Bentley Priory, Stanmore, and by the Air Defence Data Centre at West Drayton. All these centres might be attacked. The attacks might also include civil radar stations (see map) which provide a backup radar capacity.

This and the following map cover the majority of military targets which any Soviet attack on the UK would certainly include. Other major nuclear targets would be population and industrial centres, including major cities, power stations, heavy industry and oil refineries. The extent to which smaller airfields and smaller cities were attacked would depend on the total strength of the weapons the attacker had decided – or was able – to use against Britain, given that other countries would contain many similar targets.

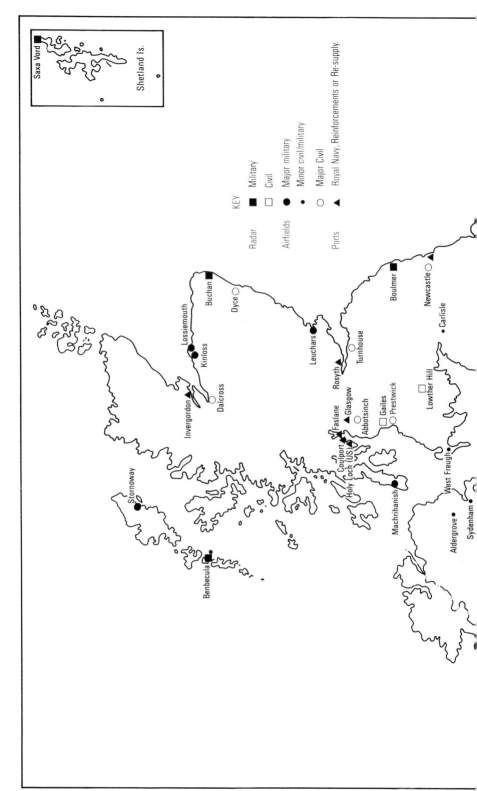

KEY

	Military	Civil
Radar	■	□

	Major military	Minor civil/military	Major Civil
Airfields	●	•	○

	Royal Navy, Reinforcements or Re-supply.
Ports	▲

Saxa Vord ■

Shetland Is.

Stornoway ●

Benbecula ■●

Lossiemouth ●
Kinloss ●
Buchan ■
Dyce ○

Invergordon ▲
Dalcross ○

Faslane ▲
Coulport ▲
Holy Loch (US) ▲
Glasgow ○
Abbotsinch
Gailes □
Prestwick ○

Machrihanish ●

Leuchars ●
Rosyth ▲
Turnhouse ○

Boulmer ■
Newcastle ○
Carlisle •

Lowther Hill □

West Freugh •

Aldergrove •
Sydenham •

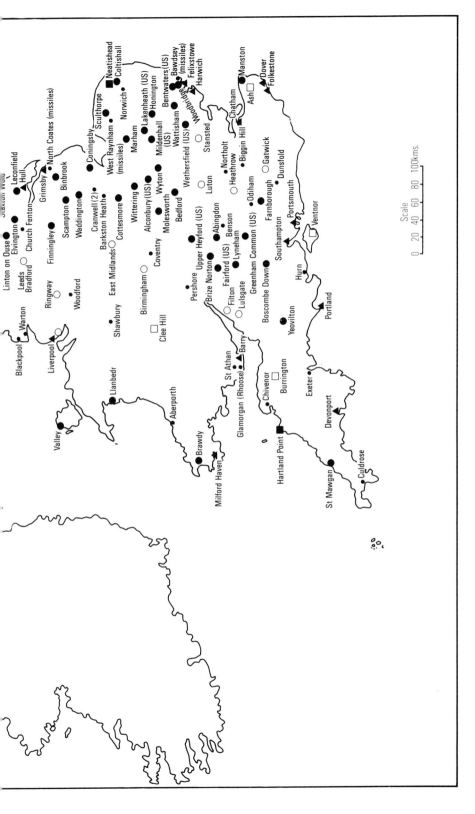

Another 'Weapons Systems Evaluation Group' report* from this period assessed the results of the planned US attacks:

The combined atomic offensives are estimated to cause a total of seventy-seven million casualties within the Soviet Bloc of which sixty million will be fatalities. Such casualties, coupled with the other effects of the atomic offensives, may have an important bearing on the will of the Soviets to continue to wage war . . . casualties of such a magnitude and the total loss of 118 out of 134 major Soviet cities would have a calamitous effect . . .

The atomic offensive would virtually eliminate the Soviet Bloc industrial capability and preclude any significant recuperation . . .

I have quoted these studies in order to demonstrate that both sides are far closer in thinking about their plans for nuclear warfare than might be imagined. There will be nothing in the least bit random about the pattern of a Soviet strike on the United Kingdom. They will set themselves the objective of total destruction which is, demonstrably, the goal of *both* sides. It is highly questionable whether the US's new objective of flexibility and restraint could ever work in practice. But it cannot work at all if the Soviets will not play: and they will not, because they distrust American motives as being intended to facilitate the US of nuclear weapons as coercive means in international (crisis) diplomacy. There are few situations where a threat of all-out nuclear warfare would be credible as a means of political pressure.

So the pattern of Soviet attack on the United Kingdom is in essence *very* predictable. They choose their own priorities from the targets listed (Table 17) and work their way through them. At some point, they will run out of forces or nuclear ammunition, or cease to be able to operate as a coherent entity. So, probably, will we. The really unpredictable feature is which sites on the target list will *not*, in the event, be attacked. The reasons would include:

(a) Failure of the delivery system or weapon; a rough esti- mate of the reliability of ICBMs and medium range missiles is about seventy per cent. For that reason, major targets will be covered twice (at least) – most military nuclear bases would be in this category.

(b) Non-availability of the delivery system through pre-emp- tive strikes on airfields or missile bases.

---

*US Joint Chiefs of Staff papers, quoted in an article by David A. Rosenberg, *International Security* (US), Winter 1981–82.

Figure 25: Target Britain – 2 (*overleaf*) Command, control, communications and intelligence centres

This map shows the major command and control centres which the Soviet Union might wish to strike in order to prevent the use of nuclear forces from Britain. The Royal Navy HQ at Northwood, and the RAF HQ at High Wycombe are primary links to British nuclear forces. The United States also has several major command centres in Britain – Naval Headquarters for Europe are in London, while the 3rd Air Force is based at Mildenhall. Mildenhall is also the base for flying war rooms – converted Boeing 707 civil jetliners – which would control all US Forces in Europe in war, if no ground headquarters had survived. Northwood is also a NATO reserve European command centre.

Links to British Polaris submarines are primarily through the three Post Office very low frequency (VLF) radio stations shown. Other communications stations, run by the Post Office at Somerton, Burnham and Dorchester (not shown) can also be used to contact Royal Navy ships. Satellite communications (marked with an 'S') enable NATO military commanders and political leaders to confer about the use of nuclear weapons in the European battlefield, and to authorise their use.

Before and during a war, signals intelligence gathered by eavesdropping stations of Government Communications Headquarters (GCHQ) would provide details of the movements of opposing forces. Stations like Menwith Hill, Edzell, and Oakhanger control many spy satellites which would be continually gathering data.

Once a first nuclear attack had taken place on the Soviet Union, these communications and intelligence centres would be used (if they survived) to discover which Soviet targets had successfully been destroyed with nuclear weapons. At the same time, high altitude reconaissance aircraft from the US air bases at Alconbury and Mildenhall would use electronic or photographic detectors to discover the progress of the war while flying high over the Soviet Union. British aircraft from Wyton would do the same, at shorter range, over targets in Eastern Europe.

Any cities or military targets which had been scheduled unsuccessfully for nuclear destruction in a first wave of attacks would then be struck using remaining nuclear forces, so long as commanders and their headquarters survived. The Soviet Union might also be checking on which targets in Britain and Europe had escaped destruction, and might use undestroyed missiles and aircraft for a second attack.

The Soviet Union might, therefore, wish to destroy all or more of the centres shown here. But the sites shown as command and control centres would – overwhelmingly – be the priority targets. If they were destroyed, it might not matter whether or not the communications stations survived.

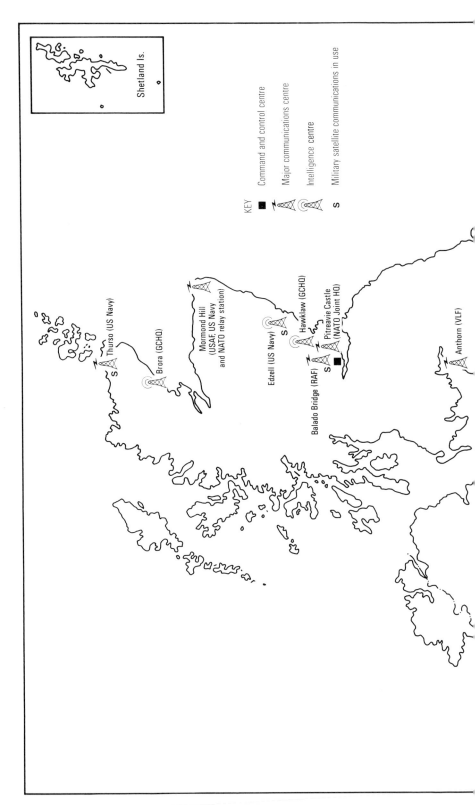

Shetland Is.

KEY

■ Command and control centre

◁◀ Major communications centre

◁◉ Intelligence centre

s Military satellite communications in use

Thurso (US Navy)

Brora (GCHQ)

Mormond Hill (USAF, US Navy and NATO relay station)

Edzell (US Navy)

Hawklaw (GCHQ)

Balado Bridge (RAF)

Pitreavie Castle (NATO Joint HQ)

Anthorn (VLF)

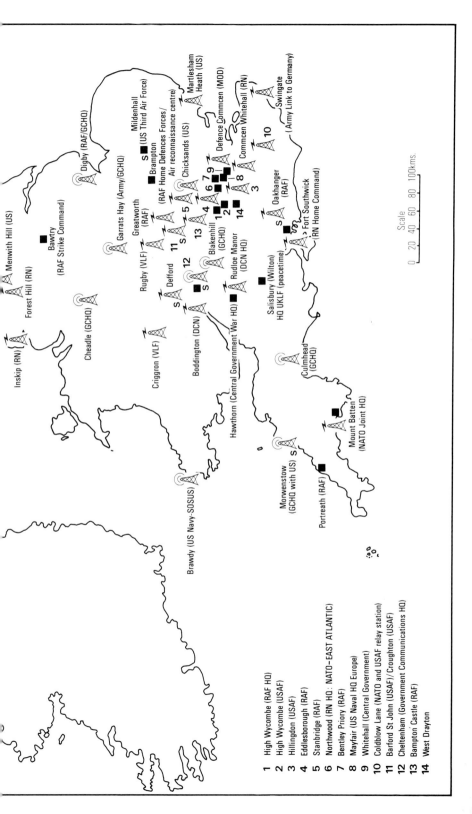

Inskip (RN)

Forest Hill (RN)

Menwith Hill (US)

Bawtry
(RAF Strike Command)

Digby (RAF/GCHQ)

Cheadle (GCHQ)

Garrats Hay (Army/GCHQ)

Mildenhall
S (US Third Air Force)

Brampton
(RAF Home Defences Forces /
Air reconnaissance centre)

Greatworth
(RAF)

Martlesham
Heath (US)

Defence Commcen (MOD)

Chicksands (US)

Rugby (VLF)

6 7 9

Commcen Whitehall (RN)

S

Swingate
(Army Link to Germany)

Defford

11
5
13 S
4
1
2
3
10

8
14

12
Blakenhill
(GCHQ)

Criggron (VLF)

Boddington (DCN)

Rudloe Manor
(DCN HQ)

S

Oakhanger
(RAF)

S

Fort Southwick
(RN Home Command)

Hawthorn (Central Government War HQ)

Salisbury (Wilton)
HQ UKLF (peacetime)

Brawdy (US Navy-SOSUS)

Culmhead
(GCHQ)

Morwenstow
(GCHQ with US) S

Mount Batten
(NATO Joint HQ)

Portreath (RAF)

Scale
0 20 40 60 80 100kms.

1 High Wycombe (RAF HQ)
2 High Wycombe (USAF)
3 Hillingdon (USAF)
4 Eddlesborough (RAF)
5 Stanbridge (RAF)
6 Northwood (RN HQ: NATO-EAST ATLANTIC)
7 Bentley Priory (RAF)
8 Mayfair (US Naval HQ Europe)
9 Whitehall (Central Government)
10 Coldblow Lane (NATO and USAF relay station)
11 Barford St John (USAF/Croughton (USAF)
12 Cheltenham (Government Communications HQ)
13 Bampton Castle (RAF)
14 West Drayton

(c) Successful defensive action (against aircraft).

(d) Inadequate or inaccurate target intelligence – this seems unlikely.

(e) Allocation of forces to higher priority missions elsewhere.

There then arises the question of the total strength of Soviet forces available for use against the United Kingdom. The range of the UK from the majority of bases likely to be available to Soviet Long Range Aviation in war suggests that first strikes on time-urgent targets would come from the rocket forces, using land based ss5 or ss20 missiles – or from submarine launched missiles. Secondary attacks may be made by the longer range aircraft in the Soviet's Theatre Forces Frontal Aviation and by elements of Long Range Aviation in Europe.

Table 18 summarises the available Soviet forces for nuclear strike on the United Kingdom, on this basis. The yields or weapon loads available are also shown. If, as NATO now says it expects, a phase of conventional warfare and long range conventional bombing precedes any nuclear attack, then it is inevitable that the forces described will have suffered at the hands of the defences, and perhaps Soviet missile sites would also have been damaged by western attacks. Such casualties may not be very severe; *Hard Rock*, for example, claims a Soviet loss rate of ten per cent (14 out of 141 sorties).

The level of attack on Britain depends on the perceived importance of the UK *vis-a-vis* other targets in Europe and, possibly, the Middle East. The UK, militarily, comes second in NATO in Europe to Germany. France would come close too; although French political visibility in NATO is low, and the French forces are detached from NATO planning, a Soviet 'worst case' analysis would have to take the initiative by assuming that French nuclear and conventional forces would, sooner or later, join with NATO against them.

Besides these three major European powers, there would be the other twelve NATO nations, from Turkey to Norway, to consider. However a much greater variety of attack systems is available for shorter range use, such as the 250 or so ss4 missiles said still to be in service. What then emerges from this kind of analysis is a picture of nuclear striking potential far greater than would be implied by the standard official British 200 megaton scenarios. We cannot, of course, know Soviet plans, but we can well see that a most probable situation would allow the Soviet nuclear forces to direct rather more than 300 weapons and perhaps 600 megatons against

Table 18 *Soviet Nuclear forces in Europe*

Carrier		Weapons carried	Total forces	
Type	Number	Type and yield	Warheads	Yield (MT)

(a) Missiles

ICBM SS 11	120	One 1MT (non-MRV version)	120	120
ICBM SS 19	60	Six 200kT (MIRV)	360	72
(In fields at Pervomaysk and Derazhnya)				
IRBM SS 4 } IRBM SS 5 }	175*	One 1 MT	175	175
IRBM SS 20	175*	Three 150kT (MIRV)	525	78
(Allocated to Europe)				
		TOTAL missiles	1180	445

(b) Aircraft

Tu 16 Badger	300	One/two free fall bombs (1MT) or two AS6 standoff missiles (200kT) (say half force in each role)	600	420
Tu 22 Blinder	130	One/two free fall bombs (1MT) or one AS 4 standoff missile (kT) say half force in each role)	195	143
Tu 22m Backfire	75	One/two AS 6 standoff missiles (200kT)	150	30
Su 24 Fencer	500	Six weapon carrying positions, say half force carrying one free fall bomb, remainder two AS 6 missiles	750	450
		TOTAL aircraft	1695	1047
		TOTAL in European theatre (75 per cent)	1270	785
		TOTAL long and medium forces in Europe, including missiles – at least	2450	1230

*Assuming two-thirds to be targetted on Europe
MT – Megaton; kT – Kiloton; MRV – Multiple re-entry vehicle; MIRV –
multiple independently-targetted re-entry vehicle; ICBM – Intercontinental
ballistic missile; IRBM – Intermediate range ballistic missile.

the United Kingdom. Yet,the Home Office computer programme has been set to an arbitrary upper limit of 300 weapons.

The weapons exist, and the targets exist. Some major targets would have two, three or even more weapons directed against them. For example, a major air base such as Upper Heyford might experience cross-targetting by missile warheads with an airburst to destroy aircraft and ground facilities, then a groundburst duplicating this, but with a DGZ on the location of the nuclear weapons store, and, finally, an air-delivered large yield groundburst bomb, to thoroughly destroy the runways and prevent long term use of the area. This is not overblown nuclear fantasy, but precisely the sort of deliberate, mechanical calculation made by strategic target planners on all sides.

Most of the weapons used would be groundbursts. These provide, as the US Air Force planners note, the 'bonus' of contamination and cratering in the target area. Airbursts are only of advantage if cities were generally targetted *per se*, and this appears to be neither the Soviet nor the American intention. Their objective in attacking non-military targets is preventing economic or military recovery. In any case, unless exceptional civil defence provisions were made for protecting the population (and countervailing action was *not* taken by the attacker), the civilian mortality from fallout radiation would compensate for the mortality 'lost' through reduced blast range.

Another factor, affecting aircraft strikes, is that free fall bombing attacks would have to be low level, and consequently groundburst, unless air defences have already been entirely suppressed. The manouevre normally adopted is 'toss-bombing', whereby an aircraft approaches its target, pulls up vertically whilst releasing the bomb into a parabolic trajectory, and then turns to head at maximum speed in the opposite direction. However, each of the major Soviet bombers can carry stand-off air to surface missiles.

The few hard targets – principally command centres like Northwood, Forth Southwick, or High Wycombe – may be attacked quickly by multiple groundbursts, not unlike the triple one megaton strike on High Wycombe which was a feature of *Square Leg*. A further hazard, of course, is water bursts – two, in the Clyde and the Thames, were part of *Square Leg* (using five megaton warheads). The potency of such an attack as a radiological weapon is considerable, besides its other effects.

Having, in the last Chapter, examined the extraordinary biases which have featured in the casualty and damage assessment pronouncements made by the Home Office and their ministers, we come to a further, apparently systematic, scaling down of the threat facing the UK in nuclear war. It may be that there is a further layer of study, well-hidden behind official secrecy, at which more pessimistic assumptions have been displayed and examined. But that is hard to believe. There is gloom enough in the Home Office's circulars, which, piece by piece, do indicate the expectation of a society wholly destroyed. They speak of 'recovery' despite it all, but have no picture of what a likely attack would add up to, certainly not on the customary military basis of 'worst case'.

Apart from the overall yield and the number of targets, there are a few important features of a worst case estimate which do not crop up. One aspect is water bursts, particularly if used as a radiological weapon. A more serious question involves the targetting of nuclear reactors or reprocessing facilities – sixteen in all, in Britain. There is no incentive – and no signs of any doctrine of mercy on either side – not to deal with these doubly essential targets with groundburst nuclear weapons. If attacked, they will in most cases distribute (given high yield or accurate targetting) the reactor's inventory of fissile material and products as fallout. As described in the previous chapter, that makes a substantial and highly adverse difference to fallout levels. Yet the voluminous and highly detailed *Technical* or *Operational Manuals* for scientific advisers do not provide any discussion of the effects and special dangers of fallout from nuclear reactors. In a category all of its own is the Windscale plant, and associated waste stores nearby at Drigg. These targets, if successfully attacked, would launch into the atmosphere fallout equivalent to many hundreds of nuclear weapons. Given the priority of targetting (a) power stations, and (b) facilities that might enable 'recovery', even in a few years, of an atomic weapons manufacturing capacity, it must be assumed that *all* reactors will be attacked.

Neither is any serious official consideration given to chemical and biological weapons, other than to produce unverifiable allegations about the size of a Soviet CW stockpile (in order to justify a comparable US programme of manufacturing and stockpiling in Europe). On chemical weapons, the *Training Manual* suggests that chemical weapons are 'a tactical hazard rather than a strategic hazard'. The view taken by the MOD in 1968, that it was 'not easy to conceive of the use of chemical weapons against a civilian population in these is-

Plate 45 The Royal Ordnance Factory at Burghfield, near Reading, is the final assembly site for most of Britain's nuclear weapons and, consequently, a prime nuclear target.

lands', the *Manual* suggests, remains valid and is 'essentially correct'. Reasonably, it is argued that chemical weapons might be used, exceptionally, to attack a UK military target, with consequent civilian casualties. But it is not a reasonable weapon for an attacker to use against the civil population; it produces a poor return, unless high value is placed on capturing some special facility or industry intact.

Biological weapons are different. 'If biological weapons are considered as a means of attack upon the United Kingdom, then they present a serious hazard to the population.' Although countermeasures – vaccines – may be developed, 'at present these preventive measures do not exist.' There would be no specific protection, and no remedy unless the disease agent were identified and its spread monitored.

On the CBW threat, there is at least consistency in government planning; as far as the SRHQs (or other non-military controls) are concerned there is no special provision for filtering to remove such agents. It would appear extremely unlikely for a biological or chemical attack to be made on its own; few possible agents used in this way would have any military utility in war or crisis between major powers. After a nuclear attack, however, the possibility arises of multiplying the death rate by a biological attack. Tests involving spraying sample fluorescent particles upwind on the UK were carried out by Porton Down in the 1950s, and proved effective: 'suitable conditions for an attack (on the UK) occur on about three days out of four.'

Nothing can be done about this sort of threat; it seems a feasible adjunct to the nuclear preparations of the US or the USSR and no particular standards or morality have hitherto been shown by nuclear planners which would seem to restrict development or use of BW. Practically, however, they may not be necessary in such a situation – survivors' poor personal and environmental health, loss of immunological protection through radiation, poor feeding and housing, may easily permit previously dormant diseases to become endemic, particularly given the virtually total loss of health care. Furthermore, development of BW has been banned since 1973 by treaty, channeling military research into other directions.

On the hazards of nuclear war, however, we have been misled or kept in ignorance as much about its likely scale, as about its direct and long-term consequences. Perhaps it is wilful deception; perhaps it is just a reflection of the unwillingness of the British establishment to think through the consequences of nuclear war and the possession of nuclear weapons – not just on its own behalf, but also on behalf of the public. When, for example, Magnus Clarke was researching for his thesis on the likely course of a nuclear war for Britain* – a thesis in no sense adopting a disarmament position – the Ministry of Defence refused to identify 'major RAF operational bases', in the context of their being nuclear targets – even though a thousand different, open publications contained all this information and more. When the MOD produced a propaganda pamphlet, at public expense of £8000, for the residents of Greenham Common and Molesworth, the prospective cruise missile bases, it assured them that the bases were not, because of the missiles' mobility, 'likely to be a priority target'. That was in July 1980; in September 1980, the two bases featured on the *Square Leg* bomb plot as high priority targets indeed. Greenham Common was one of the

The Nuclear Destruction of Britain, op. cit.

very earliest *Square Leg* targets. It would not have been dishonest for the MOD to say that the bases were almost certainly priority targets anyway, and the addition of the cruise missiles represented only a marginal increase in the mortal risk already faced in war by anyone living near the bases. Telling the truth to the public plainly and simply does not come easy to Whitehall; a suitable redraft by the Central Office of Information, on this occasion, gave an intentionally misleading impression.

Whitehall always prefers not to put such matters before the children. Meanwhile vast budgets are set aside for nuclear weapons and the means of their delivery. All the time, we still face, as a nation, the prospect of continually decreasing security. Even in the 1950s, the United Kingdom did not face the prospect of extinction as a viable twentieth century society; even in the 1960s, some still had hopes that the effects of nuclear war could realistically be mitigated. No-one has any such hopes now, and we are offered only an insulting insufficiency of half-baked, short–term, do-it-yourself propositions about a type of 'civil defence' not worthy of the name. The problem is priorities, as J. K. S. Clayton explained in the introduction to the *Training Manual*:

It is inevitable that the Home Defence share (of the defence budget) must be small; the provision of military equipment will invariably take precedence.

He continued by reiterating the link between Home Defence and deterrence policy:

No defence policy based on deterrence can be convincing if it fails to include an element for Home Defence. A potential attacker must be persuaded that *the nation is ready to accept and survive an attack, at least to the extent of being able to retaliate.*

Can we really continue to accept a defence policy predicated on an assumption of willingness to accept an attack? Can we accept any part of an official civil defence programme the avowed purpose of which is to sustain the impression, abroad, that we are 'ready to accept and survive' a nuclear attack? Is this truly a policy for national security – or national suicide?

13
The fraudulence of civil defence

The government does not care for its civil defence programmes to be called fraudulent. Yet they cannot be otherwise in a nuclear-armed state. The strategy of nuclear deterrence is based on the gamble of 'make or break', with the odds perceived as being enormously in favour of success – meaning no war. Any investment in civil defence implies that the protagonists of deterrence do not believe the odds so good; thus it undermines deterrence in the public eye. There is a further disadvantage. To the potential adversary, investment in civil defence implies a move to limit damage in a nuclear strike, and is especially dangerous if seen in the context of accompanying a potential first strike against delivery systems.

On the other hand, a policy of no civil defence suggests to the citizen that there is no protection in nuclear war or succour available if something goes wrong. And an adversary might judge the deterrent to lack credibility, if there were not definitive plans for the day it might have to be used.

So civil defence measures have to be devised, and presented to the public, with all of the professional skills of a conjurer hauling white rabbits from an empty hat. There must be an impression of civil defence for public consumption, but it should rely, somehow, on techniques which are *simple*, policies which are *cheap* and *easy to implement*, yet somehow are *effective* and *save lives*. The public must be assured that their lives and property are safeguarded, yet not encouraged to dwell to an undue extent on the horrors of war, still less on the gaping holes in the fabric of government policy. Of course when civil defence policies are examined in detail, they have as much substance as the emperor's clothes.

The disparity of resources is immense. Between thirty and fifty full time civil servants work on civil defence, and most of that work is concerned with planning for the preservation of government. Tens of thousands of civil servants and military staff work on nuclear weapons, and maintaining the equipment stockpiles necessary for their use. Whilst billions of pounds were spent on new nuclear weapons procurement, virtually every Home Office advisory circular that went out during the 1970s warned stringently against spending a penny more to provide each new item of planning. All things are feasible in civil defence, might have been the official motto, provided they involve spending no money.

Whitehall's front line troops in the civil defence game are the Council Emergency Planning Officers (EPOs) which each local authority was asked to appoint in 1974. The typical EPO is often an ex-military or ex-police officer, if not, then probably a career civil defence official who stayed near the business even after 1968. For the most part, they patiently and unimaginatively translate the Home Office circulars into local *War Books* and *War Plans*. They generally have an attitude of resignation to nuclear weapons and warfare; they say they hope their work is all in vain. Some, ex-military, more gung-ho, look forward to the prospect of nuclear war with unhealthy glee. But they are rare. The majority tend to aggrandise themselves and echo the Whitehall spirit of keeping unpleasant facts from the children by strong, considerable habits of secrecy; conducting briefings for other staff under virtual oaths of confidentiality and making free with rubber stamping 'RESTRICTED' or suchlike on their output, a meaningless gesture since – as they are not Crown Servants, or contractors – the information they themselves originate is not covered by the Official Secrets Act. Nor should it be.

Few, if any, of the EPOs give full obedience to Whitehall. Many of them are aware of the extraordinary deficiencies in civil defence arrangements, and think the remedy is major new expenditure. Many argued for years to have the *Protect and Survive* booklet made available to the public; even going so far in some counties to reproduce and circulate leaflets based on the previous version (*Advising the Householder*), when the Home Office refused to relax its copyright control on *Protect and Survive*. Meeting in regular, highly private forums, they have picked out the holes in Home Office policy, sometimes to evident official distaste. One metropolitan area's former EPO described to me, endearingly, how the Home Office circulars reaching his office would be divided according to whether they related to peace or war; those about war might as well have gone into his dustbin.

Nevertheless each county, Scottish region and the GLC has its war planner and its war plans. Some of the plans and other material produced by the EPOS show remarkable similiarity since they are all derived in large measure by 'cutting and pasting' 20–30 Home Office circulars together and having them retyped. Other local authority officials will not know this, of course, and by this means many EPOS are able to produce voluminous plans with great economy of effort. All that is needed is a little local colour to fill in round the circulars. One could give some particularly outstanding examples of the general nature of Emergency Planning Officers' work which sometimes matches the high standards of lunacy prevalent in Whitehall:

Former Squadron Leader R. W. Johnstone, an emergency planner for Strathclyde Region in Scotland, produced plans for *Square Leg* indicating casualties a day after the attack of 452,000 dead and 350,000 injured. Two weeks after the attack, there were 413,000 injured but still only 452,000 dead. Not one person had died in two weeks.

The Emergency Planning Officer for Hertfordshire, produced a particularly imaginative and visionary interpretation of the Home Office's tedious circular on *Environmental Health in War* by suggesting that the sites for mass graves of the nuclear war dead be chosen with a view to their being the shrines of a future society.

Hiroshima's Lesson – You Can Survive is the title of a uniquely cheerful pamphlet produced for the residents of Essex by their EPO, Ray Fullarton. 'A radiation check in Hiroshima in 1946 revealed that there was only slightly more radioactivity in the atom-bombed city than there was in London,' the pamphlet advised. Where this excess of zeal would ultimately lead is both disturbing and mysterious, but it should be said that more of the nitty-gritty and unpleasant material on home defence planning is disclosed to Essex County Councillors by this forthcoming official than is the case in many other authorities.

Disclosure to councillors would be the last idea to occur to ex-Colonel Ian Cameron, Emergency Planning Officer for the Lothian Regional Council in Scotland. He set up a Home Defence Planning Group in 1980 and endeavoured to keep it a complete secret from the (Labour-controlled) council. No Councillor was informed. When one senior council official declined to attend a meeting, he was told by Colonel Cameron that he would have him shot (were it wartime).

A minute of an early Lothian Region Planning Group meeting (marked 'Restricted') explained that while Home Defence must be an open subject, debated in public, 'it would be unwise to reveal plans until they had been fully discussed and were considered to be workable.' No time limit was set on this process.

A new communications network for the county of Sussex has been devised by former Chief Superintendent McWhirter, EPO for East Sussex. Communities will signal to each other by coloured flags.

The North Yorkshire War Plan, by EPO Mr R. W. Cropper, added a new dimension to nuclear war with the observation that after an attack, 'refuse collection, as we know it, would cease. . .'.

Mr Graeme Bushell, Emergency Planning Officer for Cambridgeshire, achieved exceptional economy of effort in drafting his county's War Plan by sticking unyieldingly to the texts of suitable Home Office circulars.

The Warwickshire County Council War Plan gives the lowest figures in Britain for the effects of an airburst nuclear weapon, by lowering even further the Home Office's inaccurate figures. For example, the outer blast ring ('D' ring) in Warwickshire for an 'optimal' one megaton airburst in the unique atmosphere prevailing in this county is 6–9 miles from ground zero. Everywhere else the D ring, (1.5 to 6 psi) runs from 9.5 miles to 16 miles. This is not a trivial mistake. The area damaged by such a bomb would, according to these figures, be one third of the true area. The EPO for Warwickshire, like most of his colleagues, marked the County War Plan containing this rubbish as 'Restricted . . . not to be communicated to the Press'.

Eric Willcock, EPO for West Midlands Council, offered a proposal for dealing with the problem of officials being unwilling to leave their families to go to the local authority bunker. The Chief Executive's wife, he suggested to the *Sunday Times*, should be trained as a teleprinter operator.

Most council War Plans slavishly follow government assumptions and suggestions, although there is no legal obligation preventing councils or their officials from devising their own, independent, and reasonable views of what planning they need to do.

Reading and comparing the multitude of local War Plans which have been published or leaked, a sort of monotony sets in. Here and there is the occasional new idea, or particularly ludicrous remark, but there is generally an overwhelming similarity – the same charts of chief officers of the council who will run the bunkers, the same lists and summaries of Home Office circulars, and not a voice raised amongst them (that I have seen) to challenge the hypocrisies of official policy.

One reason for the silence is that the emergency planners and many of the chief officers are periodically indoctrinated at Easingwold conferences and other gatherings. No lesser word can describe the prevalent tone of cold war mania in which discussion of east-west relations is presented. When the Civil Defence and Emergency Planning Officers gather in conference, it is Lord Chalfont who addresses them on the Soviet plans for world domination. Such tirades and such intensity do not promote independence of thought. This campaign has gained impetus in 1981 and 1982, and children in school have been bombarded with literature from the Ministry of Defence and Central Office of Information which would not have been out of place in Chancellor Hitler's Germany. There is the leaflet *How to deal with a bully*, with its now notorious image of the massive Bear (Russia) and the snapping Bulldog (British). There is the propaganda of the Foreign Office Arms Control and Disarmament Unit, which displays a map of Eurasia with boundaries skilfully drawn to show a preponderance of red over blue. Accompanying pictures say that Britain, each November, remembers the war dead at the Cenotaph, while the Russians hold a warlike parade through Moscow (to commemorate the Revolution). How much further before they are accused of eating babies?

In this ideological campaign, civil defence has a clear role in supplying propaganda and public relations material for adults.

Civil Defence is not about defences; we are substantially defenceless. When wondering why civil defence planning pays so little heed to the basic matter of the vulnerability of city dwellers or those living near other obvious targets, it is instructive to look at the 1974 Civil Defence Regulations, which are the legal instrument requiring councils to do this work, whether they believe in it or not. The Regulations say nothing about protecting *people* in the local authority's charge, and nothing about any ultimate objectives. They speak only of making *plans*.

Statutory Instrument (1974) No 70. (Regulation 4)
It shall be the function of every county council and the Greater
London Council, for the purposes of civil defence – (a) to make
plans for–
  (i) collecting intelligence on the results of hostile attack and
      distributing such intelligence;
 (ii) controlling and coordinating action necessary as a result of
      hostile attack.
(iii) providing and maintaining a service in their area for the
      billeting . . .

Remaining sections refer to preventing the spread of disease,
providing facilities for the disposal of human remains, the
distribution and 'control' of food, the repair of dwellings or
clearing of roads, etc, maintaining essential services, training
their staff – and, finally, carrying out the plans if so ordered.

There is nothing in the Regulations that prohibits a council
from deciding that some of its people live in a certain target
area, and that evacuation alone could protect them. It could
be arranged. But it isn't. It isn't government policy, and the
overwhelming majority of EPOs seem to take official policy,
however absurd, as a given factor in any plans.

The same is not true of elected councillors, nor of a significant number of senior local authority staff who are supposed to make the overnight transition from their peacetime
responsibilities to running the wartime systems. Many find
the whole business quite unconvincing and a distraction. For
example, the Solicitor and Deputy Chief Executive of Manchester City warned* that although he accepted that the threat
of nuclear war existed, he didn't believe that the plans would
work.

The decisions which will need to be taken by controllers may well
include how refugees from urban areas should be turned back
from the rural areas and how much force should be used.
Whether to feed all the surviving population or only those who
have not been exposed to the fatal doses of radiation . . .

Local authority staff were in no sense familiar with, or competent to handle, such decisions, and the fundamental issue,
of whether the designated staff would just pack a bag and
leave their families behind to their fate, had never been debated. He pointed out that a plan which simply suggested
looking round after an attack to marshall surviving resources
'cannot be regarded as a safe basis for the protection of the

*Local Government Chronicle, 13 March 1981.

community. . .' The long term survival of the population might also be in question if inadequate food resources were stockpiled:

As many as ten or fifteen million people would need provisions over an extended period after nuclear attack. The Government may feel unable to commit enough resources to guaranteeing that such a large number will receive some aid. That is a political decision, but controllers should (know) whether plans for providing for the civilian community have any reality . . . .
There is a serious discrepancy between what on paper will happen and what in practice won't. . .the sort of serious discrepancy which makes one ask whether survivors can really be protected at all.

The local authorities' movement towards 'Nuclear Free Zones' has, literally, swept the country. It represents a vital and traditional facet of British culture – the resistance of local administrations to Whitehall – and on this occasion provides a unique gauge of the strength of popular feeling for nuclear disarmament measures as the means to prevent war. It was, by coincidence, Manchester City Council which started the ball rolling, not by being the first to pass a resolution against nuclear weapons, but by being the first to circulate the resolution to other authorities with a request for similar action. It was an inspired move.

In September 1980, there were only a handful of councils – Hackney in London was the first – which had advertised a position of disobedience to Whitehall on civil defence. Six months later, there were forty. A carefully checked list* published in October 1981 gave 108. Early in 1982, the last remaining county council in Wales adopted the resolution and the total number of councils, nationwide, endorsing a position against nuclear weapons approached two hundred.

The Manchester resolution does not specifically talk about councils' civil defence commitments, although unwillingness to undertake government plans is implicit in the resolution.

We believe it is not in the interests of the people to be either the initiators or the magnet of a nuclear holocaust and firmly believe that . . . unequivocal statements would clearly indicate the overwhelming desires of the people we represent and could lay the groundwork for the creation and development of a nuclear-free Europe.

New Statesman, 30 October 1980.

The pitfall for local authorities who wish to end expenditure on civil defence is the 1948 Civil Defence Act, which gives teeth to the 1974 Regulations. The teeth have bitten in the past. During the 1950s, Coventry City Council, later joined by St Pancras Borough in London, refused to carry out any civil defence work. Their attitude, as the council of the city which had suffered the worst devastation of all in the Second World War, was that there must be no repetition of those circumstances. They viewed civil defence as a waste of time and public money; St Pancras called it a 'cruel deception'.

Nonetheless the government forced the issue, sending three civil defence commissioners to Coventry in 1954, and the bill for their work to the council. Much the same happened in St Pancras in 1957.

The threat of similar action (for which councillors might later be surcharged and disqualified from office if the council incurred extra costs in consequence) has generally kept councils back from terminating their war planning altogether. Many have cut back hard on expenditure, redistributed work, and refused to participate in *Hard Rock* 82, forcing the Home Office to abandon the planned exercise.

The councils' attitudes seem a little timorous. Firstly, a direct refusal to comply on political grounds, although it carries a legal risk, would open up a debate embarrassing to the government. A second, safer means to the same end can be read into the Regulations which, being concerned with civil defence, have ultimately to be directed towards the protection of the public, not the execution or writing of paper plans *in vacuo*. Given that the government's plans are, as far as most areas of the country are concerned, wholly unreasonable, it is open to every local authority to plan, as required, but to plan for example for mass blast shelters, or evacuation, or both. In the absence of actual expenditure, the plans would merely serve as a public demonstration of the futility of attempting to protect the population in nuclear war. They would call the government's bluff.

In extremis, the 1974 Regulations do give ministers the right to 'direct' a local authority how to plan. But this power would be extremely unpopular in use, and is not thought by the civil service to be constitutionally usual; according to the circular on the *Civil Defence Act 1948 – Subordinate Legislation* (ES1/74):

The Ministerial power to issue directions is regarded as a reserve power to be used only when the national interest is at stake and

when the long-established procedures of advice and guidance fail ·
to ensure the necessary local action.

Curiously, the Home Secretary does not exercise this power
– it belongs to the Minister of Agriculture, Fisheries and
Food.

Ministers can, one supposes, direct if they wish that black
henceforth shall be white and that the seas shall divide across
the English channel. They can, with equal effect, issue directions to local authorities to keep planning on a 'stay-put' basis
even in areas which are certain to be targets. A local authority
might then reasonably point out that its boundaries embraced
a major military or urban-industrial area; that all sides expected that particular type of target to be struck; that government policy, no less than that of the Soviet Praesidium,
was to anticipate (or mount) a massive attack, attempting to
cover all such targets; that both physics and military information suggested that a particular point might be the ground
zero of a megaton range thermonuclear device; and that in
the consequence, the entire planning process for that area
was null and void, and the inhabitants dead; and that its
proper duties as to civil defence required a different course
of action. The Minister could 'direct' them that their location
would not be a target and to carry on planning.

These arguments go straight to the core fallacies of civil
defence, and would open the stage for a debate about policy
that the government might not care to have in public. In
attacking the Nuclear Free Zone movement, a common abuse
(from the government) has been to ask, rhetorically, if Soviet
bombs or fallout will in consequence avoid the areas concerned. The question can be asked with rather greater force
as to whether the bombs and fallout will avoid urban areas
(etc) because the Minister has directed city centre dwellers to
stay put. It would be difficult, one suspects, for the Minister
of Agriculture, Fisheries and Food to go into the courts to do
battle over planning assumptions with a recalcitrant council
at, say, Southampton on the basis that all bombs and missiles
might luckily miss the Solent area.

This sort of argument was examined in more detail in 1982
by the Greater London Council under its 1981 Labour administration. The GLC became a Nuclear Free Zone shortly after
Labour came into office, voted not to play in *Hard Rock* and
announced a review of emergency planning to 'terminate the
present wasteful expenditure on so-called home defence'. Following initial legal guidelines, the Council asked officials for

a report on the 'basic' level of civil defence which they thought legally necessary. The report was creative to say the least; it suggested (with Home Office backing) that the minimum staff required should *rise* from twenty–three to sixty–three. The need for the boost as a 'minimum' arose from the government *Civil Defence Review* circular (ES1/81), and the reduced warning time it prescribed.

There had been no protests when the previous, Conservative, GLC administration had in fact reduced expenditure and staff, from thirty–one to twenty–three, after taking office in 1977. So the Council took new legal advice from Queens' Counsel, and were told that before they could make any plans, or build bunkers (as the government demanded), they had first to know the likely consequences of the possible 'hostile attack' to which the Regulations refer. If the government would not give advice – and reasonable advice at that – on the most likely consequences for London of a nuclear attack, then the GLC could not undertake its statutory duty.

This approach publicly exposes the central fallacy of NATO and government stay-put policy. It may also provide a legally secure basis on which councils could refuse to make unreasonable or impossible civil defence plans.

For some of the shire counties, Conservative run, there is more sense to civil defence on their own patches. Thus, for example, at a Home Office and local authorities' conference at Surrey University in September 1980, the Association of County Councils submitted a paper asking for protection against the 'invasions' of urban refugees. Could the Home Office advise on 'registration qualifications', they asked? Entry should be limited to the lucky (and well-to-do) owners of country cottages. At lower levels some shire counties would wish to enforce this policy whether others like it or not; East Sussex's War Plan, for example, calls for each community to have a:

security team, responsible to the Control Team Leader, to safeguard the communities' food, water, fuel and all other resources. If circumstances warrant it this team could also undertake peace-keeping duties.

In West Sussex, the EPO recruited the voluntary help of the 'League of Frontiersmen' – a right wing corps – for similar functions.

It seems likely that Nuclear Fee Zones will multiply. CND's propaganda defines these primary objectives for the zones:

The support of local elected representatives gives legitimacy to alternative policies put forward by the peace movement and focuses attention on where the responsibility lies for the arms race – central government . . . While the danger of nuclear war is not remote from peoples' homes and families, the people who have the power to take decisions are. The most important help local authorities can provide is in the form of publicity . . .

Since, of course, they cannot physically enforce the prohibition of nuclear weapons manufacture or transport as called for in their resolutions, the NFZ councils' major activities thus far have been educational; it is to be hoped that the nettle of debating civil defence policy with the government can be more firmly grasped in future, and the truth about civil defence examined.

At the same time as the civil defence debate has engaged the government, private enterprise has produced a flourishing range of private shelter designs. The boom which began early in 1980 spawned several hundred manufacturers who sought to offer an individual solution to the problem. The private shelter industry soon threw up absurdities to equal any local authority War Plan.

Some of the names were ridiculous enough – the 'Life Plan', the 'Churchill Mark IV', the 'Nuclear Lifeboat', the 'Honeycomb Bombcell', the 'Homebase 7', the 'NESST', the 'NuSafe' and so on. There was also the Aftermath company, operating out of a Pall Mall accommodation address, offering everyone details of the 'risks' in their neighbourhood, and 'survival packs' made to measure. There was an enterprising Glasgow doctor who adapted his business to become the 'Hope Medical Clinic and Nuclear Advisory Agency', setting about negotiations with British Rail for the use of disused tunnels, and flaunting his membership of a DHSS advisory panel.

Manufacturers rushed to assemble qualifications based on having exchanged the odd letter or two with the Home Office or distant parties in Switzerland. The Home Office, which itself was struggling to acquire even a moderate amount of experience or knowledge on the subject, refused to endorse anyone or anything – quite rightly – and a *de facto* ban on advertising by newspapers and radio and television was imposed, by mutual consent. The unadvised public certainly needed some warning against the more lunatic of these private enterprise efforts.

Greenhows (UK) offered shelter protection against hitherto unknown 'gamma particles' (they are, in fact, rays); these appeared after the bomb's 'outer layer of TNT is fired simultaniously (sic) which creates a massive Implossion (sic) onto the Plutonium layer . . .' Another novel thermonuclear hazard fended off by a Greenhow's shelter was 'nitric acid'. Hark Northgreaves (Engineers) Ltd advertised their patented 'Nuclear Lifeboat', comprising a transparent, pressurised inner plastic skin to be fitted into a room, to protect against 'nuclear fallout and war gas'. The Consulting Engineer whose expertise was engaged on the project clearly expected gamma radiation to be repelled by a few millimetres of polythene. An equal degree of optimism would be required to believe a claim by Ledbury Survival Shelters that their product with-

Plate 46 A private shelter to resist nuclear attack: the Goblin's Pit store at Neston, near Corsham, Wiltshire, is run by a private security company.

stood 1500 psi of overpressure, a strength rather greater than that achieved by most US missile silos.

More elaborate schemes for multi-place shelters have been proposed; for 250, in Balcombe, Sussex; for 56 in Chiswick; and two schemes for 250 people in Shepton Mendip, from 'Stronghold Engineering'. There was also the proposal from the rapidly formed Rusepalm Ltd, and Messrs Lucien Fior and Co, to let out the old Eastlays store at Corsham as a nuclear condominium. All these schemes appear to have enjoyed limited success, as do the shelter manufacturers.

Things weren't much better for some of those who took early delivery. An early customer in Reading discovered, as her shelter slowly flooded, and that the company who had contracted to do the job for £2500 normally did furniture removals.

The Home Office's offerings, when they came, were little better, and the flooding problem was one that they shared. Short (as ever) of money, the Cotterill Working Party produced five designs. There were two trench expedient shelters, which the *Architect's Journal* commented cheerily 'can be dismissed out of hand', and three other examples – the old Anderson, the old Morrison, and a typical modern reinforced concrete construction, enhanced by a certain amount of computerised engineering analysis. The trench type shelters were suggested for surface use to allow for a high water table when they were constructed, and a major reason for that was that the shelters were to be constructed in a field at Easingwold in which there was indeed a high water table. The shelters were demonstrated to the press on 22 January 1981. Shortly afterwards, when the Home Office invited a prominent US expert, Cresson Kearney, to Easingwold, they were all filled with water. It was not an impressive performance. The Home Office admitted that not one of the shelters had actually been tested (by detonating conventional explosives at a suitable range).

The 'average' private shelter offered is either constructed *in situ* in reinforced concrete, or is built around a shell, usually either glass fibre or metal sheeting. The quality of the concrete reinforcement work (if any) makes a significant difference to their ultimate blast resistance, but naturally no guarantees are available. The costs start at about £6,000 and more sophisticated designs cost up to £20,000. Only a few hundred have been sold. A few well-publicised families have had prototypes installed. A well-known BBC defence correspondent spent £10,000 on one. But they have hardly become popular.

Apart from the high costs and the possible technical deficiencies, there is a more serious problem. Whatever the government does to encourage private shelter-building or makeshift activity at the time of war, there is no insulating survivors from the aftermath. A family which has survived, exceptionally, in their £10,000 shelter a few miles from ground zero of a megaton bomb is going to have to emerge, and move around, two to four weeks later. They will already have faced immense psychological stress. If they have only taken the government–recommended amounts of food (for two weeks) they may have to move through areas still dangerously radioactive to get any food. There will be no returning to 'normal life'; 'normal life' will be over for the duration, and they like anyone else will have to make do or die on whatever resources happen to have survived.

It is not unreasonable to conclude that private enterprise has offered no solution to civil defence problems.

It is startling to see the wide variation between British civil defence organisation and those of many NATO countries – let alone Sweden or Switzerland. Home Office ministers frequently refer to these countries with disarming duplicity. Surely, they claim, the fact that neutral countries carry out civil defence proves that it is worthwhile anywhere. These ill-considered statements miss the point entirely. Switzerland and Sweden do it properly, on an extensive scale, with shelters, stockpiles, and blast protection or evacuation for everyone, even refugees. They spend real money on it. They can afford it, partly because they don't spend billions of pounds on nuclear armaments. And they face a risk of relatively slight proportions in war, because they do not threaten other countries, neither by the possession of nuclear weapons, nor by the presence of foreign military bases, nor by membership of a heavily armed alliance – Warsaw Pact or NATO.

Yet not only is the British £30 million a year, official–bunker–only and hide-under-the-table public advice programme flimsy in comparison to those of the neutral countries, who have far less to fear, it is also flimsy in comparison to average NATO efforts.

In the Netherlands, the normal strength of the *Noodwacht*, or auxiliary service, is 120,000 including conscripts not serving in the army. It would carry out the rescue, first aid, and auxiliary fire–fighting functions of the old British CD corps. There are also twenty–four emergency columns from the army reserve. In Norway, where the nuclear threat is assessed as 'not severe' for most towns and cities, there is nevertheless an extensive programme of well-protected blast shelters for public use. There are evacuation and reception plans for about one million people (the population is four million). Some forty per cent of the population can be accommodated in purpose built shelters, including 190,000 public shelter places. Although, unlike Switzerland, every small private dwelling does not have to have a compulsory shelter built-in, such shelters are common and are in any case required for larger dwellings or public buildings. There is a CD corps with 50–60,000 members, plus half that number in an industrial civil defence force. There are fourteen mobile rescue columns with special equipment.

Putting the Norwegian civil defence effort in British context, *pro rata*, there would be shelter places for 23.6 million people (including 2.6 million public places) constructed at a cost of £1.26 billion since 1948. The government's current expenditure would be about £300 million a year, not including capital spending on shelters.

Denmark is similarly well placed with 2.5 million public and 2.3 million private shelter places, for a population of five million. The quality of the shelter is somewhat poorer than in Norway, but there is substantial expenditure on rescue and first aid columns, and a warning organisation similar to the Royal Observer Corps.

West Germany began a massive shelter and civil emergency protection programme in 1970, with many thousands of places being constructed in blast proof shelters. Having started late in the day, there were only 1.8 million places available in public shelters by 1977 (for a population of 62 million). The warning and monitoring network is more extensive and more sophisticated than Britain's (it includes about 82,000 sirens), and an ARP service has recruited about 100,000 members. Some 70,000 volunteers are also enrolled in a 'Technical Aid Service'. The Federal Republic's Civil Defence budget is over £100 million a year; more still is spent by the *Länder* (regions).

The German shelter programme has involved both ambitious and expedient projects. A new underground railway station in Bonn, completed in 1979, was designed to double as a bunker shelter for 4500 people. Twenty-ton doors would cover the entrance to the station in the event of attack. The Federal German government estimates that shelter places can be had for £100–200, by converting and adapting underground garages, basements and underground stations. Some of the *Länder* provide grants and tax relief for private shelter construction.

Although the German civil defence programme is manifestly far more extensive than Britain's, it suffers from similar inadequacies. Germany faces the greatest nuclear threat of all. But official food stockpiles would last for only ten days. And the official objectives of civil defence in the Federal Republic start with 'self–protection' and continue to include 'population control' and the 'protection of cultural assets'.

German adherence to the NATO stay-put policy is not total. A major 1972 'White Paper' on civil defence suggested that very vulnerable areas should be evacuated.

Belgium has a small civil defence corps, and a shelter programme – in principal only, as progress has been slow. Italian civil defence is fairly minimal. There is no single national warning network although there are a few mobile columns for rescue and fire-fighting from the fire services and *Carabinieri,* under a Directorate of Civil Protection.

French civil defence is as derisory as is Britain's. The fact that Britain and France are the two European powers with their own nuclear weapons may well be no coincidence.

Thus, even within NATO, the attention given to civil defence can seem almost to be inverse to the real threat each country faces. Across the Atlantic, Canada has renounced the use of offensive nuclear weapons as an act of national policy, and an extensive civil defence programme approaches north European standards. The first priority of Canadian civil defence is 'to protect and preserve life and property'; the two most important civil defence programmes are dispersal and shelter arrangements. A 1960–65 nationwide study of potential public fallout shelters identified 53 million places in 70,000 public buildings (the Canadian population is 21 million). In addition, the Canadians planned, in 1970, to have blast shelters capable of resisting at least 15 psi available in hazard areas.

A Former Director General of the Canadian Emergency Measures Organisation, John F. Wallace, wrote in the *Nato Review* (February 1980) that:

It is doubtful if any hard thinking is given by military defence planners to the consequences of war on the civil populations. Certainly, if deterrence fails, it will be the civilians who suffer . . .

The Canadians, like the Scandinavian countries and the Swiss, have in varying ways adopted a policy of 'total national defence'. These policies often include conscription instead of large standing armies. They include preparation and training to deter aggression, not through the possession of nuclear weaponry, but by the determined conventional defence of territory. Military preparation and discussion is generally more open and democratic, and more accepted.

The British military tradition is in complete contrast. Wars are fought on other people's territory. The elements of the British army which remain behind in crisis are not an anti-invasion force – they couldn't hope to be – and have as their chief enemy dissent or unruliness amongst the population. No-one in Britain has been trained in simple defensive military skills of the kind practiced by the wartime Home Guard.

When the aeroplane destroyed Britain's long immunity to first hand experience of war, the British government decided that civilians, like foreigners in Europe or 'natives' in the Empire, would have to suffer, if necessary, in war. This attitude was already well set in the 1930s, as noted in Chapter 3, when Baldwin announced to the House of Commons that 'the bomber will always get through' and asserted that it was necessary to 'kill more women and children quickly' to save one's own skin.

Canadian Director Wallace regards the updated version of such thoughts – in the shape of the doctrine of mutual assured destruction – as having given a 'crippling blow' to UK civil defence, noting also that:

In some countries, an attempt has been made to enhance the credibility of civil defence by making it responsible for a whole range of extraneous activities euphemistically called peacetime emergencies or disasters.

That was precisely what the Home Office did in 1972.

Swiss and Swedish civil defence precautions are, as most people know, lavish. The Swiss have been bombarded with requests from all over the world for information on their plans, and have printed their basic advice booklets in English, Arabic and French. By early 1980, the Swiss Federal Office of Civil Defence was receiving 1–2000 letters a month from Britain. Shelter places, to an exceptionally high standard, are available for nine out of ten in the Swiss population; there are 4.5 million purpose-built places and 1.8 million adapted

PROTECTION CIVILE · PROTEZIONE CIVILE · ZIVILSCHUTZ

La vie
dans l'abri

ones. There are 74,000 protected hospital beds, including eighty–eight underground hospitals and operating centres. Swiss Civil Protection activity is both national and total; like the Scandinavian countries, their defence plans also rest on territorial defence against an invader, utilising the country's geography. One quarter of the Swiss defence budget is spent on civil defence, including preparing mountain citadels for the army.

Some of the Swiss projects are huge. The most impressive is the Sonnenberg Tunnel, on the outskirts of Lucerne. The tunnel holds bunks and complete facilities for over 20,000 people. It is the world's largest shelter, incorporating a hospital, food stores, generators and emergency supplies. The Swiss food stockpile is aimed at providing each citizen and permanent foreign resident with 2300 calories a day from the start of a crisis.

Swedish planning is on an equally grand scale. There are 5.5 million shelter places (for a population of eight million), as well as limited plans for evacuation and reception. Everyone gets basic civil defence training, and a corps of over 250,000 can quickly be mobilised in crisis. Mobile columns with a thousand staff and over a hundred vehicles would be dispersed to peripheral civil defence centres. Many of the shelters are adapted for peacetime use as cafeterias or suchlike, with heavy shutters to cover the windows. One large shelter in central Stockholm is normally used as a garage.

Extensive stocks of civil defence equipment include face-masks for anyone likely to be exposed to nuclear, biological or chemical hazards. Protection against BW is taken seriously by all the Scandinavian countries, as well as Switzerland and the Netherlands. The Swedish Civil Defence system has been under development since 1944.

Britain, with France, is at the opposite extreme of civil defence preparedness from Sweden or Switzerland. Both the United States and the USSR are somewhere in between and have far more extensive arrangements than the UK. In the United States, and generally in NATO, Soviet civil defence efforts have been interpreted as preparation to wage nuclear war and therefore proof of Soviet belligerent intentions.

Unsurprisingly, the British government has been silent on

Plate 47   A Swiss civil defence pamphlet: '*La vie dans l'Abri*' ('Life in the shelter'). Such lavish foreign programmes sharply contrast with the British government's disinterest in protecting the civil population.

this issue. It can scarcely encourage and exhort in Britain, whilst condemning the same activity in the Soviet Union as warmongering. So the government, for once, have not been adding to the American refrain about Soviet civil defence. That is wisdom.

President Reagan's Administration has not been quiescent on the subject of civil defence. In March 1982, after some deliberation by the Federal Emergency Management Agency, Reagan approved a \$4.2 billion programme for Crisis Relocation (ie, evacuation). Based on the assumption (it was said) that there would be a week in which to anticipate a general nuclear exchange resulting from hostilities, the new plan proposes the dispersal of two thirds of the US population. Some 380 high risk areas would be evacuated, including the country's 319 largest cities (those with a population over 50,000) and sixty-one counterforce target areas – missile bases, airfields, and naval ports. The Crisis Relocation Plan is claimed to double the number of Americans likely to survive a nuclear war – from forty per cent to eighty per cent. The \$4.2 billion would be spent between 1983 and 1990.

American estimates of their likely casualties in a nuclear war have ranged from 140 million to 180 million or more – eighty per cent of the population. A mass evacuation plan was devised as early as 1962 for the Department of Defense by Jeremy Stone of the Federation of American Scientists. He then recommended that they did not adopt the plan:

If you get the people out and they survive, if the cities and the economy are gone there will be mass starvation and epidemics . . .

What the Crisis Relocation Programme signified, said Stone in 1982 'is a greater American interest in limited nuclear war'.

This claim is justified. In 1974, US Defense Secretary Schlesinger outlined to the Congress the possibilities of nuclear war conducted on the basis of limited counterforce strikes. The Schlesinger proposal was for:

a flexible capability (which) would make the possibility of a US nuclear attack more credible and would thus increase the leverage provided by US nuclear forces in international confrontations.*

This proposal highlights a significant difference between US and Soviet rationales for conducting civil defence evacuation

---

* See 'Limited nuclear war', Sidney D. Drell and Frank von Hippel, *Scientific American*, November 1976.

programmes. The Soviet policy is to limit the damage in an all-out nuclear exchange as far as possible. That is the only kind of nuclear war they anticipate. They threaten massive retaliation if attacked with nuclear weapons, and are aware of the consequences for the Soviet homeland.

In contrast, the United States CRP seems partly conceived to support and give credibility to threats of 'limited' nuclear battle. In the 1970s, US planners were rediscovering the early and fundamental objections to the bomb raised by scientific critics like Patrick Blackett (in Britain) or Robert Oppenheimer (in the US); nuclear weapons are not militarily useful. The Schlesinger proposal, with accompanying civil defence programmes, is a specific attempt to make marginal nuclear warfare practicable.

The first US Department of Defense assessment of the consequences of limited nuclear warfare put US casualties at an absurdly low level. Schlesinger suggested that if each US missile silo (1054 in all) was attacked by one megaton Soviet missiles, US civilian casualties would be only 800,000. He claimed:

the likelihood of limited nuclear attack cannot be challenged on the assumption that massive civilian fatalities and injuries would result.

The Department of Defense were asked by Congress to re-calculate their assessment based on a realistic set of assumptions – in particular, on the basis that the postulated Soviet strike should try to be militarily effective. One strike suggested would kill 5.6 million but only destroy forty-two per cent of the silos; a 'comprehensive' counterforce attack would kill 18.3 million Americans immediately, and still leave the US with forty per cent of its bombers and missiles intact.

The Federal Emergency Management Agency's planning for relocation began at about the same time. But US precautions have, in general, attracted the same criticisms as the British – they are limited to plans on paper. The Director of the US civil defence effort, Badyl Tirana – a man apparently much admired in British Home Office circles – said in 1978 that little had been achieved for $2 billion spent since 1960:

We have no civil defence programme, merely the apparatus to start one. When you look at civil defense in the United States, you find (that) the emperor has no clothes*

*Quoted in *Parade* (US), 21 May 1978.

The Reagan Administration now takes the view that the Soviet Union is better prepared for nuclear war than the US, and more of its citizens would survive. This might be true of the first few weeks after an attack; it is very unlikely to be true in the longer term. As in many areas of weaponry, the Reagan government has declared the US to be facing a 'dangerous' imbalance in civil defence.

Glib optimism about the effect of civil defence measures is as common in the US as in Britain. Shortly before US spending on civil defence reached an all time high in 1961, *Life* magazine announced to its readers that ninety-seven out of one hundred people could survive an atomic holocaust. Criticism of the Crisis Relocation Plan has been blunt and frequent. Many US cities have rejected the plans to move everyone out and place them 60–100 miles away as 'unworkable'. Minor sub-plans have had their absurd sides, too; one scheme for self-evacuation was predicated on those with even-number car registrations giving way to those with odd.

Soviet schemes for civil defence are comprehensively organised. As befits a large country, considerable emphasis is placed on evacuation and dispersal; in industrial planning, it is claimed, civil defence requirements have been taken into account in order to reduce the vulnerability of the industrial base. The civil defence organisation is run by Colonel-General A. T. Altunin, a Soviet Deputy Minister of Defence. He states its object as:

> The main purpose of our civil defence together with the armed forces, is to ensure the population's defence against mass destruction weapons and other means of attack from a likely opponent. By implementing defensive measures and thoroughly training the population, civil defence seeks to weaken as much as possible the destructive effects of modern weapons. . .

Training in elementary civil defence is given to everyone, at school, in industry or collective farms. A basic handbook of precautionary measures, *Everyone must know this!*, is the Russian *Protect and Survive*. The national organisation for civil defence is extensive, and is organised along military lines. Over 200,000 civil defence troops would be mobilised for rescue work in war. There are said to be extensive, dispersed and 'untouchable' food stockpiles; industrial workers are issued with kits of personal protection apparatus, said to include nerve gas counteragents such as atropine. Fallout and blast shelters are provided in the cities and in industrial complexes, and new buildings have been required to have shelters since the early 1950s.

The Soviet authorities have made claims about the effectiveness of their precautions which equal western officials' most zealous remarks. They suggest that less than ten per cent – even as little as five per cent – of the Soviet population would die in a major attack. The American assessment is that 110 million might die (as against 140 million US casualties).

The determination of Soviet civil defence is seen in some quarters as ominous. Apprehensions are worsened by the not infrequent use of the word 'victory' in Soviet writings. But it is a very qualified usage. The appalling destruction of nuclear war is fully comprehended, and 'victory' means just salvaging a few extra lives or factories from the debris. Given the thoroughness of the American SIOP plans, the 40,000 targets, and the specific targetting of 'economic recovery capability', the victory could indeed be highly qualified. Soviet specialist Professor John Erickson regards linking the Soviet civil defence effort to 'war-fighting' ideas as 'abrupt' and unjustified; their theory of deterrence is, if anything, more straightforward than the convoluted ideas and limited war proposals made in the west.

Warsaw Pact and eastern European nations show the same sort of variation in their civil defence programmes as do NATO countries. Outside the Pact, Yugoslavia apparently has the best-developed programme of all. As in Switzerland, Yugoslavian communes are expected to organise communal shelters; regulations provide for basements to be adapted and new shelters to be constructed at public expense.

As part of the boost in the *Civil Defence Review* (ES1/81) the Home Office and Scottish Office each appointed officials to look into shelter and evacuation policy. Two early results of the greater effort were a handbook of photographs with which various dwellings' protective factors could be guesstimated (distributed as ES3/81) and a circular on *Potential Communal Shelters*. The *Communal Shelters* circular (in draft) explained that:

The 'Protect and Survive' material is under review. Advice
generally will remain 'stay put'. The proposed survey (of potential
shelters) should primarily be seen in that context.

The circular asked local authorities to start surveying suitable buildings in order to accommodate those whose homes would not give enough fallout protection (even when enhanced by ('Protect and Survive' type measures) and those caught away from home. The circular admitted that a 1960s survey had found that 10 – 15 per cent of the population lived in houses with a protective factor of 10 or less, and added that:

The conclusion then was that the number of people living in houses built by modern methods of light construction would increase; it would now be reasonable to assume that the proportion of the population living in poorly protected accommodation is well above fifteen per cent.

This observation implies that 'Protect and Survive' measures were devised in 1975 in the sure knowledge that at least one in five was too poorly protected anyway, even ignoring the degradation of fallout protection on blast damaged houses. It also recognised that flat dwellers might need communal shelters.

The *Shelters* circular contained the first hint of official reconsideration of shelter policy and possible dispersal and contemplated:

shelters (being) earmarked away from areas most vulnerable to high blast damage, ie as dispersal shelters.

But it was stressed that there would be no government funds 'to finance peacetime food storage' for shelters, or indeed for any other purpose than surveys and paperwork. The first draft of the circular suggested a massive food requirement for the pre-attack and conventional phases, which might last as long as sixty days – followed by two to four weeks in shelter. The Home Office did not explain how local authorities were expected to acquire food stocks for a month or more in a forty-eight hour warning period, at the same time as doing other work necessary to equip shelters.

The circular makes rudimentary suggestions about ventilation and sanitary requirements, and reviews US suggestions.

But the communal shelter survey just repeats the failures of *Protect and Survive*, on a larger scale. The critical decisions about shelter policy – whether to make the construction of nuclear shelters in new buildings compulsory, *à la* Switzerland, Yugoslavia, or Norway; or whether to actually spend money on communal shelters – were both politically decided in the negative before the circular was drafted. The chances of local authorities being able to complete functional, viable shelters on such a makeshift basis in time of crisis seem remote. Few buildings have a water supply, for example, in their basements, and water would have to be stocked along with other requisites. Comfort would not be a feature: 'tests in the United States have shown that mats of corrugated sandwich cardboard are comfortable enough to allow unhindered sleep.' The potential shelters would have to be planned to include improvised blast and fallout protection, ventilation plant, water and food stocks, lighting arrangements, some cooking facilities, sanitation and waste disposal. The circular did not even consider whether it would be useful to station some medical staff at the larger shelters; most countries would have regarded this as mandatory.

In its free pamphlet, *Civil Defence – Why We Need It*, the government has claimed that civil defence is an 'insurance premium'. If that is so, it is not a premium the government is prepared to pay. They are unprepared to contemplate any serious level of expenditure; even in 1982/83, they had yet (in real terms) to exceed the spending in some of the 'low years' of the mid 1970s. Non-expenditure on shelters, etc, is justified with reference to the 'slight risk of war'. For what it is worth, this demonstrates the falsehood of the 'insurance' analogy, along with many other remarks in this dishonest sheet. In the insurance business, paying the premium totally secures the insured against a loss. Civil defence doesn't work like that: it does not guarantee to replace all our human capital, so long as we keep up with the premiums. You only get what little you pay for.

'The risk of war,' the pamphlet says, 'is at present considered so slight that the enormous expense of providing shelters to every family in the land could not be justified.' Following the figures given by Swiss or German authorities, providing communal shelter and support facilities would cost, roughly, between £100 and £200* a head. Not all the British population need be protected against blast; some areas are simply not near targets, and good precautions against fallout would suffice. A suitably extensive programme of food stockpiling and industrial precautions together with evacuation re-

---

*By 1980, Switzerland had spent $2.4 billion and constructed six million shelter places, together with supporting facilities. They plan to spend $4 billion between 1980 and 2000.

ception arrangements, might double the cost. Without doubt, a comprehensive programme of civil defence for the United Kingdom, as the Home Office says, 'would cost billions'. Perhaps it would cost £7 billion at todays prices. It would take much more than a decade to complete such plans. But it would be ready earlier than the Trident submarines, and cost less. Over a decade, such a comprehensive civil defence programme would require the diversion of five per cent of the defence budget. As the government says:

The case for civil defence stands regardless of whether a nuclear deterrent is necessary or not. Radioactive fallout is no respecter of neutrality . . . we would be as powerless to prevent fallout from a nuclear explosion crossing the sea as was King Canute to stop the tide. This is why countries with a long tradition of neutrality (such as Sweden or Switzerland) are foremost in their civil defence precautions.

All that is true. In fact, the case for civil defence stands a great deal better in a nonaligned, non-nuclear armed country; and in any case, this passage does not justify government policy; the United Kingdom does not have civil defence as the Swedes, Swiss, Canadians, Russians, Norwegians, Yugoslavians, or Dutch might recognise it.

Fundamental political questions arise. There is a strand of informed civil defence opinion, represented for example by the 'Civil Aid' organisation or the private Nuclear Protection Advisory Group ('Nupag'; who have issued their own riposte to *Why We Need It*), which has argued for precisely such a massive programme of civil defence. They take a roughly neutral stance on nuclear weapons defence, pointing out that 'the only sure way to protect people is to get rid of the weapons that menace us.' In the meantime, proposes 'Nupag', postpone or cancel Trident, tax the us for their air bases to pay for civil defence projects, start a new publicly-funded shelter construction scheme – and then save money from social security funds through the extra employment thus created.

Such proposals attract criticism from divergent quarters. The government and its sympathisers call it unrealistic (meaning it is not their policy). Many in the nuclear disarmament and peace movements would regard such a programme as preparation for war. Many socialists and liberals would be appalled at the massive diversion of economic resources into such unproductive sectors of the economy. Conservatives would deplore excessive public spending on this kind of civilian defence.

The non-government criticisms can, to a considerable extent, be reconciled, I believe. Our defence policy is presently based on threatening counter-aggression; that is the essence of nuclear deterrence. We can instead offer the deterrence of defence, active and passive, of the British Isles and the population. Indeed we can try to do both. However, if what we are seeking to do is to defend, at reasonable cost, the British people and society, then we have to recognise the enormous risks – and costs of protection – which attach to maintaining nuclear weapons and US bases. As Lawrence Freedman observes*, a determined attacker can if necessary subject even massive civil defence expenditure to a law of diminishing returns by increasing the scale of attack. The Americans have responded in this way to Soviet civil defence efforts; the USSR could do it to Britain.

For the United Kingdom, limiting the damage which would be caused in nuclear war has to start by stripping away the targets. Our exceptional vulnerability since the early 1950s has rested mostly on Britain's role as the US's 'unsinkable aircraft carrier'; even in 1948. Britain was treated (in Operation *Dropshot*) as an expendable US asset, with the Strategic Air Command expecting no more than six months' use out of the place in an all-out atomic war. Since then our vulnerability has increased, and our national (and personal) security has been all but destroyed. Every pound (or dollar) not spent on preparations to mount a nuclear war from Britain is worth far more than every pound spent on civil defence measures.

I do not believe that it is either worthwhile or sensible, strategically, to undertake any civil defence programme in Britain until there has been a wholesale change in defence policy, in the direction of defensive deterrence. To spend the necessary billions on shelters in other circumstances, while retaining nuclear weapons and US bases, would suggest a posture of nuclear war-fighting to a potential adversary, would be an inexcusable further waste of economic resources, and would diminish security. We need to measure the worth of our society in terms of the calibre of the Health Service, the craft of workers and the useful output of industry, the creativity of education and the quality of life – not by the

Times, 26 March 1980, see p. 19.

number of concrete shelter places and nuclear bombs and missiles.

If Britain is to have real civil defence, then it must be on the model of allies like Norway, or neutrals like Sweden. It must be part of the 'total defence' of the country, embracing conventional military defence; we must give up a defence that is predicated on the destruction of the territory and cities of another, for in so doing we only wreak equal vengeance on our own heads. If we do not do this, then civil defence becomes merely a means of making nuclear weapons more thinkable, threatening and usable.

John Clayton, the former Home Office Scientific Advisory Branch Director suggests that the purpose of the 'element of Home Defence' is that 'a potential attacker must be persuaded that the nation is ready to accept and survive an attack'. That is an impossible impression to give. It is untrue. To accept a nuclear attack is an obscene, disgusting thing to ask of the population. What matters 'freedom' or 'a way of life' in a radioactive wasteland?

It is easy to generate emotion, of course, about nuclear war. It is also easy to whip up hysteria with propaganda about vile and dangerous enemies in eastern lands. That too is an appeal to the viscera and not to the cranium. Such attitudes create and are embedded in political doctrines that currently offer no escape from nuclear weapons and war, by accident or design. No one can say for certain to what level of population and 'survival' (or not) the post nuclear war world will come. It does not matter. What will matter is our failure to take evasive action first, now.

Britain and NATO each say they stand for 'freedom'. National independence will be defended against outside aggression. That is fine and proper. But as we have seen, the first home defence task of Britain, within NATO, is to extinguish public dissent. If war comes, freedom will already have been sacrificed to the cause of making war. That is the ultimate insult, obscenity and deception of what the British government calls civil defence; it asks citizens to die for freedom with their lips sealed and their cries unheard, lest they call out too loudly for freedom and their own independence of choice, thought and action.

Appendix 1
Government circulars on civil defence and emergency planning

Title		Comments
Home Office Civil Defence circulars (CDC)		
5/69	Earmarking of Church Premises	Originally Restricted.
2/70	Requisitioning of motor vehicles in a war emergency; arrangements for supplies of motor fuel for essential services in war	
4/71	Essential Service Routes	Originally Restricted.
Home Office Emergency Services Circulars (ES)		
1/72	Home Defence 1972–76	Start of the 70s revival
2/72	Police Deployment in a War Emergency	Confidential, police only
3/72	Police Deployment in a War Emergency	Sanitised version of ES/272 omitting mention of internment, police use of firearms, etc. Notes creation of Police Support Units.
4/72	Police Home Defence Training	
5/72	Local Authority Scientific Staff	
6/72	Tidal flooding in Greater London	London area only.
7/72	National Arrangements for dealing with Incidents involving Radioactivity (The NAIR Scheme)	Concerns radioactivity accidents in peacetime, including reactors, isotopes, etc.
8/72	Regional and Local Authority Scientific Staff	
1/73	Home Defence Regional and Sub Regional Boundaries in England and Wales	

Title		Comments
2/73	Counter Sabotage Planning	Restricted booklet by MI5, issued to police only.
3/73	Home Defence Planning Assumptions	Originally Restricted, contains basic definitions for war planning.
4/73	Amendments to Financial Arrangements	
5/73	Local Authority Scientific Staff	
6/73	Home Defence College, York	Brochure and charges for HDC courses.
7/73	Machinery of Government in War	Deals with regional and local government, but not central government plans.
8/73	Government Wartime Communications for Local Authorities – Financial Arrangements	
9/73	Essential Service Routes	Latest amendments.
1/74	Civil Defence Act 1948 – Subordinate Legislation	
2/74	Home Defence College, York	Latest charges.
3/74	Biological Weapons Act 1974	Outlaws manufacture or use of biological weapons in UK, and ratifies BW treaty.
4/74	Food and Agriculture Control in War	
5/74	War Emergency Planning for the Fire Service	
6/74	Protection of Key Points	Secret details of Key Points sent to Chief Constables only.
7/74	Key Point Protection	Restricted notes on guarding Key Points prepared by MI5, sent to police only.
8/74	Local Authority Scientific Staff: Home Defence College – Incidental Expenses	
9/74	Regional Coordination of Local Authority Home Defence Planning	
10/74	Public Survival under Fallout conditions	
11/74	Armed Forces in War	
12/74	Home Defence Training for the Police	

Title		Comments
1/75	Nuclear Weapons	Issue of HMSO booklet of the same name.
2/75	Information Services in War	
3/75	Police Manual of Home Defence	Restricted, sent to police only.
4/75	Construction Work and Building Materials in War	
5/75	Communications in War	Restricted.
6/75	Post Office Telephone Preference Scheme	Restricted, concerns peacetime use of TPS and sent to police only.
7/75	Major Accidents and Natural Disasters	The only major Home Office circular not concerned with war planning.
1/76	Fallout Protection in War	
2/76	Community Organisation in War	
3/76	Briefing Material for Wartime Controllers	Restricted and on 'need to know' basis; sensitive material concerns law and order, firing squads, summary execution for reluctant workers, and restoration of monetary and banking system.
4/76	Ports and Shipping in War	
5/76	Energy Supplies in War	
6/76	Water Supplies in War	
7/76	Homelessness in War	
8/76	Environmental Health in War	Hygiene, refuse disposal, and burial of the dead.
9/76	Advice to the Public on Protection against Nuclear Attack	Issue of samples of *Protect and Survive* (first edition) to emergency planners.
1/77	Preparation and Organisation of the Health Service for War	Home Office cover on a DHSS circular to health authorities.
2/77	Inland Transport in War	
3/77	National Arrangements for Incidents Involving Radioactivity (The NAIR Scheme)	see ES7/72.
4/77	Home Defence College, York	Brochure and charges for course.
5/77	Public Survival under Fallout Conditions	
6/77	Home Defence Planning Guidance – 1977 Onwards	

Title		*Comments*
1/78	Transmission of Radiological Information in Wartime	Deals with UKWMO.
2/78	Earmarking of Buildings for War Planning	
3/78	Home Defence College, York	
1/79	Food and Agriculture Controls in War	
2/79	Wartime Communications for Local Authorities	The Emergency Communications Network.
3/79	Emergency Communications Procedures	How to use the ECN.
4/79	Home Defence Training for the Police	
5/79	Satellite Accidents	Restricted.
1/80	Local Home Defence Training	
2/80	Advice to the Public – *Protect and Survive*	Public sale of slightly revised version of *Protect and Survive*.
1/81	Civil Defence Review	Conservative Government's enlarged programme.
2/81	Community Organisation in War; Voluntary Effort in Civil Defence	Sir Leslie Mavor appointed Coordinator of Voluntary Effort in Civil Defence.
3/81	Protection of the General Public in War; Survey of the Protective Qualities of Residential Accomodation	Pictorial handbook summarising likely PFS of typical British houses

Scottish Office circulars

In the main, Scottish Office emergency services circulars are slightly rewritten versions of their Home Office counterparts, adapted to Scottish administrative arrangements, and issued between three and eighteen months later. They are circulated by Division IA of the Scottish Home and Health Department in Edinburgh, the equivalent of the Home Office's F6 Division.

A few circulars listed opposite do not correspond directly to any in the Home Office series:

Title		Comments
ES(SCOT)		
3/75	Home Defence	General summary for Scotland.
4/77	Health Services in War	Equivalent to HO ES1/77 but classified Restricted.
1/78	Effects of Radioactive Fallout on Food, Fisheries and Agriculture	A NATO study on the subject.
5/78	Civil Emergencies – Supply of Equipment	Civil emergency use of Home Defence stores at Cambusbarron, Stirling, and Montreathmont, near Montrose (telecommunications).

Northern Ireland Office

In Northern Ireland, the administration of Home Defence is almost entirely the responsibility of the provincial government. Local authorities (some twenty six District Councils) had apparently not received any guidance circulars from the NIO by late 1981. A meeting to discuss their potential role in civil defence was held during March 1981, but no papers were circulated. In general, home defence plans in Northern Ireland appear to be about ten years behind their mainland counterparts.

Other departments

The Department of Health and Social Security, and the Ministry of Agriculture, Fisheries and Food have produced occasional circulars for local authorities (and, in the case of the DHSS, for health authorities). Most of this material is contained in Home Office Circulars ES 1/77 and ES 1/79.

Appendix 2
County Council Wartime Headquarters (including Scottish Regions)

The majority of council Wartime Headquarters are basements or semi-basements of the peacetime council offices, usually equipped with improved or improvised fallout protection, but generally no greater blast protection than the building would ordinarily afford. Standby controls are most usually located in one of the district councils' Wartime HQ sites within the county (or Scottish region), and the same comments apply. Purpose-built buildings, where known, are denoted (P). These have either been specially built above or below ground (although not necessarily for their present user), or within (ie below) a post-1960 council office development.

There is no one central source for this information, and some councils will not discusss their provision of protected accomodation for Wartime Headquarters. Thus, the appendix contains omissions and, no doubt, some errors.

In Northern Ireland, there are to be four Area Controls subordinate to Northern Ireland Central HQ – North, South, East and West areas. Home defence planning in NI is however, many years behind the mainland. One HQ (East Area) is located at Mount Eden Park, off Malone Road, in south Belfast.

Sub-Region	County	Main Wartime HQ	Standby Wartime HQ
11	Cleveland	Old Town Hall, Middlesborough	Civic Centre, Hartlepool
	Durham	County Hall, Durham	Town Hall, Darlington
	Northumberland	County Hall, Morpeth	–
	Tyne & Wear	Civic Centre, Sunderland	(New site at Kenton Bar proposed by HO)
21	Humberside	Wawne, Hull (P)	Grimsby Town Hall, Grimsby
	North Yorks	County Hall, Northallerton	–
	South Yorks	Cusworth Hall, Sprotborough, Doncaster	County Hall, Barnsley
	West Yorks	County Hall, Wakefield	Brighouse, Halifax (P)

Sub-Region	County	Main Wartime HQ	Standby Wartime HQ
31	Derbyshire	County Offices, Matlock	–
	Lincolnshire	Lincoln	–
	Nottinghamshire	County Hall, Nottingham	Severn-Trent Water Board, Gt Central Road, Mansfield
32	Leicestershire	County Hall, Glenfield, Leicester	County Social Services Office, Kettering
	Northamptonshire	County Hall, Northampton	
41	Cambridgeshire	Shire Hall, Cambridge	Town Hall, Peterborough
	Norfolk	County Hall, Norwich	County Council Office, Kings Lynn
	Suffolk	Police HQ, Civil Drive, Ipswich	District Council HQ, Bury St Edmunds
42	Bedfordshire	County Hall, Bedford	
	Essex	County Hall, Chelmsford	Mistley, Manningtree (P)
	Hertfordshire	County Hall, Hertford	District Council Office, Hemel Hempstead
51	Greater London	See Appendix 3	
61	Kent	Maidstone	
	Surrey	Technical College, Guildford (P)	Town Hall, Reigate
	East Sussex	County Hall, Lewes (P)	Horsham (P)
	West Sussex	County Hall, Chichester	Eastbourne
62	Berkshire	Shire Hall, Reading (P)	District Council HQ, Newbury
	Buckinghamshire	County Offices, Aylesbury	Bletchley Fire Station, Bletchley (P)
	Hampshire	Car park building, The Castle, Winchester (P)	
	Isle of Wight	Former RAF station, Ventnor (P)	
	Oxfordshire	Woodeaton Manor, Woodeaton (P)	

Sub-Region	County	Main Wartime HQ	Standby Wartime HQ
71	Avon	Flowers Hill, Brislington, Bristol (P)	Lease from HO to be cancelled after rent rise
	Dorset	City Library, Colliton Park, Dorchester (P)	Blandford
	Gloucestershire	Shire Hall, Gloucester	
	Somerset	Taunton	
	Wiltshire	County Hall, Truro	
72	Devon	Exeter	
81	Clwyd	Shire Hall, Mold (P)	
	Gwynedd	Caernarfon	
82	Dyfed	Carmarthen	
	Mid Glamorgan	Industrial estate, Bridgend (P)	Construction stopped after protests
	South Glamorgan	Wenallt, Cardiff	Coryton, Cardiff
	Gwent	Abergavenny	
	Powys	Llandrinod Wells	
	West Glamorgan	West Cross, Swansea (P)	Civic Centre, Neath
91	West Midlands	Fylde Green, Sutton Coldfield (P)	County Hall, Birmingham
	Staffordshire	County Buildings, Stafford	Queens Avenue, Stoke on Trent
	Warwickshire	Shire Hall, Warwick	Retreat Building, Rugby
92	Shropshire	Shirehall Building, Shrewsbury	
	Hereford & Worcester	County Hall, Worcester	Shire Hall, Hereford
101	Cumbria	Carlisle	
	Lancashire	West Leigh, Lea Road, Preston	
102	Greater Manchester	Mill Lane, Cheadle	Municipal Buildings, Earle Street, Crewe
	Merseyside	Walker Art Gallery, William Brown St, Liverpool	Southport
Scotland			
Eastern zone	Lothians	Alderston House, Haddington	
	Borders	Newton St Boswells	

Sub-Region	County	Main Wartime HQ	Standby Wartime HQ
Western zone	Strathclyde	Clippens House, Linwood	
	Central	32 Buchanan St, Balfron	
	Dumfries & Galloway	Dumfries	
Northern zone	Fife	Kirkcaldy	
	Tayside	Craigiebarns, Dundee	
	Grampian	Woodhill House, Aberdeen	Durris House, South Deeside Road, Aberdeen
	Highlands	Raigmore, Inverness	

Appendix 3
Wartime Headquarters in Greater London (Region 5)

Other public organisations have emergency control centres equally remote from London; British Gas would be at Staines in Middlesex, the CEGB at East Grinstead in Surrey. These major, regional level headquarters are all twenty to twenty–five miles from the centre of London. Subordinate to SRHQ51, at present, are five Group Controls, also in the outer suburbs. These are, in turn, linked to each London Borough (or the City of London) War HQ. Many inner London boroughs have refused to maintain or modernise the War HQS – as has the Greater London Council.

Regional
Armed Forces HQ 5: Wilton Park Barracks, Beaconsfield
Sub-Regional
SRHQ51: Kelvedon Hatch, Nr Brentwood, Essex
Police
Emergency Control Centre (South): Merstham, Surrey. Emergency Control Centre (North): Lippetshill, Essex

North Group

Group War HQ: Partingdale Lane, Mill Hill (temporary use of military and Barnet Council site) (Control 51A)
Police District War HQ: Enfield Police Station, Baker Street, Enfield

Enfield: Town Hall, Enfield (P) (A1)
Haringey: Town Hall, High Road, Wood Green, N22 (A2)
Islington: Town Hall, Upper Street, N1 (P) (A3)
City of London: Guildhall, Basinghall Street, EC2 (A4)
Westminster: Queens Terrace, St Johns Wood, NW8 (P) (A5)
Camden: Town Hall, Esuton Road, NW1 (A6)
Barnet: Partingdale Lane, Mill Hill, NW8 (P) (A7)

North East Group

Group War HQ: Northumberland Avenue, Wanstead Flats, E12 (Control 51B)
Police District War HQ: Romford Police Station, Main Road, Romford

Havering: Town Hall, Main Road, Romford (B1)
Barking and Dagenham: Civic Centre, Wood Lane, Dagenham (P) (B2)
Newham: Deanery Road, Stratford, E15 (P) (B3)

Tower Hamlets: Cheviot House, Philpot Street, E1 (B4)
Hackney: Town Hall, Stoke Newington Church Street, N16 (P) (B5)
Waltham Forest: Town Hall, Forest Road, E17 (B6)
Redbridge: Town Hall, Ilford (B7)

South East Group

Group War HQ: Lunham Road, SE19 (Control 51C)
Police District War HQ: Bromley Police Station, Widmore Road, Bromley

Greenwich: Southwood Road, New Eltham, SE9 (P) (C1)
Bexley: Civil Offices, Broadway, Bexleyheath (P) (C2)
Bromley: Town Hall, Widmore Road, Bromley (C3)
Croydon: Town Hall, Catherine Street, Croydon (C4)
Southwark: 28 Peckham Road, Camberwell SE5 (C5)
Lewisham: Town Hall, Catford SE6 (C6)

South West Group

Group War HQ: Church Hill Road, Cheam (Control 51D)
Police District War HQ : Sutton Police Station, Carshalton Road West,
  Sutton

Wandsworth: Municipal Buildings, High Street, SW18 (D1)
Lambeth: St Matthews Road, Brixton, SW2 (P) (D2)
Merton: Town Hall, Wimbledon, SW19 (D3)
Sutton: Civic Offices, Throwley Way, Sutton (D4)
Kingston upon Thames: Guildhall, High Street, Kingston upon Thames
  (D5)
Richmond upon Thames: 91 Queens Road, Twickenham (D6). Church
  Road/Kew Road, Richmond upon Thames (P) (after 1982).

North West Group

Group War HQ: Beatrice Road, Southall (Control 51E)
Police District War HQ: Harrow Police Station, 74 Northoldt Road,
  Harrow

Harrow: Civic Centre, Harrow (E1)
Brent: Town Hall, Wembley (E2)
Kensington and Chelsea: Central Library, Hornton Street, W8 (E3)
Hammersmith and Fulham: Town Hall, King Street, W6 (E4)
Hounslow: Civic Centre, Lampton Road, Hounslow (E5)
Ealing: Beatrice Road, Southall (P) (E6) (shared with Group War HQ)
Hillingdon: Civic Centre, Uxbridge (P) (E7)

Controls are numbered hierarchically; thus Enfield's full designation is
  Control 51A1. (P) indicates a purpose-built bunker either
  underground or within a recent council development. The
  remainder are generally basements of town halls, strengthened and
  fallout protected. Most have emergency generators and other
  facilities installed. About 1500–2000 officials would staff these
  controls.

Appendix 4
Major underground factories and depots of World War II

Site	World War II use	Post war use(s)
Ministry of Aircraft Production		
Spring Quarries, Hawthorn, Corsham, Wilts 2,250,000 ft² (215,000m²)	Aircraft production factory for Bristol Aeroplane and other companies; (later) RAF Fighter Group HQ, communications and switching centre	Central Government War Headquarters (but identified only as Property Services Agency Supplies Division); Headquarters of Defence Communications Network.
London underground tunnels, Redbridge, Ilford, etc East London 300,000 ft² (28,000m²)	Electrical equipment and electronics factory for Plessey company	Factory was in new extension for the Central Line, which came into orthodox use after the war.
Dudley cavern, Dudley Zoo, Dudley, Worcs. 32,600 ft² (3000m²)	BSA Company of Small Heath, Birmingham (arms mfrs); were to have used, but scheme took too long and cavern was used for ammunition store instead	None known.
Warren Row, near Henley on Thames. (adapted chalk caves) 30,000 ft² (2800m²)	Aircraft parts manufacture	Regional Seat of Government (RSG) 6, from 1959–64, then SRC61. Closed in 1971, but reopened for Ministry of Defence use in 1980–1.

Site	World War II use	Post war use(s)
Drakelow tunnels, Drakelow, near Kinver, Worcs 300,000 ft² (28,000m²)	Rover Aero Engine Factory, dispersed from Coventry in 1942	Regional Seat of Government (RSG) 9 from 1959, then SRC91, then SRHQ92.
Tunnel, Austin Works, Longbridge, Birmingham 25,000 ft² (2250m²)	Spare capacity for Austin motor factory	None known.
Workshop, Short Bros, Rochester, Kent 12,000 ft² (1110m²)	Additional workshop space for Short Bros factory	None known.

Ministry of Supply

Henley on Thames (tunnel scheme) 15,000 ft² (1400m²)	Engineering works: Godley and company	Engineering works on lease from MOD.
Copenacre Quarry, Corsham, Wilts 630,000 ft² (60,000m²)	Ordnance store	Royal Naval Supply Depot and Computer Centre
Valley Works, Rhydymwyn, Flintshire (now Clwyd)	Massive tunnelled store for reserve supplies of mustard gas and other poison gases	Maintained as government 'Special Site' for central government evacuation but not refurbished or re-equipped.

RAF Ammunition Stores

Chilmark, Dinton, Salisbury (11MU) (Maintenance Unit)	Stone quarries converted 1940; still used as major RAF bomb store, believed also to hold central nuclear weapons stocks.
Fauld, Burton on Trent, Staffs (21MU)	RAF, later USAF bomb store in converted alabaster mine. Now allocated to the Royal Navy.
Linley, Salop (21MSU)	Not in RAF use.

Site	Post war use(s)
Harpur Hill, near Buxton, Derbyshire	Specially constructed tunnels; site was proposed for an SRC in 1960s; now Safety in Mines establishment.
Rowthorne (28MU)	County unknown.
Butterton Tunnel, Butterton, Staffs (28MU)	Not in RAF use.
Grange Quarry, Holywell, Flint (now Clwyd)	Now used as private military museum.
Newlands (59MU)	County unknown.
Llanberis Quarries, Gwynedd (31MU)	In use 1941–56; cleared 1969–75.
Rhiwlas, Bangor, Gwynedd	Commercial Store.

Other Air Force and aircraft production sites

Bristol Aeroplane Company, Farland Quarry, Portbury, Near Bristol	Used by Bristol Aeroplane Company.
Temple Cloud, Midsummer Norton, Avon	Two factories used by Parnall Aircraft; one now used as jet engine test bed.

Admiralty underground oil fuel and ammunition storage sites

Plymouth, Portsmouth, Harwich, Immingham, Dover, Invergordon, Lyness	Fuel Depots.
Dean Hill, near Salisbury, Hants	Tunneled underground store still in use.
Trecwyn, near Fishguard, Dyfedd	Tunneled underground store still in use.
Benarty, Fife	Tunneled underground store, apparently now demolished.
Fishguard (Neyland) Exmouth Plymouth (Ernesettle) Five other sites	

Art treasures

Manod Slate Quarry, Blaenau Ffestiniog, Gwynedd 16,000 ft² (1500m²)	Still maintained for the same purpose.

Site	Post war use(s)
Westwood Quarry, Bradford on Avon, Wilts	Stored British museum treasures, also housed engineering works; now disused except for stone quarrying.

Ministry of Home Security: Air raid tunnel schemes

I New tunnels	*Length of tunnels*	
Ramsgate, Kent	2.5 miles	(4.1 km)
Tranmere, Birkenhead	1.3 miles	(2.1 km)
Foxenden Quarry, Guildford	0.33 miles	(0.55 km)
Portsdown Hill, Portsmouth (2 sites)	1.8 miles	(2.9 km)
Riddlesdown Pit, Kenley, Surrey	0.4 miles	(0.65 km)
Epsom Downs, Surrey	0.44 miles	(0.71 km)
Brighton Road, Coulsdon, Surrey	0.2 miles	(0.33 km)
Ashley Road, Epsom, Surrey	0.46 miles	(0.75 km)
Valley Road, Chipstead, Surrey	0.06 miles	(100 m)
Luton (4 sites)	0.9 miles	(1.5 km)
Stockport, Cheshire	2.5 miles	(4 km)
Townfield Quarry, Easington, Durham	0.3 miles	(0.5 km)

II Existing tunnels	*Comment*
London – disused tubes at Leytonstone, Liverpool Street, Southwark, and Aldwych	Disused old tube tunnels.
Dover, Kent	Various existing caves.
Loftus, Yorks	Old iron mine – accomodated 400–500.
Runcorn, Cheshire	Old quarry haul roads – total 0.5 mile (0.8 km).
Chislehurst	Old quarry workings.
Newcastle upon Tyne	Victoria tunnel, 2.5 miles (4 km).
ditto	Ouseburn Culvert constructed 1939 0.34 m (0.55 km).
Birkenhead	Hamilton Square Subway, Mersey Railway.
Ebbw Vale, Monmouth	Old colliery drift; length 850 m.
Ramsgate, Kent	Railway tunnel and three caves—5000 shelter places.
Consett, Durham	Five old colliery drifts – 650 places.
Huddersfield	Damside Tunnel—pipe subway with 800 places.

Note: Details of all these underground storage, factory sites, or air raid shelters are from Public Records Office files declassified during the 1970s; chiefly the papers of the War Cabinet's Engineering Advisory Sub-Committee on Underground Chambers, also known as 'MISC 21'. Details of the RAF ammunition stores comes from AIR file 2/ 5692, to be transferred to the Public Records Office in 1984.

Appendix 5
British Telecom: Telephone preference scheme

Lines in Category 1 (War use)

Aircraft Control Bodies: Airport Authorities with war-emergency tasks, British Airways Board, Civil Aviation Authority.

Ambulance Services

British Rail

British Waterways Board

Broadcasting Authorities: BBC, IBA.

Carrier Warning System receiver points

Coast War Watching Organisation (HM Coastguards)

Docks and Ports war emergency control organisation

Electricity Supply Industry: CEGB, SSEB, NSHEB

Food and Agriculture: Wartime food and agricultural control organisation including MAFF peacetime regional and divisional offices, DAFS Area Offices (Scotland), bakers, buffer depots, dairies, flour mills, food manufacturers and processors, slaughterhouses, wholesale food distributors and stores and food depots, major food supply organisations, other manufacturing, processing, distributing or wholesaling food industry premises, food cold stores, manufacturers and distributors of agricultural equipment, animal feeding stuffs, insecticides, and fertilisers (not including any retail outlets).

Water authorities and internal drainage boards

Gas Supply Industry (British Gas)

Government Departments: central, regional and local offices

Regional Health Authorities, Area Health Authorities, hospitals (NHS and private), blood group reference laboratory, Lister Institute (blood products laboratory).

Local Authorities: Wartime Main and Standby Headquarters, Fire Brigade headquarters and stations, Emergency Food Control and Feeding Centres, Information and Self-help Centres, Rest and Billeting Centres, Refuse and Sewage Works.

Meteorological Services

Military Operational Establishments: Air, Army, Navy.

National Coal Board: Mines; Mines Rescue Stations

National Radiological Protection Board

Petroleum Industry

Pilotage Authorities

Police Headquarters and Police Stations

Post Office

Public Health Laboratory Service

Radio Transmitting and Receiving Stations
Regional Wartime Government: Regional HQ group locations, SRHQS, Scottish Central and Zone Controls
River Boards (where flooding is likely to take place)
Road Transport: Bus Control Authorities, Important Companies, War Emergency Control Organisation
Shipping Control
Water Undertakings
Works and Building Organisation Bases

Lines in Category 2 (Peacetime emergencies)

Advisory Conciliation and Arbitration Service
Agriculture: Veterinary Clinics, Surgeons and Inspectors
Air Transport: Aircraft Accident Investigation Branch, Aircraft Operating Companies, Airports (other than in Category 1)
Association of County Councils, Association of District Councils, Association of Metropolitan Authorities, Convention of Scottish Local Authorities
Coastguard: Coastguard Stations, Coast Watching Stations and Lookouts, official and private Residences of Designated Coastguard Officers
Confederation of British Industries local offices; including Employers' Associations
Defence Establishments
Education: Colleges, Schools, Universities (only if isolated from community, or difficult access by road, or designated emergency centre by Local Authority)
Factories engaged in production of food, war materials or dangerous (eg inflammable) materials, or commodities essential to the maintenance of the life of the community in an emergency
Fire Service: Fire Controls, Fire Stations
Foreign and Commonwealth Governments: High Commissions, Embassies, Legations, Consulates
Forestry Commission
Government Departments: Central, Regional and Local Offices; private residences of key officers
Health and Safety Commission and Executive
Highway Maintenance Depots
Homes (Local Government and Private): Nursing Homes, Homes for the elderly, children, and physically and mentally handicapped (if isolated from community or difficult access by road)
Judiciary Court Houses and Clerks of Court Official Residences, Judges' and Sherriffs' official and private residences, magistrates' official residences
Lifeboat Stations, private residences of Lifeboat Officers
Local Government: Counties, Town Halls, offices, depots, Rest Centres, including Emergency Rest Centres and Emergency Feeding Centres, private residences of: Lord Mayors and Lord Provosts, County, Scottish Regional and District Controllers (ie Chief Executives), Chief Officers with designated Wartime Appointments, County and District Emergency Committee Members, Other Key Officers.
Lord Lieutenants: official and private Residences
Manpower Services Commission
Medical Services: Blood Transfusion Supply Depots, British Red Cross

Society, St John Ambulance Brigade, Clinics, Nurses (business and private residences of community nurses and midwives), Pathological Laboratories, Dentists and Dental Surgeons, home dialysis Patients, pharmacies.

Ministers of the Crown: private residences

Mortuaries and Crematoria

National Air Traffic Control Service

Newspaper Industry: offices of national and local newspapers, news agencies

National Museums and Galleries

Police

Ports, Docks and Canals Authorities and Companies, Lighterage Companies, Ship-to-shore Lines, Shipping Companies, Major Shipyards, Trinity House Depots (and private residences of Superintendents), locks and swing bridges.

Power, Fuel and Water: UK Atomic Energy Authority: power stations and private residences of key officers, Catchment Boards – Surface Water Control and Irrigation, coal and oil depots and distributors, electricity and gas supply industries, hydraulic power equipment companies, National Coal Board, North Sea Gas and Oil suppliers, Storm Tide Warning Service and River Authorities control lines, Water Supply Companies.

Pumps, Lifts, Lighting, etc Maintenance Contractors for Government Departments

Research Stations: Laboratories engaged in Biological, Radiological or Chemical Research Stations handling potentially dangerous materials

Road and Rail Services: Roadside Telephones, Motor Passenger Transport Authorities and Large Companies, Road Haulage Organisations and Large Companies, Railway Termini (passenger and goods).

Salvage: Salvage Organisations

Secure Premises: Banks, Burglar Alarm Control Rooms, Customs and Excise Bonded Warehouses and Depots, Prisons, Borstals and Young Offenders Institutions, Remand Homes.

Staff Associations and Trade Unions: (and District offices)

Telecommunications: BBC and IBA offices, studios and stations, Radio Relay Companies (lines used for emergency purposes), Telegraph and Cable company offices and stations

Traffic Area Commissioners

Women's Royal Voluntary Service: offices and main depots

Lists from British Telecom instruction D.1.B0012 (with some abbreviation). Lines in Category 3 (the remainder) get disconnected in any emergency, leaving Categories 1 and 2 connected. In war, Category 2 lines are disconnected as well.